THE WAGER OF LUCIEN GOLDMANN

THE WAGER OF LUCIEN GOLDMANN

TRAGEDY, DIALECTICS, AND A HIDDEN GOD

Mitchell Cohen

PRINCETON UNIVERSITY PRESS   PRINCETON, NEW JERSEY

Library of Congress Cataloging-in-Publication Data

Cohen, Mitchell, 1952–
The wager of Lucien Goldmann : tragedy, dialectics,
and a hidden god / Mitchell Cohen.
p. cm.
Includes bibliographical references and index.
ISBN 0-691-03420-6
1. Goldmann, Lucien. I. Title.
B2430.G584C64   1994
194—dc20   93-40394

This book has been composed in Adobe Palatino

Princeton University Press books are printed
on acid-free paper and meet the guidelines
for permanence and durability of the Committee
on Production Guidelines for Book Longevity
of the Council on Library Resources

Printed in the United States of America

10 9 8 7 6 5 4 3 2 1

For Nicole Fermon

Then call it what you will,
Call it fulfillment! Heart! Love! God!
I have no name for it.
    —*Goethe's Faust*

Contents

Acknowledgments _____

SOME TWO DECADES AGO, as an undergraduate in a seminar on Eastern European communism, I became fascinated by Georg Lukács. Two of his books, *Theory of the Novel* and *History and Class Consciousness*, made an enormous impression on me, and as I wrote a paper on Lukács, I became both intrigued and perplexed by his renunciation of both works and his subservience to Stalinism. It was extraordinary, I thought, that this remarkable thinker had forsworn his most compelling theoretical work. So I began inquiring about the fate of his ideas— the ideas of the "young Lukács"—after he disowned them. This led me to Lucien Goldmann.

That same semester I read Goldmann's book on Kant and, frankly, probably did not understand much of it. I also read the English translation of *Les Sciences humaines et philosophie* and was taken by the sort of questions its author posed. Finally, I read Goldmann's essay "Reflections on *History and Class Consciousness*" and was impressed by Goldmann's effort to save Lukács from Lukács, both philosophically and politically. This led me, in the late 1970s, to write my doctoral thesis at Columbia University on Goldmann, but after completing it, I turned to another interest, which resulted in my writing a book entitled *Zion and State: Nation, Class, and the Shaping of Modern Israel* (in it I used a number of themes and ideas I derived from Lukács and Goldmann). Then, in the late 1980s, I returned to Goldmann, and the outcome is this book, a work larger and more mature (I trust) than the thesis, although much of the latter has been incorporated into it.

This is a somewhat roundabout way of saying that this book has a long history and therefore, inevitably, I have accumulated many debts in writing it. I am very grateful to Annie Goldmann, Lucien Goldmann's widow, for sharing generously her remembrances with me and for allowing me access to her personal archives. I am also especially grateful to Youssef Ishaghpour, a fine cultural critic and thinker who studied with Goldmann in the 1960s. He has been, during my stays in Paris, an invaluable interlocutor, always ready to share his rich insights into Goldmann's work (and into other subjects too).

A number of colleagues and friends were kind enough to read this manuscript, in its totality or in part, and offer valuable thoughts and criticisms, which have undoubtedly resulted in a better book. My thanks to John P. Diggins, Ferenc Fehér, Agnès Heller, Dick Howard,

Irina Livezeanu, Brian Morton, James Rule, Adam Seligman, Vladimir
Tismaneanu, Marx W. Wartofsky, and Richard Wolin. My debt to the
late Irving Howe goes far beyond the trenchant comments he provided on an earlier draft of this book.

Research for this book was conducted in France, Switzerland, Romania, Hungary, and Israel, as well as in New York. Students, colleagues,
acquaintances, and friends of Goldmann were kind enough to share
ideas and recollections with me, as were several people who did not
know him but were helpful in providing contextual information. I am
thankful to them all. These included the following individuals. *In
France*: Kostas Axelos, Cristina Boica, François Erval, Joseph Gabel,
Madeleine Duclos Garepuy, Maurice de Gandillac, André Gorz, Henri
Gouhier, Charles Gruber, Jacques Leenhardt, Henri Lefebvre, Michel
Löwy, Edgar Morin, Sami Naïr, Brigette Navelet, Irene Petit, Stanley
Pullberg, Jeannine Quillet, Rainer Rochlitz, Maximilien Rubel, Joseph
Spielmann, and Menahem Wieviorka. *In Switzerland*: Inhelder Barbel,
Pierre Engel, Ernst Erdöes, Yvonne Moser, and J. Jacques Vonèche. *In
Romania*: Mihail Alexandru, Mihail Florescu, Mircea Bălănescu, Mihail
Leonescu, Mihail Dragomirescu, Anna Toma, Sorin Toma, Simon Katz,
Carol Neuman (interviewed in United States), Leonte Răutu, and
sources who wish to remain anonymous. *In Israel*: S. Z. Feller, Ger-
shom Scholem, Helena Solomon, Vladimir Zaharescu, and David
Zoller. *In the United States*: Lionel Abel, Joseph Bujes, Liviu Floda, An-
nette Michelson, Hermina Tismaneanu, and Ilie Zaharia, *In Britain*:
Leszek Kolakowski.

I made extensive use of, or received assistance from, the following
archives and libraries: the Bibliothèque Nationale (Paris); Columbia
University Library (New York); Ha-Shomer ha-Tsair Archives (Givat
Haviva, Israel); the Lukács Archives (Budapest); the Romanian Acad-
emy Library (Bucharest); and the University of Bucharest Law School
Archives.

My research has been supported by grants and stipends from the
National Endowment for the Humanities, the American Philosophical Society, and PSC-CUNY (City University of New York Research
Foundation). I am grateful to these institutions for their generosity.
In addition, I am appreciative of the continual encouragement and
support I have received from my academic colleagues and the administration at Baruch College of the City University of New York. Parts
of the introduction and Chapter I appeared in a special issue on Goldmann of *The Philosophical Forum* (Fall–Winter 1991–1992), and a large
part of chapter 9 appeared as "The Concept of Community in the
Thought of Lucien Goldmann" in *Praxis International* (Summer 1986).

I wish to thank both these journals for permission to reprint the respective materials. In the final chapter, the quote from the poem "The City of Yes and the City of No" is from *The Collected Poems, 1952-1990* by Yevgeny Yevtushenko. Edited by Albert C. Todd with Yevgeny Yevtushenko and James Ragan. Copyright © 1991 by Henry Holt and Co., Inc. Reprinted by permission of Henry Holt and Co., Inc.

Finally, I would like to express special thanks to Peter Dougherty of Princeton University Press—a fine editor and friend.

New York City
August 1993

A Note on Titles, Abbreviations, and Language in the Text

ONLY SOME OF LUCIEN GOLDMANN'S WORKS have been translated. When I refer to those that have been, I use the English titles. When I refer to a text by Goldmann that has not been translated, I use the original French title. However, when I quote Goldmann, I have, in almost all cases, translated directly from the French, although sometimes in consultation with the published translations. The reader may find details about the translations of the major works and the original editions of Goldmann's books in the Bibliography. I use the following abbreviations for some of the titles of Goldmann's works in the text: *Kant* for *Immanuel Kant* (*Introduction à la philosophie de Kant*); *Novel* for *Towards a Sociology of the Novel* (*Pour une sociologie du roman*); "LH" for "Lukács et Heidegger," the short appendix to *Kant*, which was dropped after the 1945 German edition; *LH* for *Lukács et Heidegger*, the book Goldmann was writing when he died in 1970. Abbreviations are explained in the text when they are first used. Goldmann's use of French and German was without contemporary American sensibilities when it comes to sexism in language. I have tried to be as sensitive as possible in this regard, but not to the extent of anachronism—Goldmann's *l'homme tragique* cannot be rendered as "tragic person"—or awkwardness. In presenting his ideas, I have sought to be faithful to his own voice, for better or worse.

THE WAGER OF LUCIEN GOLDMANN

Introduction _____

Eppur si muove?

IT IS SAID THAT GALILEO, after recanting before the Inquisition the theory that the earth moves, arose from his knees and murmured beneath his breath, "Eppur si muove"—yet it still moves. This phrase was chosen by the Romanian-born philosopher and critic Lucien Goldmann as the title of his address in February 1969 to a conference in Stockholm organized by Bertrand Russell to protest the Soviet invasion of Czechoslovakia. Viewing the year 1968, in particular, the events in Prague and Paris, as a historical watershed for the European Left, Goldmann, though steadfastly identifying himself as a socialist, contended that "in relation to this turning point . . . the old words 'reform,' 'revolution,' 'socialism,' 'capitalism,' 'liberalism,' 'democracy,' change their meaning and will only remain valid to the extent to which one gives them new meaning."[1]

His death the following year in his adopted home, Paris, deprived Goldmann of sufficient opportunity to make such reformulations. To assert that the earth "still moved" had a dual meaning for him: it was a defiant reassertion of his own, singular version of Marxist humanism in the face of the bitter end of the Prague Spring, and it represented an insistence that the rebellions in Paris and Prague demonstrated that one-dimensional societies could not, after all, triumph permanently. During his lifetime Goldmann was most renowned for his work on the sociology of literature and philosophy. However, as Herbert Marcuse wrote in a volume of *Hommage* published not long after his friend's death, for Goldmann, "philosophy and political radicalism were one, Marxist theory was in the facts themselves; the philosophical and literary documents contained, in themselves, their translation into social reality. . . . He was an eminently political being, and the imperative to change the world was in all his ideas."[2]

Nevertheless, while others in the Left Bank—notably, Louis Althusser—staunchly upheld the "scientificity" of Marxism, Goldmann was acutely aware that Marxism was in crisis—indeed, radical crisis—and would have to reinvent itself radically if it were to survive. He had been an anti-Stalinist since his youth in Romania and through the 1960s had argued for a market socialism. Concurrently, he contested the structuralist, scientistic, and antihumanist theorizing infecting French left-wing circles in that tumultuous decade. Had he lived into the 1970s, he would undoubtedly have had little patience with post-modernism. In fact, the popularity of these trends in the Left Bank was one reason why Goldmann's own name and work were eclipsed—despite his eleven books and the acclaim of thinkers as diverse as Alasdair MacIntyre, who declared him "the finest and most intelligent Marxist of the age," and Jean Piaget, who characterized him as "a creator of ideas as one rarely meets in a lifetime" and "the inventor of a new form of symbolic thought."[3] Surveying the efflorescence of cultural theories and declamations about "texts" in recent years, it is difficult to find works with the persuasive force, originality, and depth of Goldmann's chef d'oeuvre, *The Hidden God*, which combined serious scholarship with theory.

To uphold, as Goldmann did in 1969, that "new meaning" had to be sought for basic terms of political and intellectual vocabulary was a sign of doubt and confidence. A dialectic of doubt and confidence characterizes Goldmann's writings as a whole, beginning with his early writings. This was a Marxist who did not portray his aspirations for humanity's future as an inexorable unfolding of history's laws, but as a wager akin to Pascal's in God. *"Risk,"* he wrote in *The Hidden God*, *"possibility of failure, hope of success,* and the synthesis of the three in *a faith which is a wager* are the essential constituent elements of the human condition."[4]

Few theories have had the historical impact of Marxism, and few have engendered comparable anticipations of human emancipation. Few have seen as much brutality committed in their name. The twentieth century, according to Marx's prognoses, should have issued in a free and classless society in which, as *The Communist Manifesto* proposed, the condition for the liberation of one would be that for all. Instead, the twentieth century belonged to Hitler and Stalin, to world war and cold war. Little wonder Goldmann was preoccupied with tragedy, although denying that his own thought was tragic. Still, as Goldmann himself often argued, an oeuvre takes on an objective meaning beyond its author's intentions.

This was one reason why Goldmann inveighed against the use of biography to unlock texts. His own method, which he eventually classified as "genetic structuralism," synthesized concepts drawn from two chief sources. The first was the Marxism of Georg Lukács. Ultimately no single book affected Goldmann as much as this Hungarian philosopher's tour de force of 1923, *History and Class Consciousness*. In it Lukács contended that knowledge and being would merge on the morrow in working-class consciousness and consequently in universal proletarian revolution. The second source was the "genetic epistemology" of the Swiss psychologist Jean Piaget, in particular, his contention that the basis of human knowledge was the genesis of "totalities" he called "mental structures." From Lukács's theory of class consciousness and Piaget's epistemology Goldmann fashioned his own idea of the "transindividual subject" of cultural and historical action. This subject was composed of an ensemble of individuals, whose common "mental structures" came about as a consequence of their genesis within a common sociohistorical background. The true subjects of cultural creation or historical action were transindividual, according to Goldmann. The achievement of great authors—Pascal and Racine, for example—lay in the coherent elaboration in their works of the worldview implicit in the mental structures of a social group. Discerning that worldview and the mental structures within it allows us to delineate the meaning of the writings of Pascal or Racine beyond their immediate, individual intentions.

In *The Hidden God*, this approach proved remarkably fertile. I shall, in the course of this study of Goldmann, often make use of his methodological insights. However, I will also ask the type of question he preferred to make secondary—in this case, how did Lucien Goldmann become Lucien Goldmann? Hence I begin with biography, presenting Goldmann's life until his academic career began in Paris after World War II.[5] It is, I think, intrinsically interesting as the story of the genesis of an intellectual. It will also tell us a good deal about his preoccupations with Marxism and tragedy. Still, Goldmann would be correct in contending that it does not tell the entire story—it cannot, in his terminology, fully understand and explain his work. For if Goldmann insisted that he was a dialectician studying tragedy and not a tragic thinker, and if we apply to him his own suggestion that the meaning of an author's work transcends his intentions, then we will see that Goldmann's work, while championing Marxism, coherently and acutely elucidates, embodies, and elaborates the contradictions of Marxism and its adherents—contradictions between Marxism's fecundity and its fate, between its emancipatory content and the repressive forms that were deployed in its name. Goldmann's work is structured by a dialectic of tragedy and hope, and he was a tragic dialectician.

To miss this dialectic of tragedy and hope is to miss Goldmann. Consider the caricature drawn of him by Allen Bloom. "Lucien Goldmann," he wrote, "told me a few months before his death that he was privileged to have lived to see his nine-year-old son throw a rock through a store window in the Paris of '68. His studies of Racine and Pascal culminated in this. *Humanitas redivivas!*"[6] Bloom's assumption, apparently, was that Goldmann's study of the tragic vision in seventeenth-century France ought to have led to resignation or ought to have made a neoconservative of him. This assumption is possible only by misconceiving the relation between politics and scholarship in Goldmann's work. His study of great figures of Western civilization, such as Pascal, whom he called the first modern dialectician, did not aim to save Western culture from the Left on behalf of resignation or an elite studying classics. To the contrary. Irving Howe once wrote that André Malraux achieved depth of vision in *Man's Fate* because he acknowledged the authority of defeat.[7] Similarly, Goldmann recognized the authority of tragedy, but while upholding human possibilities. He was a relentless humanist. For Goldmann, the project of the Left was not the negation of Western civilization, but its fulfillment, and he maintained that Marxist humanism represented the culmination of what was best in the European heritage. His fear was that capitalism would savage that heritage and cut it short. Marcuse wrote of Goldmann's "deep apprehension lest Western society destroy all that was dear to him," his fear that literature, art, and all of humanity's creations and creative potentials would be vanquished by adaptation to a world that valued consumption rather than culture and community.[8] The authority of tragedy demanded not a closed mind and resignation, but openness to human possibilities.

It is remarkable that from a viewpoint opposite to that of Bloom, Edward Said is guilty of the same type of misconstruing—that is, missing the dialectic of tragedy and hope that structured Goldmann's thought. In an essay on Lukács and Goldmann entitled "Travelling Theory," Said proposes that "Goldmann's adaptation of Lukács removes from theory its insurrectionary role." Said proposes that in the work of Goldmann, a "politically committed scholar," an "awareness of class or group consciousness is first of all a scholarly imperative, and then—in the works of highly privileged writers—the expression of a tragically limited social situation." In contrast, the revolutionary class consciousness ascribed by Lukács, the "directly involved militant," to the proletariat, was itself "an insurgent against the capitalist order."[9]

But between *History and Class Consciousness*, written in the aftermath of Bolshevism's triumph, and *The Hidden God*, which was presented originally as a *doctorat d'état* at the Sorbonne in 1956, came Stalin and Hitler instead of world proletarian revolution—all of which is absent in Said's interpretation. The absence is glaring, for it is only by ignoring the intervening history that Said can oppose Lukács, the "directly involved militant," to Goldmann, the "politically committed scholar." He thereby misses the vital difference: that between a Marxist intellectual who believes in 1923 that the working class is about to become the "identical subject-object of history" and a Marxist intellectual who, after Stalin and Hitler, is consumed by the authority of tragedy—yet who still insists on hope, insists that his Marxist humanism "still moves." The hidden god may have become the hidden class, but Goldmann's Pascal is a man of paradox, poised between tragedy and the dialectic. Echoing Lukács's early essay on "The Metaphysics of Tragedy," Goldmann presented tragic man as a being in the world but not of it, since real value lay in the transcendent, in a *Deus absconditus*. Since the deity is hidden, this world becomes the sole reality that humans face. Pascal, tragic thinker and harbinger of the dialectic, says both yes and no to this world. And he wagers. So, too, Lucien Goldmann, but not quite: he insisted on the yes though haunted by the no. He was a dialectician and proponent of—wagerer on—human "hope" and "possibility" who equally recognized the authority of tragedy in the human condition.

When Goldmann read Lukács seriously for the first time, in Switzerland in the early 1940s, the two texts that made a particularly profound impression on him were "The Metaphysics of Tragedy" and *History and Class Consciousness*. The first, a pre-Marxist work, envisaged an unbridgeable gap between authentic life and everyday existence, in which everything is "an anarchy of light and dark" and "nothing is ever completely fulfilled."[10] *History and Class Consciousness*, which reinjected vigorously classical German philosophy and dialectical categories into Marxism with vigor, contained a brilliant critique of bourgeois social science and philosophy on one hand, and anticipated the imminent revolutionary transformation of the totality of human reality on the other.

It is hardly surprising that both these works—one focused on tragedy, one suffused with apocalyptic utopianism—intrigued him so. Goldmann was then a refugee, and Europe was engulfed in world war. Born in Bucharest in 1913, his youth was spent in difficult straits in the Moldavian town of Botoşani. After spending the academic year 1930–1931 in Vienna, where he studied with the Austro-Marxist philosopher and sociologist Max Adler, Goldmann entered law school in Bucharest. The Romanian Right was then ascendent and anti-Semitism was fierce. Goldmann was active in—and eventually in conflict with—communist student circles. The source of tension was what might be called his premature anti-Stalinism. He received his degree but emigrated to Paris, where he lived until fleeing the Nazis, first to Toulouse and then to Switzerland. There, he befriended Piaget and immersed himself in Lukács, while becoming increasingly interested in Pascal and Racine and writing a doctoral thesis on Kant. The war's end brought him back to Paris, where he affiliated with the Centre National de la Recherche Scientifique and obtained French citizenship, though with some difficulty. He was apparently rejected more than once, and even after he was naturalized, he harbored the fear that, somehow, he might be sent back to Romania, where his former communist comrades had come to power. As one consequence, he was cautious about writing directly about political matters for most of the 1950s.[11]

In 1952 Goldmann published *The Human Sciences and Philosophy*, a withering critique of mainstream methodology in the human sciences and the first full-length exposition of his emerging methodological ideas. Their fullest elaboration and application came in his study of Pascal and Racine three years later, *The Hidden God*. This *doctorat d'état* was presented for a six-hour public defense at the Sorbonne in February 1956. As reported in *Le Monde*, at its end, an admiring though wry member of the jury, Jean Piaget, addressed the candidate: "Monsieur Goldmann, you know, no doubt, that there are interesting but false theories. There are true theories which contribute little or nothing. Yours is very interesting—perhaps it is true." As described in the weekly *L'Express*, the panel, composed of especially eminent scholars—in addition to Piaget, Jean Wahl, Henri Gouhier, Maurice de Gandillac, and Octave Nadel—was thoroughly seduced by Goldmann's unorthodox interpretation, except for Nadel. The latter characterized Goldmann as an electrician who deformed a chateau while trying to illuminate it.[12]

The Hidden God provoked rage from traditional and conservative interpreters of Pascal and Racine. Goldmann's suggestion that Pascal was a precursor of Marx was particularly irksome to some: how could a foreigner—a Marxist!—trespass on sanctified French terrain, and with such conclusions? Equally annoyed were the "orthodox" Marxists of *La Nouvelle Critique*. As two of his students, Sami Naïr and Michel Löwy, later commented, for Communist Party intellectuals, Goldmann was a non-Party spoilsport.[13] Despite—or perhaps because of—these accusations of heresy, *The Hidden God* placed Goldmann on the French intellectual map. Yet while he eventually attained secure academic status, he always remained something of an outsider and few of his leading students were French.

In the ensuing years, Goldmann played an active and prominent role in French and European intellectual life, writing on a wide array of subjects for journals of the non-Communist Left, such as *Les Temps modernes* and *Arguments*, and engaging intellectuals across the continent. "His flowing white locks," Leszek Kolakowski recalled, "and bear-like silhouette were familiar to participants in innumerable congresses and humanistic symposia at which in a bass voice and passionate somewhat aggressive tones, he would expatiate time and again on the principles of genetic structuralism as exemplified particularly in Pascal and Racine."

Goldmann appears as "Fabien Edelman" in *The Samurai*, Julia Kristeva's roman à clef about French intellectuals in the 1960s: "Graying, potbellied, smiling, with his shirt open and of course no tie, he addressed everyone by the familiar *tu* and was always ripping up existentialism and lauding dialectical reason (as overhauled by Pascal), alienation, and the New Novel."[14] (Goldmann was Kristeva's doctoral adviser upon her arrival in Paris from Bulgaria). Witold Gombrowicz, in his diary for 1965, expressed almost comic fury after an encounter with Goldmann. The latter pressed his own interpretation of Gombrowicz's play *The Marriage* against that of the playwright: "Goldmann, professor, critic, broad-shouldered Marxist, decreed that I did not know, that he knew better! Rabid Marxist imperialism! They use that doctrine to invade people! Goldmann, armed with Marxism, was the subject—I, deprived of Marxism, was the object."[15]

In 1959, Goldmann became a directeur d'études and chair of the section on the sociology of literature at the École des Hautes Études. He held this position until his death, although in the early 1960s he also founded the Center for the Sociology of Literature at the Free University of Brussels. While he continued his cultural writings, his politics became increasingly explicit. The axis of Goldmann's politics was the realization of the individual in "the authentic human community." The latter he often identified with "totality." In his first book, Goldmann had presented Kant as a thinker in quest of a totality he took to be unattainable. Lukács's contribution in *History and Class Consciousness*, Goldmann later contended repeatedly, was in returning the Hegelian—and therefore a historical—concept of totality to the center of Marxism. For Lukács, "totality" was the perspective of the proletariat, the universal class, which in understanding its own interests understood thereby humanity's interests, which in revolutionizing itself revolutionized the world. For Goldmann, as for Lukács, "totality" was a matter of both method and aspiration. Marxism, by thinking historically, dialectically, and in terms of transindividual actors, a "we," provided the possibility to actualize "totality," something impossible for Kant who could not go beyond the individual.

While the young Goldmann, like Lukács, believed that the proletariat was the historical guarantor of his wager, by the late 1950s this was no longer the case. Goldmann still posited the "objective possibility" of socialism, but he had concluded that it was no longer plausible to envision the traditional working class as the revolutionary agent—the transindividual subject—that would transform history as Marxism had conceived it. Nor, of course, would Communist parties, which, according to Leninism, ought to have rendered explicit and embodied the proletariat's revolutionary consciousness much as, on the cultural level, Pascal and Racine's work did for the tragic consciousness of the *noblesse de robe* (legal nobility) in Goldmann's interpretation of seventeenth-century France. (Goldmann's personal experiences, and not only his theoretical conclusions, could only have made him skeptical of Communist parties. The behavior of French Communists in 1968, when Goldmann supported the worker-student revolt, probably reminded him of his unhappy encounter with their Romanian counterparts when he was a youth in Bucharest in the 1930s).

While the question of class was always important for Goldmann, unlike Lukács he almost always formulated his politics as the quest for "the authentic human community." This "totality" was not one into which the individual or the particular vanished; the whole required the parts no less than the parts required the whole. Again unlike Lukács, he argued that liberal values, such as individual freedom, tolerance, and equality before the law were historical products of the emergence of market societies and that however much socialism sought—and ought—to negate capitalism, it could not negate these principles, save at its peril. Consequently, he came to conceive "the authentic human community" as a decentralized market socialism based on *autogestion*, workers's self-management. In the early 1960s he embraced the quasi-syndicalist notion of revolutionary-reformism, formulated by such theorists as Serge Mallet and André Gorz. They argued that a "new working class" had been created as advanced "organized" capitalism displaced liberal capitalism. This metamorphosis had engendered and required "new middle strata" of professionals and technicians, who would, it was proposed, lead the traditional working class in a struggle for the qualitative transformation of the workplace, in the direction of democracy and self-management. "*Autogestion*" was one of the watchwords of the "Events" of May 1968 in Paris, and the French New Left in general; Goldmann embraced it, as did the *soixante-huitards*, although not uncritically.

Throughout the 1960s, especially between 1968 and 1970, Goldmann often sounded like a man in search of a transindividual subject to win his wager. He passed from Europe's intellectual world as the 1960s did, succumbing in October 1970 to hepatitis complicated by internal hemorrhaging. In his writings, Goldmann proposed that transindividual mental structures and not biography should be the locus of research; likewise, Goldmann disregarded the biographical in himself, as his friend and rival Henri Lefebvre observed. Goldmann was neglectful of his own health, usually obese, often ill: his premature death at age fifty-seven corresponded, in a way, with his oeuvre.[16] Six volumes of his shorter works and essays, two of which he was laboring on when he died, have been published since.

Lucien Goldmann's work never received its due. While discussions of him appear in various histories of Western Marxism and several valuable, short books on him appeared in French, German, and Italian in the early 1970s, this is the first attempt to capture his work as a whole rather than in an introductory manner. In one way or another, all of Goldmann's writings are deeply engaged with previous philosophical controversies concerning method in the human sciences. For this reason, the biographical chapters in this book are followed by two chapters analyzing in some detail the debates preceding him. Goldmann's work cannot be understood or appreciated fully apart from them. Thereafter I treat, in consecutive chapters, Goldmann's theories themselves, their various applications, their engagement with the French intellectual world of his day, and finally Goldmann's politics. Goldmann tended to be a hermeneutic thinker, that is, he tended to theorize through interpreting the works of others. For this reason I have sought, throughout this book, to situate Goldmann in relation to the writers to whom he was responding or, more specifically, in relation to their arguments.

There is a decided slant toward philosophy in these pages. This is because Goldmann's principal achievement was, in my view, as a philosopher of the human sciences, and his theory of them is embedded in all his literary studies and political pronouncements. He insisted on the partial identity of subject and object and his writings on method cannot be artificially separated from the object of his studies.

If the subject is always within the object, if facts and values cannot be simplistically separated and opposed to each other, then a scholar ought not to feign a false and unattainable objectivity, argued Goldmann. Rather, the scholar's perspective should be declared openly in order to facilitate criticism of his or her work. It is a point with which I concur; and I readily declare my sympathies with his endeavor, although, again, it will be evident that I intentionally violate several of his precepts in the ensuing pages. Eppur si muove? It is unpopular nowadays—even considered futile by some—to ask this question of the work of a socialist humanist, however anti-Stalinist, unorthodox, and inventive. Goldmann's work, or at least my analysis of it, will, I trust, respond for itself.

Part One ─────────────────────────────────

GENESIS

1

A Youth in Romania

LUCIEN GOLDMANN SPOKE RARELY of his origins. Perhaps this was for personal reasons, and perhaps it was due to his own methodological strictures against biography. In any event, records of his youth are few. Indeed, they are so sparse that details must be presented with constant caveats. He did leave an important clue, however, in a passing remark he made in 1959, a quarter of a century after quitting Romania for France, in a commentary on Marc Chagall's paintings. The milieu of Chagall's adolescence, said Goldmann, was similar to that of his own.[1]

He did not elaborate. Instead, he focused on how the "mental structures" generated during Chagall's youth in the Jewish community of Vitebsk (Belorussia), at the turn of the century, found expression in his paintings. Among these structures were the separation of urban from rural existence, and especially the estrangement of Jews from peasant life. Chagall pursued an artist's career—a path taken by relatively few eastern European Jews, as Goldmann noted. This choice indicated an unease in the painter, a sense that for him the Jewish world was "problematic." In this, he was like Racine, the Jansenist turned playwright, whose tragic vision absorbed much of Goldmann's intellectual energies in the 1950s. Having quit the Jansenist world "for the 'world' at large," Racine still saw the latter "in the very categories" of the former.[2]

The same may be said, at least in part, of Goldmann, an eastern European Jew who, like Chagall, eventually made France his home. Unlike Chagall, Goldmann pursued a career well-populated by Jews— that of an intellectual. However, the Jewish and Romanian worlds from which he came were problematic for him. (One day, the Marxism he avidly embraced within them both would be problematic for him too). Isaac Deutscher's description of the "non-Jewish Jew" suited Goldmann well; he dwelled "on the borderlines of various civilizations, religions, and natural cultures"; he was "born and brought up on the borderlines of various epochs"; his "mind matured where the most diverse cultural influences crossed and fertilized each other."[3]

Indeed, here was a Romanian Jew who, immersed in German philosophy, sought to synthesize the Marxism of a Hungarian (Lukács) with the epistemological theories of a Swiss (Piaget) in a theory of culture that he applied to Pascal, Racine, and Jansenism in seventeenth-century France. Did not Novalis declare—in an aphorism prominently quoted by Lukács at the beginning of his *Theory of the Novel*—that "[p]hilosophy is really homesickness; it is the urge to be at home everywhere"? But the effort to be at home everywhere runs the risk of being at home nowhere. Goldmann's thought was structured by a dialectical tension between his restless quest for "authentic human community" and his powerful obsession with the concept of tragedy. He insisted on the possibility of the former while recognizing the authority of the latter. He was a dialectician of tragic hope. To discern the sociohistorical genesis of this dialectic, we turn to Romania at the turn of the twentieth century.

I

Shortly before World War I, Constantin Dobrogeanu-Gherea, "Romania's Marx" according to Karl Kautsky, described the country as "a monstrous mingling of old and new," in which bourgeois legal structures were superimposed on a largely peasant, precapitalist society.[4] Lucien Goldmann was born Sergiu-Lucian Goldmann on Kiseleff Street in Bucharest at 8 P.M. on June 20, 1913, and spent his youth in the town of Botoşani, in the northeastern province of Moldavia. He later returned to the national capital to attend university. In the interim, Lucian, as his name was spelled in Romanian, was exposed to all that troubled a profoundly troubled country. Romania was an overpopulated land, rife with conflict between town and country. Rural poverty was extensive and brutal. The peasantry, which composed some 78 percent of the population and was politically disenfranchised until after World War I, periodically expressed its grievances violently. Industrial development was slow, although postwar land reforms fueled a small commercial class and hurried a decline of the aristocracy. As of 1930 only 10 percent of the population could be classified as proletarians.

Romanian society was characterized by an essential contradiction, argued Gherea in his book *Neoserfdom* (1910), a minor classic of Marxist literature on underdevelopment. In the aftermath of the various European revolutions of 1848, liberal ideas and institutions had been fostered in Romania, although without any corresponding social and economic development. The 1866 constitution gave joint legislative responsibility to the king and parliament, but left the land's feudal structure in place. Politics was dominated by the Liberal and Conservative parties. There was, in brief, a bourgeois superstructure with a feudal base—in Gherea's words, a "gap between formality and actual reality."[5] Leon Trotsky, who befriended Gherea when he came to Bucharest to report on the Balkan Wars for a Russian journal in the summer of Goldmann's birth, wrote: "The fundamental question of Romanian social development, the agrarian question, cannot . . . be solved from within parties in which the tone is set by serf-owning landlords dressed in European liberal clothes."[6]

Nationality problems plagued the kingdom as well. Until 1914, ethnic Romanians comprised most of the population. World War I doubled the country's territories, however, resulting in an enlarged presence of national minorities. By the time of the 1930 census, ethnic Romanians comprised 72 percent of the population (some 13 million people); 8 percent were Hungarians (1.4 million people), 4 percent were Germans (0.7 million people), and 4 percent were Jews (0.7 million people).[7] In these circumstances, increasing numbers of ethnic Romanians found an outlet for their frustrations in a fierce racial nationalism. Chauvinist agitation, combined with the neglect of rural grievances by relatively moderate but corrupt governments in the 1920s, contributed to the rise of peasant parties on one hand, and to movements that were protofascist, antileftist, antidemocratic, and anti-Semitic, on the other (the most notorious was the Iron Guard). A. C. Cuza, the "apostle" of Romanian anti-Semitism, was dean of the law faculty at the University of Jassy, not far from Botoșani.[8] For the Romanian Right, the peasant embodied the nation; Jews, who were not legally emancipated until 1919, were viewed as aliens and competitors, particularly in the universities, the seedbed of Romanian fascism in the 1920s. Goldmann's teenage years were in a world of relentless anti-Semitism. There were, as one scholar put it, "two antipodes of Romanian social, ethnic and cultural symbolism, the Jew and the peasant." Nationalist students demanded anti-Jewish quotas, and bitterly complained of Jewish overrepresentation in professional schools.[9]

A counterforce, though modest, came from the Left. Romanian social democracy was founded in the 1890s, but socialist ideas established a (minor) presence in the 1870s and 1880s as exiled Russian and Bulgarian revolutionaries passed through the country. In 1880, Gherea, a Ukrainian Jew born Solomon Katz, published the first Romanian-language socialist pamphlet, "An Open Letter to Premier I. Bratianu by Caius Gracchus."[10] Nineteenth-century Romanian socialists were influenced not only by Russian but also by western European— especially French and German—socialist thinking.

It was mostly intellectuals who were drawn to Marxist ideas; there was no social base for a proletarian movement in this agrarian land. Populists, most famously Constantin Stere, branded social democracy an "exotic plant." Certainly, such suggestions were reinforced by the central roles within social democracy of first Gherea and then Christian Rakovsky, an ethnic Bulgarian who would later be an ally of Trotsky and a victim of Stalin's purges. Romanian rightists maintained that left-wing ideas were "foreign" and often identified Jewry with Bolshevism. Undoubtedly, they felt their views confirmed by the large number of young Jews who rallied to the Left, which consistently denounced anti-Semitism.[11]

The Romanian Social Democratic Labor party was established in 1893 under Gherea's leadership and was oriented toward the mainstream of European Marxism. Gherea believed that socialism could be born only after capitalist development displaced feudalism; it was capitalism, therefore, that was on the Romanian agenda—the existing bourgeois superstructural forms had to be given a capitalist content. The party survived only until 1900, when a bloc of leading members moved to the Right.[12] It was reconstituted a decade later; consequently, its status was tenuous when Romanian communism emerged from splits in its ranks after the Russian Revolution. (Gherea died in 1920.)

The impact of the Bolshevik and Hungarian revolutions on the Romanian Left was profound. In the postwar period, virtually every hue of Marxism could be found within the kingdom's borders, albeit each with few followers. Some writings by Lenin and Trotsky were issued in 1918 by a "Romanian Revolutionary Communist Committee," and in the ensuing decade Romanian communists published materials in numerous languages, including Romanian, Russian, Ukrainian, German, and Yiddish.[13] The progress of Romanian communism was, however, quite slow. The Romanian Communist Party (RCP) was founded in 1921 and banned three years later. It faced severe repression on one hand, and competition from Social Democrats for support within the small working class, on the other. The RCP was also hampered by factionalism and purges, born of meddling by the Comintern. It is estimated that its membership dropped from two thousand in 1922 to twelve hundred in 1931.[14] In that year, at its fifth congress (held in Moscow), it came firmly under Comintern dominion.

The RCP, like the Social Democrats, advocated a proletarian ideology in a precapitalist society. Its organizing efforts centered on three major groups: workers, peasants, and national minorities. It was a strong proponent of minority rights and recruited many Jews, especially young intellectuals, into its ranks. There was even a Yiddish-speaking Organization of Communist Jews.[15] Alexandru Dobrogeanu-Gherea, Constantin's son, was among the Jews who achieved prominence in the new party at this time, along with the future foreign minister Ana Pauker (Rabinovici) and her husband, Marcel. Among its supporters was a young Botoşani Jew named Lucian Goldmann.

II

"From a sociological point of view, the town in which I spent my youth probably differs little from many other Moldavian towns," reads an unpublished autobiographical fragment Goldmann sketched in 1956. He recalled a small city, not much industrialized, its mill having been destroyed by fire, its sugar works providing two to three months of seasonal employment each year—"one of the principal events in [Botoşani's] social life." It was a world Chagall might have painted:

> Around the town was an extensive agricultural range composed partly of large and medium sized landed estates [*exploitations*] whose owners lived in the city, and partly of a small scale peasantry and agricultural workers. The sale of agricultural products from all these lands naturally constituted the principal source of revenue for the town's inhabitants. Within it there were two communities which were numerically almost equal: Jews and Christians. The former were concentrated in crafts and commerce. Some were quite rich [but] the majority was extremely poor. [Christians] occupied all the public positions in the civil and military bureaucracy, and also [were the] manual workers and menial laborers.[16]

Botoşani was a crossroads and the site of crosscurrents. It was the capital of Botoşani district, a market town for agricultural produce and a commercial junction for goods passing to and from Austria and Russia. The municipality had a lively civic and cultural life, with a good theater and numerous publishing houses and journals. The region as a whole was vibrant in Romanian cultural history. The national poet, Mihai Eminescu, was born near Botoşani in 1850, and the nationalist historian Nicolae Iorga was born in the town in 1871, and attended the same *liceu* (academic high school) in which Goldmann would later be enrolled.

Jews first came to Botoşani in 1540, and the city's Jewish community became one of the most important in Moldavia, the second largest in the province until the late nineteenth century. In 1899 Jews numbered some 16,817 in the town, making up 51.8 percent of its population, including 75 percent of its merchants and about 68 percent of its artisans. In 1930—the year in which Goldmann left—some 11,840 Jews lived in Botoşani, composing approximately 36.6 percent of the inhabitants.[17] There were numerous Jewish houses of worship, and the town's rabbi, Ezra Zuckerman, had an excellent library of Judaica. In tumultuous times, Moldavia's Jews, town dwellers with highly visible middleman roles in a predominantly rural economy, were easy and frequent scapegoats, entrapped between estate owners and peasants. There were anti-Jewish riots in Botoşani in 1870, and Jews there, and throughout Moldavia, were particularly victimized during the peasant uprising of 1907. "It was directed at first against Jewish tenants in northern Moldavia," Rakovsky wrote, "and was prompted by the antisemitic outbursts of Romanian liberals and nationalists. After plundering the Jews's farmsteads, however, the peasants turned on the Romanian tenants and then the landlords. . . . The whole country, that is all the villages, was engulfed in the flames of the rising."[18]

This "jacquerie," which occurred just six years before Goldmann's birth, was especially traumatic for the Jewish inhabitants of Botoşani city, for the national upheaval began in their province. Peasants rampaged through the town center; local Old Believers (Russian Orthodox schismatics) plundered Jewish stores; the populist newspaper *Moldava de Sus* (Northern Moldavia) called upon "all true Romanians" to join the struggle "to save our ancestral land and our race from the plague and infernal plans of the Yids."[19] If Gherea, who wrote *Neoserfdom* in the aftermath of these events, identified the contradiction between a bourgeois superstructure and a feudal base as Romania's essential structural quandary, one could add that the Jews were in the pith of the contradiction, particularly as commercialization of Romania's agriculture began in the late nineteenth century.

Jews had no political rights and were forbidden to own rural land. (This changed only when citizenship was officially conferred after World War I.) They were, however, permitted to be *arendaşi*, managers of the estates of the large landlords. Among their tasks was the subletting of small tracts to individual peasants. "While serving as a tool of feudal exploitation," wrote Trotsky, "the rightless Jew has at the same time to serve as the lightning-conductor for the wrath of the exploited." Romania's ruling strata, he observed, not only needed Jews as intermediaries between landlords and peasants, they needed hatred of Jews.[20]

In the late nineteenth century, the number of Jewish arendaşi grew, and many were Austrian in origin. Botoşani district had the highest percentage of cultivable land (52 percent) leased to arendaşi, and the second-highest percentage (28 percent) of land let to Jewish arendaşi in particular.[21] However, unlike their non-Jewish counterparts, these Jewish managers could never hope to purchase the tracts they supervised;

their status was that of permanent middlemen with no options outside of utilizing their positions to their best, if limited, advantage. In practice, this often meant extracting the highest rent possible. At the turn of the century, these circumstances, combined with often bitter competition among both Jewish and non-Jewish arendaşi, intensified resentments towards Jews in general.

The arendaşi composed a social stratum doomed by historical developments—not unlike the noblesse de robe of seventeenth-century France, who would one day preoccupy Goldmann. A chief concern of Romanian peasants was to obtain easier conditions for agricultural leases.[22] Conservative populism, articulated in particular by Vasile Kogalniceanu, agitated on behalf of the small peasants and against the arendaşi—though not against the landlords. The chief demand was that land be rented directly by landlords to peasants, and not through the arendaşi. Similarly, the arendaşi were the targets of the Village Cooperative movement, which called for rents to be paid directly to landlords. The Liberal party, advocate of a select program of industrialization, also attacked the arendaşi, and the Conservatives, who were beholden to the big landowners, preferred peasant ire to be deflected from them toward the arendaşi.[23] Consequently, when the revolt broke out, the Jewish arendaşi were the first quarry, although the violence soon expanded beyond them. According to the report of Ilie Vasescu, prefect of Botoşani province,

> [T]he inhabitants . . . are demanding the expulsion of the Jewish arendaşi from the estates. On the pretext that they have not been getting what they wanted, armed bands of peasants have been organized who devastate and destroy everything and steal everything they find. . . . They take over the town halls and expel the communal authorities. It is therefore a complete revolution.[24]

Bucharest eventually suppressed the uprising.

Reforms enacted after World War I divided estates to the benefit of small landlords and peasants, redistributing some four million hectares.[25] The day of the Jewish arendaşi, Moldavia's quintessential rural middleman, was over, although anti-Semitism was not. During the war itself, when Goldmann was a child in Botoşani, the retreating Romanian army brutalized Jews in the town and throughout Moldavia and Wallachia. "The Jew is without any protection, [is] beyond the law" wrote an observer shortly afterwards.[26]

In short, Goldmann passed his childhood in a period of trauma, and his youth at a time of battling ideologies and prejudices. His parents were relatively prosperous and secular Jews. They rarely went to synagogue although "Gică," as Lucian was affectionately known, received some religious education, was taught some Hebrew, and had a Bar Mitsvah.[27] His father was in the legal profession and was twenty-nine when his only son was born. Joseph Goldmann died of chronic syphilis seven years later, leaving his wife Serafina (née Bernbaum) destitute. She was twenty-four when she gave birth, and came of Polish-Viennese background. Her son's file at the University of Bucharest contains an official certificate of her indigence and numerous pleas for aid by him to the dean.[28]

What his mother could not give to him financially, she gave culturally. "She was a hard woman and that was decisive for his development, along with his father's death," according to an acquaintance. "She may have been the most cultivated woman in the city, having been imbued with a profound literary culture. Their home was filled with books and languages—it was impregnated with intellectual life. This was the milk she gave him."[29] Nonetheless, the relation between mother and child seems to have been difficult. After Goldmann quit Romania in the 1930s, he had only occasional contact with her. She spent World War II in hiding, and remained in Botoşani until Goldmann arranged for her to come to Paris in the 1960s. She died not long before the death of her son.[30]

Goldmann received his secondary education at the August Treboniu Laurian academic high school, which was famed as one of the finest in the country. Founded in 1859, the Laurian became a liceu (roughly equivalent to a French lycée) in 1889, the first in northern Moldavia. It was known for its French teachers. Goldmann spoke Romanian, Yiddish, and German from his early years; the last seems to have been his native tongue.

The student body at the Laurian was mixed. Of 521 pupils in the school year 1927–1928, 162 were Jewish (31.1 percent), and 359 were Christian (68.9 percent). This represented an exceptional situation; before citizenship was granted to them, Jews were barred from state primary schools, and secondary schools opened their doors infrequently. Goldmann was an undistinguished student. He received his baccalaureate in August 1930, tenth in a class of thirty-nine, passing exams in Romanian, Latin, French, geography, natural sciences, natural history, and civics. Beyond schoolwork, however, he developed a passion for poetry, especially that of Baudelaire, Heine, and Rilke, and avidly followed literary movements abroad. He was, according to a schoolmate, "a teenager full of intellectual zeal." When this schoolmate subscribed to Henri Barbusse's journal, *Monde*, Goldmann habitually came to borrow it as soon as it arrived from Paris.[31]

Goldmann's political education began in 1927, when he became a member of the Botoşani chapter of Ha-Shomer ha-Tsair (the Young

Guard), a Zionist socialist youth movement. His mother enrolled him primarily for social reasons. At age fourteen, Lucian was fatherless, had a physical deformity—he was hunchbacked and rowed regularly on a nearby lake in the hope that muscles would disguise this fact— and was a lonely youth with few friends. In Ha-Shomer ha-Tsair he discovered a "home" in "a community of intellectual youth," in the words of David Zoller, the former head of his chapter.[32] Goldmann was an active and then a leading member for three years.

Ha-Shomer ha-Tsair was born in pre–World War I Galicia as an apolitical youth organization. Its founders were attracted to the romanticism then current in German and Polish youth movements and were also influenced by Viennese intellectual trends. Members tended to be from middle-class backgrounds, like Goldmann's, and many young Jews in Goldmann's liceu passed through its ranks. In it they were intensely educated to a vision of "youth community" in which the individual, the "I," would be fulfilled in a "We." Western materialism was shunned, lofty values embraced, and the "middleman" status of many diaspora Jews rejected as a source of vulnerability and spiritual deprivation. (Surely, the fate of the arendaşi made this poignant for Botoşani youth.) "Without being religious," comments a historian, "they were imbued with a religious spirit in the sense of a moral revivalism and inner faith."[33] (Guards) engaged in a youthful pursuit of moral perfection, turning to eclectic sources for inspiration. Their readings ranged from the Prophets, the Essenes, and the Hasidim to the New Testament, Martin Buber, and Gustav Landauer. They were particularly stirred by the romantic anticapitalism of Gustav Wyneken, the ideologue of the German Free Youth Movement, who summoned disciples to create egalitarian and pacifist youth communities based on ethical absolutism and hostility to all things bourgeois.[34]

By the mid-1920s many Shomrim sought "self-realization" as "pioneers" in communal farms (kibbutzim) in Palestine. Local chapters in the diaspora, including Goldmann's, trained members in agriculture with this in mind. In late 1925 a severe economic crisis engulfed Palestine and radicalized Ha-Shomer ha-Tsair there. The Palestinian chapter proceeded to affix Marxism to its ideology of "individual-in-community," and members turned anxiously to the writings of Lenin, Kautsky, and Max Adler for intellectual guidance.[35] A similar turn followed in diaspora chapters during 1926–1928, precisely when Goldmann joined. The ideology that emerged was a mélange of Zionism, Marxism, romantic anticapitalism, secular religiosity, and communitarianism.[36] This was the context in which Goldmann first studied Marxism. His chapter "imbued" its recruits with "humanism," according to Zoller: "We instilled in them a vision of the world." Goldmann took to his studies with great seriousness and became an important intellectual presence within the group.

It was a particular juncture in the history of Romania as well as that of Ha-Shomer ha-Tsair. The Peasant party had come to power, intensifying anti-Semitism was making Jews feel increasingly vulnerable, and the underground RCP had gained prestige as an implacable foe of these trends. According to the sociologist Joseph Gabel, who befriended Goldmann in Paris in the 1930s, the tenacity of the RCP underground had left a lasting impression on young Goldmann.[37] In the late 1920s communism and Zionism vied vigorously for the allegiance of Botoşani's Jewish youth. Ha-Shomer ha-Tsair expected its adherents to move to Palestine. Many of those who did not became communists. In the Botoşani chapter, an ideological split occurred in 1930. Among those who quit Ha-Shomer ha-Tsair was "Gică" Goldmann; his "faith" in Marxism led him toward communism.[38]

Goldmann's direction was also decisively affected by his participation in a remarkable local institution—the Botoşani Reading Circle. It was founded in 1908 by young Jewish intellectuals—there were about a hundred in the initial group—and sponsored lectures on themes ranging from literature and science to sociology and music. (The head of the Botoşani Credit Bank taught a course in Yiddish literature). Building a library was, however, the primary preoccupation. Books were purchased locally at "Zayde [Grandpa] Schwartz's Bookshop." The collection included materials in Romanian, French, German, and Yiddish, a few books in English and an array of journals in various languages.[39] The library had a particularly good sampling of left-wing literature; in fact, by 1930 it was largely a center for RCP activists.

Goldmann's talents were nurtured in the Reading Circle. He became an enthusiastic member, probably at about age sixteen or seventeen, giving lectures under its auspices and assisting in fund-raising parties to purchase books and to subsidize needy students. In his autobiographical fragment he distinguished sharply between those who simply used the library and those who actively tended to it.[40] From its ranks of sixty–seventy youngsters (many of whom had been active in Ha-Shomer ha-Tsair) came an array of talented individuals, including two future Romanian government ministers, a leading diplomat, and a noted Soviet economist. In 1938 the Reading Circle had the distinction of being closed by order of King Carol II.

By then, Goldmann was long gone. But the *vision du monde* and categories that he assimilated in Botoşani, especially those of Ha-Shomer ha-Tsair (humanism, secular religiosity, and socialism envisioned as the realization of the individual-in-community) remained within him. Or more precisely, he would reinvent them in various guises throughout his life's work, in his insistence that an "authentic human community" was Marxism's true concern, and in his belief that Marxism represented a wager in humanity's future akin to Pascal's in the existence of God.

III

Goldmann's active ties to the Communist underground developed while he was a law student at the University of Bucharest in the early 1930s. First, however, he sojourned to Austria for the academic year 1930-1931. At the University of Vienna, he had contacts with Romanian Communist students studying there; more important, he attended classes in political economy and audited the courses of Max Adler. He was already well acquainted with this renowned Austro-Marxist philosopher from his period in Ha-Shomer ha-Tsair, which had a "Max Adler tendency."[41] In the Austrian capital, seventeen-year-old Goldmann read Marxist theory voraciously, including the works of Otto Bauer, Rudolf Hilferding, Karl Renner, and Friedrich Adler. He may have encountered early writings of the Frankfurt School as well. It was here that he became acquainted with the work of Georg Lukács. Ultimately, no thinker would impress him more, although his decisive reading of Lukács took place later, in Zurich during World War II.

Goldmann's initial interest in Kant may have derived from reading Max Adler in Botoşani; it certainly blossomed in his course in Vienna. While Goldmann always referred appreciatively to Adler, he preferred to minimize the latter's impact on him. This was misleading on his part, for Adler's influence on Goldmann was decisive. Not only was Adler a neo-Kantian Marxist and Goldmann the author of a doctoral thesis on Kant, but Adler's concept of "social a priori" was almost certainly a source of Goldmann's notion of transindividuality. It is likely that neo-Kantianism also provided a link between Goldmann's flowering philosophical interests and his legal education in Bucharest, which began in 1931.[42]

Neo-Kantianism was preoccupied by the question of method and by the relation between facts and values. These themes became prominent in contemporary jurisprudence as a result of the writings of Emil Lask, Gustav Radbruch, Hans Kelsen, and Rudolf Stammler. For Goldmann, Lask was undoubtedly the most important of them. Like both Adler and Goldmann, Lask began his career in legal studies and then shifted to philosophy. He befriended and profoundly influenced Lukács and Heidegger; all three were nurtured in the milieu of Heidelberg neo-Kantianism. Goldmann later devoted substantial effort to criticizing neo-Kantianism, but he made extensive use of Lask's concepts, and singled him out for praise.[43] The references are most often to Lask's *Fichtes Idealismus und die Geschichte* (1901), but as a law student Goldmann almost certainly read the *Rechtsphilosophie* (1905). In it Lask analyzed the relation between legal studies (conceived as "cultural sciences") and "worldviews" and the relation between "cultural values" and individuals (conceived as "empirical" realities). He aimed to transcend the opposition in legal theory between natural law (with its ahistorical absolute values) and historicism (with its relativism) in order to establish the existence of objective, nonindividualized "transpersonal values."[44] Lask and Radbruch employed the terms "transindividual" and "transpersonal" in their respective theories to explicate cultural structures that linked yet superseded individuals; Goldmann would reinvent these notions in Marxist form in his theory of the "transindividual subject" of collective historical action.

At the University of Bucharest law school, the philosophy of public law received great emphasis, especially the writings of contemporary German and French theorists.[45] In addition to his legal training, Goldmann studied political economy with G. Tasca, a powerful figure at the university, who later served in the cabinet, representing the Peasant party. Goldmann's expression of gratitude to him in the preface to his *Mensch, Gemeinschaft und Welt in der Philosophie Immanuel Kants*, is the sole acknowledgment to a Romanian in his works.[46]

Following three years of study, Goldmann received his law degree (Licenta in Drept) in December 1934. It was an inopportune time for a Jewish Marxist to be studying law in Bucharest. Universities were not only at the center of national chauvinism and anti-Semitism, but they were permeated by corruption. Goldmann, like most other students, often had no choice but to bribe professors. The year before Goldmann enrolled, Salo Baron reported that in the overcrowded Bucharest law school, many students had come "unsatisfactorily prepared, and having no interest in their studies . . . spend their time and energy, in the absence of university sports, on Jew-baiting or actual Jew-beating."[47] Surviving classmates of Goldmann testify to an atmosphere of pervasive prejudice on the campus and in the city. "Anti-Semitism was ever present," according to Leonte Răutu (then Lev Oigenstein), who briefly shared a room with Goldmann and who would later, as RCP Politburo member responsible for ideology and culture in the 1950s in the regime of Gheorghiu Gheorghiu-Dej, be known as the Zhdanov of Romania. Another (non-Jewish) friend of Goldmann's, Mihail Dragomirescu, secretary-general of the Student Democratic Front, an RCP front organization of the mid-1930s, recalls that "the central question at the time was: are you an anti-Semite or not?"[48]

Goldmann frequented, and may have briefly lived at, the Schuller Dormitory, a residence for Jewish students in the Jewish quarter of Bucharest. Since Jewish students were refused admittance to most student houses, they were compelled to establish their own. The Schuller was for males (there was a lodging for females nearby), and many nonresident students came regularly for meals. It was a self-managed facility, housed in what, until 1920, was the Italian embassy. The dormitory was endowed initially by a wealthy merchant but later subsidized by the Jewish community. Its inhabitants were mainly poor and from the provinces. The Schuller bustled with politics, both communist and Zionist, and was occasionally targeted by anti-Semitic violence.

Life in the Schuller was dominated by the AGSE, the Asociațiile Generale ale Studenților Evrei (General Union of Jewish Students). In 1931, the illegal Union of Communist Youth (UCY) clandestinely asserted control over the AGSE, displacing the Zionists. The AGSE's president from 1932 to 1934, Carol Neuman, was an RCP sympathizer (who later joined the party), and his successor was Mihail Florescu (born Jacobi), a future minister under the Ceausescu regime. The UCY usually met at the Schuller under the cover of "cultural discussions," which included non-Jewish students as well. It was in this environment that Goldmann met Jewish communists, such as Răutu and Florescu, as well as non-Jewish communists, such as Dragomirescu and Miron Constantinescu. The latter, a future Politburo member and minister of education, would author the preface for the single volume of Goldmann's essays to appear in Communist Romania.[49]

Goldmann lectured regularly at the Schuller on Marxist themes, with Communist approval. He frequented popular student haunts, such as La Yogu, an Albanian dairy cafe, and the Cofetăria Pariziană, all in the vicinity of Calea Văcărești, where fashionable Bucharest cafes were to be found. Acquaintances recall him as intellectually mature beyond his years, eagerly discussing the implications of Freud and Einstein for Marxism, along with the ideas of Max Adler and Austro-Marxism in general.[50] Goldmann was once caricatured, on a wall in the Schuller reserved for posters and jest, as a young man whose head spewed forth dizzying ideas. It seems that he was especially interested in theories of sexuality as well as the opposite sex. "His head was in the clouds, but when it came to girls, his feet were on the ground."[51]

Goldmann may have written some articles at this time. With one exception, to which we will return presently, none can be identified, since police repression compelled politically active students to sign articles with pseudonyms. Goldmann was active in a Communist front group, the Poor Students Union, which published the *Poor Students' Tribune* (Tribuna Studentului Sărac). He almost certainly wrote for it.

This "newspaper" appeared in poster form and was plastered on walls, new "issues" being printed whenever authorities tore down old ones. None seem to have survived.

Whether Goldmann was actually a member of the Union of Communist Youth and, if he was, whether he joined in Botoşani or Bucharest, is unclear.[52] All Communist organization was clandestine and membership was not openly acknowledged. Goldmann did participate in various Communist and student demonstrations, and possibly in activities supporting the February 1933 railway workers' strike. This was the first significant RCP organized labor action, and some two thousand arrests resulted from clashes with the police.[53] He may have authored an article at this time under a pseudonym entitled "Dincolo de Podul Grant" (On the Other Side of the Grant Bridge). On the other side of this bridge were the miserable districts of Cringasi and Giulesti, in which the railway workers lived.[54] Goldmann's political activities led to a brief imprisonment of about two to three months without trial, although it is impossible to discern the exact time or circumstances. It might have been during the strike, but there was also a general pattern of police roundups of leftist students, particularly during May Day demonstrations and celebrations on the anniversary of the Bolshevik revolution.

Additional details about Goldmann's activities are difficult to obtain. Beyond lecturing in communist student circles, he may have engaged in agitprop work. In this context he probably met Lucretiu Pătrăşçanu, a lawyer and fellow Moldavian, who was one of the RCP's leading intellectuals (and who was married to one of Goldmann's cousins). Using the pseudonym of Andrei, Pătrăşçanu was in charge of RCP agitprop and was greatly respected by Schuller students. Goldmann, in private conversation in Zurich in the 1940s, repeatedly expressed great esteem for Pătrăşçanu, who became a prominent purge victim after the RCP came to power.[55]

Less conjecture places Goldmann as an antifascist activist. With the specters of the Iron Guard and Romanian fascism rising, the RCP tried to organize an antifascist campaign in a Popular Front mold. Prominent journalists and intellectuals began contributing to RCP-dominated publications, thanks to the efforts in 1933–1934 of Ana Pauker and Dmitri Kroshnev, who were the RCP members responsible for these efforts.[56] It was in this context that Goldmann published what was probably his first literary essay, a short study of the novels of N. D. Cocea, which appeared in the weekly *Clopotul* (The Bell) on April 13, 1934. Cocea was a renowned and flamboyant writer and publicist, the author of several satirical works of fiction and an editor of left-wing journals close to the RCP, such as *Reporter*. He occasionally addressed or read poetry to discussion groups organized by the RCP, and Goldmann may have attended some of them. The link between Cocea and the RCP was an acquaintance of Goldmann's from Botoşani (and Romania's ambassador to France in the 1950s), Mircea Bălănescu.[57]

Clopotul was published in Botoşani, and its name was probably chosen to recall Alexander Herzen's journal of the same name. Founded in 1933, *Clopotul* was taken over in February 1934 by "democratic forces"—that is, RCP supporters. It was edited behind the scenes by the RCP's representative in the town, David Salzberg, who had known Goldmann in both Botoşani and Vienna. An important organ of the National Committee to Fight Fascism, *Clopotul* was eventually suppressed. However, the authorities were unwilling to arrest the man who was officially its director and whose name lent it great prestige throughout Moldavia—Scarlat Callimachi, the "Red Prince." This eccentric scion of a wealthy and prestigious noble family lived alternately in Bucharest and in his native Moldavia. He was a radical socialist, and while he was not a Marxist, he maintained close ties to Communist circles. His other passions were French culture and the plight of the Jews; he was married to a Jewish actress and coedited, with a Jewish friend, a collection entitled *Testimony by Travellers and Strangers on Jews in the Romanian Principalities.*[58] When he was in Botoşani, Callimachi occasionally sponsored informal seminars, especially on the "historical sciences," which were often attended by young Jews from the town. Goldmann knew Callimachi in Botoşani, though not well, and it was Callimachi who asked him to write on Cocea for *Clopotul* (which frequently published Cocea's essays as well).

Goldmann had relatively little interest in Romanian literary life per se. His article on Cocea is as concerned with a French author—Anatole France—and an Austrian—Karl Kraus—as with its ostensible Romanian subject. This was natural. While there was considerable Romanian intellectual ferment in the interwar years, it was overwhelmingly right-wing and nationalist in orientation.[59] In his controversial critique of Romanian intellectual life in the early 1930s, *Nu* (No), the young Eugène Ionesco declared, "I would urge on all my young literary colleagues the greatest circumspection and the most systematic distrust towards sacred Romanian 'values.'" Romanian culture was characterized, in his view, by "a prodigious confusion of projects [*de plans*], by an extraordinary absence of critical sense."[60]

If any Romanian figure impressed Goldmann, it was probably Dobrogeanu-Gherea. This cannot be asserted with certainty, and Gherea's ideas were not in favor in RCP circles. In the late 1960s, long after he was established in France, Goldmann made a point of asking a visiting

Romanian friend to send him Gherea's works.[61] Gherea was among
the first to apply Marxist categories to the study of culture, and some
of his themes are comparable to those of Goldmann. In 1891 he wrote
a celebrated essay tracing the social genesis of pessimism in literature
to intellectuals made vulnerable by the vicissitudes of the market;
Goldmann, in *The Hidden God*, traced the genesis of the tragic vision to
the historical fate of the noblesse de robe.

Gherea suggested that orthodox Marxism could not account for segments within classes that have some interests in common with other
classes. He thereby anticipated later debates on defining new middle
strata within capitalism. This issue of middle strata reappeared
throughout Goldmann's life, beginning with his youth as a Jew in
Moldavia and continuing on through his study of the noblesse de robe.
In addition, Austro-Marxists devoted considerable efforts in the 1920s
and 1930s to analyzing this question, as did an important portion of
the French New Left in the 1960s. Goldmann's politics, in the last decade of his life, rested on the hope that a "new working class," led by
the new strata of technical and intellectual wage earners produced by
advanced capitalism, would lead a "revolutionary-reformist" struggle
for the qualitative transformation of capitalism into a system of workers's self-management.

Although Gherea was a deterministic materialist and argued that
capitalist development could not be bypassed, his Marxism was inconsistent in that he contended that an advanced (bourgeois) superstructure could precede the development of a capitalist base in underdeveloped countries (that is, in Romania). This was contrary to—indeed, it
inverts—the simplistic causality accepted by many Second International Marxists, for it presumes that superstructure can lead, and does
not simply reflect, the base.[62] The rejection of such crude determinism
was to be an essential aspect of Goldmann's future project, as was the
case with Lukács and Western Marxism in general. It is also notable
that Gherea accented themes later central to Lukács's and Goldmann's
interpretations of Marx: the alienation of labor and the commodifica-
tion and depersonalization of human relations.

Goldmann's essay on Cocea is preoccupied with the adequacy—or,
more precisely, inadequacy—of social consciousness to the historical
moment. In contrast to Gherea, he begins with an orthodox Marxist
assertion of the dependence of ideology on the material world, citing
Engels's declaration that changes in superstructure lag behind those in
the base. It is the social sources and cultural consequences of this lag
that concern Goldmann as he paints a dismal picture of European, and
especially Romanian, intellectual life.[63] "Our present society," he de-

clares, "entered its decadent phase long ago. Social crises are reflected
in the most peripheral domains of both individual and social life."
While economic misery besets the population at large, "moral and intellectual crises" corrode the ruling classes. The latter have "abandoned any intellectual or spiritual life," and lack "the courage to face
reality, let alone think of tomorrow." They only pursue their own narrowly circumscribed interests.

Goldmann then generalizes, finding a parallel phenomenon among
intellectuals. The latter are devoid of "either idealism or culture" and
are "animated by a narrow materialism, a 'modern' art and literature
mainly characterized by an absolute subjectivism" lacking any link to
"reality." Still, "in the midst of this thoroughly rotten society," writers
do appear who are motivated by the sentiments and ideology of the
previous era's bourgeoisie. In other words, they are animated by the
ideals of the revolutionary bourgeoisie, an ascending class, whose
aspirations pointed the way to human progress. He cites three examples: Cocea in Romania, Anatole France in France, and Karl Kraus in
Austria.

Goldmann's premise is one that dominated Lukács's cultural criticism (although Lukács is unmentioned): the culture that accompanied
the bourgeoisie in its rise was progressive and positive; the culture accompanying the rule and decline of the bourgeoisie is reactionary and
negative. Speaking of Cocea, Anatole France, and Kraus, he declares:

> Judging society through the revolutionary bourgeois ideal [idelilui], whose
> supreme artistic achievement is Goethe's *Faust*—an ideal of a fully devel-
> oped individual with a highly intelligent and intense inner life, who thirsts
> for knowledge, and who is eager to participate in the joys and sorrows of the
> surrounding world—these writers inevitably assume a critical posture to-
> wards the decadence and emptiness around them, and they become pam-
> phleteers and satirists.

Their thinking comes of a specific era in bourgeois development, one
marked by an unshakable belief in the power of human reason to scrutinize the world—to scrutinize it as effectively as the bourgeoisie re-
made it. Consequently, the satirical writings by these three authors
take on a critical "intellectual character," which, with style and fervor,
mocks the present world without pity. Nonetheless, Goldmann chastises their social criticism as "sterile and incomplete." Their bourgeois
ideals prevent them from grasping the essence of contemporary social
reality. Cocea's three major novels assail solely the effects of the current social crisis. Like Kraus and Anatole France, he fails to grasp the
key to the modern world: the class struggle between the bourgeoisie

and the proletariat. He presents the passionate cultured individual as the ideal alternative to what Goldmann calls the banal culture of the dominant strata (*pătură*), but Cocea never envisions a collective subject—a "we." Though he speaks of the Romanian workers's movement, he never conceives of the class as a unit. He sees only individuals in the world, some admirable, others execrable. It was not for ideological reasons that Cocea—like Kraus and Anatole France—allied himself to the proletarian movement, but out of his need for an anchor. For all three, it would be a matter of supporting "the best of the worst," says Goldmann, quoting Kraus.

Goldmann specifically characterizes Cocea, Anatole France, and Kraus as "tragic," and he does so in terms that anticipate his depictions of Pascal, Racine, and the noblesse de robe in *The Hidden God*. Cocea, Anatole France, and Kraus live "with the ideology of a social reality long gone" and are "strangers to today's class reality." They are too intelligent to seek the reinvention of the historical period of bourgeois ascendance, but they can propose no solutions; they can do nothing beyond criticizing the secondary manifestations of the crises they witness. "It isn't a coincidence," writes Goldmann, "that whenever overwhelming events shattered society, they were aware of the sterility and ineffectiveness of their own work." And they all retreated from the world—as did the Jansenists Goldmann later studied. World War I led Anatole France to isolate himself in the country, writing nothing for years. After Cocea's journal, *Facla*, was closed, he quit the literary scene for a protracted period. When Hitler seized power, Kraus wrote a poem declaring, "Ich bleibe stumm und sage nicht warum [I remain silent and don't say why]."

Goldmann draws from the autobiographical elements in Cocea's last novels to elaborate his points. One of Cocea's protagonists, Andrei Vaia, is animated by the generous, "beautiful ideology" of the Romanian bourgeoisie and rural aristocracy of the 1848 period. "Unfortunately," comments Goldmann, "he lives in the years 1920–1930." As a consequence of this contradiction, Andrei Vaia ends up writing for the journal of the reactionary National Peasant party. The discouraged hero, like Cocea, then retreats to his country estate, where he writes a novel and lives with a beautiful peasant woman. He returns to Bucharest in 1930, but now finds it a powerfully alienating environment. He seeks compensation in love, the one realm that still seems to make sense to him. His affections now fall upon an intellectual woman who frequents literary circles. But she is unfaithful to him with his best friend, a hunchbacked Jew, whom he strikes and calls "*Jidan*" (dirty Jew). The novel closes with an embittered protagonist.

Could it have been otherwise? If Andrei Vaia wants more than beautiful ideas, Goldmann determines, he must leave his literary salons; he must walk a few miles to Bucharest's Grant Bridge, which "separates the two worlds." Crossing it, he will find himself among the workers (these were the workers who were involved in the 1933 railway strike). To truly embrace their cause, Cocea must recognize that though the average, barely literate laborer "cannot become a second Faust" after fourteen hours of daily toil, the proletariat as a whole—and it alone—can. The "second Faust" must be a collective subject—the working class. By joining their struggle, the young intellectual Lucian Goldmann declares, individuals will fulfill themselves "by transforming an ideology that would otherwise remain a lovely museum piece into a living reality."

Goldmann expanded on these themes a decade later in a 1945 article on Kraus in *Lettres*, a journal published in Geneva. Here, he characterizes Kraus and Lukács as the most important German-language intellectuals of the previous half-century. He acknowledges Kraus's heroic struggle against reaction, but insists that Kraus must, despite himself, be classified as a reactionary because he judged society through the prism of classical bourgeois ideals, even though he knew those ideals to be vanquished and unrealizable:

> It is in the name of these ideas of Liberty, Equality, Fraternity, and above all in the name of the individualist ideal of the man who is entirely and harmoniously developed from the spiritual and moral point of view (the "*Bildungsideal*" of Goethe and Schiller) that Karl Kraus judged his epoch and contemporaries.[64]

With the future apparently closed to his ideals, Kraus could look solely towards the past.[65] His role, as "last paladin of an ideology which no longer represents any social class," provides "the key to everything Kraus thought, did, and wrote."[66] Although at first Kraus was intransigent in his ideals, he was compelled to compromise once engaged in real struggles demanding alliances. This finally led him to support Dolfuss on the spurious grounds that it was required to fight the Nazis. This was the "only false and anti-human position of his life," remarks Goldmann.[67] This Austrian writer, who accused the workers of acting prematurely and thereby helping pave the way for the fascists, ended up an isolated man for whom the written word was the sole weapon—a weapon quite impotent against Hitlerism.

Kraus was incapable of seeing the whole, the totality of the struggle.[68] On one hand, he was able to create characters who were "exact images of a rigorously analyzed reality stripped bare," but on the other, he was unable to imagine an alternative. In making this analysis, Goldmann came close to Lukács's famous distinction between realist literature and naturalist literature: the former truly reveals the dynamics of social reality (that is, grasps the totality and its structure) whatever the political views of the author, while the latter captures the surfaces, the "images." Here, for Goldmann, is located the ultimate flaw in Cocea, Anatole France, and Kraus.[69] The last, a "magician of style," who loved humanity, was great only at expressing his anguish and revolt. He was "a reactionary, but a great reactionary. He saw, sensed, recorded the end of a world, but he remained blind before the first symptoms of the birth of a new society," which Goldmann, at the end of World War II, believed possible.[70]

These two articles—the latter largely a matured elaboration of ideas in the first—present early formulations of Goldmann's ideas on the relation between worldviews expressed in cultural creation, and socioeconomic realities. It is striking that already in 1934, when he was only twenty-one years old, he characterized discord between worldview and reality as "tragic." In *Mensch, Gemeinschaft und Welt in der Philosophie Immanuel Kants* (1945), Goldmann presented the "critical philosopher" not only as a great bourgeois and *Aufklärer* (enlightener), but as a tragic one, out of synchrony with the weak and backward German bourgeoisie of the day. Kant's individualism ultimately stayed him from positing the possibility of a historically created totality, according to Goldmann. Furthermore, in his early essays on seventeenth-century France, and later in *The Hidden God* (1955), Goldmann discerned in Pascal's *Pensées* and in Racine's theatre a tragic worldview expressive of an ideology (Jansenism) traceable to a social class (the noblesse de robe) left in limbo as it was historically bypassed by the consolidation of the absolute monarchy.

Goldmann's *For a Sociology of the Novel* (1964) demonstrated a homology between the mental categories of capitalism and cultural creation, which, he argued, precluded anticipating a world beyond capitalism. His studies of Genet, in the 1960s, written after he had concluded that the proletariat would not become a second Faust, asked if Genet—an isolated cultural figure—did in fact project beyond the immediate, contemporary world in his plays. All this reflects Goldmann's concern both with tragedy—also a central pursuit of the young, pre-Marxist Lukács—and with the relationship between what the Marxist Lukács, in *History and Class Consciousness*, called imputed and empirical consciousness. Hope, tragedy, disjuncture—these are the categories that structured Goldmann's worldview. He was what Georg Lukács called "a problematic individual."

IV

Goldmann proposed that, like his novel's hero, Cocea ought to cross
the bridge to the workers' struggle, to turn his back on personal fulfillment in the world of literary salons. Ironically, Goldmann's encounter
with Romanian Communism led him to a life not as a militant but as
a politically committed, though unaffiliated, intellectual. Moreover,
decades later, after he had concluded that the proletariat was not
going to play the role imputed to it by Marxism, he would find himself
in circumstances not dissimilar to those of Cocea, Anatole France, and
Kraus.

In 1958, when Goldmann was rethinking the historical role of the
working class, he remarked, in a footnote, that with the rise of Stalinism, "relations between socialist intellectuals and the workers's movement have become extremely complex and problematic." The natural
situation, he suggested, had been that of 1925–1928 when intellectuals
played a role on "the first level." But this situation had "totally disappeared," displaced by a "contrary phenomenon": the socialist theoretician who was isolated from the workers's movement, and if a member
of a party, had only a secondary role in it. Such, he notes, was Lukács's
fate after the 1920s.[71] It was Goldmann's, too, although in contrast to
Lukács, his direct engagement with the communist movement was
brief.

Goldmann's activities in RCP circles lasted roughly from 1930–1931
through 1935. If his membership in Ha-Shomer ha-Tsair spanned a
crucial time in that movement's history, this was also the case with the
RCP. In the early 1930s, the RCP was being transformed from a Leninist into a Stalinist party. Ironically, responsibility for Romania in the
Comintern came into the hands of Béla Kun, the former leader of the
unsuccessful Hungarian Soviet Republic and, within the exiled Hungarian Communist leadership, the nemesis of Goldmann's future intellectual inspiration, Georg Lukács. In the early 1930s, many of the
RCP's original leaders went to Moscow to escape repression at home,
only to fall victim to Stalin's purges, as did Kun himself.

In Romania, the RCP underwent intense "Cominternization" following its 1931 congress. "The movement was very rigid," according
to Rǎutu, who added that the assassination of Kirov in December 1934
had a chilling effect on the RCP leadership. The ideological temper is
captured by Dragomirescu, who recalled the shock of meeting Goldmann on campus carrying a copy of Trotsky's autobiography: "Imagine that! Trotsky's autobiography! To read Trotsky then was worse

than being a Social Democrat. Trotsky! It was the supreme crime."[72] Later the Union of Communist Youth was purged on orders from the Communist International of Youth, and the Party initiated loyalty inquests and expulsions.

Goldmann was very much ensnared in these developments, although specifics are difficult to reconstruct and to corroborate. What can be said with certainty is that the most significant Marxist theoretician to come from Romania was either chased from Romanian Communist circles or quit them in acrimonious circumstances. Indeed, after his arrival in Paris, French Communists were warned by their Romanian sister party that he was untrustworthy.

The main point of contention was Goldmann's anti-Stalinism. To make matters worse, he repeatedly and openly criticized intolerance in RCP ranks and opposed the branding of dissenting views as "deviations."[73] Goldmann "behaved like a dissident—when there were no dissidents."[74] He was, among other things, accused of Trotskyism. There was no significant Trotskyist tendency within the RCP, although several students did identify themselves as Trotskyists at the Schuller. Trotskyist was, of course, an epithet hurled indiscriminately by Communists at this time. Furthermore, the RCP, illegal, small, besieged, and supported only by Moscow, was becoming intellectually hermetic. "In the underground conditions of the RCP," according to Bălănescu, "the question wasn't whether Trotsky or Stalin was right; it was a question of a struggle to exist. It was a question of whether we would continue."[75]

There was some justification to the Trotskyist accusation in Goldmann's case.[76] As early as 1932 and 1933, he was not only bitterly critical of Stalin, referring to him as a "murderer," but he openly expressed admiration for Trotsky.[77] One sees this esteem retained in his writings of three decades later. In his distinction, in *The Hidden God*, between two trends within Jansenism, Antoine Arnauld's "dramatic centrists," who subordinate means to ends, and Martin de Barcos's extremists, who refuse to compromise means, Goldmann echoed that made in Trotsky's writings in the 1930s between Stalin's "bureaucratic center faction" and Marxist revolutionists. (The exiled, isolated Trotsky would, one presumes, thereby become the Barcos of Bolshevism.) Goldmann's analysis of André Malraux in *Towards a Sociology of the Novel* (1964), contraposed the Stalinizing leadership of the Chinese Communist Party in Hankow to the Shanghai revolutionaries who embrace what he calls the "Trotskyist" concept of "community" in *Man's Fate*.[78] Descriptions of Goldmann and his problems with the RCP by Communist friends tend to be consistent and evasive: "His strong inclination towards ideas . . . regarded as 'unorthodox' . . . led . . . to his estrangement from the Communist movement"; "Within the anti-fascist movement he was classified as Trotskyist because of his tendency to eccentricity and nonconformism which brought him into conflict with his friends."[79]

Nonconformism had practical ramifications, one of which was to make life at the Schuller unpleasant. Goldmann's lectures there, previously with RCP blessings, were halted abruptly in late 1932 or early 1933 and he became persona non grata. Later, at an unofficial party gathering of leftist students near the Schuller, the party instructed Carol Neuman, the ASGE president, to rebut Goldmann demonstratively if he spoke, and it was prearranged for others to join in shouting him down.[80]

Goldmann's rupture with the RCP and his exit from Romania cannot be dated with precision. His law degree was dated December 3, 1934; an undated letter from him to the dean applying for the license requests that in the event that his diploma was not yet ready, a certificate be issued so that he might be admitted to the bar in Ilfov, the county encompassing Bucharest. But he never practiced law. "He simply disappeared one day."[81] His biography now becomes fuzzy. According to a curriculum vitae he prepared in the late 1950s, he arrived in France in late 1934. He seems to have visited Vienna and Lwow (where he had family) along the way. Several Romanian friends place him back in Bucharest at various times in 1935 and 1936, and one recalls him speaking to her in Bucharest enthusiastically about the French Popular Front of 1936.[82] Yet none of his Parisian acquaintances remembers him leaving Paris for a return visit to the Balkans. It is conceivable that he went back and forth a few times, although his purpose by then was clearly to settle in Paris.

Goldmann's decision to leave Romania permanently may have been due to any of an array of reasons or, more likely, their combination: fear of arrest and the increasingly restive and repressive circumstances in the country; an increasingly problematic, if not shrill, relation with the RCP; the fact that as a young Jew, especially a leftist one, he had few professional options as a lawyer or teacher; a sense that Bucharest was too provincial for him. In any event, after the mid-1930s, he never returned to Romania.

Perhaps this indicates the severity of his break with the RCP. In 1945 Goldmann wrote a letter, apparently from Paris, articulating a complex attitude toward the Communist Party. His immediate reference was to the French Party, but he clearly aimed to generalize and his words were surely rooted in his Romanian experience. The recipient was Madeleine Duclos, a philosophy student in Toulouse with whom he had fallen in love in 1940, and to whom he dedicated his study of

Kant. During the war, while Goldmann was in Geneva and Zurich, she joined the French Communist Party and married the Communist head of her Maquis unit.[83] This did not deter Goldmann's entreaties. Consequently, his letter—in which he sought "to clarify the essential objection I have to the actual Communist Party"—was written to a Party member with whom he was in (unrequited) love.

Goldmann contended that the Party treated human beings "as means, as important factors certainly, but at bottom as secondary. A true community is an *ensemble* of men who struggle in common for an ideal, and thus the humblest of tasks is as *valuable* as the most elevated. This is why there are only comrades in such a community (Kant, Marx, Lukács and Lenin knew it and said it)." Such, however, was not the case in the Communist Party. It takes discipline—something he concedes to be necessary—to an extreme. For the Party, "men, the truth, morality, have become means without value-in-themselves." This was incompatible with the "humanist philosophy" of Marx, Lenin, and Lukács.

Then Goldmann qualifies his indictment: "I know that the Communist party is the only real hope for the world today, which is why I will not attack it in public or in writing. Letters are something else. With you I don't do 'politics.'" He goes on to state that philosophy, "thought in general, knows man as such," whereas "party politics must resolve the tasks of the day." However, "there are times when these two things are extremely difficult to reconcile." He recounts that his publisher in Zurich once proposed that he edit a new journal of Marxist philosophy, to be titled *The Heritage and the Future*. While the project was abandoned, six months later, a new Communist Party publication appeared under the name *The Heritage and the Present*. Goldmann, while wondering aloud if the similarity of names was mere coincidence, discerns a more important point: the names reflected the essential differences between philosophical and party activities as he had defined them. One focuses on the future and the other on the present. He asks, "[C]an we make a *philosophy* of the present and would it be Marxist?"[84]

Goldmann had no definitive answer. He distinguished the tasks of philosophy and politics, was bitterly critical of Communist parties, yet was unwilling to renounce them entirely. With theory and practice separate, philosophical consciousness and the historical world seemed—again—at odds. In the ensuing years, his views of the Communist movement became even more negative. Events in Romania, where the RCP had taken full power by 1948, certainly shaped his attitude. Some of his acquaintances rose to prominence there; however, others he knew or admired were purged or executed. The Romanian embassy in Paris sought to contact Goldmann shortly after the war, when Pătrășcanu, then an RCP minister in a coalition government in Bucharest, made an official visit to France. Might Goldmann return to Romania? Goldmann quickly refused, fortunately for him. Pătrășcanu was soon to be purged. Goldmann told friends in Paris, only half face-tiously, that he himself would be likely to be hung were he to go to Bucharest. Goldmann's work and reputation fared poorly in Commu-nist Romania, receiving little attention besides the posthumous collec-tion prefaced by Constantinescu, a notation in a biographical diction-ary, and a summary of his literary methodology in a study of Marxism and structuralism.[85]

2

Homeless

IT WAS NATURAL for Goldmann to go to Paris. The French capital, traditionally, was western Europe's great cultural lure for Romanians, especially the young. A return to Vienna could not have enticed him for the Austrian republic and Austrian social democracy had perished violently at the hands of Chancellor Engelbert Dolfuss in February 1934. Hitler's Germany was obviously out of the question.

Paris harbored a substantial colony of Romanian students. They published their own newspapers, some of which made their way back to Romania. An article printed in one of them in December 1934, the month in which Goldmann completed his studies in Bucharest, declared that Romania's future leaders were to be found in Paris, where they were learning a discriminating attitude toward the problems of their homeland. Romania, the author averred, needed the French spirit.[1] Goldmann, however, never intended to take the French spirit back to Bucharest.

I

He arrived in early 1935 and, probably lacking proper papers, survived by taking menial jobs, from washing dishes to selling newspapers. He was often forced to borrow money and for a time he even experimented in tutoring English, a language he barely knew. After he fled France for Switzerland during World War II, he wrote a sentimental poem about his first years in the Left Bank. It spoke "of us, Bohemia" surviving "hungry and penniless" through "days of rain and cockroaches". It was "a time past in which everywhere / things seemed beautiful / when we lived aimlessly." He looked forward to the liberation, because for him Paris "would always remain Paris / the center of the world."[2] Lucian became Lucien.

Despite his straits, Goldmann earned degrees in public law and political economy in 1935 at the law faculty of the University of Paris, and three years later he completed a *licence* at the Faculté des Lettres at the Sorbonne. At the same time he absorbed the political and cultural world around him. Among the talks he heard was one by Walter Benjamin. Joseph Gabel, a Hungarian Jew who, like Goldmann, became a

sociologist in Paris after the war, met him for the first time in 1936 at
Nicolai Bukharin's lecture—his last in Paris—on "The Fundamental
Problems of Contemporary Culture."[3] Among other things, the lecture
addressed the question of "socialist humanism," later one of Goldmann's leading themes. Goldmann announced to Gabel that he had
decided to become an academic.

Paris was politically and intellectually tumultuous in the mid-1930s.
The Popular Front rose and fell; the Action Française denounced leftists, democrats, and Jews; Hegelians, Marxists, neo-Kantians, Durk-
heimians, Bergsonians, and left-wing Catholics debated in the journals, universities, and cafes. When Goldmann arrived, Hegelianism
was beginning to challenge the academic dominance of Bergsonianism
and neo-Kantianism, Léon Brunschvicg being the latter's most prominent French representative. As Vincent Descombes notes, rising interest in Marx and Hegel had been stimulated first by Russian developments and then by Alexandre Kojève's famous lectures on Hegel's
Phenomenology of Spirit at the École Pratique des Hautes Études during
1933–1939.[4] Indeed, this has been called the era of "the three Hs"—
Hegel, Husserl, Heidegger—because of the great sway of these German thinkers on the young generation of aspiring French intellectuals.
This was partly fueled by an influx of foreign academics and philosophers, such as Kojève himself, in flight from Hitler and/or Stalin.

Goldmann's interests, especially in German philosophy, were thus
attuned to Parisian currents. Perhaps because Ha-Shomer ha-Tsair had
nurtured a secular religiosity in him, he was singularly impressed by
the left-wing Catholic movement known as Personalism, centered
around the journal *Esprit* and its editor, Emmanuel Mounier. In *Kant*,
written a decade later in Zurich, Goldmann placed French Personalism
directly on the path begun by Kant and pursued by Marx and Lukács.
Personalism, Goldmann wrote, was a vital counterforce to the "psy-
chosis of anguish and despair" represented by the philosophies of Heidegger, Sartre, and Bergson:

> After the philosophical silence of G. Lukács, which has already lasted more
> than twenty years, Personalism seems to me to have been the most impor-
> tant [philosophical] event in the last years before the war. Naturally, French
> Personalism emerged from traditions very different from German human-
> ism, and was hardly conscious of a kinship with it. It is therefore even more
> significant that it spontaneously arrived at the same questions and also very
> frequently at similar responses.[5]

Those questions and responses—at least, some of the most important of them—were Goldmann's as well, and it is possible that his interest in Pascal was stimulated in part by the Personalists. Many of

Mounier's central themes parallel those of the maturing Goldmann. Mounier saw Pascal as "the father of the dialectic." He argued that communication was the basic attribute of human nature and that socialism was the realization of the gospel; that the socialist "person" was part of a community, part of a "we," in contrast to the bourgeois "individual"; that the person was definable as "a movement towards a transpersonal condition which reveals itself in the experiences of community and the attainment of values at the same time."[6]

Mounier characterized his own position as one of "tragic optimism" and proposed that the animating principles of Marxism were those of a secularized Christianity. He feared a reified world in which human beings gave themselves over to "the bondage of things." The greatest threat to humanity in his view was the advent of technocratic rule, of either the Left or the Right.[7] Goldmann's secular religiosity eventually crystallized as the claim that Marxism was a dialectical humanism that wagers on humanity's future as had Pascal on God's existence.

The author of the *Pensées* has enjoyed, for the last century, a privileged place in French intellectual life. In the decades preceding his tercentenary in 1923, a Pascal revival took place in which his anti-Cartesianism was celebrated as an "antitype" to positivism and the dominance of "scientism."[8] Pascal's tragic sense was also suited to the aftermath of World War I. One author, André Suarès, wrote in 1923: "He defined our agony . . . his experience has anticipated its extremity and horror. . . . His thought held so much of the future that in truth we still have him in our midst."[9] Pascal's thought remained present in French intellectual circles in the 1930s not only because he spoke to a sense of tragedy and despair, but because his "wager" allowed space for hope, too. After 1945, a substantial literature concerned with Pascal appeared. Notable contributions came from the Left and from authors with historical and sociological (as opposed to religious) questions to pose. Among them were Henri Lefebvre's two-volume *Pascal*, Paul Benichou's remarkable *Les Morales du grand siècle*, and eventually Lucien Goldmann's *The Hidden God*.

II

Although Goldmann volunteered for French military service in 1939, he was rejected for health reasons. From November 1939 through June 1940, he taught German at the Collège de Châlons-sur-Marne, just outside Paris. It was rare for a foreigner to obtain such a post, and apparently he secured it with the assistance of Vladimir Jankélévitch.[10] In the aftermath of the German invasion, he was dismissed. He began supporting himself by teaching philosophy at a private school and by ghostwriting theses in public law for wealthy students, mostly the children of diplomats. Fearing deportation, he fled south in the summer of 1940, to Toulouse, in the Unoccupied Zone. Here, again, his income came from ghostwriting theses for affluent students. He lived for a period at the Cité Universitaire and then in the basement of a university teacher's home.

Goldmann managed to attend classes at the University of Toulouse and devoted his intellectual energies to Kant, developing many of the ideas that would later appear in his thesis. One evening he announced to Gabel, who had fled to Toulouse with him, that he had "discovered the key to Kant." He discussed his ideas at length with Madeleine Duclos. After the war, following her marriage, a dejected and rejected Goldmann wrote to her that his book on Kant "will probably be the only real fruit of our meeting."[11] At this time, Goldmann began writing an extensive essay, perhaps projected as a book, on the European crisis. It does not seem to have survived. Of particular importance is the fact that while immersed in Kant, he attended a lecture on Jansenism in Toulouse. It aroused in him a great interest in Pascal and Racine, which he would pursue in Switzerland.[12]

Soon Jews in Toulouse had to face the specter of deportation, beginning in late summer 1942. Goldmann may have been involved at one point in helping to smuggle Jewish children over the Swiss border.[13] His own clandestine flight, via Lyon, was in October 1942, after a period in hiding. He quickly found himself confined in the *Auffangslager* (internment camp) of Gierenbad near Zurich. He remained in the camp (a former textile factory) for four or five months, living with several hundred other illegal refugees (all men—women were in another camp, not far away). While there, he told fellow internees that after the Stalin-Hitler pact, he no longer considered himself a materialist in the Marxist sense. It was Kant who concerned him.

Among those in Gierenbad was Manès Sperber. This former Comintern functionary, later a renowned novelist, had been born in Austrian Galicia. Eight years Goldmann's senior and also a graduate of Ha-shomer ha-Tsair, he had worked with Alfred Adler and became a confidant of André Malraux and Arthur Koestler. In his memoirs, Sperber described the camp as a miserable place in which the refugees slept on straw (often wet from rain or snow) and were presided over by a "vain and authoritarian" commandant and scornful guards. "Undoubtedly," he wrote, "the whole troop had received orders to treat us like lepers."

The internees included a small group of intellectuals. In their ranks were an art historian, a translator of English-language literature, and a Viennese jurist. Days were spent in the refectory, where, in a corner, despite the noise, Sperber and others gave lectures and study circles were organized.[14] Goldmann and Sperber, in a vigorous though friendly way, debated the nature of the Moscow trials. Sperber believed that Bukharin's trial had been unjust, but not the earlier proceedings against Zinoviev and Kamenev. Nor did he think Trotsky innocent. Goldmann insisted that all the tribunals had been frauds.

Later, Sperber gave two lectures on the work of Georg Lukács after a copy of *History and Class Consciousness* found its way into the camp. His presentation emphasized the heretical elements of Lukács's thought and emphasized the centrality of method in the Hungarian Marxist's project.[15] At first Goldmann tried to make Kantian counterarguments, but he became increasingly fascinated by, and then obsessed with, Lukács's work. And he soon put his new interest to use.

Goldmann's freedom from Gierenbad was secured through the help of Tsvi Taubes, the chief rabbi of Zurich, whose son, the psychologist Jacob Taubes, became his close friend. Goldmann now turned to writing a doctoral thesis in philosophy at the University of Zurich, one in which Lukács was a central presence. *Mensch, Gemeinschaft und Welt in der Philosophie Immanuel Kants* (Man, Community, and the World in the Philosophy of Immanuel Kant), completed between September 1943 and September 1944, became Goldmann's first book—it was published in 1945—and his only book written in German. Its reinterpretation of Kant was, among other things, an attempt to rescue German philosophy and humanism from the German barbarism that had engulfed Europe. Undoubtedly, the same impulse led Goldmann, immediately after the war, to translate into French Lukács's *Goethe and His Age* and *Short History of German Literature* (the latter in collaboration with Michel Butor). The *Short History* bifurcates German culture into progressive and reactionary trends in an attempt to dissuade intellectuals from discarding all German culture in the aftermath of Nazism.

Goldmann's *Kant* radiates hope; it was completed three months after D-Day. Earlier, the war had induced great despair in him, and a deepening preoccupation with the concept of tragedy. His mood is discernible in poetry he wrote during the war years and never sought to publish. There are two batches of unpublished poems by Goldmann, some in Romanian and some in French.[16] Most are in rhyming verse (in the original) and their literary merit, to be generous, is modest. Some were evidently written in Toulouse, and some in Switzerland. It is impossible to date or place the Romanian poems, which largely dwell on the same themes as do the French ones—loneliness and love. One, entitled "Night," begins, "It is sad and terrible / when in the dead of night / before the dawn / life seems so desperate." It speaks of a "cold and alien" world in which there is "Nowhere a shelter / only fear growing inside." Respite is found only in a brothel. There is also a rendering into Romanian of "Pirate Jenny's Song" from Brecht's *Three Penny Opera*, which Goldmann called "The Dream of a Waitress in a Harbor Pub."

Many of Goldmann's French poems seem to be addressed to a particular woman, very possibly Duclos. A deep yearning for a "we"— personal and political—is ever-present. One poem, "Solitude," ends, "And I, all alone, again follow the path / on which we marched together long ago / Tormented anew by doubt / And I no longer know what I want." A "Letter from an Interned Father to His Son Who Is with a Swiss Family" voices the pained regrets of a parent who is unable to be with his child on the child's tenth birthday. He tells him to "thank your God" that good people care for him. In "Vision," Goldmann speaks of a world in which "Hatred struts [*se promène*] / far and wide." Yet in this world, "Madmen and lovers / artists, women" try to preserve a faith and to stand against their times, "their souls suffering / and crying to heaven / their eternal dream / of love and beauty / of ardor and truth / and in their eyes / the reflection of God / dead on the cross."

Appeals to heaven are frequent in the wartime verse of the future author of *The Hidden God*. In a poem that indicates that, at least in private, Goldmann had profound doubts about his own beliefs, he speaks of escaping the terror of his times, in which "vengeance, hate, menace the whole world / Everywhere the human species seems sunk in a mire," by entering the tranquil courtyard of a Renaissance chateau. There, the voice of someone long dead seems to speak to him of "man," the "lamentable being," whose nature never changes and who inflicts pain on his fellows. The poet is told that "To this miserable man, God one day gave / two inestimable goods: hope and love / and when he loves he will turn towards the future / despite his pale face and blemished look." The ghostly voice declares that "I struggled like you / I lived solitary, but guarded my Faith [*ma Foi*] / in man and in the earth and I loved them." Whereupon the author enters the chateau and finds the devil.

Finally, there is a poem entitled "Letter, 1942," which is entirely structured by the poles of hope and despair. It begins, "I know that tomorrow life will be recaptured / and man will be joyous anew / I know that tomorrow / Beautiful songs to God's glory / will be heard everywhere." But, the poem continues, "Between today and tomorrow lies an abyss / and this abyss opens wide and gaping." Victory will come too late for too many. Thus while the poet believes that a better world will be born, he is no longer able to rejoice in its prospects: "Perhaps tomorrow I can recapture myself / Tomorrow, perhaps, I'll be able to forget this mass of rotting ruins, of deaths of ashes / which are always there, preventing me from praying / But I fear that it is too late—I am only a man / these three years which just passed / go beyond, I fear, the sum / of all a man can stand." He closes unable to promise a happy future.

While Goldmann did not, in his published writings, ever speak of himself as despairing (in fact he always inveighed against despair), his poems not only present another picture, but give us a Marxist who once believed in something he called God and lost his faith during the war. Who that God is, or was, is left unclear by his verse. But Goldmann leaves us with a lonely man, with a God vanquished at worst, hidden at best, much like the description found in Lukács's pre-Marxist essay on "The Metaphysics of Tragedy." Yet when Goldmann wrote *Kant* shortly after these poems were composed, his themes were humanism, optimism, human possibility, and the transcendence of despair and ahistorical tragic thinking.

III

Goldmann's time in Switzerland was one of great intellectual fertility and discovery. In the preface to the first French edition of *Kant* (1948), Goldmann declared that he wrote the volume "under the direct influence of Georg Lukács whose early works, then entirely unknown, I had discovered by chance."[17] "Chance" was in all probability his encounter with Sperber, but why the young Goldmann was so attracted to young Lukács is better explained by parallels in their intellectual developments.

A Hungarian Jew of bourgeois origins, Lukács was Goldmann's senior by three decades. He grew up in Budapest, and was especially influenced by German and Hungarian romantic anticapitalist currents, the same trends that influenced Ha-Shomer ha-Tsair. Both Hungarian and German were spoken in the Lukács family home, and Lukács gravitated to German culture, finding his native environment too constricting. Goldmann, we know, gravitated to German at home where it was spoken along with Romanian.

A central motif of romantic anticapitalism was the opposition, made most famous by the sociologist Ferdinand Tönnies, of *Gemeinschaft* (community), which was identified with *Kultur* and ethical, aesthetic, organic "German" spiritual values, to *Gesellschaft* (society), which was envisioned as *Zivilisation*, an "Anglo-French" mechanical, "external," materialist world of technical/economic advance.[18] Lukács, in his new preface to the 1962 republication of *Theory of the Novel*, wrote that romantic anticapitalism was initially "in the young Carlyle or in Cobbett ... a genuine critique of the horrors and barbarities of early capitalism—sometimes, as in Carlyle's *Past and Present*, a preliminary form of socialist critique. In Germany this attitude gradually transformed itself into a form of apology for the political and social backwardness of the Hohenzollern Empire."[19]

In central Europe, romantic anticapitalism originated largely as the ideology of those intellectuals, especially in German academia, who believed that all that they held dear was crumbling before the onslaught of "modern" (that is, capitalist) society. They harked back to a supposed world not yet contaminated by *Zivilisation*, with its rationalization and quantification of all aspects of life. In Lukács's *Soul and Forms* (1909), romantic anticapitalist categories are manifest in the counterposing of authentic "Life" (a realm of ultimate human values) and inauthentic "life" (everyday empirical existence) as an irreconcilable duality, a duality echoing Kant's distinction between the noumenal and phenomenal worlds and Plato's between the realms of forms and appearance. In inauthentic "life," no sense of wholeness was possible for the individual; the human fate was thus a tragic one.

Five years later, in *Theory of the Novel*, Lukács contrasted the cultural expressions of the modern, fragmented (capitalist) world to the harmony of ancient Greece, an "integrated" civilization. The novel, at whose center was the "problematic individual" seeking himself in a Godless universe, was contrasted to the Homeric epic, in which the hero was at home in a rounded world and at one with the community. Lukács proposed that "[w]hen the structures made by man for man are really adequate to man, they are his necessary and native home."[20] When he became a Marxist, Lukács found the means to realize this home; the proletariat was the historical force through which life would be made into Life.

Similar oppositions and categories structure Goldmann's thought, although he ultimately concluded that the proletariat would not play the role ascribed to it by Marx and Lukács. In *Kant*, Goldmann placed enormous emphasis on the distinctions made by Emil Lask between *universalitas* (reified universality) and *universitas* (content-full totality) in the critical philosophy, and between "analytic logic," which is atomistic and sees individual elements as the only authentic reality, and "emanatist logic," which assumes that one must know the whole in order to know the parts. Goldmann's quest for the "authentic human community" in which the individual would be realized, and his insistence on the centrality of totality in method (together with the attendant opposition to capitalism as well as to "scientism," positivism, rationalism, and empiricism) were his own Marxist reworking and attempted transcendence of the *Gemeinschaft/Gesellschaft* dichotomy.

Goldmann's interest in Pascal deepened while writing *Kant*. The logician K. Dürr was officially his thesis adviser, but he was primarily absorbed by the classes of Theophil Spoerri, the author of several works on the seventeenth-century philosopher. Goldmann became the center of a group of students studying Pascal and Marx. Spoerri, who was especially concerned with the concept of tragedy, occasionally attended the discussions.[21] In *Sciences humaines et philosophie* (1952), Goldmann credited Spoerri with initially suggesting to him the contrast between Pascal and Descartes as a model for the systemic study of worldviews. This paradigm would be essential to Goldmann's approach to the tragic worldview of Pascal and Racine in *The Hidden God*. Importantly, the Spoerri circle typed copies of Lukács's *Soul and Forms*, then out of print, and discussed "The Metaphysics of Tragedy." Theater was also one of their concerns, and it is likely that Goldmann began to study Racine more attentively at this time. Brecht's works especially engaged his circle, and after the war there were occasional meetings with the playwright, who stayed for a period outside of Zurich. Goldmann attended at least one of the meetings with Brecht.[22]

By the time he returned to Paris after the war, Goldmann was thoroughly conversant with Pascal's oeuvre.[23] Like Dilthey, the neo-Kantians, and Lukács before him, Goldmann would insist on the differences between the "human" or "cultural" sciences and the natural sciences. The appeal to him of Pascal was natural; Pascal was both a believer and a scientist. In a 1948 essay, Goldmann wrote that the crucial step in *"la démarche Pascalienne"* was Pascal's recognition that man is compelled to strive for a totality he will never find on earth "in an immanent manner."[24] In that same year, in the preface to the French edition of *Kant*, he stated that were he to rewrite the book, he would assert that "Pascal was the first," where he previously had pointed to Kant as first in the history of dialectical thought.[25] Goldmann concluded that a tragic vision of the world was to be found in both Pascal and Kant, and that the two pointed the way to the dialectic. Here, we again see how the tension between dialectical hope and the possibility of tragedy structured Goldmann's thinking from his days in Romania on. We found it in his portrait of Cocea, the intellectual espousing bygone ideals in order to criticize the present when he needs to cross the bridge to the workers's movement. We find it anew in Goldmann's treatment of Kant as a thinker in quest of an unattainable totality, and we discern it yet again in his use of Pascal's wager. It is also the key to his comparison of Lukács and Heidegger, the subject of a short but important essay appended to the original edition of *Kant*.

IV

It was with the parallel between Lukács and Heidegger that Gold-mann's publishing career began and ended. The theme of the appen-dix to his *Kant* was also that of his unfinished last work, which he was writing when he died in 1970. In a later chapter I will examine his com-parison of these two philosophers in more detail; here I will look at his early schematic formulation with an eye toward its place in his intel-lectual genesis.

Goldmann seeks to delineate the homologous development of these two thinkers. He sketches its roots in the Young Heidelberg school of neo-Kantianism during World War I, particularly the influence of Heinrich Rickert and Emil Lask on them. Goldmann declares that his purpose is to demonstrate how "an intellectual current that promised to pursue the line of classical German philosophy and to lead to a sys-tematic philosophical humanism" took shape.[26] He first directs our at-tention to Heidegger's 1914 doctoral thesis, *Die Lehre von Urteil im Psy-chologismus* (The Doctrine of Judgment in Psychologism), a defense of the antipsychologism characteristic both of the Heidelberg neo-Kan-tians (especially Rickert) and of Edmund Husserl's phenomenology. Then Goldmann points to parallels between Heidegger's 1915 work on *Die Kategorien und Bedeutungslehre des Duns Scotus* (The Doctrine of the Categories in Duns Scotus), which is dedicated to Rickert and praises Lask, and Lask's own *Die Logik der Philosophie und die Kategorienlehre* (The Logic of Philosophy and the Doctrine of the Categories) of 1910.

Goldmann contends that the last pages of Heidegger's book on Duns Scotus present, or retrieve, key themes of Lukács's *Soul and Forms*. He cites Heidegger's statement that "one will not achieve a de-finitive clarification of . . . [the question of the relation between form and matter] by confining it within the logical sphere of meaning and of the structure of meaning." Insisting on the centrality of metaphysics and the need for modern philosophy to come to grips with Hegel— "the most powerful system of historical vision of the world"—Hei-degger avers: "Objectively considered, the problem of the relation be-tween time and eternity, between mutation and absolute value, presents itself, in reflected form, epistemologically in history (the con-stitution of value) and in philosophy (the validity of value)."[27]

This formulation, in Goldmann's account, presents the same prob-lems raised when the absolute values of authentic "Life" are opposed by Lukács to the mundanity of "life" in "The Metaphysics of Tragedy." This essay in *Soul and Forms*, which Goldmann praises as "the most important in the book," poses "the question of the relation between this opposition [of Life and life] and the supreme limit, death."[28] Consequently, Goldmann asserts that *Soul and Forms* represents the first text of modern existentialism, "the true foundation of the modern philosophy of existence. . . . [T]he distinction which Heidegger will subsequently call 'authentic' and 'inauthentic' *Dasein* is at the center of the book."[29]

Dasein, an everyday term in German connoting ordinary existence, literally means "Being there." It is Heidegger's term in *Being and Time* (1927) for man as a being capable of ontological inquiry, that is, of inquiry into the nature of his own Being and Being in general. Goldmann attributes Heidegger's distinction between ontological and "ontic" inquiry—the latter being that of the positive sciences, technology, "facts"—to Lask.[30] Goldmann contends not only that the kinship between Lukács's *History and Class Consciousness* of 1923 and Heidegger's *Being and Time* of 1927 is obvious "from the very first pages," but that the relation of *Soul and Forms* to *History and Class Consciousness* is one of "the transcendence of tragedy." Lukács traveled from a tragic Kantianism in *Soul and Forms* by means of Hegel to the historical Marxism of *History and Class Consciousness*. From the angst-ridden, irreconcilable dichotomy of Life and life, and preoccupation with the ultimate limit, death, in *Soul and Forms*, Lukács arrived in *History and Class Consciousness* at "a philosophy of humanist existence [that is] optimistic and full of hope, a philosophy that surmounts the metaphysics of tragedy and transcends it in a Hegelian sense."[31] Lukács transcended it because he had found an agent—the proletariat, the second Faust—that would create *in history* the "authentic human community."

Goldmann constructs two parallels. The first is between Heidegger, who wrote (in his book on Duns Scotus) of the problematic historico-philosophical relation between "time and eternity . . . mutation and absolute value," and Lukács in *Soul and Forms*. The second is between Heidegger in *Being and Time* and Lukács in *History and Class Consciousness*. More precisely, Goldmann asserts that *Being and Time* is in fact a dialogue with and an attack on *History and Class Consciousness* "from the viewpoint of a philosophy of anguish and death." According to Heidegger, the ideas in *Being and Time* were elaborated beginning in 1919. This, Goldmann notes, was when the major themes of *History and Class Consciousness* were fashioned by Lukács, in the aftermath of his departure from Heidelberg, adherence to the Hungarian Communist Party, and participation in the failed Hungarian Soviet Republic. Goldmann goes so far as to claim that the words "Being and Time" are "a translation of and at the same time a response to *History and Class Consciousness* in the Heideggerian language and world-view."[32] According to Goldmann,

"True and false" consciousness in Lukács was transformed into "authentic and inauthentic" *Dasein*; the difference between essence and appearance became that of the ontological and the ontic. The practical essence of man became the existential of concern and preoccupation; the Lukácsian critique of the rational and neo-Kantian theory of knowledge is reappropriated entirely [*est entièrement reprise*] but it is applied to Descartes. Lukács's Hegelian totality became the "world" of Heidegger. To the creative action of the community and hope in the future, he counterposes "resolute-decision," the "anguish" which isolates, and life-towards-death. History as a common struggle was replaced by the great man as a model, and by history as the possibility of repetition. From the community and the *We*, only the *They* remains.[33]

The "They" is Heidegger's *Das Man*, an impersonal pronoun (*l'On* in French) that means "one" or "they" in the sense of "one does this" or "they do that." The "one" or "they" to which Goldmann refers is an anonymous "inauthentic they-self," which *Dasein* becomes when embracing an everydayness determined by others rather expressing authentic self. We can discern here the importance of Heidegger's terminology for Goldmann's own thinking, for Goldmann always spoke of his own goal as the "authentic" community. The anonymous one/they is inauthentic; it is the historically constituted "we" that creates the authentic community. This is not only a key to Goldmann's thought; it is the crucial point at which he sees Lukács and Heidegger, two thinkers preoccupied with a similar problematic, as parting company.

In *History and Class Consciousness*, the attainment of class consciousness by the proletariat entails grasping historical totality. Since according to Lukács's Marxism, the commodity is an object that embodies the entirety of capitalist relations of production, and since the worker is commodified in that he sells his labor power for a wage, self-consciousness, that is, the class consciousness of the proletariat is equivalent to the self-consciousness of the commodity. Thus its commodity status is overcome; subject and object are identical; and this is the basis of the future, socialist, nonreified community. Consequently, while,

for Lukács this transition [to true consciousness] is only possible by an establishment of the true unity of subject and object, in the transition to the *We*, in the practical action of the class struggle. Heidegger recognizes but one path as just and possible—the exact opposite. "Isolation," tearing away from the They [*l'arrachement à l'"On"*], recognition of limit, life-towards-death, in short, the true realization of the *self* [*du Moi*], isolation from consideration of the surrounding world, the destruction of unity between subject and object.[34]

We find this same preoccupation with the "We" and *Das Man* in an unpublished dialogue of just over five typed pages written by Goldmann around the time he completed *Kant*. It manifests the particular impact of Kant's *Critique of Judgement* on him, and is entitled "Dialogue dans une Buffet de Gare."[35] The "Dialogue" is between P. and G. P. begins by declaring that no philosophy had as yet accounted satisfactorily for "human beauty." G. responds, in Socratic manner: is not this impossible if we do not first address the question of beauty in general? This he defines as the question of "form," which he in turn specifies as *"the incarnation of a human reality in a material given [une donnée matérielle]"* (emphasis added). Beauty, he elaborates, synthesizes the "theoretical" and the "practical," "the finished and the unfinished," "nature and the human spirit." Goldmann's touchstone is evidently Kant's claim that the aesthetic and teleological theories of his *Critique of Judgment* provide a bridge between his two earlier critiques, which have for their respective subject matter epistemology and nature (*The Critique of Pure Reason*) and morality and freedom (*The Critique of Practical Reason*).[36]

To illustrate "the incarnation of human reality in a material given," G. turns to poetry, choosing as an example poetry about forests among different peoples. Such poetry "incarnates" a multiplicity of quotidian sentiments; forests are a mysterious force, a shelter, a friend, "a place of repose and dream, in any case something human and not just brute reality."[37] What is of the essence in this (very German) example is not merely a relation between two elements—the human reality and the material given—but their complete fusion "to the point of creating *one* new reality, the aesthetic reality." The criterion of a true "allegorical incarnation" is *totality*. G. explains:

> Every brute material reality is part of an infinite whole of spiritual and temporal relations. It is only a link [*une maille*] in a network which extends itself to infinity in all directions [*se prolonge à l'infini de tous côtes*]. Through incarnating a human reality, it is wrested from this network in order to become a total and independent reality, without extensions or bonds [*sans prolongements ni attaches*]. This is what creates a work of art.[38]

We find here a reworking of Kant's assertion that the judgment of taste—that is, the aesthetic judgment that something is beautiful—is not cognitive or logical, but is "disinterested"; that is, the object of the judgment obtains of no interest save contemplation of it. Such a judgment comes from the "free play" of our faculties of understanding and imagination, and it claims intersubjective validity; it proposes that we all ought to agree with the judgment, though there is no way to compel such concurrence. If we declare an object beautiful on the grounds of experience of its form alone—irrespective of the object's purpose—Kant calls its beauty "free," and such beauty is the concern of the judgment of taste. Its object is defined by "purposiveness without purpose," a "finality without end." Through reflection, Kant says, it is possible to see "a finality of form, and trace it in objects . . . without resting it on an end."[39] This is in contradistinction to purpose in teleological judgment or to the Aristotelian notion of nature as a purposeful whole. It is experience of the *form* of purposefulness in the art object, apart from any actual purpose that may or may not be there, that is beauty. This form provides the basis of shared aesthetic experience. Thus "the determining ground of the judgment of taste" is

> the subjective finality in the representation of an object exclusive of any end (objective or subjective)—consequently the bare form of finality in the representation whereby an object is *given* to us, so far as we are conscious of it—as that which is alone capable of constituting the delight which, apart from any concept, we estimate as universally communicable.[40]

When G., in Goldmann's dialogue, is asked by his interlocutor if there is any utility to be discerned in the origins of judgments of value and aesthetic judgments, he responds, "Yes and no," and then begins to move beyond Kant's "free" disinterested beauty. "Utility," however, is deemed to be a concept too subjective and individualistic. G. speaks instead of "the interest of the human community," though he insists that "interest" be broadly understood, and that "community" denote something altogether different from "society," "social," or "collective." G. derives a notion of community out of Kantianism, but goes beyond Kant. Human values, be they "the true," "the good," or "the beautiful," can be understood solely on the basis of "the two constitutive and fundamental elements of the human condition: the *community* and the *action* that constitutes it."[41] The "human person" is the goal of action, insists G., citing Kant's categorical imperative: every person is an end in himself, part of "the kingdom of ends." It is action toward this goal that creates for the individual "the sole manner of self-transcendence [*la seule manière de se dépasser*], of finally finding the true meaning of life, of the real community, the *we* which can realize the 'self' [*moi*]."[42]

Goldmann has taken us in a circle in order to construct a whole. Having presented "the beautiful" as a totality defined by form, which, in turn, is created by human action ("incarnation"), G. proposes that judgments of value and aesthetics be conceived not as a matter of disinterest, but in broad terms of the community's interest. The individual, the self, is part of the community, of the "We," through his or her participatory action in constituting it, in the same sense that he or she may create something of aesthetic value that is intersubjectively valid when it is experienced as beautiful. The theoretical, the practical, and the beautiful are thereby rendered as a totality. When P. asks what determines the "We," G. replies, "The subject of common action. Its supreme form will be such that the subject will be the whole of humanity."[43] In other words, it is universal, like Kant's kingdom of ends or Marx's communism—although there is no allusion to Marx by G.

G. recognizes that some human groups do not act in a universal manner; they act against others, in hatred. This hatred is, however, "not constitutive of man," and such groups are always threatened by disintegration because they are bound by false consciousness. Such false consciousness substitutes "the 'they' and the 'I' [*le 'on' et le 'je'*]" or the "social" and the "individual" for "the 'we' [*'nous'*] and the 'self' [*'moi'*], the community and the person."[44] By means of a mixture of Heideggerian and Lukácsian language within a framework of argument alternately Kantian and Hegelian, Goldmann has given us a Marxian reinvention of the romantic anticapitalist distinction between *Gemeinschaft* and *Gesellschaft.* It is posed, as P. puts it, as "an attempt to resolve the antinomy of the collective and the individual." Not only have the two discussants strayed from aesthetics proper, but P. concludes that "since beauty is not action, it is before anything else contemplative." Even so, G. responds, all feelings or emotions (*toute affection*) originate in action. The impressions experienced when facing a forest are "the function of a real action, past or present, of the community."[45]

P. takes the more properly Kantian position: beauty, especially human beauty, is free (*gratuite*), disinterested, remote from action. This, according to G., is an illusion. He delineates two aspects of the human condition, both of which he claims are anticipated by Kant. (This is in fact only the case with the first; the second has a strong Freudian resonance). On one hand, there are "sensibility and understanding." These, of course, compose the a priori according to Kant. On the other hand, there are, according to Goldmann, "eros and the need to act together, to create." Eros differentiates humans from the "archetypal intellect" (God), and reason distinguishes them from the other beings on earth:

> However, this reason is *"action"*; because it is in the *realization* of the "WE," in the general community of human action that we make the decisive step towards the absolute. But on this general foundation there must always be the reality of eros, the community of two [*la communauté à deux*], *love.*

But, G. adds, sexuality is usually substituted for love. He then comments that while Sartre's *Being and Nothingness* provides "a penetrating analysis of this phenomenon," its author "totally ignores action" (an odd criticism of Sartre) and therefore concludes that "love is impossible, a simple illusion."[46] This counterposing of Sartre's to G.'s views of love and the human condition is notable since *Being and Nothingness* became the central text of existentialism after Heidegger's *Being and Time*. We can perceive here how Goldmann's thinking is structured by the relation between existentialism (and/or tragedy) and his own dialectical vision (and/or hope). We have already observed this in his counterposing first of *Soul and Forms* and *History and Class Consciousness* and then of Lukács and Heidegger.[47]

Sartre's discussion of love and hate occurs fairly late in *Being and Nothingness*, in the section on "Being-for-Others." It is modeled partly on the celebrated discussion of Master and Slave in the *Phenomenology of Spirit*. In Hegel's parable two "self-consciousnesses" engage in a life-and-death struggle for recognition, as "it is only through staking one's life that freedom is won."[48] The struggle for selfhood is through confrontation with an Other and death. He who is less resolute and fears death becomes a bondsman, slave to a master, his apparent opposite. But through labor, and through the self-disciplined use of his powers, the slave transforms himself, learns his own capacities, and that the world is not fixed. He can finally cast off dependence. In the meantime the master reaches an impasse because having made an Other his slave, the latter's recognition can yield no satisfaction.

Sartre calls love one of the possible "concrete relations with Others." For him, each person is engaged in an ultimately futile effort to obtain recognition and esteem from others. In love, one wants an Other to be dedicated totally to one's own freedom. I try, in love, to possess the Other's freedom and subjectivity, all the while demanding that the Other's love be freely given to me. This, however, is only possible "if I get hold of this freedom and reduce it to being a freedom subject to my freedom." Love is "to possess a freedom as freedom."[49] This project cannot but be frustrated because in asking to be everything for the lover, there must be "a gluing down of the Other's freedom." Hence Sartre declares, "What the Hegelian Master is for the Slave, the lover wants to be for the beloved."[50] With an important caveat: the lover wants the beloved's affection to be freely chosen. Love, finally, turns into strife, as each is seduced into being an object for the Other; each seduces the Other's freedom in the demand for love. *Being and Nothingness* tells us that "conflict is the original meaning of Being-for others."[51]

A concept of "we" such as Goldmann's is an ontological impossibility for Sartre. P. poses a Sartrean question to G.: "Are you sure that love is not 'pour-soi' [For-Itself], that it does not annihilate one being for the benefit of the Other?" *Pour-soi* is Sartre's term for consciousness as a "negating" or "annihilating" force, that is, as a "nothingness," which surges forth toward and acts on the world, changing things from what they were. Thus P.'s question is whether or not love is ultimately a destructive projection from the self. G. rejoins with an unequivocal no. Nonetheless, he admits that this is more often than not the case in the contemporary, decadent world, a world in which "we are obliged to go through a great deal of our life outside any real community." It is a world "in which the baker makes his bread not for those needing it, but to sell it and to earn the most possible. He only thinks of himself, of how the service he renders will bring him a surplus."[52]

It is a world in which everyone is a means for the Other, contrary to Kant's kingdom of ends. In it, most people live "a false, artificial form" of life. P. summarizes G.'s claims as follows:

> In your view ... there is an essential distinction to be made. There is the "We" which is radically different from the "They" [*du "On"*]. What distinguishes human society from the realm of termites [*la termitière*] is, in sum, man's possibility of realizing his "SELF" [*MOI*] in the "WE." ... Each of us [*nous*] *knows it or comes to know it.*
>
> But all this supposes the stability of the human condition. Your philosophy is only defensible and has universal validity in time and space if there is something fixed and eternal in man.[53]

G., whom we assume speaks for Goldmann, concurs. He insists that, though a rarity, love does exist "*in our world.*" Like art, it synthesizes sensibility and understanding, transforming "sexual union into a community of struggle for the ideal."[54] This is only possible if the goal of the struggle, of action, is "the human person, the human community in general." Otherwise the inauthentic substitutes itself for love, be it the anonymity of "the They" or the bourgeois notion of the family as a respectable haven.

Once more, Goldmann makes a Hegelian move: he tries to bring truth, beauty, love, and action into a totality. G. is now able to return to his initial question, and to define "human beauty" as "*the synthesis of two fundamental elements of man, eros and ideal, incarnated in the same being*" (Goldmann's emphasis). Importantly, it is incarnated in "the community of action" when it becomes one with the struggle for "the ideal."[55] Authentic love between two individuals entails mutual involvement in a larger project, something beyond the individual—the building of a community. It thereby becomes the union of "eros" and "the 'We.'" Love, says G., is the union of Venus and Prometheus. (Two decades later, in *For a Sociology of the Novel*, this concept will govern Goldmann's analysis of the relation between Kyo and May in Malraux's *Man's Fate*.) The aspiration of Goldmann's life's work remained consistent: individual fulfillment in a community of ends in opposition to the reified modern (capitalist) world—a community understood as a totality linking the theoretical, the moral, and the beautiful.

V

What provides the link between the individual and the community, between the part and the whole? Goldmann's answer rests finally on his concept of the "transindividual subject," which synthesizes the insights he drew from his two masters, Lukács and Jean Piaget. Goldmann's personal links with these two men were radically different in character, though both were forged during his stay in Switzerland. He met Piaget during the war, and their relationship was mutually enriching. Goldmann dedicated *Recherches dialectiques* (1959)—the title may be rendered, significantly, as either "Dialectical Quests" or "Dialectical Studies"—to Piaget, "Master and Friend." It is perhaps not coincidental that the Swiss psychologist's second book, written at age twenty-two in 1918, was a novel entitled *Recherche*. Its protagonist, Sebastian, is obsessed with the relation of science to faith and morality. For him, "science gives the laws of the world, faith its engine; in between these two social forces, social salvation is the equilibrated result."[56] The interests of the young Piaget were precisely those of the youthful, as well as the maturing, Goldmann.

Their first meeting was as startling as it was memorable for Piaget. He left the following account of it:

> He [Goldmann] arrived unannounced one fine day at my home and declared to me simply that he was a Marxist and had consequently come to work with me for a year or two because I was the most authentic dialectician, at least in the West. Although he had never published anything, he had a number of projects in mind, among them a study of me etc. In brief, at the outset, he said everything he could have to frighten me . . . and I began to swear to him that I had never read a single line of Marx or of Marxist theoreticians and had no intention of doing so either. "All the better," was his response, "I will explain them to you and without the deformations or omissions to which Marx's thought is ceaselessly victim."[57]

Goldmann, who came to argue that there was a close parallel between Piaget's "genetic epistemology" and Marx's dialectical method, convinced Piaget to read and reconsider Marx.[58] In a September 1945 letter to Fred Pollock supporting Goldmann's request for a grant from the

Institute for Social Research, Piaget commended Goldmann's doctoral thesis as a work that "renews the problem of interpretation of Kantian thought." His young acquaintance, he wrote, was "full of projects concerning the sociology of Marxist thought, and I personally have great hopes for Goldmann's current and future works."[59]

Goldmann's relation to Lukács was much more complicated. He often seemed to be an uncritical admirer of Lukács, or at least of the young Lukács. In a 1963 letter, Goldmann told Lukács, "[Y]our work seems more and more important to me every year . . . it becomes increasingly lucid." He called Lukács "one of the towering figures of the twentieth century."[60] That same year, Theodor Adorno warned Goldmann to qualify his praise of Lukács. "I do not exaggerate," Adorno declared, "when I say that it was Lukács's early writings, primarily *Theory of the Novel*, that motivated me to take up philosophy and I will never forget him for that." At the same time, said Adorno, it was essential to recognize the limits of young Lukács's work, in specific, the romantic lauding of antiquity ("der romantschen laudatio temporis acti") in *Theory of the Novel* and the "metaphysical glorification of the party as *Weltgeist*" in *History and Class Consciousness*. Unqualified paeans to Lukács were dangerous "because—as you know—he repudiates exactly those writings that you and I hold in high esteem, even though his prestige among progressive intellectuals rests solely on these very writings."[61]

In fact, Goldmann's attitude toward Lukács had already become nuanced two decades before Adorno's letter, in the period between the publication of the first (German) edition of *Kant* in 1945 and its French translation in 1948. In his preface to the latter, Goldmann stated that while he had once placed Lukács on a par with Kant, Hegel, and Marx, he no longer thought that to be the case. He regarded Lukács as "the most important twentieth century philosophical thinker," but he believed it more accurate to describe him as a "great essayist" and not a systematic philosopher. Lukács's work thus foreshadowed a fuller system, and Goldmann, no doubt, saw himself as its elaborator.[62]

This shift may be partly due to Goldmann's personal encounters with the Hungarian Marxist, although these were few. They took place shortly after the war in Switzerland. An intermittent, and usually quite formal, correspondence continued after Goldmann settled into academic life in Paris. Goldmann first met the author of *History and Class Consciousness* in 1946 at the Rencontres Internationales in Geneva. Lukács spoke there on "The Aristocratic and Democratic Worldviews." It was a dogmatic Marxist presentation and led to an acerbic dialogue with Karl Jaspers. Disappointed, Goldmann—or so he later told his wife—privately approached Lukács afterwards. Why, he asked, did you permit the party to write your lecture? Lukács was irritated by Goldmann's brash—although perhaps not entirely innocent—insinuation, having just returned to his native Budapest, after surviving the 1930s and World War II in Stalin's Moscow. Some time later, however, they had a more congenial encounter in the Odéon Cafe in Zurich.[63]

Lukács described his first meeting with Goldmann to one of his students as ridiculous. According to Lukács's version, his young admirer wanted to discuss *History and Class Consciousness*. Lukács proposed that Goldmann overcome this infatuation and, instead, pursue his project on Pascal and Racine. "The poor Goldmann!" Lukács declared subsequently. "Undoubtedly a decent man and an adherent of mine; I only cannot understand what he can find in my immature works like *Soul and Forms* and *History and Class Consciousness*."[64]

What Goldmann found in those early works is revealed in *The Hidden God* (1955). He took only half of the Hungarian's advice, for he wrote the book on Pascal and Racine, but remained faithful to (though modifying) the ideas of the young Lukács. He sent a copy to Lukács on March 2, 1956, inscribed, "To Georg Lukács with my respect and an admiration which finds expression on every page of this work."[65] Lukács did not respond for three and a half years. This was due, at least in part, to events in Budapest. After the Soviet invasion of Hungary in the autumn of 1956, Lukács, who had joined Imre Nagy's ill-fated revolutionary government as minister of culture, was deported to Romania. He remained there until the following April, and after his return to Hungary, where he refused to repent, his movements and contacts were constricted because he was placed in a form of "internal exile" in Budapest.

It was October 1959 before Lukács finally wrote to Goldmann to express thanks for both *The Hidden God* and *Kant* (which Goldmann apparently had sent to him earlier). He explained that he had not responded sooner because of "a very peculiar intellectual situation which renders dialogue by letter very difficult, if not impossible." He did not define the "situation" as his political difficulties (although they were undoubtedly a factor). Rather, it was a question of Goldmann's relation to Lukács's oeuvre as a whole:

> If I had died around 1924 and my unaltered soul were to look at your literary activity from another world, it would be filled with genuine gratitude for your intense occupation with my early works.
>
> However, since I have not died and have created my life's work proper during these thirty-four years—and this life's work does not exist at all for you—it is very difficult for me as a living person whose main interests are, naturally, focused on his own present activity, to take a position on your expositions.[66]

Lukács then qualified his rebuff:

> Please don't misunderstand me. This does not imply any reprimand against
> you, nor any sensitivity on my part. I know very well that every published
> work lives a life independent of its author's initial intentions and later in-
> sights. And from your standpoint you are fully entitled to take into account
> my early works alone and to ignore my life's work proper. If we were to
> meet somewhere in person, naturally we would, without difficulty, find
> plenty of subjects for a dialogue. By letter, however, this is practically im-
> possible. Therefore I must restrict myself to thanking you in a very formal
> way.[67]

Finally, Lukács asked his proponent for a favor, as he would several
times in ensuing years. Would Goldmann look into the fate of one of
Lukács's books, long scheduled for French publication?

In a handwritten reply, Goldmann cheerfully agreed to help, even
though the book in question, *The Meaning of Critical Realism Today*, embodied just those aspects of Lukács's "life's work proper" that he had
studiously ignored. (It should be recalled, however, that Goldmann
had translated two of Lukács's later literary works). Goldmann responded, tellingly and directly, to Lukács's criticisms:

> As far as my position toward your work is concerned, it is quite simple. I
> owe you far too much to comment publicly on my disagreements with you
> either in your early or later works. Such a procedure would seem utterly
> petty to me. On the other hand, I have always tried to do everything possi-
> ble to assure the publication of your post-war writings in France, which
> seemed much more important than a debate.[68]

As a rejoinder, this was generous and loyal. Goldmann's concerns,
however, were not only personal. He was writing to the foremost
Marxist intellectual of the century within three years of Khrushchev's
"secret speech" denouncing Stalin's crimes at the Twentieth Congress
of the Soviet Communist Party and the Soviet invasion of Hungary.
These events had sent Western European Marxists reeling. In their aftermath in France, there was an exit (or purging) from the French
Communist Party of leading intellectuals (such as Henri Lefebvre).
Concurrently, France was immersed in the Algerian crisis, which led
to the return of de Gaulle. During these events, the Left was largely
ineffective. Goldmann was so terrified by de Gaulle's specter—he
thought it potentially heralded a new French fascism—that he considered fleeing again to Switzerland.

Given these circumstances, Goldmann was ill inclined to criticize
Lukács in public, believing that Lukács's intellectual stature remained
essential for the revival—indeed, the survival—of an intelligent Marx-

ism. He pleaded with Lukács to participate in a conference on dialectics scheduled to take place in France in the spring of 1960: "[T]he French Marxist philosophers, or those who are close to Marxism, are undergoing a severe intellectual crisis at present and many of them are about to throw out the baby with the bath water. To most of them you are—and rightfully so—one of the last intellectual authorities to have survived from the Marxist camp."[69] Lukács did not attend. On the contrary, he was at this time denouncing the translation into French of his most celebrated contribution to Marxism, *History and Class Consciousness*.

There is little of philosophical content in the modest correspondence that continued between Lukács and Goldmann. Most often, Goldmann requested Lukács's participation in various colloquia or proposed to Lukács that he contribute to various collections. Lukács invariably declined with courtesy, though occasionally offering to permit translation into French of one essay or another. The Hungarian Marxist could not have accepted Goldmann's invitations to travel in any event, for after his return to Budapest in 1957 it had been made clear that were he to go abroad he would be unable to come home. In late 1962, Goldmann tried to engage him in a multiauthor, multivolume *History of Marxist Thought*. Lukács responded with considerable enthusiasm for the project and made various suggestions but, once more, refused to collaborate: "Presently I am so busy with the preparation of my *Ethics* that I cannot possibly allow myself any digression. Considering my age, you will certainly understand that."[70] Goldmann's *History* never came to fruition.

After Goldmann's death in 1970—the year before his own—Lukács was asked to contribute to a commemorative volume entitled *Hommage à Lucien Goldmann*. He declined to write an original contribution. Instead, he submitted for translation an article written in 1910. In other words, "Remarques sur la théorie de l'histoire littéraire" was an essay by the young Lukács so admired by Lucien Goldmann. Perhaps this choice indicated a grudging gratitude on the part of the old Georg Lukács to his unrequited protagonist.

Part Two

THE PHILOSOPHICAL BACKGROUND

3

A Short History of Method

IN THE PLACE DE LA SORBONNE, a few meters from the venerable buildings of the University of Paris, stands a bust of August Comte. Together with Descartes, Comte represents the touchstone of modern French thought. Descartes's *Discourse on Method* (1637) presented a famous set of rules of method at a time when the scientific revolution was turning the European mind topsy-turvy. Comte, writing two centuries later, in another epoch of scientific advance but also after the fall of the ancien régime, proposed that the world be grasped by one method, that of natural science. His "positive philosophy" rendered "a uniform manner of reasoning that is applicable to all subject matters that the human spirit can occupy itself with."[1]

The question of method was central to all of Lucien Goldmann's writings. Positivism was his bête noire. Repeatedly, he contrasted it to dialectics, and his initial ambition was to write a history of dialectical thought. *Kant* was intended as its starting point in order to emphasize the importance of the critical philosophy for the genesis of the dialectic. Study of Pascal reoriented Goldmann, and part of the originality of *The Hidden God* is its suggestion that Pascal represented a dialectical French countertradition—or the foundation of one—to Cartesianism (and by extension to positivism).

I

Goldmann's preoccupation with positivism and "scientism" was almost inevitable given the French trajectory of his career. The France to which he came as a young man had not only been the land of Descartes in the seventeenth century and of Comte in the nineteenth century; it was that of Durkheim in the early twentieth century. According to Durkheim, "[A]side from Cartesianism, there is nothing more important in the history of French philosophy" than positivism, whose founding was "the most impressive event in the philosophical history of the nineteenth century."[2]

Yet if France provided the venue of Goldmann's postwar work on method and his critique of positivism, the sources of that work were in German philosophy, specifically, the debates on the "human" or "cultural" sciences in the late nineteenth and early twentieth centuries. Of those who argued about method in Paris in the 1950s and 1960s, Goldmann was a rarity, for his point of departure was the German disputation of three-quarters of a century earlier, rather than the French intellectual environment alone. With few exceptions—Raymond Aron was one—most participants in the French exchanges wrote as if Dilthey and the Heidelberg neo-Kantians had never existed, even though these German philosophers anticipated almost all of the issues discussed later in Paris. It is against both the German and the French backdrop that Goldmann must be situated to discern the fecundity of his thought.

Positivism originated in the subversion by science of the totalistic aura—Christianity—that was cast over all forms of inquiry in the Middle Ages. There was, of course, a scientific discourse in the Middle Ages, but it posed few essential challenges to religion in comprehending the world. Medieval science was dominated by Aristotelianism, an organic tradition, and the ideas of Ptolemy and Galen; explanation was teleological, presuming final causes, for everything in the universe had its natural place. Aristotelian science combined induction and deduction, viewing causation as a union of matter and form—that which is particular and that which renders something a member of a class. Change was "potentiality" attaining "actuality." Medieval thought assumed a sole, divine origin for—and, consequently, regularity in—the physical laws of nature and the "natural laws" of morality that were presumed to govern (or to be those that ought to govern) social and political life.

This mode of thinking was challenged by the scientific revolution of the seventeenth century. Once Galileo proposed that "this grand book, the universe" had been "written in the language of mathematics" and declared that the universe was one great mechanism written in "triangles, circles, and other geometric figures"[3] understandable by human beings, then both the beliefs in and the mysteries of God's purpose were in danger of dissolution before the advance of human knowledge. The mechanistic and corpuscularian worldviews that underlay, rose with, and were consequent to the scientific revolution threatened religion, and undid the dominance of the Aristotelians in science. Corpuscularianism rested on atomism: everything in the universe was composed, ultimately, of small irreducibles existing in the void. Geometry, as the science of shape, and mechanics, as the science of motion, became the basis of science in general.[4] Causation was no longer a matter of teleology, but rather of mechanism, and the action of corpuscles on one another.

Hence Galileo rejected Aristotelian teleology, but not the "inductive-deductive" method, which he would recast as the "composite-resolutive" method of reasoning from observations of phenomena to principles and then back to phenomena.[5] If the universe had a telos, it no longer came within the domain of scientific explanation. Physics, for Galileo, had to be distinguished within philosophy. Newton later conceived physics as "natural philosophy" and embraced the "inductive-resolutive" method, renaming it "analysis-synthesis."[6]

Descartes, who was praised by Comte for "rendering to the world the glorious service of instituting a complete system of positive philosophy,"[7] sought to generate his rules of method in Euclidean manner by establishing fundamental axioms from which he would derive consequences. His *Discourse on Method* tells us to accept nothing but what is self-evidently so, "clearly and distinctly" to the mind; to divide each problem into as many parts as possible; to think in a linear mode, beginning with what is simplest and building up slowly to the complex; to enumerate carefully and examine thoroughly each link in a problem.[8] These precepts left a permanent and dramatic imprint on scientific discourse and all French thought, equaled only by the Cartesian theory of the Cogito—the positing of the self as a singular thinking something that is opposed to the world outside it, and the starting point from which all knowledge is deduced.

Comte's "social physics," later renamed sociology, averred the methods of natural science to be appropriate to the study of society; in both cases the goal was "savoir pour prévoir." He insisted that "any proposition which is not strictly reducible to the simple enumeration of the facts—either particular or general—can have no real meaning or intelligible meaning for us."[9] The "scientific spirit" subordinates imagination to observation, restricting the former "to discovery and perfecting the coordination of observed facts and the means effecting new researches."[10] While "facts" are his ultimate reference, Comte insisted that whereas in inorganic sciences we know the parts better than the whole and must move from the simple to the compound, the reverse is the case in social studies and biology: perspective must first come from the whole. How his stress on "facts" is epistemologically reconciled with this claim is not clarified adequately.

Nonetheless, he distinguished "social statics," the aspect of "social physics" that delineates elements in a structure at a given instant, from "social dynamics," which seeks to delineate the history of the structure. As a "scientist," Comte demanded a strict separation of facts and values: "Astronomers, physicists, chemists and physiologists neither admire nor blame their respective phenomena."[11] John Stuart Mill, in his important chapter "On the Logic of the Moral Sciences" in *A System of Logic*, concurred strongly:

> A scientific observer or reasoner merely as such, is not an adviser for practice. His part is only to show certain consequences follow from certain causes and that, to obtain certain ends, certain means are the most effectual. Whether the ends themselves are such as ought to be pursued, and if so, in what cases and to how great a length, it is no part of his business as a cultivator of science to decide, and science alone will never qualify him for the decision.[12]

Mill, however, rejected Comte's holism, that is, the claim that to study society we have first to see it as a whole. Instead, Mill argued that the "sequences and co-existing" of even the most complex phenomena "result from the laws of the separate elements. The effect produced, in social phenomena, by any complex set of circumstances amounts precisely to the sum of the effects of the circumstances taken singly."[13] On the other hand, while Comte believed that his positive philosophy represented the scientific successor to theological and metaphysical stages of human knowledge, Mill contended that the "backward state" of the "moral sciences" had to be corrected by "applying to them the methods of physical science, duly extended and generalized."[14] Durkheim, who did not classify himself as a positivist per se, declared the "principle objective" of his *Rules of Sociological Method* to be the extension of "scientific rationalism to human behavior." He demanded the value-free study of society. "Social facts" had to be viewed as "things," data, external to the observer.[15]

II

The "classical age" of German thought and culture reached its pinnacle with Hegel's speculative system. After his death, however, the advances of science in the nineteenth century challenged the very validity of such thinking. Yet if "science" opened up unbounded possibilities for positivists, the subsuming of all knowledge under the categories of (natural) scientific method deeply unsettled many philosophers, especially in Germany. None was more unsettled than Nietzsche, whose critique of values and whose call for a transvaluation of values was one direct response to the rise of "scientism."

Rickert complained at the turn of the twentieth century that philosophy was so under the shadow of natural science that its "historical sense" had been paralyzed. Consequently he would seek out, as his most important book was entitled, *The Limits of Concept Formation in Natural Science*.[16] In the South-West German (or Heidelberg) neo-Kantian school, a response to what was effectively an identity crisis of philosophy was fashioned. The summons "Back to Kant," issued in 1865 by the Tübingen philosopher Otto Liebmann in *Kant und die Epigonen*, represented a turn from Hegelianism, materialism, and positivism to critical philosophy as a model for the relation between philosophy and natural science.

The German debate germinated as well in the development of hermeneutics—*hermeneuein* means "to interpret" or "bring to understanding" in Greek—as a discipline for Bible studies. Integrating philosophy and linguistics into its practices, hermeneutics became secularized as a general method of interpretation, which Friedrich Schleiermacher, in the early nineteenth century, tried to establish as a "science" in which one "understood" a text by reexperiencing the author's mental processes.[17] Understanding was conceived as a circular process in which one grasps something by referring it to something else known; through the "hermeneutic circle," understanding becomes a dialectical process of knowing an element only by knowing the whole of which it is a part, and knowing the whole only by its parts. We thus know a sentence through its parts—words—but we know the meaning of the words only by reference to the sentence.[18]

Wilhelm Dilthey proposed to look not just at literature but at history as a text to be interpreted. Although not a neo-Kantian, he fashioned a "critique of historical reason," arguing that the interpretive character of historical science demarcated it from natural science and that the "transcendental" conditions of historical knowledge had to be specified. "Transcendental" was defined as referring to "every determination which has as its basis something transindividual."[19] Kant had argued that knowledge results from the imposition of order by the structure of mind on the data of experience. Our "sensibility" receives sense perceptions through a priori forms of "intuition," time and space, and our understanding (*Verstand*), which is composed of a priori "categories," synthesizes the manifold of sense data. Kant's "Copernican revolution" lay in his assertion that to be known, objects must conform to our minds, not the reverse. He thus distinguished two worlds, the "phenomenal" one, which we can know—objects as they appear to us and are organized by the a priori "categories"—and the unknowable "noumenal" realm of "things-in-themselves" behind what appears to and is organized by the mind.

The conditions of scientific cognition are thereby established: the phenomenal world is organized by the intuitions of the sensibility and the categories of the mind through which we think what is intuited.

Dilthey, who wanted to establish the concepts by means of which we know history, sharply distinguished the *Naturwissenschaften* (the natural sciences), whose conditions of cognition were presented in Kant's first *Critique*, from the *Geisteswissenschaften*. Employment of the word *"Geist,"* which is usually translated from the German as "mind" or "spirit" and means both, illustrates the importance of Hegel's legacy for Dilthey. *"Geisteswissenschaften"* would be most precisely rendered as "the sciences of the mind" or of the "spirit," and Hegel envisioned human history as the journey of *Geist* writ large to self-knowledge and self-realization. Dilthey states that his own use of *"Geist"* is similar to those employed by Montesquieu, Hegel, and Jhring when they spoke, respectively, of the "spirit" of the laws, "Objective Spirit," and "spirit of Roman law."[20] The actual usage of *"Geisteswissenschaften"* originated in the German translation in 1863 of Mill's chapter title "On the Logic of the Moral Sciences" as "Von der Logik der Geisteswissenschaften oder moralischen Wissenschaften."[21] Goldmann used the French term *"les sciences humaines,"* and we shall speak of "the human sciences," which is now its customary use in English.

Dilthey writes:

> *Every single expression of life represents a common feature* in the realm of . . . objective mind. Every word, every sentence, every gesture or polite formula, every work of art and historical deed is intelligible because the people who express themselves through them and those who understand them have something in common; the individual always experiences, thinks and acts in a common sphere and only then does he understand.[22]

In Hegel's use of *"Geist,"* complained Dilthey, "communities" are "constructed . . . from the universal rational will." In contrast, it is necessary to

> start from the reality of life, life contains the sum of all mental activities. Hegel constructed metaphysically; we analyze the given. . . . Thus we cannot understand the objective mind through reason but must go back to the structural connections of persons, and by extension, of communities. We cannot assign the objective mind a place in an ideal construction, but must start with its historical reality.[23]

The task of the *Geisteswissenschaften* is to provide concepts to determine how knowledge in the human sciences is possible. This makes the relation between history and human consciousness a fundamental preoccupation:

> Man does not discover what he is through speculation about himself or through psychological experiments, but through history. Dissecting the products of the human mind which is designed to give us insight into the

origin, forms and function of mental structure, must combine the analysis of historical products with the observation and collection of every available part of the historical *processes* by which they were produced. The whole historical study of the origin, forms, and working of man's mental structure depends on the combination of these two methods.[24]

Dilthey engages in a humanist hermeneutics of both literature and history, "reading" history and social phenomena as texts and as the meaningful expression of human mental states.[25]

On this basis Dilthey distinguished explanation (*Erklären*), which we use to pursue knowledge in the natural sciences, from understanding (*Verstehen*), which is required of the human sciences. In the natural sciences, we examine "facts which present themselves to consciousness as external and separate phenomena," while in the human sciences our concern is "the living connections of reality experienced in the mind." Nature has no "meaning," while the products of human endeavor— which are intentionally done—do. Natural sciences delineate "connections within nature through inferences by means of a combination of hypotheses," whereas the human sciences base themselves on "directly given mental connections." He goes on:

> We explain nature but we understand mental life. Inner experience grasps processes by which we accomplish something as well as the combination of individual functions of mental life as a whole. The experience of the whole context comes first; only later do we distinguish its individual parts. This means that the methods of studying mental life, history, and society differ greatly from those used to acquire knowledge of nature.[26]

Thus historical studies must be interpretive, and in the human sciences the key question is the relation among experience, expression, and understanding. Understanding entails intuitive reexperiencing of the original actor (or writer), a "rediscovery of the I in the thou."[27] We can understand history for the simple reason that humans are historical beings; it is never a matter of something totally external to them, but rather of the objectifications of "the mind-constructed world."[28]

Mental life, according to Dilthey, is purposeful and structured. A "mental structure" is "the inner-relationship between various processes within the person."[29] Dilthey insists that values are imminent in life and that the human scientist cannot avoid examining the object of scrutiny in light of values external to it. Facts and values cannot be simply opposed to each other. It is not rationality or empirical "facts" alone that structure our consciousness, but "*Erlebnis*," lived experience in which "reality is there-for-me."[30] Where *The Critique of Pure Reason* gives us the categories of the understanding (*Verstand*), Dilthey gives us "categories of life," which structure our interaction with and knowledge of the world. It is this that makes Dilthey's notion of understanding (*Verstehen*) possible. (To avoid confusion in this chapter, I shall henceforth use only the German "*Verstand*" to denote the understanding in Kant's sense. For the notion of interpretive understanding in the various senses used by Dilthey, Weber, Goldmann, and others, I will continue to use "understanding.")

The first of Dilthey's categories is totality, or, as he puts it, the category of the whole and the parts: "The whole must be understood in terms of its individual parts, individual parts in terms of the whole."[31] The other four basic categories are "means and ends," "power," "inner and outer," and "value." Dilthey sees these categories as historically produced and also as part of human nature: "[T]he environment acts on the subject and is acted upon by him."[32]

The mechanism enabling this dialectic is the "acquired psychic nexus." It contains "the rules on which the course of individual mental processes depend." The nexus is experienced as a structure, a whole— never as a consequence of "parts growing together; it is not compounded of elementary units." Life forms "a pattern which develops through the constant absorption of new experiences on the basis of older ones."[33] Consequently, Dilthey argues, humans discover themselves through analyzing historical products and the processes that compose those products. Life, Dilthey writes, is the "interweaving of all mankind," and each individual is "a point where webs of relationships intersect."[34] The acquired psychic nexus is the site where the subjective and the objective meet; history must be viewed as a meaningful totality. Since Dilthey insisted that history is made by individuals, he believed poetics and biography to be especially valuable means of access to human psychic processes and to history. The unconscious conditioning of the nexus may reveal the cultural values of an author's or actor's times.

The tool Dilthey proposed for his historical and cultural hermeneutic was the worldview, or "*Weltanschauung*"—an "intuition which springs from our involvement in life,"[35] a historically created effort to grasp the world coherently. Because the human mind is "oppressed by the restless change of impressions and destinies and by the power of the external world," it finds itself in search of meaning. This takes form in a pursuit of "permanent evaluations of life and firm goals."[36] The result is a structured totality composed of a "world-picture"(*Weltbild*), an evaluation of life, and ideals of conduct. Since mental life is teleological, in a worldview "what the enigma contains as a bundle of tasks is elevated into a conscious, necessary system of problems and solutions."[37] From that system, or "ideal," principles of behavior are deduced, and worldviews are expressed and can be studied in religion, poetry, and metaphysics. Dilthey delineates three different *Weltan-schauungen*. The first, "naturalism," can be found expressed philosophically in Democritus, Hobbes, and Hume and in literature in Stendhal and Balzac. It has no religious expression; indeed, it is irreligious. Here, humans see themselves first and foremost as part of nature, are determined by nature's uniformities, and must manipulate those uniformities. The human will is always viewed as subordinate to human instincts, and thought and action aim to satisfy humankind's animal nature. The battle cry of naturalism is "the emancipation of the flesh." Its epistemology is sensualist; its metaphysics are materialist.[38]

In contrast, the "Idealism of Freedom" *Weltanschauung* asserts "the mind's sovereign independence from all given facts; the mind knows itself to be differentiated from all physical causality."[39] In philosophy, it is expressed in Plato, Kant, and Fichte; in literature, it is expressed in Corneille and Schiller; in religion, it is expressed in theism. Consciousness, moral will, and freedom are here counterposed to naturalism's determinism: "The idealism of freedom found firm ground for a valid solution to the enigma of life in the facts of consciousness; it postulated the existence and ascertainability of general, not further analyzable characteristics of consciousness which, with spontaneous power, shape life and a world view from the material of outer reality."[40]

Finally, the *Weltanschauung* of "Objective Idealism" is found in philosophy in Heraclitus, the Stoics, Spinoza, Schelling, Hegel, and Schleiermacher; in literature in Goethe; and in religion in pantheism. It is a contemplative worldview, in contrast to naturalism, which sees reality as something to be manipulated, and the Idealism of Freedom, which sees reality as something for the conscious, moral will to act on. Reality, for Objective Idealism, objectively bears in it ideal values, and "all the discords of life are dissolved into universal harmony."[41] The world is apprehended in terms of parts making a whole. The differences among the three *Weltanschauungen* can be conveniently summarized by Dilthey's application of them to literature:

> Stendhal and Balzac see in life a web of illusions, passions, beauty and decay, aimlessly created in a dark impulse of nature herself. In this kind of life, the strength of egoism prevails. Goethe sees in life a creative force which unifies organic products, human development, as well as the regulations of society in a valuable whole. Corneille and Schiller see in it the stage for heroic deeds.[42]

Despite his frequent—though rarely developed—criticisms of Dilthey, Goldmann's debt to Dilthey's endeavor will become increasingly manifest. For the moment, I will only point to several crucial, common Diltheyan themes (most with very strong Hegelian echoes) that were transformed, elaborated on, and reinvented by Goldmann in Marxist and "genetic structuralist" guise: the distinction between the human and the natural sciences; antipositivism and anti-Cartesianism; the dialectical emphasis on totality expressed in the hermeneutic circle; the use of the notion of worldview to grasp a commonality of coherence in literature, philosophy, and religion; and the refusal of the fact/value dichotomy.

III

The first important neo-Kantian critique of Dilthey was that of Wilhelm Windelband, father of the Heidelberg school. Windelband, following Kant's phenomenon/noumenon distinction, insisted on separating the "is" and the "ought," and this became a central tenet of neo-Kantianism. A corollary was the assertion that since "values" were nonempirical, they could never refer to facts, or to that which "is." The problems of value were posed most famously in the late nineteenth century by Nietzsche; though not Nietzschean, the term "value" was all-important in neo-Kantian vocabulary, which generalized to philosophical usage a term whose ancestry was in classical political economy. In the latter, however, nonempirical exchange value was ascribed to empirical objects, such as commodities. Rudolf Hermann Lotze, a progenitor of neo-Kantianism and Windelband's professor, distinguished between empirical "cognition" and "validity" in order to argue that while that which exists "is," values had "validity"; values therefore could be considered "objective," though they could not be said "to be." Value denoted "an ideal moment which we observe in a thing, going beyond our empirical awareness of the facts."[43]

Windelband defined the history of philosophy as "the process in which European humanity has embodied in scientific conceptions its views of the world and its judgments of life."[44] Faced, like Dilthey, with the rise of a scientism that brought philosophy itself into question, Windelband, like Kant, sought to cast out metaphysics from philosophy and to argue that philosophy was not at all opposed to science but, rather, had its own realm, "its own problem." This he defined as "those values of universal validity" that serve as organizing principles for all the functions of culture and civilization and for all the particular values of life. Philosophy treats these values as norms, not facts.[45] Consequently, for Windelband, the most important of philosophical questions was the "binding link" between "being" and "value."[46]

Philosophy's task in a scientific age, contended Windelband, is to discern the principles behind the specialized sciences. Philosophy finds the norms that serve as the foundations of valid knowledge. He assumed that to speak of logic, ethics, and aesthetics, we must presuppose ideal standards of the true, the good, and the beautiful. These "objective norms" function as "rules of judgment" in examining and evaluating causal events. As a foe of relativism, he wanted to discern universal values in individual events; as a Kantian, he spurned both correspondence theories of truth and epistemological realism. Knowledge always comes of the mind's imposing form on the matter of experience.

Thus Windelband saw philosophy as a science of "normative consciousness" (Normalbewusstsein), that is, of transcendental consciousness, in the Kantian sense, in contrast to individual empirical consciousnesses. In "normative consciousness" is constituted the conditions of knowledge in general rather than the possibilities of a particularly situated individual's knowledge. It posits absolute values, or standards, which apparently function as do Kant's regulative ideas of reason. Kant posited God, freedom, and immortality as necessary but unprovable "ideas of reason," which our minds tend toward and must assume in the employment of Verstand. These principles are "regulative" in that they monitor Verstand and direct its operations. They press us toward systematization in our search for knowledge. Verstand works with sensibility on empirical data; Vernunft (reason) is the intellect trying to go beyond the empirical, not just toward systematization but toward knowing the nonempirical, which for Kant is impossible. Vernunft is governed by its own ideas ("Pure Concepts"), which try to specify the "unconditioned," that is, nonempirical, entities: the soul, God, the "world as a whole." It insists that we systematize and consequently demands that we think of nature as a unity; when we engage in scientific study, we proceed as if nature were a unity, though we cannot possibly know or prove this.

Kant insisted on separating scientific knowledge from moral and aesthetic judgments. Windelband insisted that fidelity to Kant meant going beyond him; whereas the first Critique set out to delineate the general conditions of knowledge and established them as those of the natural sciences, Windelband argued this to be inadequate if the question of history were to be approached. Kant's identification of science per se with natural science—actually the Newtonian quest for laws—excluded historical science because for Windelband history can be addressed solely in terms of unique and contingent events. Consequently, the positivist notion of a unitary scientific method for all realms of knowledge was rejected, though both historical and natural sciences were viewed as empirical. Windelband objected to Dilthey's distinction between Naturwissenschaften and Geisteswissenschaften on the grounds that it was not the object of examination—*Geist* or *Natur*—that distinguishes sciences, but their methods and their logic. The issue was "modes of investigation," not "the contents of knowledge itself." The principle of classification is "the formal property of the theoretical or cognitive objectives of the science in question."[47]

Historical science, then, is distinguished from natural science by its methodological logic, not the content of its object (history). Therefore, when Windelband rejected the notion of a unitary scientific method, it was not on ontological grounds; that is, it was not on the grounds that different realities or types of being, such as Dilthey's *Geist* and *Natur*, are being studied. Deploying Kant's distinction between the "generalizing" and "particularizing" "interests" of reason, Windelband declares natural science to be "nomothetic" and historical science to be "idiographic." The former seeks to establish laws and to place facts under general laws. Logic is therefore nomothetic in principle. Psychology, argues Windelband, is a nomothetic science; consequently, he criticized Dilthey's use of psychology as a basis for the *Geisteswissenschaften* and for distinguishing the *Geisteswissenschaften* (as a science of the psyche) from the *Naturwissenschaften*. The neo-Kantians, because of their opposition to psychologism (the reduction of epistemology to psychology) preferred to speak of the *Kulturwissenschaften* rather than *Geisteswissenschaften*.

The *Kulturwissenschaften* are "idiographic" according to Windelband. They seek to elucidate nonrepeatable, individualized events. The goal of an idiographic, as opposed to a nomothetic, science is "a complete and exhaustive description of a single more or less extensive process, which is located within a unique, temporally defined domain of reality."[48] In contrast to Dilthey's ontologically based distinction between *Geist* and *Natur*, Windelband gives us *Kultur* and *Natur*, but founded on the contraposition of *Gestalten* (unique configurations) of events to laws (of natural science). This does not mean that something cannot be studied both nomothetically and idiographically, as long as the two dimensions are not confused. It is a matter of two different interests of knowledge, different "cognitive or theoretical use of facts." Thus,

> Natural science seeks laws; history seeks structural forms. In the natural sciences, thought moves from the confirmation of particulars to the comprehension of general relationships; in the historical sciences, it is devoted to the faithful delineation of the particulars. From the perspective of the natural scientist, the single datum of observation never has any intrinsic scientific value. . . . The historian's task . . . is to breathe life into some structure of the past in such a way that all of its concrete and distinctive features

acquire an ideal actuality or contemporaneity. His task, in relation to what really happened, is similar to the task of the artist, in relation to what exists in his imagination. This is the source of the relationship between historical accomplishment and aesthetic creativity, the kinship between the historical disciplines and *belles lettres*.[49]

According to Windelband, "law" and "event" are "the ultimate, incommensurable entities of our world view."[50] From the perspective of history, events are unique and unrepeatable; they can be said to have "value." In contrast, if seen from the cognitive goal of natural science, an event is simply an exemplar of a rule under which it is subsumed. If history is concerned with the individual and must reconstruct the past out of "raw material," a principle for selection of "facts" is required. All phenomena are not of interest, and every datum must be placed within a larger whole. Thus general propositions are a part of idiographic inquiry. But it does not follow that history should abandon singular facts, as positivism does, in Windelband's view. When positivism formulates laws in order to make a natural science of historical studies, it produces only trivial generalities.[51] The selection principle for the natural sciences—determining what is and what is not worth examining and using in research—depends, ultimately, on the assumption of generally valid values or norms posited by the normative consciousness, much as Kant's *Verstand* posits principles for the natural sciences.[52] These are the ideal standards, "rules of judgment"— indeed, the "objective" standards of the true, the good, and the beautiful (following the objects of the three *Critiques*). As the laws of understanding and the regulative ideas are "objective" for Kant's first *Critique*, so are such norms. Hence historical science requires an idiographic method, but one basing its effort on universal values. Philosophy's task is to set forth these values.

Rickert, Windelband's student, sought to constitute a historical "science" of the individual based on "objective" norms or values. To make sense of this effort, it is useful to follow Guy Oakes in proceeding not directly (and chronologically) to Rickert but, rather, to one of Rickert's students, who had an important influence on Lukács and Goldmann: Emil Lask.[53] In his *Rechtsphilosophie* (Philosophy of Law), Lask analyzed law as a *Kulturwissenschaft*. He declared that according to the "critical theory of values" the only "reality" is empirical reality. However, empirical reality is also "the scene or substratus of transempirical values or meanings of general validity."[54] Lask distinguishes between an unrepeatable "individual" value—"as unique as the infinitely manifold empirical substratus of reality to which it is attached"—and the type of value to which philosophy addresses itself, which he calls "common" or "typical" in that it belongs "to a plurality of distinct contents of reality."[55] These typical values, removed from the concretely given, embody "the absolute standard of an unlimited number of instances of its realization." Thus philosophy—*Rechtsphilosophie*, in this case—as a theory of typical values had to find "the universal formula of legal value," its "transcendental locus" or "typical value-relation" in order to place law within the context of worldviews.[56] Lask insisted that a line be drawn between the "solely empirical" within reality and the embodying of values within reality.[57] Consequently, an "ought" can never be derived from an "is"; facts and values are distinct. There is a "cleavage" between the philosophical and the empirical "significance" of the concept of a norm. An "ought" in philosophy cannot be based on any "empirical authority;" an "ought" is grounded in absolute values.[58]

The task of the cultural sciences was, according to Lask, the "working out" of the "empirical and temporal factuality of the appearance of cultural meanings," not establishing the validity of those meanings. This requires "methodological selection" in the face of the original "materials" of reality.[59] Since there is an "immense gap which separates reality and being," and since Lask accepts the idiographic/nomothetic distinction, his question becomes how to form the concepts with which to know historical and cultural objects.[60] Lask proposes that conceptualizations of reality can be according to one of two logics: analytic or emanatist.

Analytic logic is atomistic; concept formation is through abstraction from individual entities. Emanatist logic, on the other hand, sees in individual existences the embodiment of the content of concepts. According to Lask's 1901 doctoral thesis, *Fichtes Idealismus und die Geschichte*, analytic logic, of which Kant is an exemplar, considers "the unlimited number of particular objects which can be experienced empirically" to be the "only reality" and "the unshakable basis from which concept formation originates." A concept is "artificial" and incapable of existing on its own; it is solely "the outcome of thinking." Concept formation comes about through "analysis of the immediately given."[61]

Consequently for Lask, as for the neo-Kantians in general, the more general the concept, the more distant it is from the empirical. Analytic logic presumes that between immediate empirical reality and the concepts used to comprehend it, there is a *hiatus irrationalis* (a term Lask borrowed from Fichte). Empirical reality is "brute" and particular. Philosophical deduction is incapable of leaping from the indeterminate to the determinate; that is, it cannot conceptually arrive at "the particular concrete determination." This is because "Bruteness is the sole and absolute 'law' of reality [*Brutalität ist das 'Gesetz' der Wirklichkeit, das einzige und absolut*]." The *hiatus irrationalis* comes necessarily of the "sudden breaking of all threads of speculation vis-à-vis the fact of brute reality." It is unbridgeable; while the "self" may "produce" the object in the Kantian sense of supplying the a priori means of cognition of brute reality, there can be no accounting for the "coming into being" of the actual object. The object is located, says Lask, following Fichte, "between projection and projectum [*zwischen Projektion und Projectum*]," where "it is dark and empty . . . the projectio per hiatum irrationalem."[62] Lask points out that Fichte "translated" this into analogies pertinent to the logic of the natural sciences; here, too, "laws" do not "allow us to penetrate into their singular manifestation in the concrete case."

Consequently the "absolute hiatus" reappears in the impossibility of specifying "how the forces of nature operate" and how they manifest themselves according to laws.[63] In analytic logic a concept abstracts a commonality from a series of phenomena and represents them as moments of the concept. The concept has no ontological status; as thought, it is something apart from the "brute" existents it conceives. Thus while concepts, of course, are not irrational, the gap between concept and reality is—and is unbridgeable.[64]

In contrast, for emanatist logic, of which Hegel is an exemplar, concepts do not abstract from reality; rather, individual existents instantiate the content of concepts and emanate from them. Therefore, as Goldmann notes in *Kant*, the whole must be known in order to know the parts.[65] Individual existents are subsumed under concepts, which are real and have ontological status. Logic, metaphysics, and ontology become inseparable, a whole. There is no antithesis of concept and reality as concepts are real and individualities emanating from them are rational.[66] Max Weber, in his 1903 essay on "Roscher's 'Historical Method,'" follows Lask in seeing emanatism epitomized in Hegelianism and summarizes with a clarity absent in Lask:

> Suppose one accepts the Hegelian theory of concepts and attempts to surmount the *"hiatus irrationalis"* between concept and reality by the use of "general" concepts—concepts which, as metaphysical realities, comprehend and imply individual things and events as their instances of *realization*. Given this "emanatist" conception of the nature and validity of the "ultimate" concepts, the view of the relation between concept and reality as strictly *rational* is logically unobjectionable. On the one hand reality can be deduced from the general concepts. On the other, reality is comprehended in a thoroughly perceptual fashion: with the *ascent* to the concepts, reality loses none of its perceptual content. The maximization of the content and the maximization of the extension of concepts are, therefore, not mutually exclusive. This is because the "single case" is not only a member of the class,

but also a part of the whole which the concept represents. . . . The conceptual contents function as metaphysical entities: they stand behind and buttress reality. Reality is a necessary consequence of these contents in a sense similar to the sense in which the propositions of mathematics "follow" from one another.[67]

Lask argues that in the emanatist approach the concept has "logical supremacy" and empirical reality is viewed as dependent on its higher reality. Hence the concept is "richer in content than empirical reality and ought not to be thought of as part of it." There is an "organic . . . communion between category and particular reality." It is because "the concept releases . . . the particular moment of realization from its abundant profusion" that Lask uses the term "emanatist."[68]

For Hegelian logic, the more general the concept, the more concrete it should be. In Lask's words, "[T]he highest level of the general is at the same time the highest level of concreteness."[69] There is an identity of content and breadth, which is a consequence of "overcoming [*überwindet*] the difference between generality and totality [*Allgemeinheit und Totalität*]," the term "generality" being one of quantity. As a consequence, "the breadth then becomes the content realizing itself and the content becomes the vital movement passing through the entire breadth; the growing of the breadth goes together with the augmentation of content and vice versa."[70]

In his *Rechtsphilosophie*, Lask classified natural law theory as emanatist because it sees law as emanating from a higher source or essence, and then hypostatizes legal values as legal realities. Lask opposes natural law, as a metaphysical and ahistorical rationalist view, to the legal positivist (and presumably analytic) view that law is the order of he who has the power to command, that is, of external authority. The emanatist "eliminates the criterion of the community authority and replaces it with reason as a higher formal source of law, from which law 'emanates' without and against any human enactment, so that law conflicting with reason becomes formally void."[71] Lask, importantly, "opposes historicism" to natural law on the grounds that the former is something like naturalism, "an empirical scientific method" pretending to be a worldview. Lask warns against the confounding of "individuality of values and historical factuality" as a consequence of failing to recognize the *hiatus irrationalis* separating meaning from being. He argues:

> Historicism is the exact counterpart of natural law, and this constitutes its significance on principles. Natural law wants to conjure the empirical substratus out of the absoluteness of value; historicism wants to conjure the absoluteness of value out of the empirical substratum. It is true that natural

law by its hypostatization of values destroys the independence of the empirical. But its basic belief in transhistorical, timeless values has not been an error refutable by the historical enlightenment of the present as many think; rather this has been its immortal merit. Historicism, on the other hand—not by any means history itself nor the historical view of the law—destroys any philosophy, any worldview. It is the most modern, most widespread and most dangerous form of relativism, the levelling of all values. Natural law and historicism are the two rocks of which legal philosophy has to steer clear.[72]

In other words, Lask wishes to avoid absolute transhistorical values on one hand and relativism on the other. To do so he uses a Kantian notion of value that has "transindividual validity."

According to the critical philosophy, a human being's free will—that is, an autonomous will acting solely from a sense of duty—is his (or her) "absolute law." Consequently, says Lask, the end of social life must be the unification of duty-bound individuals in the "community of men of free will." The "absolute" in social institutions is to be found in the "community," a fusion of what individuals deem universally valid.[73] This presumes a contract between the ethically autonomous individuals. The attempt to fuse socialism with a Kantian "community idea"—individuals in the kingdom of ends—was prominent within the Marburg neo-Kantian school (Stammler, Hermann Cohen, Paul Natorp, and Karl Vörlander, among others). Such a kingdom was only possible, according to Lask, to the extent that such a socialism went beyond the scope of individuals.

For Lask, Kant's "community" is not a concrete group of individuals, but, rather, a belief in the abstract value of humanity. Stammler was correct, Lask argues, to discern the idea of community in Kant, an attempt to point beyond the individual. Writes Lask:

If justice is really to express a specific and intrinsically valuable idea, any resort to it as a concept implies a fundamental departure from ascribing value exclusively to the individual personality, a departure toward an idealizing view of community life. Even a legal philosophy of Kantianism—indeed that of Kant himself—thus contains the starting point of a trend beyond social-philosophical individualism.[74]

This last point was essential to Goldmann's reading of Kant. However, for Lask, who was a neo-Kantian and not a Marxist, concepts and reality remain "incommensurable." Lukács's Hegelian Marxism responded with the theory of subject-object identity; Goldmann later used the attenuated and modulated formula of "partial" identity of subject and object.

Rickert attempted to show how, given the hiatus and the irrationality of reality, one can speak of the possibility of historical knowledge. For him, the world presents itself to us as an inchoate, infinite mass of objects and matter of which no knowledge can be complete. In speaking of it as a "whole" in the first place, "reality" must be treated like a Kantian regulative idea of reason: we presuppose this "reality," but cannot "prove" its existence. No Hegelian essence lurks behind or within it, and knowledge of it "as a whole" is impossible. Our concepts are never adequate to what experience presents to us, though concepts are requisite to anything we call experience or knowledge. "Reality" confronts us with an "infinite manifold"; any single object we experience is composed of an infinite combination of events and processes with no delimitations of time or space. It is impossible to discern "reality" totally. Reality is "extensively infinite." At the same time, the events and processes of the extensive infinity are "intensively infinite"; that is, they can be divided into an infinite number of elements, and each element, in turn, has an infinite number of constituents.[75] Knowledge, therefore, presupposes a selection process, conceptualization, because an effort pictorially or otherwise "to reproduce an exact reproduction of what has no limits is an absurd enterprise."[76] Nor can knowledge be a correspondence of propositions to reality.

Selection implies conceptualization, which results in "representation" ("the logical form that must necessarily be taken by the *result* of scientific work").[77] However, Rickert argues,

> The content of reality can be an object of immediate "experience" or "acquaintance." But as soon as we attempt to conceive it by means of natural science, precisely those properties that constitute it as reality always escape us. We have access to the full content of reality only through the immediacy of life, never by means of natural science. . . . The more completely we develop our natural scientific theories and representations, the further we depart from reality as unique, perceptual and individual—in other words, from reality as such. . . . *What fixes the limits of natural scientific concept formation and which the natural sciences can never surmount, is nothing but unique empirical reality itself.*[78]

Rickert, like Windelband, is arguing that the cognitive interest of natural sciences is in generalizing, that is, in establishing laws as abstract as possible, while the cultural and historical sciences are individualizing. Natural science seeks the universal and invariable beyond a particular object's spatiotemporal reference. Consequently, "the complete logical articulation of a concept in natural science depends on the extent to which empirical perception or sense perception is eliminated from its content."[79] Its validity depends on its abstraction from the individual, on its distance from the immediately real. This defines for Rickert the limit of concept formation in natural science:

> In comparison with natural science . . . which always moves from the specific to the general and thus to the unreal, we can designate history as a *science of reality*. . . . The historian attempts to represent the distinctiveness and individuality of reality. Even if he cannot reproduce the content of reality itself, his concepts still stand in a relationship to unique and individual reality that is in principle different from and actually *more proximate* than what holds true for the concepts of generalizing natural science.[80]

The key problem for historical knowledge is concept formation and drawing "lines of demarcation" so that "indeterminable heterogeneity" can become "a *determinate* domain of *discrete* objects."[81]

Natural science employs universal concepts on this "indeterminable heterogeneity," while, according to Rickert, historical, or cultural, science uses "values." As a science, history's concern is nonrecurring individuality. Like Windelband, Rickert claims that individuality alone has value, has intrinsic worth, because it is not simply a moment of a generalization. Indeed, "value" is possessed by all cultural phenomena, since they embody human purpose. Nature is "whatever comes to pass of itself." It is born and grows of itself. Culture is created or fostered by humans with valued goals:

> [V]alues always attach to cultural objects. . . . If we abstract every value from our conception of a cultural object, we can say that it thereby becomes the same as a mere object of nature or that it can be scientifically treated as such. The presence or absence of *relevance to values* can thus serve as a reliable criterion for distinguishing between two types of scientific *objects*. . . . Apart from the value attaching to it, every real cultural phenomenon must be capable of being regarded as connected with nature and even a part of nature.[82]

Rickert defined culture as "the totality of real objects to which attach generally acknowledged *values* or complexes of meaning constituted by values which are fostered with regard to these values."[83] Like Windelband, he assumes that objects may be seen from both natural and cultural scientific perspectives.

Rickert's distinction between cultural and natural sciences thus has two bases: Logically, natural and cultural sciences are distinguished on the methodological grounds that the former generalize and the latter individualize, and they also are distinguished by "value-relevance"

(*Wertbeziehung*). Natural sciences, aiming at abstraction and universal laws—and thus not at the distinctly individual—have no value-relevance, while cultural sciences, concerned with nonrecurring and meaningful events, must. Here, we can see why Rickert used the term "*Kultur*" and criticized Dilthey's use of "*Geist*." The concern of *Kulturwissenschaften* is not the mind per se, but, rather, cultural products, institutions, and their meanings. Using "*Geist*" implied that the mind and psychological processes are the object of investigation, and this led to the danger of psychologism. "*Kultur*," argued Rickert, refers to "real historical *life* to which a meaning is attached that constitutes it as culture. In addition, we can also understand by culture the nonreal 'content' itself."[84]

By speaking of "nonreal" content, Rickert meant to distinguish culture (as something transindividual) from the mental "reality" of "what takes place temporally in single individuals."[85] A nonreal spatial configuration is something noncorporeal, as opposed to mental, that is, actual psychological, events. When one uses such terms as "Greek," "German," "Renaissance," or "Romanticism," one employs "names for concepts of unreal meaning configurations that can be more or less completely grasped in common by many persons within a people or an age."[86] Dilthey's error was in confusing "the nonreal meaningful content of culture that is situated in the realities of history with the real psychic existence that actually occurs in the mental life of single individuals."[87] Consequently, Rickert, who believes that general values "obtain only among human beings who live together in some sort of *community*," that is, among human beings who have shared meanings, speaks not of an "acquired psychic nexus," as does Dilthey, but, rather, of an "individual social nexus" and of "social individuals." Individuals, and culture, exist in a transindividual context.

Rickert declares value-relevance to be the logical principle of the cultural sciences. "Individualizing concept formation" is "value relevant," and thus it opposes "the value free concept formation" that obtains in natural science. He argues that "the *values* that govern value-relevant concept-formation in history and determine what the object of history is, are always drawn from cultural life or are *cultural values*."[88] In contrast to nature, which is "devoid of meaning," the criterion of the objects of historical science is relevance to values, and it is the concept of value that "*establishes the relationship between the mental and the historical*."[89] Values, however, do not "exist." They are valid or invalid. They cannot "correspond" to reality, which, unconceptualized, is irrational. Furthermore, to be "oriented" toward values in historical science, Rickert claims, is not to posit evaluations. Here, he draws on the analogy with classical political economy:

"[S]piritual" existence, i.e. the psychical acts of valuation, should be conceptually distinguished from the values themselves and their validity, just as real goods must be differentiated from the values attaching to them; and one should realize that what is important in "spiritual values" is not the spiritual element, but the *values*. Then one will no longer be disposed to base the distinction between nature and culture on the psychical.[90]

He later adds:

Values are not realities, either psychical or physical. Their nature consists entirely in their *acceptance as valid*: they have no real being as such or existential *actuality* in their own right. However, values are *connected* with real entities. . . . In the first place value can "attach" to an *object* and thereby make it into a *good*. In addition it can be connected with an *action* of a *subject* in such a way that this action becomes a *valuation*.[91]

There is value-relevance in history inasmuch as subjects accept values and denote objects as goods. To say this, Rickert insists, in a murky argument, is to raise a question of an "is" and not an "ought." History does not try to determine the validity of such values. It is value-relevance that permits historical science despite the *hiatus irrationalis* and allows the study of history despite the problem posed by intensive and extensive infinitude. But despite his denial that evaluation is entailed, he assumes that in delineating a historical object, historical scientists must use or "refer" to the values they accept or to the community of which they are a part. Rickert writes:

[T]he objectivity of a *particular* historical investigation is in no way threatened by the fact that a cultural value serves as the guiding principle in the selection of the data regarded as essential, for the general acknowledgement of the values that endow the objects under consideration with significance is a *fact* that the historian can point to. He thereby achieves the highest degree of empirical objectivity.[92]

How?

Only after what is historically essential has already been *established* on the basis of its relevance to some cultural value can one inquire retrospectively into causes or prospectively into effects and include in one's representation the factors uniquely responsible for the occupance of the historically essential event.[93]

In sum, Rickert wants to argue that what makes historical science possible are universals—what he calls "values"—which are the basis of selection. While these values derive from a historian's community, this does not mean that evaluation occurs in actual historical study. The

latter is not concerned with the validity of the values, just their existence. These values function as "objective norms," and while Rickert
admits that there are as many historical truths as there are cultures, he
assumes that a day will come when atemporal absolute "objective"
values of the true, the good, and the beautiful will be accepted by all
and serve as standards for the individualizing science of history.

IV

It is in Max Weber's methodological essays that these debates find
their most acute reformulation. According to Weber, "'mental' or 'intellectual' phenomena—regardless of how these ambiguous terms
might be defined—are just as susceptible as 'dead' nature to an analysis in terms of abstract concepts and laws. . . . [T]he real question is
whether the generally valid laws which may eventually be discovered
make any contribution to the *understanding* of those aspects of cultural
reality we regard as *worth knowing*."[94] Even if one accepted Rickert's
methodological differentiation among sciences, says Weber, these are
not the sole distinctions. Even if the objects of both internal and external experience are "given" to us in the same way, "both the course
of human conduct and also human expressions of every sort are
susceptible to a *meaningful interpretation*. As regards all other entities
we can find an analogue for this interpretation only in the sphere of
metaphysics."[95]

Weber did not, however, embrace a Diltheyan notion of *Verstehen*.
On the contrary, while not negating the uses of empathetic reexperiencing, and while insisting that history must be grasped as the result
of purposeful individual human activities, Weber insisted on the possibility of objective analysis of subjectively constituted (or partly subjectively constituted) human behavior. He contended that such action
can be intelligible and grasped by means of replicable "logical" constructs—through ideal-types.

The ideal-type is an abstraction from "reality," which serves not
as a hypothesis but as a tool for rational imputation in research. It
gives means by which a description of reality—that intensive and extensive totality—can be expressed, but it is not itself a description. It is
constructed

> by the one-sided accentuation of one or more points of view and by the
> synthesis of a great many diffuse, discrete, more or less present and oc-
> casionally absent *concrete individual* phenomena, which are arranged ac-

cording to those one-sidedly emphasized viewpoints into a unified *analytical* construct [*Gedankenbild*]. In its conceptual purity, this mental construct [*Gedankenbild*] cannot be found empirically anywhere in reality. It is a utopia.[96]

There is no pure capitalism that can be empirically discerned, but an ideal-type of capitalism, constructed from the essential traits of the economic regime called capitalist, provides a conceptual tool against which to examine empirical capitalisms.

The ideal-type's relation to empirical realities thus parallels that between Kant's regulative ideas of reason and the world. The ideal-type is a logical means for research and not a conceptualization of an existing manifold. It is a means, too, by which one can do historical research despite the *hiatus irrationalis*. The ideal-type's function is "comparison with empirical reality in order to establish its divergences or similarities, to describe them with the *most unambiguously intelligible concepts*, and to understand and explain them causally."[97] It provides "rational, empirical-technical constructions" by means of which we can delineate what a behavior or thought pattern would be like if it were consistently rational, empirical, and logical. Thereby we can explain a subjectively rational action in which mistakes can nonetheless be made as a goal is pursued. And by constructing an ideal-type that depicts a rational course of action or the rational functioning of a system, we can discern the irrational deviations from the model.

Consequently, Weber's notion of *Verstehen* (understanding), unlike Dilthey's, is desubjectified. Weber recognizes that the actions of human beings are unlike those of atoms or chemical reactions; humans act meaningfully and purposefully. Yet, he does not conclude that empathy satisfactorily grasps human behavior: "When one begins to think, *first-person* experiences are replaced by reflection upon third-person experiences which are conceived as an 'object.' "[98]

Causal explanation of "subjective," or meaningful, human action is possible. To understand Caesar one need not be Caesar.[99] Whatever the value of Diltheyan empathetic reexperiencing, scientific analysis of behavior must employ ideal-types and the presuppositions of rational action to make human actions and interactions comprehensible. In "explanatory understanding" we apprehend an actor's purposes and explain what causes him or her to act. In other words, we link *Verstehen* and *Erklären* (explanation): we rationally understand the meaning of the act; and we explain its cause. Motivation (subjective intent) is linked to causation. We grasp "in terms of *motive* the meaning an actor attaches to the proposition [that] twice two equals four when he states it or writes it down, in that we understand what makes him do this at precisely this moment and in these circumstances. This is rational understanding of motivation which consists in placing the act in an intelligible and more inclusive context of meaning."[100] We can directly observe and understand chopping wood; when we know the woodcutter's purpose is a wage or firewood, that is, when we know the "sequence of motivation," we have explanatory understanding. A scientific explanation of "the subjective meaning of action . . . requires a grasp of complex meanings in which an actual course of understandable action thus interpreted belongs."[101] We understand the motive, and we explain the cause of action by situating the action in a broader social context of purposes and meanings. To "understand" is

> to identify a concrete "motive" or complex of motives "reproducible in inner experience," a motive to which we can attribute the conduct in question with a degree of precision that is dependent upon our source material. In other words, because of its susceptibility to a meaningful *interpretation* and to the extent that it is susceptible to this sort of interpretation—individual human conduct is in principle intrinsically less "irrational" than the individual natural event. Insofar as it is susceptible to a meaningful interpretation: if human conduct cannot be interpreted in this way, it is no different from the fall of the boulder from the cliff.[102]

With this argument, the methodology debate has come full circle: the stress on individuality in Weber's immediate predecessors engendered the distinction between the *Geistes/Kulturwissenschaften* and *Naturwissenschaften*. Weber's argument, however, challenges their formulations in a fundamental way. Because human action is intentional and, in principle, can be rational, that is, because it can consciously posit ends for itself and can be analyzed through ideal-types, it can also be presumed to be less "irrational" than nature's mere events. For Weber,

> A correct causal interpretation of a concrete course of action is arrived at when the overt action and the motives have been correctly apprehended and at the same time their relation has become meaningfully comprehensible. A correct causal interpretation of typical action means that the process which is claimed to be typical is shown to be both adequately grasped on the level of meaning and at the same time the interpretation is to some degree causally adequate.[103]

The "logical content" and "validity" of an object of knowledge, Weber continues, are dependent on concept formation, and not on the object's "'substantive' qualities," its ontological status, or "the kind of 'psychological' conditioning required for its acquisition." Whether the object is a mental one or external nature, whether it is "knowledge of processes 'within' us" or "those 'without' us," the concepts are the same "from a logical point of view." Moreover,

> to identify the "self-evidence" of "empathy" in the actual or potential "conscious" inner "experience"—an exclusively phenomenological quality of "interpretation"—with a unique empirical "certainty" of processes "susceptible to interpretation" is an even more serious mistake. Physical and psychical "reality," or an aspect of "reality" comprehending both physical and psychical components, constitutes an "historical entity" because and insofar as it can "mean" something to us. "Meaningful," interpretable human conduct ("action") is identifiable by reference to "valuations" and "meanings." For this reason, our criteria, for *causal* explanation have a unique kind of satisfaction in the "historical" explanation of such an "entity."[104]

Weber believes that the social scientist's work is always "value-relevant." The selection of the object of study is always informed by the scholar's own cultural or value system. How else might something be deemed worthy of study in the first place?

Yet once the value-relevant choice is made, argued Weber, the intrusion of values into the actual process of study is dangerous and avoidable through causal analysis. However, Weber proposes that there is no "absolutely 'objective' scientific analysis" of culture and social phenomenon, or, more precisely, that there are none that are independent of the "one-sided" perspectives that select, analyze, and organize them in the first place:

> The type of social science in which we are interested is an *empirical science* of concrete reality [*Wirklichkeitswissenschaft*]. Our aim is the understanding of the characteristic uniqueness of the reality in which we move. We wish to understand on the one hand the relationships and the cultural significance of individual events in their contemporary manifestations and on the other the causes of their being historically *so* and not *otherwise*.[105]

In speaking of why something is "*so* and not *otherwise*," Weber raises the issue of "possibility," or, more specifically, what he called "objective possibility," a concept he uses in attempting to analyze historical causality. Here again, he employs imaginary mental constructs. To find out what caused a given occurrence, that is, to find out which of the complex of antecedents that produced a given result were essential to its appearance, we need to ask, What if some of those antecedents had not occurred?

We can accomplish this by constructing an imaginary sequence of events and comparing it with the actual historical events. We elaborate an "unreal" construct to discern what the "objective possibilities" were, and we compare this to what in fact happened. Weber provided a famous illustration of this procedure in his analysis of Eduard Meyer's discussion of whether the Persian defeat at Marathon by the Greeks was decisive for the future history of Western culture:

> The assessment of the causal significance of an historical fact will begin with the posing of the following question: in the event of the exclusion of that fact from the complex of facts which are taken into account as co-determinants or in the event of its modification in a certain direction, could the course of events, in accordance with general empirical rules, have taken a direction in any way different in any features which would have been decisive for our interest?[106]

Here we have the basis for judging "objective possibility." What would have happened to Western civilization had the Hellenes lost at Marathon?

If it can be demonstrated that the development of Greece would have been significantly different than it was, we can make a legitimate claim of "adequate" historical causality. We do this by studying what took place where Persia *was* victorious and what Greece was like at the time. Weber concludes that such analyses based on objective possibility would show that a Persian victory at Marathon would have led to the imposition of Persian religious motifs on Greece, which would have transformed Greek religion in such a way that the incipient rationalism within Greek culture would never have flowered. A very different evolution for Western civilization as a whole would have resulted. If Persia had been victorious, this would have been "adequate" (sufficient) to yield another development of Europe: "[I]f we 'conceived' the effect as having actually occurred under the modified conditions, we *would* then recognize those facts thus modified to be 'adequate causes.'"[107] To conceive causation, we posit counterfactuals.

Purposeful human behavior has hereby been grasped through constructing a logical model, rather than relying on "reliving" or "re-experiencing." This brings us back to the fact/value problem. Weber, like Rickert, wants to insist that a value judgment (*Werturteil*) is not the same thing as value-relevance (*Wertbeziehung*). Value judgments are "practical evaluations of the unsatisfactory or satisfactory character of phenomena subject to our influence."[108] We make them throughout our lives, and all history must in some way be linked to values. But analyses of history or society do not, Weber argues, have to evaluate; indeed, value judgments cannot, he insists, be derived from factual statements. Values are a matter of faith and cannot be proven. Competition among them will forever be a fundamental feature of our world: "Science can make [one] realize that all action and

naturally, according to the circumstances, inaction, imply in their consequences, the espousal of certain values—and herewith—what is
today overlooked—the rejection of certain others. The act of choice itself is his own responsibility."[109]

The historical and social sciences can instruct us as to the adequacy
of various means toward various ends. They make no judgment about
the ends themselves. They tell us what can be done, not what ought to
be done. Ironically, Weber thus replicates in his own way Kant's distinction between noumenal and phenomenal realms on one hand, and
Mill's distinction, in *The Science of Logic*, between the adequacy of
means and the evaluation of ends in the role of the social or moral
scientist.

4

Lukács, Marxism, and Method

"THE PRIMACY OF THE CATEGORY of totality is the bearer of the principle of revolution in science."[1] When Georg Lukács published these words in 1923 in *History and Class Consciousness*, he had been a Marxist for five years. His book's reinjection of the categories of classical German philosophy into Marxism made a profound impression on an array of intellectuals, who, beginning in the late 1920s, rejected the dogmatism that had come to dominate "official" Marxist thought of both the social democratic and Third International varieties. These intellectuals became known as Western Marxists, and some of the most gifted among them composed the Frankfurt School. It was a tradition with which Goldmann strongly identified.

Lukács defined Marxist orthodoxy as a matter of method. This orientation was, in part, a consequence of the period he spent, during World War I, in the neo-Kantian milieu of Heidelberg. It was there that he encountered Lask and became a valued interlocutor of Weber. In the opening essay of *History and Class Consciousness*, "What Is Orthodox Marxism?" Lukács proposed that were all Marx's individual theses to be proven wrong, the orthodox Marxist could accept such findings and remain orthodox. The issue was not "the 'belief' in this or that thesis, nor the exegesis of a 'sacred' book." Rather, orthodoxy referred "exclusively to *method*" and "the scientific conviction that dialectical materialism is the road to truth and that its methods can be developed, expanded and deepened only along the lines laid down by its founders."[2]

Lukács declared, "What is crucial is that there should be an aspiration towards totality."[3] This was always his own aspiration. In *Soul and Forms*, totality—"wholeness"—was sought, but unattainable; the consequence was his preoccupation with "the metaphysics of tragedy." In *History and Class Consciousness*, totality was attainable by means of the working class, which would, through historical action, simultaneously grasp and create historical "totality." In his 1967 preface to the book's republication, Lukács characterized this as "an attempt to out-Hegel Hegel."[4] Rickert wrote, "The totality of reality always remains an 'Idea' in Kant's sense of the word, that is, a necessary but theoretically insoluble task. Only as a logical 'value' is the 'world' to be understood philosophically."[5] Lukács the Marxist saw totality not solely as a concept required to apprehend reality, but as the essential, and practical, feature of reality itself.

I

Young Lukács matured within the milieu of romantic anticapitalism, which longed for idealized, organic *Kultur* embedded in Gemeinschaft, which it opposed to the utilitarian *Zivilisation* of Gesellschaft.[6] *Soul and Forms* presented an irreconcilable dualism between the realm of ultimate values ("Life") and the inauthentic chaos of empirical, everyday existence ("life"). Both Platonic and Kantian motifs are discernible here: Plato counterposed the permanent and real world of "forms" accessible to our reason to the fluctuating empirical world perceived by senses. Kant's theory gave us the "noumenal" world of moral freedom and the "phenomenal" world of natural causation. Lukács, in a 1909 letter, declared his aesthetics to be based on "the assumption that all genuine and profound need for expression finds its own typical way—its scheme if you will—which is the form."[7] These "forms" were meaningful atemporal structures by means of which human beings express their ever-unfulfilled possibilities, possibilities ever stymied in the face of inauthentic everyday "life." A tragic vision of the world emerges from the "foundering of form against life." In the unavoidable conflict between life and Life, "is" and "ought" are inevitably opposed to one another.

These themes have their origins in part in Lukács's studies in Berlin with Georg Simmel in 1909–1910, around the time he was writing *Soul and Forms*. Simmel, like his neo-Kantian contemporaries, asked how "the raw material of immediate experience" gives rise to "the theoretical structure which we call history." To provide an answer, Simmel, like Dilthey, sought to determine "the a priori dimension of historical knowledge."[8] In other words, a priori categories "form" the events of "history," as for Kant the a priori categories form "nature" by imposing epistemological order on the sensuously given data of the physical world. Thus the separation of form from content, for Simmel, became methodologically essential; "forms" were conceived by him as categories with their own logic that constitute history and structure worldviews. Without them, life and the world would be unintelligible.

We see here an essential source of the worldview of *Soul and Forms*; "culture" for Simmel is a "form" that comes of the interaction of human beings. It is Objective Geist in that it embodies human purpose in language, morals, technologies, and artistic creations. Objective Geist cultivates human existence; it may, however, become an hypostatization, too, thwarting the expression of life. Since objective culture takes on its own autonomy from individuals who create it, it may become reified when means acquire the value of ends, as Simmel sought to show in *The Philosophy of Money*. His purpose was to derive the noneconomic consequences—the consequences for human values and interrelations—of the modern money economy by showing how "economic objects" are invested with "a quantity of value as if it were an inherent reality," and then handed over "to the process of exchange; to a mechanism determined by those quantities, to an impersonal confrontation between values, from which they returned multiplied and more enjoyable to the final purpose, which was also their point of origin: subjective experience." This, says Simmel, is "the source of that valuation which finds its expression in economic life and whose consequences represent the meaning of money."[9] Consequently, the individual is confronted by an "objective realm" of circulating objects. Money embodies that which is common to "economic objects"; it "objectifies the external activities of the subject which are repressed in general by economic transactions." Money is *"a reification of the general form of existence according to which things derive their significance from their relationship to each other."*[10] This process, which results in means being increasingly taken for ends, is at once a great danger and an unavoidable result of the human need for the use of symbols and abstractions. Simmel compares it to another "tool" that "circulates," language:

> Just as my thoughts must take the form of a universally understood language so that I can attain my practical ends . . . , so must my activities and possessions take the form of money value in order to serve my more remote purposes. Money is the purest form of tool . . . , it is an institution through which the individual concentrates his activities and possessions in order to attain goals that he could not attain directly. . . . What money mediates is not the possession of an object but the exchange of objects.[11]

Money is the most poignant case of means becoming ends, something Simmel insisted was dependent on the "cultural tendencies" of an epoch. He contrasted the ancient Greeks, for whom means and ends were not radically opposed and for whom money only served consumption, to the modern world, in which money serves production. When some of his contemporaries claimed that "the ideas of antiquity displayed socialist tendencies," Simmel ascribes this to the "organization of consumption but not productive labor" in antiquity.[12]

With the centrality of the opposition of means and ends in the modern economy, "one of the major tendencies of life—the reduction of quality to quantity—achieves its highest and uniquely perfect representation in money."[13] The world becomes "a huge arithmetical problem," with everything quantified, the division of labor increasingly developed, and human beings—especially workers—and human values increasingly stunted. Simmel argues that the "life-style of a community" rests on the relation between "the objectified culture" and "the culture of the subjects," and that the diremption of subjective and objective culture is the necessary result of the division of labor in modern society. The process of specialized objectification of culture results in the alienation of subject from object with vital consequences: "Whenever our energies do not produce something whole as a reflection of the total personality, then the proper relationship between subject and object is missing."[14]

The "peripheral in life" and its means, its tools (such as money), become life's masters. Simmel is not led, however, to explain this process as a historical and therefore transcendable function of capitalism. He may echo Marx's theory of commodity fetishism, but he defined his own analysis of money as an "attempt . . . to construct a new story beneath historical materialism."[15] It represented only one aspect of the general phenomenon he called "the tragedy of culture." The conflicts between life and form, between means and ends, between subjective and objective culture—indeed, between subject and object—are inevitable and irreconcilable. For Simmel, as for his student Lukács, with the latter's opposition of Life and life, a whole cannot be made.

II

In his 1962 preface to *Theory of the Novel* (a book written in 1915–1916), Lukács declared that "the author" had not been "looking for a new literary form but, quite explicitly, for a 'new world.'"[16] As J. M. Bernstein observes, in *Soul and Forms* Lukács discovered that questions of aesthetic forms engendered questions of ethics, for the form that can make life meaningful—that makes life into Life—must be ethical. The foundering of form against life requires an ethical and historical response.[17]

In his unfinished *Philosophy of Art*, written in Heidelberg in 1912–1914, Lukács sought such wholeness in art. He concluded, however, that this was an illusory and utopian quest. Having eliminated art and everyday life as paths to salvation, and with World War I surrounding him, Lukács turned to Dostoevsky. But in the work he produced, *Theory of the Novel*, the Russian novelist only makes a brief appearance at the end. What is of importance is the transformation of Lukács's notion of form in this book and the way this change leads toward the concept of totality found later in *History and Class Consciousness*. In *Theory of the Novel*, Lukács links literary forms to the civilizations that produced them. This historical and sociological approach is a marked contrast to *Soul and Forms*, where he declared "the Gods" of history to be "rash." It is not, however, alien to other early works by Lukács; in his study of modern drama, he explored a theatrical form as the product of modern, fragmented bourgeois society. He contrasted that society to the organic society of the Greek polis and its cultural products.

In *Theory of the Novel*, the contrast between the Greek and modern worlds is again essential. This is, of course, an old theme in German culture, extending back to Goethe and Hegel. The latter presented an idealized picture of the polis as the embodiment of *Sittlichkeit* (ethical life), an organic whole with which the individual is identified and in which he is at home. "In an *ethical* community," Hegel wrote in *The Philosophy of Right*, "it is easy to say what a man must do, what are the duties he has to fulfil in order to be virtuous: he has simply to follow the well-known and explicit rules of his own situation."[18] For Hegel this totality with which the individual merges was flawed because it lacked "subjective freedom." The parts, one might say, vanished into the whole.

Socrates posed the problem of subjective freedom to his society. According to Hegel, "[T]he tendency to look deeper into oneself and to know and determine from within oneself what is right and good appears in ages when what is recognized as right and good in contemporary manners cannot satisfy the will of better men."[19] Such people become what Lukács called "problematic individuals," and the possibility of a higher complex totality, a community of difference within unity, of an objective whole in which the parts—individuals—are also subjectively free, is posed. The breakdown of the *Sittlichkeit* of the polis and the emergence of subjective freedom are prerequisite for this higher complex totality in which the particular (the individual human being) is essential to and part of, and thus never dissolved into, the totality. We can never go back to the more simple whole.

Lukács does not reach a complex totality at the end of *Theory of the Novel*. His book is structured by the claim that the novel is the "epic" literary form of the fragmented world, in which the individual is "transcendentally homeless" and "problematic." He contrasts this to the "homogenous," "rounded," "integrated civilization" of the polis, in which the individual is at home—more precisely, in which the epic hero is "never an individual" for that hero bears "not a personal destiny but the destiny of a community . . . the omnipotence of ethics,

which posits every soul as autonomous and incomparable, is still unknown in such a world."[20] Briefly, in the Ethical Life of the polis, there
was no thought of ethics per se. "Is" and "ought" were one; one lived
the ethical life of one's community. As in Hegel's description, there is
no individual subjectivity.

For the Greeks there were "only answers but no questions . . . only
forms but no chaos." The Greek's community was "an organic—and
therefore intrinsically meaningful—concrete totality."[21] Lukács insists
that "[e]very form is the resolution of a fundamental dissonance of existence" and "[e]very art form is defined by the metaphysical dissonance of life which it accepts and organizes as the basis of a totality
complete in itself."[22] According to Lukács,

> [T]otality as the formative prime reality of every individual phenomenon
> implies that something closed within itself can be completed; completed be-
> cause everything occurs within it, nothing is excluded from it; and by attain-
> ing itself, submits to limitation. Totality of being is possible only where ev-
> erything is already homogenous before it has been contained by forms;
> where forms are not a constraint but only the becoming conscious, the com-
> ing to the surface of everything that has been lying dormant as a vague
> longing in the innermost depths of that which had to be given form; where
> knowledge is virtue and virtue is happiness, where beauty is the meaning of
> the world made visible.[23]

In other words, the individual phenomenon is one with the whole, the
totality, the community, and form emerges out of the very life of the
community; it is intrinsic to its reality. It is an "extensive totality," in
which the meaning of life is immanent. This is no longer so in our age,
the age of the novel, an age that Lukács, using a Fichtean phrase, calls
the "epoch of absolute sinfulness." The "immanence of meaning in
life" in the modern world is problematic, although this age "still thinks
in terms of totality." Once subjective freedom emerges, once we find
"the only true substance within ourselves," form is no longer to be
seen as immanent to the extensive totality in which we live, but rather
as that which must be created by us. This makes our world larger,
richer, and more dangerous than that of the Greeks, "but such wealth
cancels out the positive meaning"—the totality—upon which their life
was based.[24] And for Lukács, as for Hegel, one cannot go back to this
home anymore, once the question of individual autonomy, subjective
freedom, and thus ethics, becomes something real, for there is no
longer a unity of "is" (the empirical world) and "ought" (the form that
world ought to be). The "metaphysical life" of the Greeks was in a
"circle" that was "smaller than ours," and the circle has been broken.
Once subjective freedom and "the productivity of the spirit" are in-

vented, we can no longer "breathe in a closed world." The "cracks" are "irreparable."[25]

Consequently, it is the differing "historico-philosophical realities" faced by authors that result in different epic forms: that of the Greek epic (by which Lukács means Homer) and that of the novel. The novel's hero "is the product of estrangement from the outside world" and the "inner form of the novel" is the "problematic" individual's journey towards himself in a fragmented world in which he is not at home, in which he is engaged in the "adventure of interiority" in a world abandoned by God, by totality.[26] If one is not at home, one must find oneself. Again, this is not merely a literary matter for Lukács; in posing these issues, he clearly believes there is an homology between the novel and the reality in which it is born, for "the structural categories of the novel constitutively coincide with the world as it is today."[27]

In that world, totality and meaning are no longer directly given and the structures that "the soul, in the process of *becoming-man*" confronts "lose their obvious roots in supra-personal ideal necessities," and become conventions that simply exist; they are there not as "natural containers for the overflowing interiority of the soul," but as an "all-embracing power" confronted by the soul. Convention offers not meaning but, rather, strict laws; it appears as a "second nature," "the nature of man-made structures." Like nature itself, it appears as a realm of necessity, not as human-made and thus human-alterable realities. Here, we see the lasting influence of Simmel's analysis of subjective and objective culture. Lukács writes: "This second nature is not dumb, sensuous and yet senseless like the first; it is a complex of senses—meanings—which has become rigid and strange, and which no longer awakens interiority; it is a charnel house of long-dead interiorities. . . ." Thus the question becomes when "the structures made by man are really adequate to man," for then they will be "his necessary and natural home."[28]

In *Theory of the Novel*, Lukács had no way home, no path beyond the "epoch of absolute sinfulness" in which he found himself. But he detected "intimations" of something new on the horizon, coming from Russia, expressed abstractly in Tolstoy but portentously in Dostoevsky, whose work, according to Lukács, went beyond the novel. In direct contrast to the crude Marxist determinism that reduced cultural change to a reflex of socioeconomic change, Lukács detected world-historical change foreshadowed in the appearance of a new form of culture represented by Dostoevsky's novels-beyond-novels. Lukács, who never went on to write his Dostoevsky study, does not really explain what this new art form is or may be. The Lukács of 1923—now a Marxist for five years—had the means by which to make the world whole again, to make the structures created by humans adequate to them: the world-historical action of the proletariat. The theory of "second nature" will become his theory of reification and the claim that in the capitalist world of the market, one form, one moment of Objective Spirit, becomes dominant—the commodity. And in one particular commodity—the worker, whose labor power is purchased for a wage—there was the possibility of an identity of the objective and the subjective in revolutionary consciousness. The dichotomy between "is" and "ought" would thereby be transcended, as would the opposition of Life and life. Indeed, life would become Life. What Lukács sought in Dostoevsky—a condemnation of the epoch of absolute sinfulness and a secularized religious projection of its opposite, a communion (or community) of souls—could take actual objective shape when the universal class recognized itself as exploited humanity incarnate, overthrew capitalism, and established the socialist future—a new totality.

Lukács proposed to transcend virtually all the philosophical and methodological issues by means of Marxism's power to unify theory and praxis; this unification was possible because of the relation between Marxism as "science" and a historical force, the proletariat. Furthermore, when Lukács assailed positivism in History and Class Consciousness, his target was not solely "bourgeois" social science, but also the positivism and simplistic materialism that had infected Marxism through the work of the later Engels and later that of Karl Kautsky. Lukács asserted that the key to Marxism was its method and that this method could not be detached from the practical activity of the working class:

> Only when a historical situation has arisen in which a class must understand society if it is to assert itself; only when the fact that a class understands itself means that it understands society as a whole, and when in consequence, the class becomes both the subject and object of knowledge; in short, only when these conditions are all satisfied will the unity of theory and practice, the precondition of the revolutionary function of the theory become possible.[29]

Since Lukács insisted that the historical dialectic of subject and object is the essential interaction grasped by Marxist theory, his own task became the articulation of a dialectical theory of consciousness. Accordingly, he rejected any view of history as a process of "natural" evolution based on the unfolding of "objective" laws.

Engels, in his famous speech at Marx's grave, declared his longtime collaborator to be the Darwin of human history. Both authors of The Communist Manifesto often stressed that theirs was a scientific, not a utopian, approach to socialism. Whether their "scientific" approach represented an intrusion of "positivism" or "scientism" depends in part on how one understands their use of the word "science." Here, circumspection is required, and not only because, unlike Engels, Marx combined admiration with caution in his view of Darwin. The underlying issue is one that has been exhaustively debated and redebated: Marx's relation to Hegel. Louis Althusser, the foremost proponent of Marx's "scientificity" in postwar France, claimed that an epistemological rupture must be discerned in Marx's work; the young Marx was a philosophical (and naive) humanist, still rooted in Hegelianism, whereas the older Marx was a scientist of society and history. Althusser initially dated this transformation between 1844 and 1845, that is, between Marx's *Paris Manuscripts*, with their famous theory of alienated labor, and *The German Ideology*, in which Marx and Engels elaborated their theory of history. There was, Althusser argued, not development in Marx's thought, but radical discontinuity, a turn to "reality"; dialectical materialism displaced idealism.[30]

But when Hegel used the word "science" (*Wissenschaft*), he did not conceive science as something apart from philosophy. (It is worth recalling that the Latin *scientia* literally means "knowledge" and comes from *scire*, the verb "to know."[31]) In the preface "On Scientific Cognition" to the *Phenomenology*, Hegel declared, "To help bring philosophy closer to the form of Science, to the goal where it can lay aside the title '*love* of knowing' and be *actual* knowing—that is what I have set myself to do. The inner necessity that knowing should be Science lies in its nature and only the systematic exposition of philosophy provides it."[32]

For Hegel, the object of philosophy is "the Truth," and "the true is the whole."[33] The principle of totality is the heart of Hegel's method. But Hegel's purpose was not to model knowledge on natural science. Rather, *Wissenschaft* for him is rational knowing, a system of necessary propositions, something that demonstrates and articulates. "Dialectic" was a matter of consciousness and development, and he rejected the notions of a dialectic of nature and the evolution of organic nature—in direct contrast to *Geist*, which does develop. In the *Phenomenology*, Hegel insists that "organic Nature has no history; it falls from its universal, from life, directly into the singleness of existence."[34] Hegel's view of *Geist*, as opposed to nature, is consequently contrary to that of Engels, who insisted that there was a "dialectic of nature." The later Engels believed that his materialism saved the dialectic from Hegelian mystification, but it is more accurate to say that Engels accepted both an important positivist premise—the unity of scientific theory, understood as natural science—and a Darwinized Hegelianism by claiming that "in nature . . . the same dialectical laws of motion force their way through as those which in history govern the apparently fortuitous-ness of events."[35] Engels's "dialectical laws"—the transformation of quantity into quality, the interpenetration of opposites, the negation of the negation[36]—applied equally to nature and history; for him, we have knowledge when those laws are reflected in our minds.

In short, what we find in Engels is a materialist and Darwinian con-flation of Hegel's distinction of the dialectical development of *Geist* and the nondialectical development of nature. Consciousness then be-comes a "reflection" of the material world, much as superstructure re-flects base. Freedom lies in knowledge of historical and natural neces-sity, that is, knowledge of the laws of history and nature, which have the same moving principles. On this basis, scientistic determinism be-came a feature of Marxist orthodoxy, especially in the work of Karl Kautsky, the dominant figure in German social democratic theory in the era after the death of Engels. Marx displayed a positivist bent in various writings, perhaps more so in the later works. Windelband called him a "peculiar" cross between Comte and Hegel, and Rickert criticized historical materialism for being more a product of party pol-itics than of science. Not only did it rest "on definite *valuation*" but its attack on idealism only substituted "new ideals for the old ones."[37] However, while Marx never devoted a work to method, he did make important scattered pronouncements about it, and those often sharply distinguish his work from positivism. In a note in *Capital*, Marx ap-plauds Giambattista Vico's recognition that "human history differs from natural history in this, that we have made the former, but not the latter."[38] In his afterword to the second German edition of *Capital* (1873), Marx declared that his own method was the opposite of Hegel's; Marx's starting point was the material world as "translated into various forms of thought," while for Hegel, "the life-process of the human brain, i.e., the process of thinking, which, under the name of 'the Idea,' he even transforms into an independent subject, is the demiurgos of the real world, and the real world is only the external, phenomenal form of 'the Idea.'" Mystification though this be, it was still Hegel, according to Marx, who first comprehensively worked out the "general form" of dialectic. "With [Hegel]," however, said Marx, "it is standing on its head. It must be turned right side up again if you would discover the rational kernel within the mystical shell."[39]

As Marx noted, Hegel's starting point is "the Idea." Hegel's logic was at the same time an ontology: "Reason governs the world and has consequently governed its history."[40] Logic is in the nature of things and gives us the rules of thought as we experience them in particular. The unity of the true and the whole is the result of *Geist*'s develop-ment. *Geist* posits its subjectivity in the objective world and returns to itself as the absolute, the identical subject-object, whose self-knowledge is knowledge of the whole. Totality, in Hegel's account, is not, however, the simple expression of unfolding *Geist* in which particularity vanishes; rather, the particular is the requisite means for the instantiation of the universal. "The notion of the whole," says Hegel, "is to contain parts; but if the whole is taken and made what its notion implies, i.e. if it is divided, it at once ceases to be a whole."[41]

Marx vanquished Hegelian *Geist* and replaced it with the historical development of material forces and a specific universalizing force, the proletariat. The concept of totality thus remained the structuring principle of his endeavor, but was reconceived. The *Grundrisse* articulates this in its assertion that production, distribution, exchange, and consumption are not "identical" but, rather, form "members of a totality, distinctions within a unity." In other words, Marx's materialism, like Hegel's Idealism, understands totality as complex, as a diversity within unity. What is required is a "concrete" and not "a chaotic conception [*Vorstellung*]" of the whole.[42]

Marx's notion of concrete totality closely parallels his view of the dialectical relationship between the individual and community, and in this parallel we can see how method and aspiration are inseparable in Marx's project. He tells us that his starting point is "[i]ndividuals producing in society—hence socially determined individual production." He intends this to contrast with the "Robinson Crusoe" image of the individual, that is, the view that the individual is first and foremost a "natural individual" who enters society from without; Marx chastises this notion as one of the "unimaginative conceits" of classical political economy. This misconception, says Marx, underlies the perspectives of Adam Smith and David Ricardo, who see man as "not arising historically but posited by nature" and "not as a result of history but as history's point of departure." For Marx, on the contrary, "the more deeply we go back into history, the more does the individual, and hence also the producing individual, appear as dependent, as belonging to a greater whole."[43]

The individual, then, must be grasped within larger totalities, within history, within social relations, not outside of them. The individual is part of a larger whole, is dependent on it, yet remains an individual. Human beings are "social individuals," autonomous within the whole but not undifferentiated from it. They become themselves only within the whole:

> The human being is in the most literal sense [*zoon politikon*], not merely a gregarious animal but an animal which can individuate itself only in the midst of society. Production by an isolated individual outside society—a rare exception which may well occur when a civilized person in whom the

social forces are already dynamically present is cast by accident into the wilderness—is as much of an absurdity as the development of language without individuals living *together* and talking to each other.[44]

Marx rejects abstract notions of the individual and insists that the human being is individuated within and through society. The part is individuated within the whole, as the whole is not an abstract mass, or a simple totality, but is a complexity composed of—requiring—the parts and their interactions to be a whole. Thus language is required for the communicator to communicate, but there must be the activity of communication by individuals; the communicator uses language, a social institution, in an individualized manner. There is, in Marx, always a subject-object dialectic.

For Lukács it is precisely the dialectic of subjectivity and objectivity that constitutes history; it is for this reason that *History and Class Consciousness* attacks not only bourgeois social science, but also Engels's dialectics of nature and the philosophical underpinnings of Second International Marxism. Indeed, late in life Lukács went so far as to declare that it was "a fortunate circumstance for his development"—a circumstance he did "not at all regret" that he took his "first lessons in social science from Simmel and Max Weber and not from Kautsky."[45]

However, Lukács envisioned his critique of Engels, Kautsky, and others as a critique on behalf of Marx. In his explication of method, he moves, like Hegel and Marx before him, from the abstract to the concrete in order to subvert common sense and thereby reveal a deeper profundity behind appearances. It is true, says Lukács, that all knowledge begins with "facts," but these "facts" are nothing but abstractions. Usually we think of "brute" "facts" as concrete, or self-evident. They are there before us. A fact "is." Hegel began his *Logic* by demonstrating that pure Being—the simple "isness" of what is—is nothing but an abstraction, equivalent to saying nothing unless one makes what is determinate.

Similarly, Marx rises from the abstract to the concrete by conceiving society as a concrete, complex totality. For Lukács, only "blinkered empiricists" believe that facts "are" simply "there" to be enumerated and added up, producing a coherent picture named "knowledge." If we take two or three or four "facts" and link them in some way, we are using theory; there are no "facts" without theories that constitute them, just as there are no theories (of any value, that is) without "facts." "Knowledge" is not the result of a linear process, but a circular one.

Lukács presses this further. He argues that "when 'science' maintains that the manner in which data immediately present themselves is an adequate foundation of scientific conceptualization and that the actual form of these data is the appropriate starting point for the formation of scientific concepts, it thereby takes its stand simply and dogmatically on the basis of capitalist society."[46] Why? Because such a "science" places "facts" in "space" but not in "time." Just as capitalism hypostatizes the individual and conceives him or her as a natural "fact," so such a science makes "facts," in general, ahistorical. However, to speak of facts in a meaningful way, we must not see them as immediately given, but rather as historically placed; they are comprehensible only within the larger whole. Consequently, Lukács's argument must be both against "building" a science through aggregating "isolated facts" and against specialized disciplines of research. The dialectical method, he writes, "is concerned always with the same problem: knowledge of the historical process in its entirety. This means that 'ideological' and 'economic' problems lose their mutual exclusiveness and merge into one another. *The history of a particular problem turns into the history of problems.*"[47]

How, then, does this method deal with "facts?" By simultaneously recognizing and transcending them. This Lukács calls the "dialectical nexus." To recognize and transcend "facts" means that one must, first of all, deal with "facts," things as they appear, but one can only make them meaningful by going beyond them, so to speak, by grasping them as integrated into a "concrete totality." Knowledge of the concrete totality provides "the conceptual reproduction of reality." Lukács insists that "[c]oncrete totality is . . . the category that governs reality" in the sense of Marx's statement (in *The Critique of Political Economy*) that "[t]he concrete is concrete because it is a synthesis of many particular determinants, i.e. unity of diverse elements."[48] Lukács, following the Hegelian distinction between appearance and reality, argues that one must distinguish the "real existence" of these elements from their "inner core." Phenomena—"facts" that appear before us—must be detached "from the form in which they are immediately given and discover the intervening links which connect to their core, their essence."[49] The essence is discernible only in terms of the historical whole.

Clearly, positivism, empiricism, and economic determinism are incompatible with Lukács's concept of history and dialectical method. It is from the perspective of totality that one sees them as one-sided. And since totality is conceived in terms of the subject-object dialectic, Marxism's chief concern, history, cannot be grasped in the same way as natural science. History has a subject—human beings—while nature does not. There can be no dialectic of nature. The assertion of theoretical and practical verisimilitude of the historical and natural worlds leads to "objectivist" and politically passive conclusions: as in Darwin's vision of evolution, the socialist revolution will come about as if a natural event. This, Lukács maintains, is the catastrophic flaw in the Second International Marxism of Kautsky and others. Their scientistic materialist method, in the end, disarms them politically by turning into an economic determinism. They have mystified "facts" and "science" along with the bourgeois social scientists. But

> [i]t is not the primacy of economic motives in historical explanation that constitutes the decisive difference between Marxism and bourgeois thought, but the point of view of totality. The category of totality, the all pervasive supremacy of the whole over the parts is the essence of the method which Marx took over from Hegel and brilliantly transformed into the foundations of a wholly new science.[50]

It is the continuity between the methods of Hegel and Marx that Lukács stressed, while simultaneously asserting that the two part company decisively "at reality itself": one maps the journey of *Geist*; the other, the processes of history. In fact, Lukács goes so far as to suggest that Marx's polemics against idealism were aimed more at Hegel's ideological epigoni than at the master himself. "For the Hegelian—dialectical—identification of thought and existence," he writes, "the belief in their unity as the unity and totality of a process is also, in essence, the philosophy of history of historical materialism."[51] Marx did not convert Hegel's dialectic into the principle of a "science of revolution" through merely giving it a "materialist twist." Rather, Marx's theory became such a science "because of the validity of the method itself viz. the concept of totality, the subordination of every part to the whole unity of history and thought."[52]

One of the striking aspects of Lukács's formulations and definitions of "totality" is that while he, like Hegel and Marx, states that totality is not a self-identical or undifferentiated or a simple whole,[53] his wording repeatedly subsumes the particular within the whole, rather than articulating the relation between whole and parts. Totality, we read, means "the all pervasive supremacy of the whole over the parts [*die allseitige, bestimmende Herrschaft des Ganzen über die Teile*]."[54] In defining the dialectical method, Lukács does not describe ideological and economic problems as moments of the totality, but declares that they "merge into one another."[55] By this formula, the autonomy of the parts is lost in the whole—in which case, it is not clear why they should be called parts.

Despite himself, Lukács would appear to be guilty—or close to guilty—of the error of which Hegel accused Schelling: proposing a simplistic totality based on an identity of subject and object in which "A=A," a "night in which . . . all cows are black." For Hegel the problem was also Schelling's intuitive rather than conceptual grasping of the whole, that is, Schelling's "single insight, that in the Absolute everything is the same, against the full body of articulated cognition."[56] To the extent that the parts vanish into Lukács's totality, Lukács, too, gives us a night of black cows. (Lukács appears to have recognized this problem in his 1967 preface to *History and Class Consciousness*. He cites Hegel's criticism of Schelling and praises Hegel's "healthy sense of reality," but criticizes him for never demonstrating concretely how the Hegelian alternative might be accomplished).

It is possible to read Lukács's passages as overstatements in a battle against the fetishism of empirical facts. However, if totality is for him a question of both method and aspiration, then we find this problematic formulation of totality reproduced politically in Lukács's definition of Communist Party discipline as the "unconditional absorption of the total personality in the praxis of the movement [*das bedingunglose Aufgehen der Gesamtpersonlichkeit eines jeden Mitgliedes in der Praxis der Bewegung*]." He declares this to be "the only possible way of bringing about an authentic freedom."[57] Lukács's philosophical position not only lends itself easily to Leninist centralism, but to the extent that Lukács absorbed the particular/individual into the whole—be it totality in general or the party—rather than articulating the particular as an autonomous moment within what he himself calls a complex dialectical totality, it provides a philosophical justification of his later deference to Stalinism.

III

The dialectic of totality is conceived by Lukács as a historical subject-object dialectic. Totality is not something simply grasped by savants at their desks; it is the perspective of the universal subject, the working class. Marxism, the science of society based on the principle of totality, is a class ideology. The working class alone is capable of the perspective of totality; consequently, the self-understanding of the proletariat—Marx's "universal class," in whom all suffering could be seen and whose interests were the interests of all—is the understanding of society as a whole. In *History and Class Consciousness*, we are instructed that "the rise and evolution of its [the proletariat's] knowledge and its actual rise and evolution in the course of history are just the two different sides of the same real process."[58] When Lukács wrote these words shortly after World War I, he believed that the West was on the brink of revolution. However, he understood this possibility on the basis of a dialectical concept of subjectivity that was, in part, a reaction to the fetishized notion of "objectivity" and the "natural" unfolding of history of Second International orthodoxy. The epigram he chose for his renowned chapter on "Class Consciousness" came from Marx's *The Holy Family*: "It is not a question of what this or that proletarian, or even the whole proletariat, at the moment *regards* as its aim. It is a question of *what the proletariat is*, and what in accord with this *being* [diesem *Sein*] it will be historically compelled to do."[59] In brief, Lukács posed the question of class consciousness as one linking epistemology and ontology, the knowledge and the being of the proletariat. In this framework, however, the essential question becomes the relation between what individual proletarians at a particular moment regard as their aim and the consciousness required by the proletariat's "being."

Lukács's answer, not surprisingly, is that this must be grasped through the principle of totality. He does so, strikingly enough, by integrating Weberian concepts and motifs into his argument, and retooling them. Lukács constructs an ideal-type of class consciousness, but, in contrast to Weber, for whom the ideal-type is strictly a heuristic device, he expects its historical actualization. More precisely, it is a matter of objective possibility, given the "being" of the proletariat. The "future" is therefore a crucial temporal dimension of his concept of totality. Lukács writes that "by relating consciousness to the whole of society it becomes possible to infer the thoughts and feelings which men would have in a particular situation if they were *able* to assess both it and the interests arising from it in their impact on immediate action and on the whole structure of society."[60] In what might be called a neo-Kantian/Weberian/Marxist counterpart to Lenin's distinction between trade union and revolutionary consciousness, Lukács distinguishes between the "empirical" consciousness of workers, that is, the existing immediate consciousness of proletarians in a particular sociohistorical conjuncture, and true, "imputed" or "ascribed" class consciousness. This he defined as

> [t]he appropriate and rational reactions imputed [*zugerechnet*] to a particular typical position in the process of production. This consciousness is . . . neither the sum nor the average of what is thought or felt by the single individuals who make up the class. And yet the historically significant actions of the class as a whole are determined in the last resort by this consciousness and not by the thought of the individual—and these actions can be understood only by reference to this consciousness.[61]

In other words, the contrast between empirical and imputed consciousness is possible by relating the empirically given to a concept of totality. This, in turn, is linked to the problem of revolutionary practice, for when the final economic crisis of capitalism comes about, the revolution will depend *"on the ideological maturity of the proletariat i.e. on its class consciousness."*[62] Indeed, Lukács identifies the postwar Council movement—the emergence of revolutionary self-organization of the workers—as a barometer of class consciousness.[63]

Lukács seems close to embracing a Luxemburgist perspective in his stress on spontaneity and the emergence of class consciousness. Defending Luxemburg and attacking Blanquism, he writes that the party is the "form" taken by the class consciousness of the proletariat. He chastises "mechanical vulgarizers," who see the party solely as a type of organization. It was Luxemburg's merit to see the party as the likely effect, rather than the cause, of the revolution. Similarly, the proletariat "can constitute itself only in and through the revolution," declares Lukács. The party is the "bearer of the class consciousness of the proletariat and the conscience of its historical vocation." Class consciousness is "the ethics of the proletariat," and Lukács refers to a party that establishes itself as the objectification of the proletariat's will; when it does so, the masses will "spontaneously and instinctively" turn to it.[64] Despite these Luxemburgist formulations, Lukács insisted on his Leninism. In the essay in *History and Class Consciousness* entitled "Towards a Methodology of the Problem of Organization," he emphasized the vast gap between empirical consciousness and class consciousness—a gap that must be mediated by—indeed, filled by—the Leninist party, in which the "whole personality" of the member is subordinated.

What emerges is an unresolved tension between Leninism and Luxemburgism in *History and Class Consciousness*. Why? Because, as Lucien Goldmann pointed out, Lukács failed to provide "an explicit description of the relation between class consciousness and individual consciousness."[65] In fact, Lukács, in developing his dialectical theory of subjectivity, posits his contrast between class and empirical consciousness and discusses—brilliantly—blockage of the transformation of the latter into the former (that is, reification), but he lacks a theory of cognitive development of group consciousness on one hand, and of the relation between the group (for example, class) and the individual's cognitive development, on the other. The consequence is that Lukács reinvents the *hiatus irrationalis*—into which the party steps.

IV

When Lukács said that the workers' councils were a barometer of class consciousness, he also declared that they spelled political and economic doom for reification. Lukács's theory of reification gives unity to his theory as a whole. Its roots are complex.[66] First, Lukács operates with the Hegelian distinction between appearance and reality. In appearance, in what is immediately before our eyes, capitalism is a rational system. In its essence, however, it is filled with contradictions. This becomes evident only when we see that appearances are only aspects ("moments") of the totality. Lukács asserts that "[t]he central, structural problem of capitalist society in all its aspects" is that of commodities; the "commodity-structure" penetrates all dimensions of a capitalist world. In his celebrated discussion of "the fetishism of commodities" in *Capital*, Marx contended that since workers do not produce goods for use value, but rather for the exchange value that can be realized on the market by the capitalist who pays the workers' wages, in capitalism exchange values not only dominate but displace use values in shaping the world and perceptions of it. The commodities appear to their creators not as objects socially produced by them to satisfy human needs, but as "things," whose prices seem as natural as their physical properties. In the commodity, "the social character of men's labour appears to them as an objective character stamped upon the product of that labour; because the relation of the producers to the sum total of their own labour is represented to them as a social relation, existing not between themselves, but between the products of their labour." Thus, "a definite social relation between men . . . assumes . . . the fantastic form of a relation between things."[67]

Lukács, building on Marx, returns to his own concept of "second nature." This world of "things" constitutes a "second nature" of appearances. In it, human labor power and its products do not appear as a process in which human purpose is realized by working up the objective world to satisfy human needs, but, rather, as an autonomous "objective" reality, which dominates those who actually created it by their labor power. As Lukács formulates it,

> Neither objectively nor in his relation to his work does man appear as the authentic master of the process; on the contrary, he is a mechanical part incorporated into a mechanical system. He finds it already pre-existing and self-sufficient, it functions independently of him and he has to conform to its laws whether he likes it or not. As labor is progressively rationalized and mechanized his lack of will is reinforced by the way in which his activity becomes less and less active and more and more contemplative.[68]

This transforms "the basic categories" of the individual's "immediate attitude towards the world." In particular "time" is denuded of its "qualitative, variable, flowing nature" and is frozen into a "continuum and filled with quantifiable 'things' . . . in short, it becomes space."[69] The qualitative is turned into the quantitative, and the individual is atomized, made passive, in a fragmented world he must participate in, which he created, but which he cannot control; he sees it as natural and unchangeable. On the level of appearances, this commodity system of buying and selling for the market seems quite rational. But Lukács generalizes that the process of reification produces a world in which means become ends and social, human products take on a mystified form, a "phantom objectivity," as independent things, which not only dominate the workings of economic life, but of culture and all aspects of human existence.

Reified views of the world preclude going beyond appearances in order to grasp social formations as a historical totality. Classical political economy, for example, fails to see capitalism as a historical rather than a natural product; it imagines individuals as Robinson Crusoes, fetishizes "facts," and cannot comprehend the historically structured substratum of the empirically given capitalist economy. Second nature, "petrified factuality," is taken for permanent reality. Consequently,

> only when the theoretical primacy of the "facts" has been broken, only when every *phenomenon* is recognized to be a process, will it be understood that what we are wont to call "facts" consist of processes. Only then will it be understood that the facts are nothing but the parts, the aspects of the total process that have been broken off, artificially isolated and ossified.[70]

Reification is intrinsic to bourgeois thought because, tied to capitalism, it is incapable of the perspective of totality. It is not merely "wrong"; it is ideological.

It is on this basis that Lukács, who matured in a neo-Kantian environment, pursued a vigorous critique of the critical philosophy. It "springs," he states, "from the reified structure of consciousness."[71] In *History and Class Consciousness*, Kant is presented as the representative philosopher of the bourgeois era, exponent of a philosophical position fundamentally hostile to Marxism. Classical German thought, Lukács asserts, is able

> to think the deepest and most fundamental problems of bourgeois society through to the very end—on the plane of philosophy. It is able—in thought—to complete the evolution of class. And—in thought—it is able to take all the paradoxes of its position to the point where the necessity of going beyond this historical stage in mankind's development can at least be seen as a problem.[72]

It "tore to shreds" all past "metaphysical illusions," but it also became an "insuperable barrier" to progress by constructing a dogmatic metaphysic of its own though the notion of the *Ding-an-Sich* (thing-in-itself).

The hiatus between the noumenal and phenomenal worlds in Kant is like that between Life and life in the young Lukács. But the Lukács who wrote *History and Class Consciousness* follows Hegel in insisting that forms of knowledge, that is, the categories, cannot be known outside of using them and that using them means transforming the knower and the tools of knowledge. To do otherwise, argued Hegel, is to imagine that one can to learn to swim without jumping into the water.[73] Once one accepts Hegel's critique of Kant, one can no longer maintain a fixed set of categories or the notion of the *Ding-an-Sich*; knowing means going into the water. Going into the water changes the knower, who learns his own power to swim.

For Lukács, there is a parallel between a reified world of "things" that obscures human relations and Kant's opposition of a world that appears to us to noumenal reality. Kant believed he had delivered the coup de grace to traditional metaphysics by demonstrating that we could have only "conditioned" knowledge, that is, knowledge that comes about when our *Verstand* synthesizes as "thought" the empirical manifold perceived by our senses. There can be no "knowledge" of the "unconditioned," of that which traditionally preoccupied metaphysics—God, freedom, immortality. Kant distinguished *Verstand* from *Vernunft* (Reason) precisely on this basis. We employ *Vernunft* in an ever-unsuccessful, but natural, effort to go beyond appearances "to find for the conditioned knowledge obtained through the understanding the unconditioned whereby its unity is brought to completion."[74] Verstand cannot grasp totality, but *Vernunft* demands of our knowledge that it be a systematic whole. But by Kant's account, we cannot, "know," for example, that nature is a causal system, as conceived by Newton, which corresponds to our comprehension of it. What we know are appearances ordered by our a priori sensibility and *Verstand*. Nonetheless, we proceed—*Vernunft* tells us to do so—as if it were such a causal system, which does correspond to our comprehension of it.

Hegel countraposed a historical process of knowledge to Kant's rigid categories. Since he rejected the notion of *Ding-an-Sich* and insisted that one cannot speak of knowing the instruments of knowledge without their employment, he refused to separate the categories of thought from their content. This content is determinate of the forms of the categories, and "the categories and modes of thought derive from the process of reality to which they pertain. Their form is determined by the structure of this process."[75] This process, however, is *Geist*'s journey to self-knowledge, its positing itself in the world and returning to itself on a higher level, that of knowing the whole, which is itself. For Hegel, rejecting the noumena/phenomena distinction, it is *Vernunft* that enables one to grasp the whole, the totality, rather than the province of immediate appearances that the understanding understands.

For the Marxist Lukács, the process is not one of Hegel's *Geist* but, rather, of the material development of human history through the subject-object dialectic. As one of his former students put it, Lukács saw in Kant's achievement a refusal to conceal the "intractability" of the antinomies resulting from the acceptance of "the socio-historical form of objectivity (and the corresponding relation of the subject to it) created by capitalist society as the untranscendable forms of 'our thinking' in general."[76] In other words, Kant's ahistorical categories imply the impossibility of transcending capitalism; apprehension of the whole is excluded by the notion of *Ding-an-Sich*, and the dichotomization of reality into the phenomena we apprehend and the noumena behind them precludes a grasping of essential reality and the processes composing it. As a result, totality may play a crucial (regulative) role in the critical philosophy, but it is necessarily a contentless, formal concept, something we aspire to but cannot achieve. Similarly, Lukács conceives Kant's ethic to be trapped within individualism. It is *"purely formal and lacking in content."*[77] Here, again, is the problem of form versus life, and the problem is inescapable if we accept the premise of the *Ding-an-Sich*. But for Lukács, "the essence of praxis consists in annulling *that indifference of form towards content* that we found in the problem of the thing-in-itself."[78]

Lukács moves beyond his critique of Kant via Fichte to Hegel. Fichte disposed of the problem of the *Ding-an-Sich* by rejecting the subject-object dichotomy (and Kant's timeless categories of the subject); he proposed a subject-object identity made possible through action. Indeed, "this unity is *activity*."[79] Hegel, says Lukács, decisively recasts the issue as one of the historical dialectic and Hegel "consciously [recasts] all problems of logic by grounding them in the qualitative material nature of their content, in matter in the logical and philosophical sense of the word. This resulted in the establishment of a completely new logic of the *concrete concept*, the logic of totality"—albeit in problematic (idealist) form. Lukács continues:

> Even more original is the fact that the subject is neither the unchanged observer of the objective dialectic of being and concept . . . nor the practical manipulator of its purely mental possibilities . . . : the dialectical process, the ending of a rigid confrontation of rigid forms, is enacted essentially between the *subject and object*."[80]

In brief, Hegel is able to end the confrontation of rigid forms because he insists on the dialectic as a historical interaction of subject and object. However, this poses an essential problem: that of *"the subject of action, the subject of genesis."* The subject of history for Hegel, his "we" ends up being "the World Spirit, or rather, its concrete incarnations, the spirits of individual peoples."[81] It is here—with the notion of *Geist* unfolding in history—that Hegel's great achievement became mystified, because his idealism, which "failed to discover the identical subject-object in history," was compelled to go "beyond history and, there, to establish the empire of reason which has discovered itself."[82]

Marxism, for Lukács, had discovered the true identical subject-object of history: the proletariat. The worker, we recall, becomes within capitalism a thing, an object, a commodity to the extent that his labor power is sold on the market with other commodities. All of the capitalist system is implicit in the commodity structure. The worker, however, is unlike other commodities on the market, for the worker can become self-conscious and "recognize himself and his own relations with capital."[83] Self-consciousness of this commodity "brings about an objective structural change in the object of knowledge," for the object *is* the subject. Achieving such self-knowledge, recognition of the proletariat's true role as the exploited motor making capitalism run, is "practical" knowledge because it transforms the object into an active subject. Revolutionary class consciousness engenders rejection of the capitalist system as a whole, for "since consciousness here is not the knowledge of an opposed object but is self-consciousness of the object, *the act of consciousness overthrows the objective form of its object.*"[84]

History, Lukács tells us, is the story of the endless overthrowing of "the objective forces that shape" human lives.[85] But here the objective force is human beings themselves in their role as objects, as commodities in a reified world. It is the proletariat's self-knowledge through revolutionary class consciousness that makes it the identical subject-object of history; a material subject-object as opposed to Hegelian *Geist*. Lukács writes that "the self-knowledge both subjective and objective, of the proletariat at a given point in its evolution is at the same time knowledge of the stage of development achieved by the whole society."[86]

Since in the case of the proletariat, knowledge of the object is a matter of self-consciousness; since the bearer of self-consciousness is a commodity; and since in the commodity we find the whole of capitalist society, class consciousness of the proletariat is knowledge of the concrete totality, and concrete totality is the perspective—the imputed perspective, that is—of the proletariat. Lo, we have found the historically achievable subject-object in whom knowledge and reality merge. Should this be seen as an apocalyptic confession that Marxism is a religious faith, Lukács scornfully retorts that this "so-called religious faith is nothing more than the certitude that regardless of all temporary defeats and setbacks, the historical process will come to fruition *in our deeds and through our deeds*," something that "can be guaranteed methodologically—by the dialectical method," although there can be "no 'material' guarantee of this certitude [of capitalism's doom]."[87]

In other words, it is a matter of "objective possibility" conceived not in terms of method alone but as historical potential. Here we can see how Lukács brings all the debates we have examined full circle. These debates on method, on science, on conceptualization versus reality, are functionally transformed, by Lukács's reinjection of classical German philosophy—Hegel in particular—into Marxism so that "totality" becomes a question of both method and aspiration at once; philosophy finds its means of realization in the proletariat, as the young Marx put it. In presenting this case, *History and Class Consciousness* provided a brilliant dissection, recasting and illuminating the central questions of both philosophy and society in the modern (capitalist) age. Through his quest for a dialectical theory of subjectivity, through his critique of Kant, through the theory of reification, and through his attack on the presuppositions of scientistic and deterministic Marxism, of neo-Kantianism, of the *Geisteswissenschaften* debate, and of bourgeois social science, he compelled Marxism to rethink itself, and, consequently, to refocus on questions of consciousness and culture, to the detriment of simplistic popular versions of the base-superstructure model. It is because of all this that *History and Class Consciousness* became the cornerstone of "Western Marxism."

But shortly after its publication, Lukács repudiated his own book. He later became subservient to Stalinism, professing this necessary because of the rise of fascism. Yet it was also due to the fact that the working class did not become the identical subject-object of history. An inevitable question arises: if Marxist orthodoxy is solely a matter of method, as Lukács defined it, and if the method appears to produce false theses—at least in historical prognostication of objective possibility—what then is left of it? Why remain "orthodox"?[88] This is precisely the problem that faced Lucien Goldmann, although his rejection (or at least his explicit rejection) of traditional Marxist claims about the revolutionary role of the proletariat came after the development of his own discourse on method. That discourse championed Lukács's early work, while seeking to detach what was rational from what was mystical in it. Appropriately, Goldmann's first book was on Kant.

Part Three

FAITHFUL HERESY, TRAGIC DIALECTICIAN

5

The Dialectics of Lucien Goldmann

In 1958, in a lecture to the Philosophy Society of Toulouse, Lucien Goldmann proposed that "official Marxism," which had dominated all Marxism for the previous quarter-century, had not produced a single work of theoretical importance. Consequently, "it was essential during this period that a few researchers did not submit to the pressure of any body or orthodoxy, and devoted themselves to demonstrating on the level of concrete studies in one domain or another, the *actual* possibilities [*les possibilités* actuelles] and the fertility of [Marxism's] method." This is what Goldmann saw as his own accomplishment in writing on seventeenth-century France. It allowed him to show that the dialectical method was indeed "the most efficacious [method] when it is a question of understanding those particularly complex phenomena which are the great philosophical and literary works of the past."[1] Goldmann's success in this endeavor was a function of his own synthesis of Lukács and Piaget, which was rooted in his Marxian reading of Kant. It is to his reading of Kant that we must turn before elaborating his theory as a whole.

I

The German title of Goldmann's book, *Mensch, Gemeinschaft und Welt in der Philosophie Immanuel Kants* (hereafter *Kant*), immediately tells the reader that the author's ambition is to recast the central issues in Kant's writings.[2] Goldmann explicitly declares that his work is one of "philosophy" and not "Kant philology."[3] Later he would comment that this book initiated a quest for "a new method of understanding and explanation of cultural creation."[4] A report written in 1944 by Henri de Man recommending its publication lauded *Kant* not only as an academic dissertation worthy of habilitation, but as "an important contribution . . . to the debate between the Marxist vanguard and the neo-Kantian arrière-garde."[5] Goldmann characterized his own position as "post-Kantian [*nachkantischer*] and humanist."[6]

In important respects, it is a post-Kantian, humanist, Marxist reading of Kant, rather than a Lukácsian (Hegelian), Marxist one. Goldmann's presentation of Kant is based on two fundamental and interrelated claims. The first is indicated by the title of his conclusion: "What Is Man?" Deriding specialists who saw Kant solely as an epistemologist or a moral philosopher, Goldmann insists that "the theme of 'man and human community'" was at the center of Kant's philosophy and all modern philosophy.[7] Philosophy, as Goldmann presents it in *Kant*, is a generic response to the problems of man qua man; its realization is humanity's self-realization. While this echoes the young Marx, an important Marxist link is missing in Goldmann's formulation: the proletariat is posited neither as the universal class realizing philosophy nor as an identical subject-object:

> Expressions such as German or French, bourgeois or proletarian philosophy only have meaning to the extent that they seek to show that a philosophy was born among Germans or the French, the bourgeoisie or the proletariat, or that its insights were made possible only by the social or economic situation of these groups. In any case, they cannot indicate that the philosophy solely concerns itself with the problems proper to the French or the Germans, to the bourgeoisie or to proletarians, nor that its results would be valid for them alone. In this sense, a German or bourgeois or proletarian philosophy would be as contradictory as squaring a circle. At most it could be spoken of as ideology, as political propaganda.[8]

Consequently, Goldmann's emphasis, unlike Lukács's stress on class struggle, is on the realization of an "authentic human community." In the preface to the first French edition of *Kant* (1948), Goldmann said that he wrote the book under the "direct influence" of Lukács's early works. Yet, reflecting on his book almost two decades later, he noted that while *Kant* focused on the importance of the idea of totality in the critical philosophy, the issue of subject-object identity was neglected. This issue was central in *History and Class Consciousness*, and Kant had played a crucial role in elaborating it.[9] These comments indicate that Goldmann's decisive reading of Lukács was not in Vienna in 1930–1931, but in Switzerland during the war; they also indicate that it was a selective rediscovery of the Hungarian's works, especially *History and Class Consciousness*.

In Goldmann's reading, Kant was profoundly political even when not addressing political questions. The same is true of Goldmann's book; his philosophical commentary on Kant is a moment in his own quest for socialist community. For Goldmann, like Lukács, totality was a matter of aspiration and method. However, Goldmann's departures from Lukács in *Kant* are almost as important as his fruitful employment of Lukácsian insights. Goldmann generally refrained from direct criticisms of Lukács. But his separation of the question of totality from that of subject-object identity, together with his accent on socialist community rather than class struggle, are of great import for his future theories and politics and for his differences with Lukács.

Goldmann's second fundamental claim about Kant is that he is a philosopher in quest of a totality he knows he cannot attain, not in the realm of knowledge and not in the realm of human life. For precritical Kant, Goldmann argues, the structure of the world rested on a system of causation ultimately bound to something external to humanity— God. Kant, however, was awakened from his "dogmatic slumber" by David Hume's empiricist argument on causation: knowledge is a matter of factual connections resting on habit and the association of ideas. Writes Goldmann:

> Hume had directed his attacks against the concept of *cause* and even in Kant's first works . . . the entire edifice of the intelligible world rests on this concept. It is because the form of the sensible world (time and space) must have a cause that there necessarily exists an intelligible world, a God, taught Kant. "Cause" is only a way of designating the association of empirical representations. Hence one does not have the right [on the basis of the notion of cause] to conclude that something exists which is not empirically given.[10]

Since habitual factual connections cannot presuppose a whole—there are no intrinsic links—empiricism must negate the idea of totality. Kant's recognition of this, says Goldmann, led him to conclude that his previous (precritical) position was mistaken. He was then led to posit totality as a possibility within humankind rather than outside it. This brought Kant to the theory of transcendental subjectivity and the categories, which all human beings share.

For Goldmann, "The fundamental postulate of the critical philosophy is that the authentic destiny of man is to strive towards the absolute [*tendre vers l'absolu*] and Kant frequently repeats that it neither has to be, nor can be, proven [*cela ne doit ni peut se prouver*]."[11] At various places in *Kant*, Goldmann identifies "the absolute" with totality, noumena, God, and community. Kant strives toward each of these, he argues, but is unable to reach them in any realm but aesthetics, and there only subjectively.[12] For Goldmann, the history of dialectical thought is a movement from this Kantian failure though Hegel to Marxism in which the absolute is humanized and historically placed, finally becoming the authentic human community. The movement begins with the "I" as subject and arrives at what Goldmann calls the Marxist notion of the "We."

For Lukács the Kantian cup was half empty; for Goldmann it was half full. Lukács accented those dimensions of Kant's philosophy that failed to effect—indeed, inhibited—the transcendence to dialectical thinking. Goldmann emphasized how, despite its limits, the critical philosophy points beyond itself, and is, consequently, a crucial step toward dialectical thinking. Lukács emphasized the bourgeois character of Kant's thought alone; it was thus by definition contradictory and ensnared in antinomies. Goldmann, too, emphasized the bourgeois nature of Kant's thought, but instead he characterized it as tragic. According to Goldmann, when Lukács underscores his differences with Kant (on the question of human beings attaining totality), he "neglects the fact, which is just as important, that the necessity of attaining and realizing totality constitutes the point of departure and the center of Kantian thought."[13]

In Goldmann's theory of the human sciences, great philosophy, literature, and culture are coherent elaborations, on the conceptual and imaginary planes, of worldviews implicit in the "possible" consciousness of social groups. In *Kant*, Goldmann presents an early formulation of his notion: "[T]he truly great thinker is he who achieves the maximum of *possible* truth beginning from the interests and social situation of a group, and formulates it in a manner which confers on it real scope and real effectiveness." Expounding this in a footnote, he states that the term "greatest *possible* knowledge" indicates that the thinker must be in the vanguard of the group. Goldmann cites Lukács's distinction between imputed and empirical consciousness here, but, strikingly, he prefers to speak of "*possible*" consciousness rather than ascribed or imputed consciousness, thereby accentuating its immanent potential.[14] Kant's worldview, writes Goldmann, was "the most representative system of the German bourgeoisie," rivaled only by Hegel's later formulation. That worldview had three main elements: liberty, individualism, and "juridical equality" (equality before the law).[15] Goldmann always emphasized the contributions of bourgeois liberal ideas to the development of human freedom, and he insisted on seeing Marxism as the culmination of Western thought, not its repudiation. For him, "the two fundamental categories of human existence" are "*liberty* and *autonomy of the individual*" on one hand, and "the *human community*, the *universe, totality* as the meaning and product of this liberty in the action of free men" on the other.[16]

Kant, in Goldmann's view, articulates the positive values generated, though they are unrealizable, by liberal capitalism—equality, respect for the individual, and tolerance. It is because these are unfulfillable given the limits of the bourgeois world, and because Kant strives to go beyond those limits, that his worldview ultimately becomes tragic. That worldview is thrown into sharp relief when he tries to answer three questions, which correspond to the concerns of the three *Critiques*: What can I know? What must I do? For what may I hope? Goldmann, we know, asserts that the fundamental postulate of the critical philosophy is that human beings strive for the absolute. In Kant, however, this striving is finally frustrated because of the limits imposed on what one can know, do, and hope for by the noumena/phenomena distinction and by the fact that the categories—and thus human nature—are fixed, rather than historical. For Kant, totality is unattainable, and what Kant takes for human nature, Goldmann sees as a product of reified capitalist society. Kant's accomplishment was to raise the problem of totality; he was "the first modern thinker who recognized anew the importance of *totality* as a fundamental category of existence," even though its character was problematic for him.[17]

Consequently, Goldmann (in contrast to the neo-Kantians, among others) places enormous emphasis on "The Transcendental Dialectic" in the *Critique of Pure Reason*, where Kant shows how *Vernunft* carries us into illusion when we seek to know the noumenal realm. The neo-Kantian return to Kant was, in Goldmann's view, only a partial return; it was a return to the transcendental aesthetic and analytic of the first *Critique* (that is, to Kant's theory of the a priori forms of sensibility and the categories), but not to the dialectic, which, because of the *Ding-an-Sich*, was viewed as incomprehensible. Striving for totality is thereby removed from the Kantian picture, and this, Goldmann argues, corrupts the true spirit of Kant's philosophy, and obscures its tragic grounding. Rickert, for example, turns Kant's philosophy of history into what Goldmann calls "an elaboration of concepts of the human and historical sciences. In Kant, all the categories are oriented towards the future; in Rickert they are oriented towards the past or at most towards the present."[18]

Kant's "antinomies of pure reason"—cases in which *Vernunft* presses us to employ concepts beyond their limits, that is, to apply them to the unconditioned—leads to what seem to be contradictory assertions with equally compelling proofs and conclusions. All that is true and false in the initial theses and antitheses in each case is due to reason's natural, but unrealizable, quest for the unconditioned. Goldmann focuses on the third antinomy. In Kant's words, the thesis here is: "Causality in accordance with laws of nature is not the only causality from which the appearances of the world can one and all be derived. To explain these appearances it is necessary to assume that there is also another causality, that of freedom." The antithesis is: "There is no freedom; everything in the world takes place solely in accordance with laws of nature."[19] In short, the thesis and antithesis pose the traditional questions of free will and natural necessity, or more simply, freedom and necessity. Goldmann perceives in these antitheses a counterposing of active and passive modes of looking at the world.

Kant resolves the antinomy by arguing that each assertion deals with a separate realm, the first noumenal and the second phenomenal. Kant saw "the causality of freedom" as a "causality of reason," and thus he asserted that freedom consists in the autonomous following of rational principles rather than the heteronomous following of the empirical world. The antinomy is resolved when we realize that two different realms are being addressed. Goldmann, in turn, transforms the antinomy into the following assertions:

1. "Man is free and his will can and must be determined exclusively by his intelligible end";
2. "From the contemplative and theoretical viewpoint one can consider human actions as mechanically determined by the past";
3. "There is no contradiction between these two affirmations."[20]

In the third assertion, Goldmann embraces refusal of contradiction, and presents it as a step in a Kantian demarche toward the Marxist view of history as one of purposeful human action within a set of social and historical conditions. Goldmann thinks that Kant's separation of theory and practice by means of opposing two realms is explicable by the social reality of Kant's Germany; unity of theory and practice could not then be achieved by the weak German bourgeoisie. Consequently Kant reified the phenomenal realm and opposed it to the noumenal one.

Goldmann contends that the neo-Kantians were likewise trapped within reified categories. They conflated thought in contemporary society "with thought in general."[21] Here, however, Goldmann turns to the one neo-Kantian he admired. Emil Lask had distinguished between two categories that Kant, in his essay "Idea for a Universal History with a Cosmopolitan Purpose," had tried to reconcile: *universalitas,* or atomistic, fragmented "universality," (a "generality" presumed by rationalism); and *universitas,* or "concrete totality." Kant presents this as the question of how individual acts, apparently capricious, seem to advance the capacities and purposes of the species as a whole.[22] Universalitas, says Goldmann, embodies "reified universality," and *universitas* embodies "community." (This distinction immediately brings to mind that between *Gemeinschaft* and *Gesellschaft.*) Goldmann, who refused to separate questions of knowledge from the social world in which they are posed, writes:

All social life presupposes a minimum of categorical forms without which men could not understand one another. Where the social character of life— whatever its level—appears openly, the human character of the categories can also be more or less transparent. But it is entirely otherwise in the bourgeois and individualist modern social order. Here there is no transparent community (*communauté transparente*). . . . The fundamental social relations of men, the relations of production, are those of buyers and sellers of commodities; only antagonism resulting from the desire to buy cheap and sell dear is allowed into consciousness. What unites men despite everything, the fact that the buyer only has meaning if there is a seller and vice versa, must be realized [*doit se réaliser*] despite and against their consciousness, in a reified form. The fact that production is, despite all, a social fact, expresses itself solely in the price of commodities. On the Bourse "wheat rises," "steel falls," etc. Man has disappeared.[23]

Goldmann praises Lukács for showing the intrusion of reification into all aspects of life, ranging from the daily existence of the worker to philosophical logic and epistemology. For Goldmann, ultimately, the possibilities for human knowledge will correspond to the possibilities for community; totality is both a question of method and aspiration. Thus he insists,

This difference between *Universitas* and *Universalitas*, concrete totality and reified *a priori* universality, constitutes one of the cornerstones of Kant's theoretical and practical philosophy. *A priori* universality is what characterizes given, limited man. Determining its possibilities and limits is one of the most important tasks of the critical philosophy; totality, *Universitas*, is only given today on the formal level (space and time), and could find its perfect realization only in a higher, supra-sensible state, in the archetypal intellect, in the holy will, in the knowledge of the thing-in-itself etc. Kant obviously did not transcend reification, but he described it with exactitude and defined its limits.[24]

Goldmann argues that there is a close methodological kinship among the Kantian positing of the archetypal intellect; Hegel's, Marx's, and Lukács's dialectical method; and Lask's notion of emanatist logic. We recall that Lask contrasted emanatist logic, which is based on the principle that one must know the whole in order to know the parts, to analytic logic, which is atomistic, sees individual elements as the only authentic reality, and views concept formation solely as a process of abstraction from individual entities with common properties. Kant, Hegel, Lukács, and Lask, according to Goldmann, all perceived an important flaw in modern thought: its inability "to unite the general and the individual, the possible absolute with the real given" because of "the absence of the category of totality, of the *universitas*."[25] By means of the distinction between formal *universalitas* and concrete *universitas*, Goldmann can argue—here, against Hegel and Lukács— that it is incorrect to see Kantian totality as merely formal. Rather, as György Markus puts it, totality "becomes concretized in the concept of a never justifiable but uneradicable aspiration and hope, alone constituting a valid motive for free, ethico-social action."[26] Again, for Goldmann, the Kantian cup is half full, while for Lukács, it is half empty.

Consequently, whereas Lukács saw Kant's ethics as purely formal, contentless, and unable to "test its strength on concrete problems," for Goldmann, "just as on the theoretical level the authentic meaning of human life is to strive [*tendre*] from the formal totality of empirical spatial and temporal existence to the *totality—encompassing content—*of the *Universitas* and noumena, so on the practical level man's duty is to take the *content-full totality* [*la totalité du contenu*] as his sole directive and to act as if its realization depended on his current action alone."[27] Kant's fundamental moral principle, that the maxim of one's action should be universalizable, receives various formulations in his works, and it is on one formulation in particular that Goldmann fastens in defining the actual "content" of the categorical imperative. What is that content?

> It can . . . only be a categorical rejection of individualist man as he is today. And in effect Kant is able to concentrate in a few words the most radical condemnation of bourgeois society and formulate the foundations of all humanism to come: *Act so that humanity, whether in your own person or that of any other man, is always an end for you, and never merely a means.*[28]

This, Goldmann maintains—and Lukács is clearly the target—is an "ethic of content," which in fact condemns production for the market. In such production, people use others as means to their own ends of profit. They join the world of things. Goldmann liked to recount how a student came to him horrified after a lecture on Kant's ethics. The young man had concluded that according to the categorical imperative, his father, a businessman, was immoral: he could not possibly consider each of his customers as ends in themselves. For Goldmann, the Kantian ethic yields a supreme value: "[T]his supreme value is humanity in the person of each individual man. Not the individual alone as with the rationalists nor totality alone in its different forms (God, state, nation, class) as in intuitionist and romantic mystiques, but the human totality, *the community embracing all of humanity*, and its expression, the human person."[29]

Goldmann's arguments here bear close affinity to those of neo-Kantian socialists, such as Hermann Cohen and Karl Vörlander, who averred that the categorical imperative is in itself a demand for socialist community. But Goldmann, in contrast to them, found in Kant a stage in the evolution toward Marxism, and rejected the neo-Kantian view that Marxism needed to be "supplemented" or "completed" by Kant's ethic. In this he was in general agreement with one of the foremost analysts of the relation between Kant and Marx, Max Adler. In opposition to Adler, however, Goldmann emphasized the inseparability of fact and value.

In *Kant*, Goldmann places Adler within neo-Kantianism and alternates between criticism of and laudatory remarks about him. In a 1957 article, his one lengthy discussion of the Austro-Marxists, Goldmann wrote that they were among "the most brilliant thinkers of socialism" before World War II, and he singled out Adler as a "writer and thinker of the highest order" whose work "greatly enlightened several generations of young students in central Europe."[30] Goldmann was, of course, one of those students, even if he did not acknowledge it directly. He discusses Adler in the context of an analysis of the relation between fact and value in the history of Marxism. Goldmann attacks the major theorists of the "so-called orthodox Marxism" of the Second International for turning "the dialectical concept of 'scientific social-ism'" into a "*scientistic* concept of science" that radically opposed judgments of fact (science) to judgments of value. According to Goldmann, this type of thinking was encapsulated by the famous formulation of the French mathematician and philosopher of science Henri Poincaré: from premises in the indicative, one can never derive conclusions in the imperative.[31]

The task of the workers' movement according to "scientistic" socialist theorists was to accelerate what was historically inevitable. Such determinism, Goldmann insisted, was more Spinozist than Marxist. Pointing to the "Theses on Feuerbach," Goldmann contended that Marx was no determinist and that truly dialectical thought, which is based on the subject-object dialectic, precluded determinism. Thus Goldmann had contempt for Kautsky's argument that "scientific" Marxism precluded ethics because it shows what is, not what ought to be. To the extent that facts and values get "confused" occasionally in Marx's own writings, claimed Kautsky, this was an uncontrollable function of the struggle against capitalism, which, as a matter of course, engenders indignation. Kautsky, in Goldmann's view, implicitly recognized "the *theoretical* superiority of Vörlander's ethical positions" over Kautsky's own "scientism" and that of Plekhanov.[32]

Not that Vörlander was right when he argued in "Kant und Marx" that Marx's thought itself was bifurcated between claims of objective science and a separate but implicit ethics. Goldmann notes shrewdly that Kautsky and Vörlander, although one emphasizes science and the other ethics, ultimately find themselves in the same place: both believe indicatives cannot yield imperatives. Lacking the perspective of totality, they both take one-sided positions, expressed not only in epistemological and moral theory, but also in politics. They both become reformists. Reformist socialism, says Goldmann, long based itself on ethical socialism, while orthodox, "scientistic" Marxism—"the conception of socialist politics as a matter of social technique founded on an objective science"—presented itself as revolutionary (as did Stalinism).

But the two ended up reformist, and while Goldmann does not state it explicitly, he clearly thinks that this is because they are one-sided and fail to grasp the whole, which requires grasping the subject-object dialectic. The ethical approach sees only the subjective aspect of the equation; the "orthodox" approach sees only the objective.

The Austro-Marxists, says Goldmann—he means primarily Adler and Otto Bauer—sought a synthesis between these two positions. Adler agreed with Vörlander, Kautsky, and Plekhanov that facts and values had to be radically separate. He agreed with Vörlander that there was a close link between Kant's and Marx's thought, and that in the consciousness of individual militants, socialism often takes on ethical form. Finally, he concurred with the "orthodox" Marxists in rejecting any ethical foundation of socialism. In Goldmann's mind, this is both an original conclusion and the most satisfactory one if one's premise is the opposition of facts to values. For Adler, Marx was primarily a sociologist; indeed, Adler identified sociology with Marxism per se, maintaining that socialism would be the result of causal processes, not ethical imperatives. Goldmann quotes Adler's claim, in his *Kant und Marxismus*: "The fact that the product of causality is at the same time justified from an ethical point of view is in no way secondary and an accident for a Marxist. But this convergence of the causal necessities of evolution with ethical justification is a *sociological* problem." What Marx provided was a "system of sociological knowledge," which needed no ethical justification.[33]

The important link between Kant and Marx that Adler established, according to Goldmann, was in a different vein. Adler's originality lay in

> making the Kantian a priori a sort of first discovery of the collective consciousness and [making] Kant the creator of the first epistemological elements which rendered sociology possible. Marx is thus situated on a direct continuum from Kant, who discovered the existence of social consciousness, through Fichte, who introduced the idea of action, to Hegel, who makes this social consciousness historical and poses the problem of the laws which rule its dynamic. The sociology of Marx becomes, for Max Adler, the result of classical German philosophy.[34]

These are links to which Goldmann, in his various efforts to delineate the historical path taken by dialectical thinking, would return frequently. Goldmann's concept of "transindividuality," the idea that the subject of historical action and cultural creation is a plurality of individuals with common structures of consciousness, is a further step on this continuum. The continuum includes Adler's effort to define collective consciousness in a nonmetaphysical manner that does not negate the individual. Kant's a priori categories established the conditions of knowledge for all human beings. For Adler, the foundation of Marxism was the fact that humans are social beings. He argued that since social association is a transcendental condition of experience, like time, space, and the categories in Kant's first *Critique*, we must therefore speak of a "social a priori." The study of social life presupposes synthesizing forms of understanding that are functions of but not simply derived from experience.[35] Transcendental consciousness implies sociability. Human thought entails "both a separate individual consciousness and also a manifestation of consciousness in general." It is

> the transcendental ground which alone makes possible the interaction and cooperation of human beings in the process of bringing about the knowledge of truth. For it is only thus that what is intellectually necessary becomes universally valid, so that there is a community of human existence . . . to which every empirical individual consciousness can be related, in its intercourse with others, as to a unity comprising them all. . . . In order to grasp the fundamental significance of the concept of "consciousness in general" and also to bring out the specific novelty of Marx's basic idea of the socialization . . . of the individual, it cannot be sufficiently emphasized that the true problem of society does not originate in the association of a number of human beings, but simply and solely in the individual consciousness.[36]

In brief, social being is implicit in each individual because of his rational communicative capability. The Kantian system of transcendental subjectivity implies sociability and, consequently, a category of "social a priori". Reason in Kant, as read by Goldmann, is not solely a theoretical faculty of knowledge or practical wisdom, but "the communicable spiritual faculty [*la faculté spirituelle communicable*] which makes us strive towards the realization of the supreme ends of man."[37] Communication between human beings, Goldmann continues, must presuppose that each individual can transform what is immediately given to him in various circumstances in such a manner that another person "understands what is communicated to him and can relate it to his own given, to the matter of his immediate apprehension; but it implies as well the possibility that each understand the matter proper to his experience as a partial aspect of knowledge held in common and that his knowledge is dependent on that of all other men."[38]

Not incidentally, Goldmann calls the principles of the transformation of matter, the given, into experience "form."[39] Thus the problem he has posed is the same one Lukács struggled with in his passage from *Soul and Forms* to *History and Class Consciousness*. For Goldmann, as for Adler, social life rests fundamentally on the possibility of communication, the social creation of forms in which people are at home, as it were. They both pose the question of what, in the consciousness of a multiplicity of individuals, enables collective action. Here again, we see why Goldmann proposes Kant as a "tragic" thinker. Kant asks, "What ought I to do?" He answers with the moral law, yet is unable to get beyond an eternal, autonomous "I" to a historical "We" as the subject of action. Human beings can never have the means to be moral in the Kantian system. Thus while the critical philosophy points toward "totality" and posits the human community as the supreme value, it cannot posit its realization. It is bound to the "Je" (or "Ich") and the "Je" cannot get beyond *Universalitas* to *Universitas* because it is social groups, the "Nous" (or "Wir") that make history, not isolated, atomized individuals. Goldmann, consequently, will follow a continuum from Kant's transcendental subjectivity via Hegel's historical *Geist* and Adler's Marxist "social a priori," to his own notion of the "transindividual subject." The two additional, crucial elements that will shape this are the genetic epistemology of Piaget—which Goldmann insisted both shares its basic principles with Marx's epistemology and has a Kantian character[40]—and Lukács's theories of totality, class consciousness, and subject-object relations. Goldmann will transform all of these for his own purposes.

II

The first chapter of *The Hidden God* is entitled "Le Tout et les parties" (The Whole and the Parts). At the outset, Goldmann indicates his intention not only to contribute to the understanding of Pascal and Racine, but to elucidate "the structure of facts of consciousness and their philosophical and literary expression." The reader will quickly grasp that a Marxist theory of the structure of consciousness is Goldmann's underlying quest and that through this endeavor he aims to elaborate a Marxist methodology for the human sciences. He presents two premises:

> **1.** *"[A]bstract and isolated empirical facts are the sole point of departure for research"*; and
> **2.** *"[T]he sole valid [valable] criterion* for judging the value of a method or philosophical system is its capacity to understand these facts, and their meaning [*signification*], and to derive laws from them [*d'en dégager les lois*]."[41]

The problem is to establish the nature of these "facts" and to determine what it means to understand or explain them. Goldmann follows Hegel and Lukács in rejecting the fetishization of "facts." It is an indisputable "fact" that in 1793 the head of one Louis of the House of Bourbon was severed from the rest of his person (this example is mine, not

Goldmann's). A variety of other "facts" may be listed that are pertinent to this event: that the unfortunate in question was France's monarch, was condemned by something known as the Convention, had a wife named Marie Antoinette, and so on. Yet if we attempt to comprehend this execution beyond the facts that on a certain date a certain fellow lost his head—if, in other words, we try to attribute any significance whatsoever to this event, or to make sense of it—we do not simply establish facts. Rather, we impose referential form(s); that is, we impose some order that makes the "facts" intelligible. We see them as part of processes in space as well as time. We do not merely make a sum of them from which a general picture emerges.

Consequently we must speak not just of facts but of facts constituted in relation to other constituted facts; we must speak of the links among the facts and thus must recognize that there is always some form of totality in which facts are placed. Had Edmund Burke written his *Reflections on the Revolution in France* after Louis's death, he would, no doubt, have seen the fact of execution not as a biological occurrence—a man's death—but as another example of reason-worship run amok. A Marxist historian, say Alfred Soboul, saw the same fact as one event in the cataclysmic transition from feudalism to capitalism. A liberal historian, like François Furet, later challenged the Marxist interpretation, and Georges Lefebvre, Tocqueville, and Michelet had their own analyses at earlier dates. Ought we to assume that these differences are due to one historian's possessing more "facts" than do the others? Should we assume that Michelet knew "more" facts than Tocqueville or that Soboul knew fewer than Furet, thereby permitting one to add up more units of "knowledge" than did the other in order to reach a more "accurate" picture of "reality"?

Obviously not. Furet certainly had more information at his disposal than Michelet because Furet wrote after a century more of scholarship. That research may have provided crucial new "facts" for our understanding of various events. But this does not explain his differences with Soboul; facts are not added and subtracted as if they were autonomous entities on an historical ledger. That we begin research with what Goldmann, following Lukács, calls "abstract and isolated facts," on one hand, and must integrate them into a framework, on the other, makes the nature of the interrelation between "facts" and "method" crucial, if not immediately self-evident. Hegel made a similar point when he denounced the idea that the truth is to be conceived in a proposition that is a "fixed result" or "immediately known." One can obtain a direct answer to the questions of when Caesar was born or what the square of a hypoteneuse is, but "the nature of a so-called truth of that kind is different from the nature of philosophical truths."[42]

The point is that we never comprehend anything solely on the basis of "the facts." Facts are always constituted and placed within a larger whole, which in turn shapes the facts. Hence Goldmann, again echoing Lukács, asserts that at the foundation of all dialectical thought is the principle that "knowledge of empirical facts remains abstract and superficial unless it is concretized by its integration into a whole which alone allows transcending [*dépasser*] the abstract and partial phenomenon to arrive at its concrete essence, and implicitly, its meaning."[43] In short, we always place facts into a constellation that gives them meaning, makes them intelligible, and thus we interpret them the moment we try to comprehend them. This applies whether we are analyzing history, the works of a philosopher, or those of a playwright. An individual is not a "fact" unto himself or herself, and his or her work cannot be viewed as such. He or she is part of a social world and social groups, and an author's intent may not always coincide with the objective meaning of his or her text. This is one of the points Goldmann will illustrate at great length in his study of Pascal, Racine, and the tragic worldview.

Goldmann argues against what he calls unquestioned starting points in rationalism and empiricism: innate ideas (in Descartes) and sense perception (in Hume). From these beginnings, in Goldmann's view, both philosophers proceed in a "linear" manner; be the procedure deductive or inductive, "facts" become for them forms of definite knowledge pointing their ways along a line. For Goldmann, the crucial methodological dichotomy is not between rationalism and empiricism. Rather, he places both these on one side in opposition to dialectical thinking. Following Lask, he argues that for rationalism and empiricism, both of which he insists are ultimately atomistic, parts are added up to attain a sum, with the assumption being that incontestable stages of knowledge are built along the way.

Whereas Hobbes wrote that "we may not, as in a circle, begin the handling from what point we please," for Goldmann, the relation between the whole and the parts is always circular.[44] Similarly, our own work is never to be regarded as a fixed point of knowledge, but rather as something which will later be transcended. Goldmann insists on his own Marxist hermeneutic circle, though he does not employ this term. Its origins, in his case, may be traced to Hegel before Dilthey. In his *Logic*, Hegel argued that a concept can have meaning only in relation to what he calls the entire system of concepts. A concept is determined in terms of the other concepts which it is not. "The true is the whole," he told us in the *Phenomenology*, ". . . knowledge is only actual and can be experienced as Science or as *system*." Therefore, "a so-called basic proposition or principle of philosophy, if it is true, is also false, just because it is *only* a principle."[45]

A circle has 360 degrees, each of which may be considered in itself but only takes on significance—only becomes a "degree"—when seen as a moment in the whole circle, that is, in relation to the other degrees. As Hegel puts it,

Each of the parts of philosophy is a philosophical whole, a circle rounded and complete in itself; in each of these parts, however, the philosophical Idea is found in a particular specificality or medium. The single circle, because it is a real totality, burst[s] through the limits imposed by its special medium, and gives rise to a wider circle. The whole of philosophy in this way resembles a circle of circles. The Idea appears in each single circle, but at the same time, the whole Idea is constituted by the system of these peculiar phases, and each is a necessary member of the organization.[46]

Each degree points to another, and is thus teleological and originary at once; each degree is its "self" only in relation to the whole that it partly constitutes and that in turn constitutes it. Since Hegel's circles give rise to other circles, it might be more appropriate to speak of a conceptual spiral rather than a circle. In any event, Goldmann takes Hegel's circle of circles out of the realm of Idealism and turns it into the fundamental principle of his own dialectical method:

Both rationalism, which starts from innate or distinct ideas [d'idées innées ou évidentes] and empiricism, which begins with sensation or perception, assume at each moment of research a certain amount [une ensemble] of acquired knowledge from which scientific thought advances in a straight line, with more or less certitude, without, however, having normally and necessarily to return to problems already solved. On the contrary, dialectical thought affirms that there are never any certain starting points nor problems definitely resolved, and that thought never advances in a straight line since every partial fact only takes on its true meaning [signification] by being placed in the whole, in the same way that the whole can be understood through progress in the knowledge of partial truths. The advance of knowledge thus appears as a perpetual oscillation between the parts and the whole, which must elucidate each other.[47]

The reason for Pascal's appeal to Goldmann is immediately evident from Goldmann's contraposition of Pascal to both rationalism and empiricism, and his citing of the following passage from the Pensées immediately after the above statement:

If man were to begin by studying himself, he would see how incapable he is of going beyond himself [passer outre]. How could it be possible for a part to know the whole? But he may perhaps aspire to a knowledge of at least those parts which are on the same level as he himself. But the different parts of the world are all so closely linked and related together that I hold it impossible to know one without knowing the others and without knowing the whole.

Thus since all things are both the result and the cause of causes, both helpers and receivers of help, both mediately and immediately linked together by a natural and imperceptible chain which connects things most distant and distinct from one another, I hold it to be equally impossible to know parts without the whole and to know the whole without having a particular knowledge of each part.[48]

Within three years of the publication of *Kant*, Goldmann had concluded that it was Pascal, not Kant, who was the starting point for modern dialectical thought. For Goldmann, Pascal became not only the first dialectician, but the ideal French foil against Cartesian rationalism. After all, Descartes and Pascal were contemporaries, and both were scientists and mathematicians, but with opposing worldviews. Behind the opposition between Pascal and Descartes, for Goldmann, lies that between dialectical and "scientistic" thought, between *Vernunft* and *Verstand*, between socialist community and the atomistic individualism of reified capitalism.

Dialectical thought, argues Goldmann, rejects the "atomized individual" as it rejects the "abstract fact" as a starting point. Yet it envisions a whole that does not negate the individual and the fact. Here, Goldmann subtly departs from Lukács's *History and Class Consciousness*. Lukács insisted that were all Marxism's assertions to be proven wrong a Marxist could still remain orthodox because orthodoxy was a matter of method, whereas for Goldmann, a dialectical method cannot conceptualize without its object. Method "is not an end in itself," as he put it in 1968, for "centering on method as something autonomous is positivism in the worst sense; we discuss method simply to the extent to which method is subordinate to the thing, to the necessity of understanding facts."[49] How can a method and program for research be conceptualized on the basis of these premises? For Goldmann, this is equivalent to asking how we can fashion tools both to interpret and to change the world. Like Hegel, Goldmann does not believe we can examine the tools apart from their employment. The key to his approach is found in the preface to *The Hidden God*: "The central idea of this book is that facts concerning man always form themselves into global *significative structures* which are at once practical, theoretical and emotive [*affectif*], and that these structures can be studied in a positive manner, that is, they can be both explained and understood only in a *practical* perspective based on the acceptance of a certain set [*ensemble*] of values."[50] These claims are best seen in light of Piaget's "genetic epistemology," which Goldmann believed confirmed the epistemological foundations of Marxism. Piaget is melded with Lukács to create the Goldmannian method, "genetic structuralism."

Piaget is best known for his theory of child development. In it, the processes of knowledge and learning come of the genesis and evolution of mental operations within individuals. "Piaget wants to begin where the genetically fixed forms of perception and cognition end," notes Marx W. Wartofsky, "where instinct is replaced by intelligence, and where phenotypic modes of adaptation and maturation develop beyond the genotype."[51] The Swiss psychologist characterized these operations as evolving, structured wholes. As children mature, they invent and reconstruct various concepts and operations—such as time, space, causality, object—in increasingly sophisticated ways. These operations become the means by which they will know about the world, learn about it, and be able to act in it. At a young age, a child can grasp certain relations or actions only by going through them. The child must act them out. At a higher stage of cognitive development, the child can raise them in his or her imagination. Out of simple mental structures, complex ones have developed. The individual develops a priori mental structures, but these change and evolve as he or she interacts with the world. Piaget delineated stages of a child's development (each having substages), which can be broadly sketched as follows.

In the sensory-motor stage (up to eighteen months), children learn to coordinate and locate themselves in the world. They learn to distinguish themselves from the surrounding world and discover the permanence of objects outside themselves. Then, as "preoperational" cognition evolves into concrete thinking operations (eighteen months to around age eleven or twelve), children become capable of interiorizing actions conceptually and develop "reversibility," a key step in the emergence of logical abilities. They can now reverse a temporal sequence of events, for instance, or recognize that if they reshape a piece of clay, it remains the same matter, and can be returned to its previous form. This stage represents the passage "from the sensorimotor scheme to the concept," a movement "from action to thought."[52] However, in this stage, children are still oriented to the "concrete" in their thinking; that is, they still focus on what is before them. At the highest stage, this is no longer necessary, and hypotheses and deductions become possible. The salient characteristic of the formal operational stage (beginning at about age eleven or twelve) is the "capacity to deal with hypotheses instead of simply with objects." Importantly, at this point, children can deductively derive conclusions from hypotheses.[53] At about age fifteen, the individual has a more or less stable system of mental structures. Goldmann was less preoccupied with the scheme of child development per se, than with the broader epistemo-

logical principles incorporated in it. One can see immediately, however, that Piaget's analysis of cognitive development parallels, in important respects, the structure of Hegel's developmental scheme, in
which we rise from the brute facticity before us—a here, now, and
there—to the use of our understanding to establish universals with
which to define particulars, before attaining the highest conceptual
level.

Piaget's notion that mental operations are structured wholes is clarified further if we compare it to the alternative psychological schools he
criticized, sometimes implicitly and sometimes explicitly, in elaborating his theory. As Gruber and Vonèche note, Piaget's structural wholes
are not reducible to simple elements (such as primary sensations on
which experience ultimately rests, and on whose basis mental structures are formed), and they cannot be regarded as invariant structures
(such as stable structured wholes that organize experience).[54] Such
were the positions maintained, respectively, by elementarist psychology and Gestalt psychology. (Piaget also rejected behaviorism as a
form of elementarism, which "chained" simple habits together to explain complex behavior and hence concerned itself solely with observ-
able behavior.)

While Piaget appreciated the Gestaltist assertion that experience is
not a chaotic process but is structured from the beginning, he faulted
it for envisioning structures as static. In contrast, Piaget insisted that
mental structures always evolved and are always in genesis, in processes of what he called structurating and destructurating. Gruber
and Vonèche capture this succinctly: "[T]he elementarists said, 'from
elements, structures'; the Gestaltists answered, 'no elements, only
structures;' and Piaget rejoined, 'out of structures, new structures.'"[55]
Goldmann saw a parallel between Piaget's challenge to earlier psychological schools and the challenge posed by dialectical thought to previous philosophical schools. Furthermore, Piaget's critique of the Gestaltists on the grounds that mental structures transform in interaction
with the world, leading to increasingly advanced conceptual categories, is strongly reminiscent of Hegel's critique of Kant: the tools of
knowledge (that is, the categories) are not static, but must be used and
in being used are transformed, just as the swimmer gains the capacity
to swim only by going into the water.

Knowledge is therefore always in genesis and never fixed; the structured wholes that Piaget called mental structures underlie all our experiences, and our possibilities for learning. Piaget complained, "The
common postulate of various traditional epistemologies . . . is that our
knowledge is a fact and not a process and that if our various forms of

knowledge are incomplete and our various sciences still imperfect, that which is acquired is acquired and can be studied statically."[56] Elsewhere, he elaborates:

> Scientific knowledge is in perpetual evolution. . . . As a result, we cannot say that on the one hand there is the history of knowledge and on the other its current state today, as if its current state were somehow definitive or even stable. The current state of knowledge is a moment in history, changing just as rapidly as the state of knowledge in the past has ever changed and in many instances more rapidly. Scientific thought, then, is not momentary; it is not a static instant; it is a process. More specifically, it is a process of continued construction and reorganization. This is true in almost every branch of scientific investigation.[57]

In other words, knowledge does not advance through building one certitude upon another (in what Goldmann called a linear manner) with each stage definitely resolving certain problems. Knowledge is a process, not a fact, and therefore cannot be conceived as a composite of static, "known" invariants.

Every organism, Piaget tells us, strives to adapt to and seek an equilibrium within its environment. In this endeavor the organism acts on the environment while the environment acts on it. Individuals develop mental structures through this interaction, through processes of "accommodation" and "assimilation." They accommodate to the external structures of the world—their mental structures, in other words, cope with the demands of the world—while assimilating into them by acting on the environment on the basis of their own, changing mental structures. Hence there is always a subject-object relation, and the human being as the subject of knowledge is always an active subject, a transforming subject who is in turn transformed in acting. Adaptation is thus "an equilibrium between assimilation and accommodations, which amounts to the same thing as an equilibrium of interaction between subject and object."[58]

When Piaget insists that "a structure" denotes a totality, he means that a structure is a self-regulating system governed by what he calls laws of transformation. In other words, structure is not static. He is at pains to differentiate structure, for which wholeness is "a defining mark," from a simple aggregate, and to insist that there is *"no structure apart from construction."*[59] The processes of assimilation and accommodation are never-ending, and compose evolving logical models. Importantly, there is "a parallel between the progress made in the logical and rational organization of knowledge and the corresponding psychological processes."[60]

According to Goldmann, this theory is dialectical in nature. For both Marx and Piaget, he argues, "man is neither an all powerful creator or a simple spectator; he is an actor, a being who acts on the world, transforms it, and is himself modified by the impact of these transformations [*et se modifie lui-même sous l'action de ces transformations*]."[61] Piaget, he notes with approval, rejects rigid oppositions between instinct and intelligence, thought and action, whole and parts, facts and values. Piaget came to define the relation between genesis and structure as a dialectical one: "To the extent that one opts for structure and devaluates genesis, history and function, or even the very activity of the *subject* itself, one cannot but come into conflict with the central tenets of dialectical thought."[62] On the basis of his theory of evolving structured totalities, Piaget saw knowledge as the outcome of a "circular" relation between a whole and its parts, rather than as a linear progression from the simple to the complex. For Piaget, says Goldmann, consciousness and action are "partial and *inseparable* aspects of the same reality," since to know, in Piaget's theory, means to act and "to invent."[63]

The inference Goldmann drew from this was that subject and object can be conceived neither as opposed to each other nor as identical with each other. Goldmann maintained that Piaget's view of the adaptive nature of intelligence parallels Marx's view of the dialectical relation between labor and nature, a parallel Piaget himself accepted.[64] In the first volume of *Capital*, Marx depicts labor as a process of interaction between man and the world around him. Man, a part of nature, consciously acts on it and appropriates it to satisfy his needs. He acts on the external world while it acts on him, changing him, and allowing the development of new powers.[65] Thus, according to Goldmann, "the role of 'Nature,' of 'matter,' of the object is identical in the psychology of Piaget and historical materialism."[66] Both insist that a person is an active—not a passive—subject of knowledge, who, though not all-powerful, transforms the world and is transformed by it in the same process. Human beings always search for and are in a process aimed at equilibrium within their environment. Marx's claim that social being determines consciousness, and his assertion in the third "Thesis on Feuerbach" that "revolutionizing practice" must be conceived as "the coincidence of changing circumstances and of human activity," make, in Goldmann's view, the same epistemological claims as those made by Piaget; people assimilate and accommodate as active subjects by means of their structuring and destructuring mental structures.

Piaget himself noted that it is Marx's emphasis on the activity of the subject in relation to the object that makes Marx a *dialectical* materialist.[67] Marx's merit was "to have distinguished in social phenomena an effective infrastructure and a superstructure oscillating between symbolism and adequate recognition [*la prise de conscience adequate*] in the same sense . . . where psychology is obliged to distinguish between behavior and consciousness." Consequently, the "social superstructure is . . . to the infrastructure what the consciousness of the individual man is to his behavior."[68] For Goldmann, Piaget is part of a tradition of dialectical thought that harks back to Pascal, Kant, Hegel, and Marx, though, again, Piaget did not reach his conclusions by contemplating them. Since Piaget was neither a Marxist nor a philosopher, Goldmann saw his work as an independent confirmation of Marx's endeavor.

It is in this context that we can grasp Goldmann's statement that facts concerning man form global significative structures to be explained and understood by a practical perspective based on a set of values. By "significative" structure, Goldmann intends a "meaningful" one in the sense that "human facts" must be grasped as part of an ensemble of relations representing the efforts, usually purposeful, of human beings to adapt to the world. (The French *significative* can be translated as "significative," "significant," or "meaningful.") These ensembles are totalities, which must be comprehended in terms of their internal coherence (Goldmann will call this the process of "understanding") and in terms of the environment in which they exist, an environment that is itself composed of significative structures. Since structures are totalities in genesis, and since totality is the "first, principal idea of dialectical thought," one must consider structures not in terms of a static present, but in dynamic, temporal terms of past, present, and future. A few weeks before his death, Goldmann defined the methodological principle of totality as "the idea that one can only understand a phenomenon by first inserting it in a broader structure of which it is part and in which it has a function which is its objective meaning [*sens*], whether or not the men acting and creating it are conscious of it; it is the category of significative structure which can only be understood by inserting it in a much broader signficative structure and in the whole of history [*l'ensemble de l'histoire*]."[69] We again find ourselves in Hegel's circle of circles.

For Goldmann, significative structure is the foremost tool for comprehending most human facts. He uses it in ways that parallel Weber's use of the ideal-type and Lukács's notion of imputation, though without confusing the imputation with the object in reality. Thus when Goldmann delineates the concept of reification, he declares himself to be examining the consequences of production for the market in a "pure" capitalist society, one which, he specifies, never existed. The empirical reality of capitalism always contains precapitalist survivals and manifestations of future changes. Reality is always in a process of becoming.[70] Because of the genetic character of structures, we must always perform a *"découpage"* (carving out) of a portion of changing reality for the sake of study. The totality we carve out is always a "meaningful one" in that it presents the efforts of human beings, on the basis of past experiences, to deal with their current and future realities.

"Significative" or "meaningful" is therefore not simply a subjective category, and Goldmann would later substitute the word "functionality" for the sake of precision.[71] All human actions make sense as part of the adaptation process, whether or not the given individuals are immediately aware of it. Every historical event must, as such, pose the question of history as a whole; inversely "every attempt to understand global history not as a sum of more or less remarkable events but as the history of the necessary significative behavior of the men who make it implies ... the study of the conscious and intellectual life of men and the study of the correlations between the transformations they have undergone and the transformations of other sectors of social life."[72]

By delineating a significative structure, we may elucidate the object of study in terms of both its subjective and objective reality. It is here that Goldmann enters the *Verstehen* debate with a position sharply at odds with Dilthey and close to the spirit of Weber. Dilthey claimed that we "understand" in the human sciences through reexperiencing, while we "explain" in the natural sciences. Goldmann, too, will sharply distinguish the human from the natural sciences, but with a very different argument. (Goldmann was unwilling to recognize that both he himself, in his use of the notion of worldview, and Lukács owed to Dilthey a substantial intellectual debt.)[73]

In the human sciences, argues Goldmann, we must both "understand" and "explain." One explains a significative structure by situating it within structures that encompass it (that is, the world around it). One understands it in terms of the purposeful structure of its internal dynamic and coherence. As both processes are necessary for adequate work, Goldmann rejects any opposition between "objective" explanation (*explication*) and interpretive or hermeneutic understanding (*comprehension*); such an opposition inevitably loses sight of the totality. Explanation and understanding must be employed as part of the same endeavor, and represent two moments of *découpage* of the object investigated:

> The constitutive structures of human behavior are not, in reality ... universal data [*données*], but social facts born of past genesis, and in the process of undergoing transformations which outline a future evolution. Now, on the level of the *découpage* of the object, the internal dynamism of the struc-

ture is not only the result of its own dynamic contradictions, but of a much larger structure which embraces it and which tends itself towards its own equilibrium.[74]

In short, all social phenomena must be envisioned as relative totalities in constant transformation, to be grasped with reference to their internal coherence and structure, and the manner in which they fit into and help constitute the surrounding world.

"What we look for in human facts," writes Goldmann in *The Human Sciences and Philosophy*, "is less their material reality"—their thing-ness—"than their *human signification* which, obviously, cannot be known outside of their material reality."[75] On this basis, Goldmann distinguishes the human and natural sciences. The natural sciences examine facts outside of men and women; that is, they look at facts "in their sensible reality" as external entities, not as consciously realized actions.[76] There is in the natural sciences a clear separation between the subject and the object of knowledge. We assume that solving a problem in physics or chemistry will yield the same results in Moscow, Nairobi, or Paris, and that the social or class background of the scientist is irrelevant. Inasmuch as a value is entailed, it is simply that of human mastery of nature.[77] Simply put, in the natural sciences, the results of research should be totally disinterested.

While humans are, of course, part of nature, Goldmann reiterates over and again that in the human sciences, in contrast to the natural sciences, the subject of knowledge is always part of the object of knowledge. This is because social life is "a process made by men, created by men, having a human meaning. It is precisely a question of understanding ... ourselves."[78] Goldmann consequently rejects the positivist opposition of subject to object; significantly, he does not, in consequence, embrace Lukács's notion of subject-object identity. Consistent with his claim that knowledge emerges from an oscillation, not a merging, between the whole and the parts, an oscillation that never gives us a whole picture, he proposes that one must speak of "partial identity" of subject and object in the human sciences. The positivist position is not just epistemologically false, but impossible, because we are part of the object studied. But we are not the entire object. Lukács's pursuit of total identity represented to Goldmann a formulation too extreme, too idealistic, and too Hegelian. It was linked, Goldmann came to argue, to the untenable political posture of *History and Class Consciousness*, which saw the proletariat as the identical subject-object of history. Partial identity, on the other hand, is a variable identity, in need of constant clarification during research because of changing circumstances.

Positivism, therefore, represents for Goldmann the opposite of Lukács's position. Positivism dichotomizes the relations between subject and object and between fact and value; it imagines that the individual can step out of historically conditioned *mental structures*, which are, after all, not immediately evident. He writes:

> Facts and values, freedom and necessity, are not autonomous entities and still less are they opposites; they are elements mutually conditioned within one and the same totality [*des elements se conditionnant mutuellment d'une seule et même totalité*]. Reality structures values and values transform reality, social conditions determine action and the thought of men which, in turn, transform social conditions. Man is thus neither free nor determined. He is a product of history from within which, as a product of anterior conditions, he must act and assure the future march of humanity towards freedom.[79]

No epistemology is possible outside human praxis, and there is no human praxis independent of the external world. Consciousness is a fundamental part of reality, but only a part of it.

If such is Goldmann's conceptualization of the problem of social knowledge, if such is his view of the situation in which researchers unavoidably find themselves, and if human behavior is "a *total* reality" (*un fait* total), then to separate "its 'material' and 'spiritual' aspects can only in the best of cases, be provisory abstractions always implying great dangers for knowledge."[80] The notion of partial identity compels us to recognize that "objectivity" in the human sciences is not the same thing as it is in the natural sciences.

It should be noted, however, that Goldmann's theory is vulnerable from an angle he seems not to have suspected; he never challenges positivist notions of natural science. Thomas Kuhn, Paul Feyerabend, and Gaston Bachelard all presented theories of scientific change posing questions about method in natural science parallel to those Goldmann raises in the human sciences. Goldmann does not, outside of a brief discussion of Koyré and Lenoble, substantively address himself to such matters. He specifically characterizes scientific technique and its results as cumulative.[81]

This problem aside, we can see why Goldmann contends that though Durkheim wanted to study "social facts" as external "things," he failed to ask if this is epistemologically possible in the first place:

> In the human sciences it is . . . not sufficient, as Durkheim believed it to be, to apply the Cartesian method, placing acquired truths in doubt and being entirely open to all facts, because the researcher generally approaches facts with categories and non-conscious, implicit preconceptions which close off to him the road of objective understanding in advance.[82]

Any inquiry *"only poses certain questions of reality and chooses the facts in light of those questions."*[83] Valuation is inherent in such a process.

Given Goldmann's argument, Weber's position may be seen as intermediary between positivism and dialectical thinking. To Weber's claim that valuations must intervene in selecting what we study, but do not have to—indeed, should not—impose themselves on the study itself, Goldmann responds that if values effect selection, there is no reason why they should not continue to interject themselves as we direct ourselves to the various questions raised within research. The question must inevitably go beyond posing a topic of research to the posing of questions within the inquiry. Only a dialectical method based on oscillation between the whole and the parts permits this. *History and Class Consciousness* stands out, in Goldmann's mind, as the dialectical alternative to Weber and Durkheim, albeit an alternative in need of modification through the concept of partial identity. Thus, while consciousness can never be identical with reality as a whole—there can be no identical subject-object—what we must learn from Lukács is that the "knowledge a being has of itself is not science but consciousness."[84]

Hence not only is it incorrect to identify the methods and purposes of natural and human sciences, it becomes questionable whether we should call the human sciences "sciences" at all, save in the broad sense of the German word *Wissenschaft*. In a paper written not long after *The Human Sciences and Philosophy*, Goldmann addressed this point directly. He differentiated "thought," "science," and "consciousness" in the theory of knowledge in a way that follows the Hegelian mode of "rising" from the abstract to the concrete. Logic and mathematics, he writes, are "thought" and proceed in a "hypothetico-deductive" way in which noncontradiction and rigor are the criteria; this "thought" is abstract and "indifferent" to all relations to the real and to action. Physics and chemistry, on the other hand, are the domain of "science" and proceed in an "nomothetico-experimental" fashion in search of general laws to which the real and action conform. Here, the criteria of truth are those of "thought," but with the important addition of empirical and experimental confirmation. Finally, there is historical and social "consciousness," which corresponds to the dialectic. Its criteria of truth include those of "thought" and "science"—logical noncontradiction, conformity with mathematical truths, empirical data—but a third criterion is added: "action and the transformation of the very laws which structure the real in the sense of the realization of values." Here there is partial identity of subject and object, and facts and values are inseparable. "It is the only form of knowledge," he writes, "which bears on *concrete* and *individualized* objects, localized in time and space...." These three forms of knowledge—thought, science, consciousness—are presented by Goldmann as a totality, that is, not as "separate sectors, but as particularly pregnant structures—tied by multiple intermediary structures—in a continuing series of forms of thought which graduate [s'échelonnent] from mathematical abstraction through dialectical knowledge of concrete individualized reality."[85]

At this point, at least three linked questions need to be posed to Goldmann's method: (1) What practical conclusions may be drawn from a theory of partial identity? (2) Since all research implies valuation, must we not make a value judgment among the different valuations, and if so, on what basis? (3) Finally, do we not need a considerably more elaborate grasp of the subject of knowledge in order to claim that valuations *must* always intrude throughout research?

To the first query Goldmann has the following response. Partial identity cannot but imply valuations. Since we cannot oppose the subject to the object of knowledge, and since we therefore cannot separate facts and values, we ought not to make false pretenses to the type of objectivity and neutrality in the human sciences that we would in the natural sciences. Rather than seeking to rid our work of valuations, which is virtually impossible, we should render our biases explicit. Our readers will therefore be better able to criticize our effort, which, like all research, will one day be surpassed. This being the case, the criterion for judging different valuations becomes all-important. Valuations informing research may be conceived on various levels. Goldmann claims, for instance, "[W]ere I to write a book tomorrow on the French revolution, I would write it with concepts that were in part elaborated by the French revolution itself. The French revolution would thus intervene in this book, which will be on the men who made the revolution."[86] For Goldmann, we study history in the first place in order to search for "values and ends." He goes so far as to posit—as he implied in the "Buffet Dialogue"—the idea of "community" as a "universal value."[87] We look for relevant human meaning in any study of human facts, in social or political life, and the "value" of the human community underlies any such research.

Why, however, should one valuation be accepted rather than another, including the "universal value" of community? In the first place, as a Marxist, Goldmann must believe that certain positions enable us to understand the world better than others do. He suggests that when a valuation is capable, in a manner others are not, of clarifying both other valuations and itself as social phenomena by revealing their infrastructure through an "immanent critical principle," such a valuation is superior. By way of example, he cites the relation between Marx's thought and that of Saint-Simon as depicted by the sociologist Georges Gurvitch. Gurvitch emphasized Saint-Simon's influence on Marx, and in this Goldmann, of course, concurred. However, Goldmann insists that stating this "influence" does not properly clarify what is important in the relation between the two thinkers. Saint-Simon, he acknowledges, provided a trenchant account of the struggles between the bourgeoisie and the nobility during the ancien régime. In doing so, however, he wrote from the perspective of the Third Estate, and therefore could not conceptualize the emerging antagonism between the bourgeoisie and the proletariat. In fact, Saint-Simon, the mentor of Comte's positivism, assumed an identity of interests between the bourgeoisie and the proletariat. Once the captains of industry held power, all the miseries of the proletarians would be eradicated as proper organization and technique spread throughout society. Marx, on the other hand, conceived class struggle as the key to understanding history and therefore recognized the conflict between bourgeois and proletarian. Ergo, on a "purely scientific level," Marx's theoretical perspective had to be superior. Marx is therefore also capable of giving us an understanding of Saint-Simonism, both as an ideology and as a social and historical "fact," which Saint-Simon cannot do for Marxism. Furthermore, Marx enables us to understand Marxism as the ideology of the proletariat.[88]

Goldmann's assertion of Marxism as a valuation engendering better understanding of reality, philosophers, and writers than that gained from Saint-Simonism may well be true; his proof, however, is not satisfactory and is close to a tautological argument. If one accepts Marx's historical theory, the period of the French Revolution does engender at least a partial, temporary convergence of bourgeois and proletarian interests in the displacement of feudal relations of production by capitalism. But Goldmann assumes the basic Marxist tenet of class struggle between the bourgeoisie and the proletariat, and then proceeds to claim that Saint-Simon's failure to recognize this shows Marxism's superiority. If the premise of class struggle is rejected, the argument cannot stand. Ironically, Goldmann himself would eventually question the Marxist view of the working class. But this would come after the formulation of the argument we have been presenting, which was in a book published in 1952. Here he has only provided a proof from within Marxism: Marxism recognizes the centrality of class struggle, and Saint-Simon does not; accordingly, Marxism is superior.

III

When he rejected the traditional Marxist conception of the proletariat, Goldmann also had to reject Lukács's vision of its role as the subject of history. It is in his conceptualization of the subject of knowledge—be it a philosopher or the proletariat—that Goldmann made perhaps his

most important contribution to social thought. His goal was to explain
the nature of "collective" behavior and the structure of consciousness
of social groups. He argued that almost no human actions, be they defined historically, politically, culturally, or otherwise, are solely those
of individuals, of Robinson Crusoes. Everyday life demonstrates that
it is the "We"—not the "I" or the "you and I"—that acts.[89] In one of his
favorite illustrations, he queries how to understand three men moving
a piano. If we imagine that one of the movers "has the status of subject
. . . this would mean that we assimilated the two others to the piano as
the objects of thought and action of the first."[90] To comprehend the
action without severing the tie between the consciousness of the three
men and their activity—in other words, to keep sight of the whole and
the parts of the action at once—is to see the three men as a collective
subject of action with the piano as its object. The three have a common
structure of consciousness, a common set of intrasubjective relations, in
performing the task. They are what Goldmann calls a "transindividual
subject."

Goldmann employs the word "transindividual" rather than "collective" in order to emphasize his aversion to the notion of a "group
mind." "Transindividual" directs us toward an ensemble of individuals with common mental structures, which develop as they adapt to an
environment on the basis of a similar situation. Consciousness per se,
Goldmann reiterated frequently, resides solely in individuals; collective consciousness, far from signifying a group mind, must be understood solely as "an operational notion which designates an ensemble
of individual consciousnesses and their structured interrelations. As
early as his "Dialogue dans une Buffet en Gare," Goldmann had expressed his dislike for using the word "Mind" (*Esprit*) on the grounds
that it generated too many misunderstandings—"willful or involun-
tary." More important, in the "Dialogue," G. declares that "true mind
[*le vrai esprit*] is only one aspect of action, as true action is only one
aspect of this human reality that could be called mind [*cette realité humaine qu'on pourrait appeler esprit*]."[91]

In the development of his notion of the transindividual subject
Goldmann was surely indebted to Lask's Kantian argument that while
the sole "reality" is empirical reality, it is also the "substratum" of
"transempirical values" (that is, of transindividuality); to Max Adler's
concept of the social a priori; and possibly to "transpersonal" themes
in the work of Mounier.[92] It is the theoretical elements that Goldmann
takes and synthesizes from Piaget and Lukács that give his own theory
its particular coherence. Goldmann seeks to extend Piaget's genetic
epistemology beyond the individual per se and use it to comprehend
group and class behavior. Men and women develop sets of mental

structures as a result of a common social background, and this serves as a foundation for what they can, do, and should project as life possibilities. This foundation, of course, is always in processes of structuration and destructuration. Goldmann writes:

> Just as the psychologist must conceive the psychic life of the individual as a complex effort towards a unitary and difficult to establish equilibrium [*un effort complexe vers un équilibre unitaire et difficile à établir*] between the subject and his milieu, the sociologist must study every group as an effort to find a unitary and coherent response to the common problems of all the members of the group in relation to their [common] social and natural milieu.
>
> It goes without saying that for each of these individuals, these problems are only a—more or less important—sector of his consciousness, the totality of which is tied to all the other groups to which he belongs.[93]

Now this does not—at least in principle—become a matter of what we might call transindividual reductionism. An individual, according to Goldmann, is part of many differently composed transindividual subjects and has, as a result, numerous sets of mental structures, which are of varying consequence and which may modify each other. Some transindividual subjects may have but temporary reality (such as three men moving a piano) while others may be long-lasting (such as families, social groups, and classes).[94] In history, cultural creation, political behavior, or even in the scholarly community engaged in the human sciences, action is never singular. Rather, it is the product of, or derived or elaborated from, a transindividual subject whose mental structures in genesis provide the social a priori basic categories for praxis and consciousness. Thus proletarians will have a certain set of mental structures qua proletarians on account of their place in the relations of production (which is, of course, not their sole set of mental structures).

Finally, a researcher in the human sciences does not exist outside transindividual subjects, but within them. This is to say no more than that the researcher exists in history and in society. The only alternative would be for the researcher to be the Robinson Crusoe construct Marx criticizes in the *Grundrisse* (in which case it would be difficult to discern just why, or, indeed, how, the researcher could become interested in the human sciences). It is Goldmann's argument that once we accept the thesis of the transindividual subject, we must accept that in the human sciences, the subject is always within the object of thought (human society), and the object is within the subject's mental structures. The conclusion is, again, that there is a partial identity of subject and object. For the human sciences, "science is at least partially affected by social consciousness. When dealing with the human sciences, cultural creation, historical action, one cannot separate science from consciousness, theory from practice, and judgments of fact from judgments of value."[95] It is within this systematic framework that we can finally place Goldmann's assertion that there is no such thing as a human scientist who eliminates value judgments from his work (and can see why Goldmann would see little value in the tortured neo-Kantian distinction between "validity" and "valuation"). The human scientist who eliminates value judgments is one without mental structures—that is, one who does not live within society and history. There is no such human scientist. Goldmann's point takes on more force because he claims that mental structures are neither conscious nor unconscious; they are "nonconscious."

By "nonconscious" he means "implicit." Goldmann illustrates through a physiological example. When I run, I am not conscious of the biological basis of my action. I do not decide step by step where my feet are to land or to make my heart quicken. Likewise, on "the psychical level" I am not conscious of the structure of formal logic, although I use it regularly in a variety of ways.[96] Nonconscious mental structures are a necessary component of an individual's membership in any social group(s); indeed, they are an unavoidable product of life in society. As such, mental structures necessarily have a social character. They are not comparable to the "unconscious" in the Freudian sense, and Goldmann repeatedly distinguished his theory from Freudianism. Lukács was sharply hostile to assimilating consciousness to psychology (a theme both neo-Kantian and Husserelian), but Goldmann's point is somewhat different, since he distinguishes libidinal from cognitive psychological questions. Goldmann's psychological questions are Piagetian, not Freudian. Thus he insists on sharply distinguishing mental structures from the individual unconscious that is the psychoanalyst's object of study:

> When it is a question of psychoanalysis and the libido, it is necessary to render conscious a repressed desire, to surmount an obstacle: the censor [*la censure*]. Thanks to Freud and the psychoanalysts we know the specific difficulties presented by the operation. But when it is a question of non-conscious psychic structures, the passage to consciousness does not know obstacles of this genre. They have a status in some ways analogous to that of nervous and muscular structures of which we are not conscious, although we easily become so if they are properly studied and made known. This can be done without having to surmount any censor.[97]

Elsewhere Goldmann defines the nonconscious as "the intellectual, affective, imaginary, and practical *structures* of individual consciousness. The nonconscious is a creation of transindividual subjects and has, on the psychical plane, a status analogous to nervous or muscular structures on the physiological plane."[98] In other words, it is a matter of social consciousness and learning rather than a Freudian struggle with the id or superego. Goldmann thus presents the individual on two levels, the libidinal and the transindividual. On the first level, the subject is strictly individual, whereas on the second he or she is part of a transindividual subject that goes beyond, yet resides in, him or her. Freud, in Goldmann's view, was unable to get past the libidinal level.

Goldmann's distinction between mental structures as an object of study and the Freudian unconscious has a basic validity in that the questions raised by Piaget and Goldmann are those of cognitive development in contrast to the Freudian concern with libidinal development. However, the relation between cognitive and libidinal development, in either individuals or groups, is not adequately posed or examined by Goldmann, and Freud's view of the psyche is not at all reducible in its entirety to a "libidinal" individualism. Goldmann, consequently, fails to explicate the relations between the two levels of the individual's development, libidinal and transindividual. He ignores, for instance, Freud's effort in *Group Psychology and the Analysis of the Ego* to delineate the relation between the individual conscious and the group. Freud saw individuals as seeking fulfillment of libidinal needs in a group whose leader steps into the shoes, as it were, of their superegos and whose individual members consequently identify their egos with those of the other group members. On the purely structural level of the interaction between the individual and the group, Freud's analysis might have been a fruitful source for developing a theory of the socially relevant relations between cognitive and libidinal development. Goldmann also never addressed the efforts of such theorists as Marcuse, Adorno or Reich to integrate Marxist and Freudian insights. Consequently, however original is the notion of the transindividual subject on the level of cognitive theory, Goldmann fails to elaborate it in regard to these other theories, and this represents a serious lacuna in his theory.

In any event, Goldmann argued that transindividual subjects must be the locus of research in the human sciences and that this locus characterizes Marxist thought.[99] The principle that we must oscillate between the whole and the parts here becomes the imperative to oscillate between a transindividual totality and its parts (that is, its members) in research. While Goldmann does not pursue this on the libidinal level, he does, by means of the transindividual subject, respond to an essential lacuna in Lukács's theory, the cognitive gap between empirical and ascribed consciousness. By means of the transindividual subject, it is possible to describe, as Lukács failed to, the structured relation between class and individual empirical consciousnesses. The notion of socially created mental structures in historical genesis and the notion of the transindividual subject account for what Goldmann characterized as the dual nature of our thought as deductive and empirical. Goldmann accomplishes this as follows.

1. By positing common mental structures among a group of individuals from a common background, Goldmann posits intrasubjectivity as a defining characteristic of human groups. Mental structuration is the constitutive factor in this intrasubjectivity, while structures reside solely in individuals as individuals. For Goldmann, as a Marxist, one's place in the relations of production is the most important component of that background. He agrees with Lukács that the imputation of class consciousness is fundamental to all research and to all cultural and political analysis. He avers that "possible consciousness" is "the principal instrument of scientific thought *in the human sciences*."[100] In the human sciences—again, as opposed to the natural sciences—our concern is with actors who consciously seek to realize goals they set for themselves. This is why "the possible" is so essential in understanding and explaining them. While for individuals in a given group, transindividuality may be said to exist in their consciousnesses as single, empirical instantiations of a mental stucturation shared with others, we may posit what a fully elaborated consciousness of the transindividual subject might be. Indeed, Goldmann assumes that just as Kantian man strives beyond *Verstand* towards *Vernunft*, empirical individuals tend towards possible consciousness.

The fully elaborated possible consciousness of the individual members of a transindividual subject is the self-consciousness they would achieve if they fully grasped themselves and their place in the world as a function of that one transindividuality. Such self-consciousness would, as such, be the content of that transindividual subject's consciousness as an identical subject-object. To delineate this, a researcher would have to provide a more or less pure elaboration. Such an ideal-type would have to be free from the intrusion of other mental structures of other transindividual subjects also residing in the individual. If, however, we take this off the level of research and speak instead of members of a transindividual subject in their quotidian existence—for example, the empirical human beings who comprise a class—this is impossible. They may ever tend towards that possible consciousness, as Kantian man strives towards totality, but there can be only partial identity of subject and object. Therefore, Goldmann writes, "Real consciousness is the result of multiple obstacles and deviations that the different factors of empirical reality pose and submit for realization by . . . possible consciousness. . . . [Real consciousness] results from limitations and deviations that class consciousness submits to from the actions of different social groups, natural and cosmic factors."[101]

This is the basis on which Goldmann would have us comprehend the relations between real (empirical) consciousness of members of a social group/class and "possible" or "imputed" consciousness. In "La Réification," Goldmann, in a strikingly original classification, divides the modern workers' movement into two categories. The first is exemplified by Blanquism, anarchism, and Trotskyism. These are working-class versions of idealist subjectivism that underestimate objective conditions and overestimate man. The second is exemplified by Stalinism, reformism, and economism. These are forms of objectivist materialism that underestimate man and overestimate objective conditions. Goldmann contends that what is required is a dialectical alternative to these two, and maintains that Lukács's theory of class consciousness supplies it.[102] Yet if our analysis is correct, Lukács lacked a crucial element—the cognitive theory that Goldmann found in Piaget. This permitted Goldmann to construct the dialectic missing in Lukács, although it led to basic questions about Marxist and Lukácsian prognoses and hopes, which Goldmann himself eventually recognized.

2. Hegel and Marx were correct, Goldmann argues, to criticize Kant's opposition of sensible content to pure forms of mind (the categories). However, Hegel and Marx were unable to explain the dual nature—deductive and empirical—of thought.[103] Goldmann's explanation of this duality rests on the concept of evolving mental structures. Here, again, we may see his theory as the culmination of a process that begins with Kant's transcendental subjectivity and journeys via Hegel's *Geist*, Marx, Adler, Lukács, and Piaget to the transindividual subject. Kant, whose philosophy Goldmann called "resolutely non-genetic," posited a priori categories that enable us to order our experiences. Hegel, Marx, and Lukács posited a historical, and therefore genetic, subject-object relation with the world around us. Adler fashioned his notion of a priori sociability on the basis of the possibility of communication. When synthesized with Piaget's genetic epistemology, all these elements become a new totality in Goldmann's hands—the theory of the transindividual subject. Our thought is deductive and empirical because of the interrelation between possible consciousness and the mental structures in genesis that tend toward it and give us the infrastructure for grasping reality and possibilities in the world. The relation between ourselves, as empirical, social beings with mental structures, and the empirical world around us is a subject-object relation, or more specifically, one of objects and transindividual subjects. In the *hiatus irrationalis* between Lukács's ascribed class consciousness and the empirical consciousness of proletarians—a hiatus that we have

suggested Lukács could fill only with the party—Goldmann places the theory of the transindividual subject.

Weber argued that Marxist laws were in fact ideal-types.[104] We have suggested something similar about Lukács's notion of imputed consciousness. But it was at once an "ideal" *and* to be realized—thereby necessarily losing its ideal character. If this is so, one can turn Hegel's critique of Kant against Lukács himself by means of the concept of the transindividual subject. For Lukács, it is by jumping into the revolutionary process that the proletariat learns to swim. His underlying assumption, based on his ascription of class consciousness, is that the swimmer could not possibly drown, and that there is only one direction in which the swimmer will swim—and with only a single stroke. In contrast, the idea of transindividual subjects conceived as ensembles of individuals with historically created structurating and destructurating mental structures, assimilating and accommodating to the world, provides a cognitive theory that takes into account social, historical, and plausibly individual vicissitudes. (I will return to the specific—and important—political implications of this in a later chapter.)

The idea of the transindividual subject is not restricted to class. Consequently, one must ask what specificity class has for Goldmann, especially since he insisted on his fidelity to Marx. In *The Human Sciences and Philosophy*, Goldmann points to three major structural elements of social life. The first is the special impact of economics on society. This, however, must be construed broadly and not be reduced to economic determinism:

> Man is a conscious and living being placed in a world of religious, intellectual, political, social, and economic realities and so on. He is acted upon by all that happens in this world and he, in turn, acts on it [*Il sumit l'action globale de ce monde et réagit à son tour, sur lui*]. This is precisely what we call a dialectical relation. And it is precisely because—save in very rare exceptions—individual consciousness does not have any watertight compartments exempt from the influences of the rest of his personality, that he will always constitute a *more or less* coherent unity. This suffices to explain and confirm the privileged position of the impact of economic factors in contemporary and past history. Men are so constituted that in order to love, think, or believe, they must live, feed, and clothe themselves. These domains of human activity can, no doubt, have little impact on thought and other activities *provided that the needs to which they correspond are satisfied and largely assured, and that men devote a relatively small part of their total activity to them.* Now for the great majority of men this is still not the case.[105]

In other words, given proper social and economic organization in a society of adequate material abundance, the impact of the economy would recede. Also, we may, consequently, regard economics as a structure at the very foundation of all societies, but the various moments of the social whole must still be conceived as having at least potentially relative autonomy as parts within a totality; in other words, it is not a simplistic base-superstructure paradigm as in crude versions of Marxism.

The second structural element Goldmann points to is what he calls the predominant historical function of class. One's class, he says, is defined in most materialist studies on the basis of two interdependent but not identical factors: function in production and social relations with other classes. He adds another element, which is, for him, a decisive one: "From the end of antiquity through our times *social classes constitute the infrastructure of worldviews.*"[106] It is with his concept of worldview that Goldmann reinvents Lukács's notion of ascribed consciousness as a methodological and political tool that takes the insights of Piaget's epistemology into account and links consciousness to social being. In *The Hidden God*, Goldmann characterized a worldview as "that ensemble of aspirations, sentiments and ideas, which unites the members of a group (most often a social class) and which opposes them to others."[107]

This does not mean that all members of a group are cognizant of the worldview in actuality. Individuals have such worldviews in potential when they are members of the same transindividual subject, that is, when they have common mental structures consequent to developing out of a similar situation. When fully elaborated, this vision represents what Goldmann calls the maximum possible consciousness of a given type of transindividual subject.[108] Here, Goldmann specifically identifies the worldview of a social group with its collective, that is, transindividual, consciousness. A worldview, like class consciousness, becomes the self-knowledge of the transindividual subject in question. Goldmann—at least the Goldmann who, until the late 1950s, more or less accepted Marxist assumptions about the future role of the proletariat—argues that a class is a privileged subject because it instantiates an entire perspective about the relations between human beings and their world. Goldmann states this—or, rather, as a Marxist, he assumes the global nature of class—rather than proving it. In *The Hidden God*, Goldmann writes:

All groups based on common economic interests do not . . . constitute social classes. These interests must be oriented towards a total transformation [*une transformation globale*] of the social structure (or in the case of reactionary classes towards maintaining the current overall structure). They must therefore express themselves on an ideological level through a vision of contemporary man as a whole, of his qualities and faults. This vision must express an ideal of humanity's future, of what relations between man and his fellow men and with the universe must be.[109]

It is only social classes, Goldmann argues, that have truly specific "scales of value" (*les échelles de valeur*). They each aspire to

> *a different ideal* of social *organization* as a whole [un idéal différent d'organ-isation *sociale d'ensemble*], so that collaborations between classes can only be a temporary and provisory means to attain essentially different ends. Classes may be temporarily in accord on the political level so that a common adversary can be fought, for example. Each class, however, still aspires to a different ideal of man and social organization.[110]

This does not mean, however, that different worldviews correspond to each different class throughout history. The very structure of the human personality, argued Goldmann, indicates that the number of human responses to varying historical situations is limited. Visions are thus reborn in different circumstances and at different times, each, one might say, with a historically designed wardrobe. Goldmann repeatedly asserts the need for a "scientific" typology of worldviews, but never himself fully specified the full range of visions; rather, he devoted his energy to exploring two or three of them in detail. Indeed, in one essay we find him pointing to four major visions—the Enlightenment vision (which includes both rationalism and empiricism), the tragic, the romantic, and the dialectical—while in other places he speaks of the tragic vision as a transition from the rationalist to the dialectical vision, or subsumes rationalism under "classicism" (he even speaks of Platonism as a worldview).[111] Nonetheless, he consistently claimed that worldviews are generated from differing socioeconomic and historical conditions. The "tragic vision" is discovered by Goldmann in Pascal, Kant, and in the young Lukács, for examples.

To recapitulate, Goldmann's conceptualization of the place of class rests the assertion that as physical survival is prerequisite to all human endeavor, economics, broadly conceived, must be considered a privileged aspect of social life. The historical role of class makes one's class the most important of social groups to which one can belong. Class must, however, be seen as a totality; it must be grasped not solely in terms of its material basis, but in its role as the infrastructure for the elaboration of forms of consciousness. The worldview provides the perspective of the world ideally projected by the class. That perspective is at odds with those projected by other classes.

Like "totality," "worldview" and "maximum possible conscious-ness" have a dual usage for Goldmann; they are a matter of both method and aspiration. They represent *"historical* and *social* facts" ascribed to a group as well as tools for analyzing that group's role, cultural aspirations, and historical potentials.[112] Goldmann cites Lenin's program on the peasant question in 1917 to illustrate the application of maximum possible consciousness in analyzing political situations. "In social and political action," he writes, "it is evident that alliances between social classes can only be made on the basis of a minimum program *corresponding to the maximum possible consciousness of the least advanced class."*[113] Lenin, to the chagrin of Marxists who looked toward the collectivization of agriculture and the abolition of private property in land ownership as the only possible socialist agrarian program, endorsed the redistribution of land to the peasantry at a critical moment in the revolutionary process. This shift was not because he had embraced small plot ownership as an agricultural model. Rather, he recognized that the collectivization of agriculture was beyond the grasp of the possible consciousness of the peasantry and the proletariat needed the peasants for the victory of the revolution. The proletariat's global worldview—a universalizing one, since it is by Marxist definition the universal class—projected a future society owned by all; this was not the purview of the greatest possible consciousness of the peasants.

Goldmann will later raise similar questions about the proletariat's possible consciousness. Before examining this, however, we turn to the application of Goldmann's theory in his major studies in the sociology of culture, and we will then place his entire enterprise in relation to the two major intellectual currents—both of which have their Marxist versions—of postwar France, existentialism and structuralism.

6

From a Hidden God to the Human Condition

GOLDMANN COMPLETED *The Hidden God* in 1955, and *Towards a Sociology of the Novel* (hereafter *Novel*) was published in 1964. In the interim, Goldmann began to classify his method formally as "genetic structuralism" and to employ the term "transindividual subject," although both notions were conceptually present, or in gestation, in almost all of his earlier work. The use of "genetic structuralism" was partly a response to the rise of structuralism in French thought, but Goldmann's formulation owes its origins to Lukács and Piaget. It was also during this decade that Goldmann reoriented his intellectual project, and started to articulate his political ideas more explicitly.

The first chapter of *The Hidden God* announces that it is part of "an overall philosophical enterprise."[1] The Zurich edition of *Kant* was subtitled "*Studien zur Geschichte der Dialektik*"; the first French edition (1948) lists opposite the title page a series of studies by the same author—of Pascal, Goethe, and Marx—"to appear." Hegel, curiously, is not listed. The project was never realized beyond *The Hidden God*. With its publication, Goldmann turned from French classicism to modern culture, specifically, to the sociology of the novel. This brought a methodological shift; he focused now not on worldviews but on homologies.

The change in object engendered a change in the tools of knowledge. It was a necessary move for a dialectician. At the same time, however, he seems to have begun to falter. In the 1960s, his writings became increasingly repetitious. This was surely linked to an increasing unease with Marxist prognoses; his wager seemed jeopardized, save for a brief moment in May 1968. Perhaps this is why, at the decade's end, Goldmann returned to the history of dialectical thought in the form of a study of *Lukács et Heidegger*.

I

In *The Hidden God*, Goldmann defined group consciousness as "the tendency common to the sentiments, aspirations, and thoughts of the members of a class, a tendency developed specifically as a result of an economic and social situation which engenders an activity whose subject is the real or potential community constituted by the social class [*qui engendre une activité dont le sujet est la communauté, réele ou virtuelle, constitutée par la class sociale*]."[2] When scholars delineate the worldview or maximum possible consciousness of a class or group, they do so recognizing that not all—indeed, probably few—members of the class or group have attained such consciousness. It is not "a given empirical reality" but a conceptual extrapolation for research.[3]

What Goldmann detected in great cultural works is the coherent elaboration on the conceptual or literary plane of the worldview of the social class or group—the transindividual subject—from which the author comes; or rather, within which the author's primary mental structures developed. The transindividual subject, not the solitary author, is the subject of cultural creation; it is the mental structures of the transindividual subject that the author shares and elaborates. Thus Pascal, philosophically, and Racine, nonconceptually, elaborate in their works the tragic worldview, which Goldmann will link to Jansenism and the noblesse de robe in seventeenth-century France. Pascal, the philosopher, confronts the concept of death, while Racine, the playwright, presents to us Phèdre dying. The author's achievement lies not in a singular cultural and creative quest or accomplishment, but in attaining "a completely integrated and coherent view" of what a given transindividual subject is and can be. The successful work of cultural creation elaborates the maximum possible consciousness of the group.[4] Worldviews are psychic expressions of a group's adaptation to its environment, and Goldmann insists that the number of coherent responses a group can have are limited "by the very structure of the human personality. . . ." There are rebirths of the same vision in different guises at different historical junctures.[5] Sometimes the vision can be revolutionary, sometimes reactionary. "Platonism" can be applied to both Plato and Augustine. In *The Hidden God*, Goldmann identifies four worldviews: rationalist, empiricist, tragic, and dialectical.[6]

In brief, Goldmann proposes that a work be grasped in terms of a worldview and the mental structures of a social group, and not by means of the author's biography. The libidinal individual and the transindividual subject are at opposite ends of a line. Most forms of individual consciousness and behavior take place between the two poles. Cultural creation, however, represents for Goldmann the transindividual qua transindividual—at least great cultural creation does. A given text must be viewed as expressive of a greater whole, a worldview, which elaborates the mental structures of a group. In studying Pascal and Racine, Goldmann oscillates between the whole and the parts; he goes from the work of Pascal and Racine to a worldview, and back to the work. He goes from the vision to the group/

class of which it is expressive, and then back to the vision. Each level, through this dialectical movement, elucidates and illuminates the others and the whole. He will "understand" the internal coherence of the individual whole, and then, in turn, "explain" this relative totality by inserting it within a larger whole, which encompasses it. Goldmann will explain the tragic vision in Pascal and Racine's works by Jansenism, a significative structure, which must in turn be understood. He will explain Jansenism by understanding the noblesse de robe as a significative structure. His analysis of the noblesse de robe enables him to grasp the expression of a tragic worldview at a given historical time and place in the writings of Pascal and Racine.

A brief outline of the complex period Goldmann studied will facilitate our discussion of his arguments. In the early seventeenth century, the modern French state was consolidating in the aftermath of bitter religious wars; it pursued a "convulsive progression," as Perry Anderson puts it, towards absolutism. An essential feature was the struggle between monarchs and the parlements. The latter were legal institutions that served as courts and appeals tribunals responsible, among other things, for registering and promulgating royal decrees. The king's charges could be effectively rejected by a refusal to register them.[7] The rise of French absolutism—indeed, the modern French state—was conditioned on asserting the crown's prerogatives over the powers of local nobility and clergy and feudal institutions, such as the parlements.

Such was the historical backdrop when Jansenism appeared. This religious movement, reminiscent of Puritanism in various ways, owed its name to the bishop of Ypres (Spanish Netherlands), Cornelius Jansen. His 1,300-page *Cornelii Jansenii Episcopi Iprensis Augustinus*, published in 1640 (two years after his death), reasserted the Augustinian notions of irresistible and unmerited grace, and chastised both Jesuits and Protestants. Such Augustinian revivalism, however, unsettled both the French crown and the Catholic church, though for different reasons. In the previous century, the Reformation and the religious wars pitted Catholics against Protestants, whose theological starting point was Augustinianism. The Huguenots, for all practical purposes, had a state within the French state until they were effectively crushed by the crown in the late 1620s. The Vatican knew that the French circles in which Jansenism found favor were Gallican in orientation, that is, they supported the medieval French tradition of resisting ultramontanism (centralizing of Vatican power).

Jansenism's emergence in France was due to the popularization of Jansen's ideas by a former schoolmate, Jean du Vergier de Hauranne. As abbot of St.-Cyran, he was responsible for the nuns at the convent of Port-Royale des Champs—among them Pascal's sister, Jacqueline—and this became the center of the movement. He gathered a number of *solitaires* around him, and gained support among the Gallican clergy, the *parlementaires*, and especially the noblesse de robe. The latter, of Third Estate origins, staffed the parlements and were dependent on their judicial offices, in contrast to the Second Estate's hereditary *noblesse de race* (nobles of "race") and *noblesse d'épée* (nobles bound for military careers).[8] After his arrest (by Richelieu) and death in prison in 1643, the leadership of Jansenism came to Antoine Arnauld, scion of a distinguished legal family and brother of Mére Angélique, who became the prioress at Port Royale.

The Estates-General had not met since 1614, and the Parlement of Paris was seeking to fortify itself in the face of growing royal power. Jansenism gained great strength within the *Tiers* (the Third Estate), especially among the noblesse de robe. Here, then, was a religious movement with a social base that placed the interests of the Church Universal before those of the consolidating absolutist state. A clash was unavoidable. The Jansenists were determined, but no less so than the crown. Louis XIII, as a recent biographer notes, "presided over more political executions than any other ruler in French history."[9]

Thus a wide variety of political and religious issues blurred into one another. The Jansenists eventually would be repressed by both secular and religious authorities. The abbot of St.-Cyran was imprisoned by the crown in 1637, and the *Augustinus* was condemned by the Inquisition in 1641. Its seven (later reduced to five) major points—mostly focusing on grace—were condemned in a papal bull in 1653. The Sorbonne followed suit in 1656, and also censured Arnauld after the publication of his *De la Fréquente Communion* (1643). This led to a fervent counterattack on Jesuit casuistry in the *Provincial Letters* of Pascal, who had undergone a mystical conversion in 1654. Louis XIV later ordered his book burned.

In 1660 intensified persecution sent many Jansenists into hiding. As one historian notes, referring to the nuns at Port-Royale, "[T]here is probably no parallel in monastic history to their resistance on a doctrinal issue to their bishop, to the clergy of their own national church, to their king, and to the pope. . . ."[10] However, in 1669 the Jansenists acceded to an uneasy "Peace of the Church," according to which they accepted the Church's "right" to demand their renunciation of offensive propositions in the *Augustinus*, while insisting on the "fact" that such principles were not to be found there.

Goldmann linked Jansenism to the tragic worldview. This vision's three chief elements composed a structured whole, to which he dedicated successive chapters in *The Hidden God*: visions of God, of the world, and of man. Sophocles was, of course, the father of tragedy, Goldmann commented, for in his work, the Gods "are no longer united to men in the same cosmic totality."[11] But Goldmann's orientation toward tragedy came first and foremost from Lukács, and especially from "The Metaphysics of Tragedy." Here, "the Gods of reality, of history" are declared "obstinate and rash."[12] Lukács's basic categories are, in fact, ahistorical, and the questions consuming him concerned death and human limits. Consequently, as we have already seen, he opposed "authentic life" to everyday empirical existence (or "life" with a small "l"). The former is always "unreal," always "impossible," in the midst of the latter.[13] In graphic language, Lukács declares that:

> Life is an anarchy of light and dark; nothing is ever completely fulfilled in life, nothing ever quite ends; new confusing voices always mingle with the chorus of those who have been heard before. . . . To live is to live something through to the end: but *life* means that nothing is ever fully and completely lived through to the end. Life is the most unreal and unliving of all conceivable existences; one can only describe it negatively—by saying that something always happens to disturb and intercept the flow.[14]

In ordinary life our experience of ourselves is "peripheral." But in tragedy, there is a "threshold of life-possibility" and "pure-experience of self" in this great moment.[15] Indeed, "the deepest longing for human existence is the metaphysical root of tragedy: the longing of man for self-hood, the longing to transform the narrow peak of his existence into a wide plane with the path of his life widening across it, and his meaning into a daily reality."[16]

For Lukács, "forms," particularly literary forms, come of human efforts to impose coherence on the world. The "miracle" of tragedy is "a form-creating one." Its essence is a struggle for "self-hood," which is a struggle "to create the All," in which the tragic self is "shattered against the All."[17] Lukács's use of "form" is one key to Goldmann's use of "structure" and "worldview." In a 1964 presentation on Lukács and Kierkegaard, Goldmann explained, "For Lukács . . . man searches to give coherent expression to fundamental attitudes that he can take facing life and the universe. When they attain an almost rigorous level of coherence, these expressions become forms, privileged realities for human life in general and for cultural creation in particular."[18] Lukács declares, "Form is the highest judge of life. Form-giving is a judging force, an ethic; there is a value-judgment in everything that has been given form."[19] It is because Lukács sees forms as atemporal that his worldview is tragic. Absent a notion of form in history—and thus a concept of historical change—human possibility vanishes. "Authentic life" is tragic because it is a conscious quest for an unattainable absolute, just as Kant, in Goldmann's interpretation, is a tragic figure, who posits, in his "Dialectic", an inevitable and necessarily unsuccessful striving beyond *Verstand* toward *Vernunft*, and thereby the inability to reach totality.

The consequence of the tragic quest is solitude; everyday existence is valueless. Lukács writes, "A drama is a play about man and his fate—a play in which God is the spectator. He is a spectator and no more; his words and gestures never mingle with the words and gestures of the players. His eyes rest on them; that is all."[20] Totality is present, yet hidden—hence the tragedy of human life as presented on stage. Man must live in the chaos of the empirical world, yet he is not of it, would he be authentic. He strives for authenticity through his attempts to give form to his existence and thereby to create meaning. Yet his failure is inevitable, and so he struggles ceaselessly and unsuccessfully in the face of his own limits, and especially his ultimate limit, death.

In all tragic visions Goldmann detects "a profound crisis among men and the social and cosmic world [*le monde sociale et cosmique*]."[21] It takes on particular acuity in Pascal's *Pensées*. Here, the tragic mind emerges in struggle with *Deus absconditus* in seventeenth-century France; it faces the world at a watershed, the metamorphosis of the medieval into the modern universe. In Descartes and Pascal—the former educated by Jesuits, the latter a Jansenist—Goldmann discerns two coherent responses to this transformation. In Descartes, an emerging bourgeois (rationalist) vision is articulated by a man of science who is also concerned to prove God's existence; Pascal, too, is a man of science, but he eventually rejects the world. His vision will be tragic; he will wager on God's existence, becoming, according to Goldmann, the first modern dialectical thinker as well. For Goldmann, Descartes's "reason" is Hegel's *Verstand*, and it is Pascal who opens the way to *Vernunft*.[22]

Two worldviews are counterposed. What does Cartesianism represent? We have seen how Goldmann, using Lask's distinctions, underlines the similarities, rather than the traditional differences, between rationalism and empiricism. In contrast to the dialectical circle of the whole and the parts, both rationalism and empiricism envision the world in terms of parts adding to a sum and knowledge as a linear procedure, each stage of knowledge building on a previous stage.[23] The premises of rationalism and empiricism, for Goldmann, are ultimately atomistic and individualistic. They thereby provide a one-sided picture of reality. They are expressive of the emergence of a particular class and its worldview. The bourgeoisie aspires to remake the world and thought about the world in its own image—that of "free" market competitors. Goldmann did not see this as purely negative since it brought with it the ideas of individualism, freedom, and equality before the law.[24] In the feudal world, each person was status bound in a hierarchical totality; Christianity provided its ideological halo. In contrast, competition on a free market demanded equality before the law of competitors requiring contracts among themselves. The starting point is the individual and *his* rights, not the good, or the perspective, of the whole. While the individual vanished into the medieval whole, the notion of community dissipates in the bourgeois world, displaced by the individual, an atom among atoms.

It is this that produced both rationalism and empiricism, according to Goldmann:

> Reflecting the atomistic structure of bourgeois society in its ascendent period, rationalism and empiricism saw in the universe an assemblage of autonomous parts and, consequently, each is understood in itself, independent of its relations with others. Inversely, the universe only appeared understandable by an analysis which first of all breaks down its parts in order to reconstruct it. Descartes's clear and distinct ideas, sense-perception for the empiricists, Fichte's Ego—these are all so many absolute starting points of individualist thought.[25]

In thought, as in the realms of history and politics, Goldmann's goal is a dialectical transcendence. The medieval world, with its all-embracing corporate system and all-encompassing worldview, is negated by bourgeois society, to be negated—or so Goldmann wagered—by the socialist community and the self-conscious social individual. From an undifferentiated whole, we move to a world of parts, and finally arrive back at a whole, which is now a unity of diversity.[26]

In *The Hidden God*, Goldmann's particular focus is on the contrast between Descartes's rationalism and Pascal's tragic worldview. Behind the contrast between Pascal and Descartes will be two other contrasts: between dialectical and "scientistic" thought and between socialist community and reified capitalism. Pascal's tragic vision appeared when philosophical rationalism and its attendant mechanistic attitudes were displacing Aristotelianism and Thomism. Notions of "community" and the "universe" were replaced by notions of the "isolated individual" and "infinite space." Goldmann quotes a letter by Descartes to Princess Elizabeth of Bohemia:

> God has so established the order of things and has fastened men together so tightly in society, that even if every man were to be preoccupied only with himself, with no charity towards others, he would still, in the ordinary course of events, be working on their behalf in everything that lay within

his power, provided that he acted with prudence, and, especially if he lived in a century in which morals and customs [*les moeurs*] had not been corrupted.[27]

Ultimately, says Goldmann, God has no function in such a universe.

In the preface to *The Hidden God*, Goldmann remarks that Hegel's discussion of "The Ethical Order" in *Phenomenology of Spirit* particularly shaped his argument. "Ethical order," *Sittlichkeit*, is usually rendered into English as "ethical life." It is Hegel's term for participation in a community of values and customs. He contrasted the all-encompassing community he took the Greek polis to have been with the separation of public and private spheres characteristic of Christianity—with its demand to render unto Caesar and heaven their separate dues—and the bourgeois world. Immediately before Hegel's discussion of *Sittlichkeit* is an important section on "Virtue and the Way of the World." Its preoccupation is most likely pietism, and one cannot say if Pascal and the Jansenists of Port-Royale were also in his mind. However, they were surely in Goldmann's when he reread Hegel.

"Virtue and the Way of the World" is part of a discussion of forms of "the actualization of rational self-consciousness through its own activity."[28] Hegel aims to demonstrate how individuality presupposes *Sittlichkeit*. He does so by examining three relations between individuality and social life. First he offers a critique of hedonism as an unsatisfying pursuit of enjoyment. Then he turns to "the law of the heart," by which he means romantic assertions of the sovereignty of feeling. These are repugnant to the rational apostle of the Concept (*der Begriff*); they result in self-indulgence, a "heart-throb for the welfare of humanity . . . [which] passes into the ravings of self-conceit." In this "derangement," the heart "or the individuality of consciousness" mistakes itself for universality.[29] A consciousness "which sets up the law of *its* heart meets with resistance from others, because it contradicts the equally *individual* laws of their hearts." The effect is a Hobbesian *bellum omnium contra omnes*. This, says Hegel, is "the way of the world." It is a "play" of "nullifying individualities" rather than universality. "Virtue" enters Hegel's story as an attempt to transcend and "nullify" the individuality of the law of the heart and the conflicting egoisms that come of it.[30] The problems posed by Hegel's discussion of this "virtue" inform Goldmann's discussion of the Jansenist withdrawal from the world.

Hegel's "virtuous man" is disillusioned, having recognized his failure to transform the world. He finds himself in the world and outside it. He pompously proclaims his own disinterested virtue, and turns from the way of the world, denouncing individualism and egoism on behalf of the universal. "The virtuous consciousness . . . enters into conflict with the 'way of the world,' as if this were something opposed to the good."[31] But he is classified by Hegel, with considerable sarcasm, as a "knight of virtue." By distancing himself from the world, he embraces a "universal," which obliterates particulars; he embraces a narcissistic nihilism, making of his virtuous declamations naught but gestures. It is "a sham-fight," which even he cannot "take seriously" for absent the world, his "virtue" would not have arisen in the first place. And if he is separate from the world, his virtue has no use. Denunciation of the way of the world is empty, and virtue, ultimately, "is conquered by the 'way of the world.'"[32] He cannot escape. One immediately sees the parallel with Pascal, Racine, and the Jansenists; Goldmann, however, will see tragedy where Hegel sees "knights of virtue"; Goldmann will see Pascal and Racine trapped between Augustine's City of God and City of Man.

Earlier in the *Phenomenology*, following the famous Master-Slave dialectic, Hegel presents Stoicism, Skepticism, and the "unhappy consciousness" as three attempts to retrieve independence in a frustrating world. The Stoic recognizes the futility of trying to escape the world and seeks freedom through withdrawal into thought; that which cannot be controlled is rejected. Skepticism denies that anything can be known or said intelligibly about the world. Objective reality is not rejected; it is denied to the point of incoherence. The consequence is the emergence of "the consciousness of self as a dual-natured merely contradictory being,"[33] a bifurcated being who has an empirical self on one hand and an eternal self on the other. This ruptured being is the self of Christianity. While Hegel does not speak of Augustine, Augustine's vision of two cities, of God and of Man, jumps out of the page. It is a vision of human reality outside the world and within it, on which the eyes of *Deus absconditus* are cast. It is the tragic vision of Pascal's world as Goldmann presents it to us.

Here is the foundation of Goldmann's claim that Pascal and Kant represent steps to dialectical thought. The "*unhappy, inwardly disrupted* consciousness," according to Hegel, "*is* gazing of one self-consciousness into another, and itself *is* both, and the unity of both is its essential nature. But it is not yet explicitly aware that this is its essential nature or that it is the unity of both."[34] The unity of both, the empirical and the eternal, would make this world holy, make the City of Man into the City of God; it would create Kant's kingdom of ends, turn Lukács's life into Life—in short, it would win the wager of Goldmann's secular religion by historical action. It would create the "authentic human community" in which the individual is realized in and through community—the individual-in-community, rather than the isolated egotist or a being subsumed by a universal. In short, the way is pointed to the

individual conceived as the concrete individual, not an abstract particular. Indeed, this is the entire point of Hegel's discussion of "Virtue
and the Way of the World": individual life finds its meaning within the
social world. There is no virtue in the individual's pretending to be
outside the world, for, in Hegel's words, "the movement of individuality is the reality of the universal."[35] In the chapter on *Sittlichkeit*, Hegel
presents a celebrated analysis of *Antigone*. Goldmann remarks that the
"fundamental meaning" of Sophoclean tragedy is "the affirmation of
an insurmountable rupture between man, or more precisely, certain
privileged men, and the human and divine world." For Oedipus,
Creon, and Antigone, "the world has become confused and obscure,
the gods are no longer united in the same cosmic totality, subject to the
same fatalities of destiny, the same demands for equilibrium and mod-
eration."[36] It is an ambiguous—indeed "unbearable"—universe for
man, because the gods are separated from him, have become his master and make contradictory demands of him.

For Hegel, the ancient Greek polis represented an ideal, though immature, stage in human development. In the polis, says Hegel, "Spirit
is the *ethical life* of a nation in so far as it is the *immediate truth*,—the
individual that is a world."[37] By "immediate truth," Hegel means that
Sittlichkeit is not mediated; it is not grasped conceptually. The individual is not self-reflective and is one with the community, which composes the truly universal.[38] Hegel presents a contradiction between
"human" and "divine" law. Human law is that of human practice, established by state and custom. It pertains to the individual in relation
to the community—to a particular community; while it appears universal, it is parochial. Divine law, on the other hand, is truly universal.
Its province is not the individual in relation to this or that state, but the
individual per se.[39] It is "the simple and immediate essence of the ethical sphere." The family, says Hegel, maintains the divine law as "the
natural ethical community," and is thus in conflict with the *Sittlichkeit*
of the community.[40] In Sophocles' tragedy, Antigone is bound by irreconcilable obligations, by two sets of laws. In decreeing a proper burial
for Eteocles, who defended Thebes, but not for Polyneices, who attacked the city, her uncle, Creon, as regent, embraces *Sittlichkeit*, human law, *raison d'état*. Antigone defies him, and thus Thebes, in the
name of family loyalty and divine law. For this Creon condemns her;
to do otherwise would jeopardize the authority of the community:

> Since it sees right only on one side and wrong on the other, that conscious-
> ness which belongs to the divine law sees in the other side only the violence
> of human caprice while that which holds to human law sees in the other
> only the self-will and disobedience of the individual who insists on being
> his own authority. For the commands of government have a universal pub-

lic meaning open to the light of day; the will of the other law, however, is locked up in the darkness of the nether regions, and in its outer existence manifests as the will of an isolated individual which, as contradicting the first, is a wanton outrage.[41]

Hitherto Antigone identified with the community (and its *Sittlichkeit*) in an unreflective and immediate way; now, she has, in the name of divine law, been differentiated from it. The consequences are the crises she suffers, and those her uncle faces as Theban regent. It is the family, the repository of divine law, that inters the dead. Death itself is natural, but the deceased, if unburied, is prey to the ravages of nature. Yet proper burial makes the departed one with the community again; this is precisely what Creon cannot permit for Polyneices.[42]

Now how does all this—the situation of Antigone, the conflict between divine and human law—shed light on Goldmann's exposition of the tragic vision in Pascal and Racine? For Goldmann, the "tragic mind" in seventeenth-century France recognizes the validity of the burgeoning new sciences, but refuses to accept them as the only valid world. Like Antigone, irreconcilable laws demand all of the tragic mind; like Kant, the tragic mind strives for the impossible, strives to transcend *Verstand* to *Vernunft*. The resultant vision is transitory for it is in history and history changes, while the perspective and categories of tragedy are ahistorical; they cannot posit a new, future historical community. Rationalism accepts atomized man, and the vanishing of community. These, tragic man recognizes and refuses. Rationalists saw proof of God's greatness in the notion of infinite space; Pascal finds this notion incompatible with God's existence, for it makes isolated atoms the criteria of all things. God has no function and morality no ultimate foundation in such a world. Seventeenth-century rationalism discovered infinite geometric space. But "*God no longer speaks in the space of rational science*," argues Goldmann, for in order to elaborate this notion, "man must renounce every truly ethical norm."[43] Genuine norms require something beyond atoms—be that something God or the "authentic human community." The rationalist's God has no personal reality and only secures original order in the world. Pascal's God, says Goldmann, is always present and absent at once: "*Vere tu es Deus absconditus.*" It is a deity that imposes Lukács's question: how can man live with a hidden God's eyes on him, an Almighty who aids him nought and who—unlike the God of the rationalists—grants man's powers, especially reason, no validity, all while this *Deus absconditus* makes demands of man and judges him.[44]

Goldmann, echoing Piaget, tells us that forms of consciousness represent temporary balances between individuals and the world. When the balance is upset, they become preoccupied with their relation to the outside world. The tragic vision of God is thus inevitably linked to the tragic view of the world. The world is conceived as all and nothing at once, just as God is present and absent. Thus God's presence makes this world meaningless, yet his absence makes it human reality. Tragic man refuses the world from within it; he must say both yes and no to it at once. The next step is vital: "Pascal drew the ultimate conclusions of Jansenist thought" when he extended doubt and the wager beyond the question of individual salvation to the very existence of God.[45] By saying both yes and no, by embracing paradox, Pascal became both a tragic philosopher and the creator of modern dialectical thinking. He refuses the world from within it, and then questions God's existence, proceeding to wager on it. Tragic man is in quest of totality, faced with a world that is all and nothing at once. Real value can lie only in the transcendent, in a God who is hidden from man—for whom the world remains the only reality. Pascal recognizes that with all his scientific knowledge, he can never "prove" God's existence, and can therefore only wager on it. God plays the spectator, Lukács told us, but a spectator whose eyes rest upon us. Goldmann like Lukács, asks: Can human beings live under these circumstances?

Unable to prove a hidden God's existence, Pascal responds to earthly ambiguity by refusing compromise, demanding absolute values, and wagering. Goldmann underscores "Pensée 353," in which Pascal says, "One does not demonstrate one's greatness by being at one extreme, but by touching both at once, and by filling the space in between."[46] This "yes and no" is no search for a mean. It is, on the contrary, the insistence on both at once, a demand for clarity within necessary ambiguity. The tragic being must explain his existence by means of paradox. Authentic values, Goldmann says, are "synonymous with totality." Compromise is unacceptable, but tragic man knows totality is inaccessible. His thinking points, therefore, to dialectics for dialectical thinking recognizes reconciliation of opposites. Tragic man demands absolute values, while simultaneously being an extreme realist:

> But it is precisely this *yes and no*, both equally complete and absolute (the *yes* as an *intramundane* demand for the realization of values, the *no* as the refusal of an *essentially inadequate* world *in which values cannot be realized*) which permit tragic consciousness to obtain a hitherto unachieved degree of precision and highly advanced objectivity on the level of knowledge.[47]

If God is absent and present, so too is man in a world to which he says both yes and no, one in which he demands absolute but unattainable values. Thus "placed between a silent world and a hidden God who never speaks, tragic man has no rigorous or grounded theoretical basis on which to affirm the existence of the divine." It can but be a "certainty of the heart" (Pascal's phrase), a wager on an unprovable possibility.[48] Pascal addresses this hidden God in the only way he can—through a monologue. And this is precisely what the *Pensées* are, says Goldmann, for if the *Pensées* were addressed to human beings, the possibility of human community would be supposed and tragedy transcended.

Goldmann seeks to delineate the key structures of the tragic vision in the *Pensées*. He goes from the text to the vision, and the obvious next step is to place that vision within the context of a social group or class, which he must then place in the broader whole composing the socioeconomic and historical worlds. All these are, in Goldmann's mind, necessarily linked, each a part of the circle of the whole and the parts; yet each must also be viewed as an "individual whole" with a "whole structural meaning," or, rather, a "significative structure." This concept, we know, derives from Piaget's genetic epistemology and Lukács's notion of imputed consciousness. It is essential to Goldmann's claim that facts about human beings compose meaningful patterns to be explained and understood. Human "facts" are to be grasped through their place within an ensemble of relations representing human efforts to adapt to the world. Understanding is a matter of comprehending internal coherence; we have just seen how Goldmann delineates a coherent vision of the world—a tragic one. The next step will be to place it within the broader meaningful totalities.

The worldview in Pascal's *Pensées* and Racine's theater comes of Jansenism and articulates the "maximum possible consciousness" of a social group in profound crisis. The noblesse de robe was composed of legal officers and administrators of Third Estate origin who were ennobled by the centralizing monarchy as a foil against the rest of the nobility. The birth of Jansenism in French legal and religious circles in 1637–1638 coincided with the consolidation of absolutism and the displacement of the noblesse de robe by a corps of royal bureaucrats.

Goldmann presents three stages of absolutism's evolution, following Edourd Maugis's massive *Histoire du Parlement de Paris de l'avènement des rois Valois à la mort d'Henri IV*. The first stage was the feudal monarchy. The king's power was mostly indirect during this period. The sovereign began to ally himself with the Third Estate. The second stage was centralization. The crown, backed by the Third Estate and legal and administrative officers, extended its dominion over the feudal nobility. The final stage was consolidation. The king's power became independent of the nobles, the Third Estate, and the parlements (the *Cours souveraines*) and was exercised through the *corps de commis-*

saires. In contrast to the *officiers,* who purchased and could bequeath their positions, *commissaires* served at the king's pleasure. During the reigns of Henri IV, Louis XIII, and Louis XIV, the royal bureaucracy was consolidated. Before the religious wars, recruitment came largely from the *Cours souverines.* But following Henri IV, recruitment of *commissaires* was extended beyond *officiers,* who by the end of the sixteenth century had come to imagine themselves essential to royal administration but now had to face the emergence of—and their displacement by—a new bureaucracy.

Goldmann argues that this final stage was made possible by "a balance of power" between classes, particularly between the nobility and the Third Estate. This equilibrium permitted the monarchy to establish itself as an absolute apparatus above classes.[49] Goldmann's argument follows that of Engels in *The Origins of the Family, Private Property and the State.* Absolutism, Marx's colleague argued, was an historical interregnum during which the modern state began to take shape as class conflict between the feudal lords and the emerging bourgeoisie reached a (temporary) stalemate. A balance of class power permitted the absolutist state to rise above them, giving it the semblance of autonomy as arbitrator among the struggling social interests. This type of argument was also used by the Austro-Marxist leader Otto Bauer to explain the emergence of the first Austrian Republic after World War I and to justify initial social democratic participation in its regime. Austria's was no ordinary bourgeois republic, he argued, but one which arose consequent to a balance of class forces.[50]

The tragic vision, in Goldmann's analysis, is engendered by the fate of the noblesse de robe as the needs of the French state altered with changes in class relations, and the relations between class and state. Jansenism first appeared in the transition between Maugis's first and second stages, that is, when the monarchy, backed by the Third Estate and the legal/administrative officers, was ascending over the nobility. As centralization of royal dominion succeeded, Richelieu augmented the power of the *intendants,* provincial administrators beholden to the crown. But this threatened local parlements, bastions of the noblesse de robe, who had been one of the monarchy's weapons against the old nobility. As the limited monarchy was transformed into an absolute monarchy, a centralized governmental apparatus dependent upon the king was consolidated. In the seventeenth century, it rested on the *conseils* and intendants and was fashioned at the expense of the Third Estate, especially the officers, and the older nobility, all of whose interests were linked to the limited monarchy.[51] Having been used to weaken the old nobility under the limited monarchy, the noblesse de robe, like the Moldavian arendaşi of Goldmann's youth—indeed, like the Romanian Jewish community—found its role subverted by history.

Goldmann marshals evidence to demonstrate the formidable presence within Jansenism of individuals from the urban middle class and noblesse de robe. These included aristocrats angered by, but too weak to oppose, the monarchy's growing strength, and also *avocats*, officiers, and others linked to the parlements. And among them were Port-Royal's prominent champions like Arnauld, Pierre Nicole, and Pascal. Goldmann maintains that the relationship between Jansenism and the noblesse de robe typifies that between "between an ideological movement and the social group to which it corresponds."[52]

An ideology is not enunciated by all the members of the social group, but by ideologists, such as St.-Cyran; it spreads through "fellow-travelers," in this case, the elite within legal circles. While these circles came of the Third Estate, they were at the time of Jansenism's emergence relatively autonomous, according to Goldmann. Indeed, if they did not compose a social class "in the most rigorous sense of the word," they were something very close to it.[53] What prevented the officiers of the *ancien régime* from constituting a social class in "the full sense of the word" was their own functional and economic dependence on a monarchical state whose growth they resisted, both ideologically and politically. This was the paradoxical situation par excellence—it furnished "the infrastructure for the tragic paradox of *Phèdre* and of the *Pensées*"—for they were opposed to a regime that they could not seek to undo, let alone radically transform.[54] Henri IV's "Paulette," a degree that enabled hereditary transmission of their offices, intensified the bind (although the king could rescind this right at will). Consequently, the situation of the officiers and Jansenism were linked in that the officiers were antagonistic but bound to an absolute monarchy that offered no prospects of mollifying their situation and Jansenism's tragic ideology insisted upon "the *essential* vanity of the world" and that "salvation [*salut*]" was solely to be found "in seclusion and solitude."[55] And after rising for three decades, the prices of offices declined in the 1630s.

Goldmann summarizes with several contentions: the period during which Jansenism was born, 1637–1638, was one of particular tension between the officiers and the commissaires, a tension rooted in the conflicting processes leading to the rise of the absolutist state. Jansenism paralleled this rise, and in particular, that of the new bureaucracy; it was closely bound to those sectors of society most affected by it, the noblesse de robe and the legal and parlementaire circles. The monarchy's dependence on the conseils and intendants presupposed a balance of class powers between the nobility on one hand and the officiers and Third Estate, on the other.[56] The noblesse de robe initially weakened the nobility. This done, the king allied with the nobility, while keeping offices—those of both officers and commissaires—largely in the hands of the middle class to ensure balance. In brief, between 1620–1650, the officiers steadily lost ground to the commissaires; between 1635 and 1640, a crucial juncture, clashes between the crown and the parlements intensified, the intendant system consolidated, and the price of venal offices declined; among the officiers, discontented elites emerged. Two trends were discernible, one championing active opposition and one supporting a philosophy of withdrawal. The latter became Jansenism.

How does a worldview emerge within these historical developments? Goldmann argued that previous scholars, himself included, tended to homogenize Jansenism. This was not because of poor research, but because of improper *découpage* of the object. Proper *découpage* required proper use of the notion of worldview, which, in turn, would lead the researcher where it led Goldmann: to positing several major currents in Jansenism. Goldmann's *découpage* revealed that different worldviews were to be discerned in Pascal's *Provincial Letters* and the *Pensées*. Consequently, given his theory of the transindividual subject—he did not yet use the term—there had to be two subjects of cultural creation.

This led Goldmann to posit that there was not just one Jansenism, but a "moderate" faction identified with Antoine Arnauld ("Le Grand Arnauld"), and an "extremist" faction. After prodigious research, Goldmann confirmed his deduction by uncovering the leader of the extremists, Martin de Barcos, who had succeeded Duvergier de Hauranne as abbot of St.-Cyran following the latter's death in 1643. Barcos's influence had been great between 1643–1661, yet his name had vanished from history books. Having deduced the existence of such a person by delineating the two different worldviews, Goldmann began a hunt through European archives until he unearthed proof: the correspondence of Barcos himself in archives in the Hague and the Municipal Library of Troyes. (Goldmann published these letters in a companion volume to *The Hidden God*). The hitherto unknown (forgotten) Barcos, Goldmann professed, was "the Jansenist par excellence," the man in whom Jansen's key concepts cohered, despite his conflicts with the other "friends of Port-Royale."[57]

Goldmann was inconsistent in demarcating tendencies within Jansenism—at times he indicates four, but generally he uses a threefold distinction based on what Alasdair MacIntyre calls, quite properly, different responses to the problem of "an Augustinian God and a Cartesian world."[58] These three responses were as follows.

The nontragic moderate position was espoused by the original abbot of St.-Cyran, Arnauld, and his collaborator Pierre Nicole. Goldmann at one point calls their position "dramatic centralism."[59] Pascal's *Provincial Letters* is linked to this tendency, as are Racine's "social dramas," such as *Esther* and *Athalie*. What distinguishes this group is its response to the Vatican's assertion of its prerogatives, in particular, Rome's condemnation of the "Five Propositions" (originally seven) of the *Augustinus*. Arnauld and his followers sought their own compromise: "right" (*droit*) and "fact" (*fait*) would be separated. Condemnation of the offending propositions would be accepted—Rome's "right" to do so was legitimate. However, Arnauld denied that the propositions were in Jansen's text "in fact." Goldmann finds this similar to the Cartesian (and by implication positivist) opposition of values and facts. He argues that Arnauld's epistemology, in his *Des Vraies et fausses idées*, also bears important similarities to Cartesianism. It distinguishes "right" and "fact," and claims that truth is discovered by first finding the clearest and simplest things, as Descartes did in his rules of method. Such principles, maintains Goldmann, are in accord with *The Provincial Letters*, which reflect a nontragic, moderate Jansenism.[60] In them, Pascal stated that he accepted the Vatican's definition of heresy, but that Jansen's opus was innocent. Here, Pascal and Arnauld are Thomistic; for them the tasks of man are both in the world and in the Church. They were "centrists," and consequently Arnauld was willing to compromise with the established powers, especially after a (temporary) "Peace of the Church" in 1669 ended a decade of persecution of the Jansenists.[61]

The extremist position was set forth by Barcos, who believed that Arnauld was slipping from Augustinianism into Thomism; Barcos broke with Port-Royal after the "Peace of the Church." His position represented "the tragedy of unilateral refusal [of the world] and appeal to God."[62] Since he insisted on "all or nothing," he counseled withdrawal into the life of a *solitaire*, and opposed all activity in the world and in the Church.[63] Or, as MacIntyre puts it, whereas Arnauld sought to render unto Descartes and unto God that which was respectively theirs, Barcos insisted on the impossibility of serving Descartes and the Deity in a synthetic way.[64] Goldmann sees Racine's "near-tragedy" *Andromaque* and the tragedies of *Bérénice* and *Brittanicus* as expressive of the Barcos position.

The position of "tragic paradox" is the one Goldmann finds "most coherent"; it is found only in Pascal's *Pensées* and Racine's *Phèdre*. Historically, Goldmann argues, Pascal backed Arnauld until 1657, and then shifted to the extremist position articulated in the *Pensées*. This accounts for the two different worldviews in, respectively, the *Provincial*

Letters and the *Pensées*. Racine pursued the opposite direction, moving finally to Arnauld when the persecution of Jansenism intensified. This explains the differences among Racine's tragedies.

"Tragic paradox" is a posture of refusal of the world from within it, the position of Pascal's famous wager; "whenever Barcos says *no*, Pascal responds in a paradoxical manner *yes and no*." This raises the theological problem "of the paradoxical being *par excellence*," the righteous sinner (*juste pecheur*). The question of the righteous sinner represented "if not the essence, then at the very least the permanent temptation, the final limit of extremist Jansenism."[65] The Church branded this notion fundamental to Jansenist heresy. Arnauld condemned it as well. For him, the world was composed of the saved and the damned; the virtue of the former was due solely to unmerited grace, and the evil of the latter to original sin. As grace is God's to give and take, sin must be fought in this world. Barcos would have to reject this program, along with the notion of the righteous sinner. His God was radically hidden, so there was no possibility to know how his victory, and that of truth, could be attained in this abandoned world.[66] However, says Goldmann, it is precisely radicalized Jansenism that presupposes the ideas of the wager, refusal of the world from within the world, and the righteous sinner. It is these ideas that provide coherence to the *Pensées* and *Phèdre*; absent them, these works would be incomprehensible.

We can see why Goldmann perceives a "dialectical position" emerging from tragedy. Arnauld's yes is opposed to Barcos's no; they are transcended by the yes and no of Pascal and Racine. Arnauld leans towards Cartesianism and distinguishes between *le fait* and *le droit*; Barcos moves toward a totalism of *le droit*. "Tragic paradox" seeks a synthesis of "yes and no," of *le fait et le droit*, though it is never able to achieve it, for its categories are ahistorical. There is a symmetrical structure in Goldmann's contrast, following Lask, between analytic and emanatist logic. He implies that their opposition is transcended in dialectical logic, and in his own political vision of individual-in-community. The latter embodies transcendence of both medieval holism and capitalist atomism.

Goldmann, we know, argued that worldviews are limited in number, are responses to human circumstances, and are reinvented in different guises in different circumstances. His distinctions within Jansenism bear a striking resemblance to distinctions within Bolshevism in the 1920s and 1930s. Stalin's "socialism in one country" represented a compromise with the world; once it appeared that revolution was not on the international agenda, he accepted this *fait* while insisting that the USSR embodied Marxist orthodoxy. Fact and value were thus separated, as Arnauld's compromise with the Church distinguished *le fait* from *le droit*. Goldmann calls Arnauld and his followers "dramatic centralists"; Trotsky classified Stalin and his backers as the "bureaucratic center faction." Trotsky and the "Left opposition" refused the world on behalf of permanent revolution. Trotsky, it seems, was the Barcos of Bolshevism, insisting on "all or nothing," appealing directly to a hidden God—the international proletarian revolution. Goldmann, whose youthful intellect was nurtured in the secular religiosity of Ha-Shomer ha-Tsair, with its demand for ethical absolutism and its romantic vision of community, was clearly taken by Barcos/Trotsky. Yet as he rejected both opposition of subject to object, fact and value (the positions of Arnauld/Stalin) and their identity (the position of Barcos, Lukács, and Trotsky), and since Goldmann would argue for partial identity, so he, believer in the individual-in-community, would wager, as had Pascal, from within the world. He would simultaneously enunciate yes and no and eventually would champion "revolutionary-reformism."

In fact, in the 1960s, Goldmann often sketched a threefold classification of the history of Marxism. In it, both German social democratic reformism and Stalinism represented systems of compromise with reality. In contrast, Lukács (in *History and Class Consciousness*) and Rosa Luxemburg embodied radical refusals of capitalist society. Their positions, however, were formulated before Stalin and Hitler, and were based on absolute surety of the role of the working class in history. Luxemburg did not live to see the events of the 1930s and 1940s, but Lukács, who was defeated by Béla Kun in factional fights within the exiled Hungarian Communist Party in the 1920s, did and withdrew from active political life (at least until 1956). Goldmann also witnessed—and experienced—Stalinism and Hitlerism and the failure of the proletariat to play its ascribed role; he, therefore, can only wager, which is to say yes while admitting—being haunted by—the possibility of no. Goldmann repeatedly contended that he was a dialectician studying tragic thought and not a proponent of tragic thinking, yet here, again, we see that it is a dialectic of tragedy and hope that structures his thought. It is his own thinking that parallels the "position of tragic paradox" that he presents as Pascal's; Pascal is, for Goldmann, the first modern man, and modern man cannot have the absolute faith of medieval man.

For most intellectual historians, the first modern man is not the Jansenist Pascal, but the (Jesuit-educated) Descartes, for Descartes—mistakenly—believed he had reconciled his religious beliefs with his rationalism and scientific convictions. Not surprisingly, *The Hidden God* provoked a welter of criticism and debate when it appeared. Goldmann's Marxism was not the sole reason; his arguments were at odds not only with mainstream scholarship, but with most Marxist commentary on Pascal, including that of Lukács. In *The Destruction of Reason*, a history of modern German philosophy completed in early 1953 (two years before *The Hidden God*), Lukács makes passing remarks on Pascal, whom he sees as the father of modern irrationalism, a man "flinching from social and scientific progress." The claim is hardly surprising since this, Lukács's most reductionist, Stalinist work (and possibly his worst), simplistically bifurcates the history of all German thought into progressive and reactionary trends, with no middle ground. While Pascal may have recognized the dehumanizing consequences of capitalism, he was, according to Lukács, the exact opposite of what Goldmann later claimed him to be. The author of the *Pensées* "made an about-turn precisely where his great contemporaries went on in the direction of a dialectic."[67]

Pascal spoke to Goldmann and his times, but not to Lukács, and not to Henri Lefebvre, who wrote a book on Descartes in 1947 and two volumes on Pascal in 1949 and 1954.[68] Lefebvre was, like Lukács, a Communist Party member writing during the Cold War. Like Lukács, his initial prewar renown was due to his suggestive, unorthodox (Hegelian) reading of Marx. And again like Lukács, he was a vituperative intellectual pointman in the Communist assault on Sartre's existentialism and efforts to establish a "Third Force," neither communist nor capitalist, in postwar France. Pascal, through his influence on Kierkegaard, was regarded by Lukács as a predecessor of existentialism; Pascal's alienation, his paradoxes, his sense of internal conflict had little appeal for members of Stalinist parties, such as Lefebvre and Lukács. After all, Pascal could only remind them of their own compromises.

While Goldmann and Lefebvre were often on amicable terms— theirs might be called an equivocal friendship—their polemics on Pascal took on a certain ferocity; they clashed publicly at a seminar at the Centre d'Études Sociologiques and most famously in a 1956 debate at Royaument. Lefebvre's exit from the Communist Party came shortly afterwards, as did an intellectual autobiography, *La Somme et la reste*. In it Lefebvre commended Goldmann's "non-Stalinist independent Marxism," but impeached *The Hidden God* as "adventurous" and false.[69] In contrast to Goldmann's claim that the noblesse de robe was "almost" a class, Lefebvre argued that "[i]n the compromise between the nobility and the bourgeoisie in the seventeenth century, it constituted an intermediary social group, a transition between two dominant classes, a mediation between them, an articulation, a vehicle of compromise."[70] Lefebvre, employing dogmatic Marxist categories rather than the supple ones for which he was previously famous, resisted ascribing a separate or autonomous social status as a middle stratum to the noblesse de robe; it had to be part of a major class. If so, Goldmann's claim that Pascal was the first modern man as articulator of the tragic worldview becomes tenuous, for Goldmann himself maintained that worldviews were "global" and as such must be engendered by social classes. For Lefebvre, the noblesse de robe was more properly classified as a *noblesse de bourgeois*. The concept of "tragic vision" became, at least in this case, "dialectically uncertain." He found it preferable "to speak of 'tragic consciousness,' in seeking out contradictory historical situations and (conceptual) ideological elements which permit this consciousness to emerge and to be formulated."[71]

It is noteworthy that some of Lefebvre's ideas were shaped in discussions with Lukács in Budapest in 1950. In these talks, Lukács criticized what he called the simplistic theories of class in *History and Class Consciousness*. They failed to account for "fractions of class," imputing instead a consciousness to the working class as a whole, ignoring differentiations within it. (*The Destruction of Reason*, which he was then writing, shows little urge for similar nuances). Was the noblesse de robe not best understood as a fraction of a class, Lukács asked Lefebvre? And then, which class? The two philosophers did not resolve the matter in 1950, but in the second volume of *Pascal*, Lefebvre concluded that the "dominant trait" of the noblesse de bourgeois was "bourgeois"; its feudal characteristics were recessive. Yet the issue remained: "A structure of consciousness, a 'vision,' can be attributed to a group endowed with a strong internal cohesion: a class. Supposing one could attribute such a structure to classes, it is extremely difficult to attribute it to a faction of a class."[72]

In contrast, an argument strikingly similar to Goldmann's was presented twenty years before him by another Lukács admirer, Franz Borkenau. In *Der Übergang von feudalen zum bürgerlichen Weltbild*, Borkenau presented the mechanization of the *Weltbild* (picture of the world) of philosophy and the natural sciences as symmetrical to the emergence of the manufacturing mode of production beginning in the seventeenth century.[73] Late in the book, he proposes that the Hobbesian worldview—that of "homo homini lupis"—is "the essence" of human relations under capitalism, and criticizes Descartes's "rationalist-optimist" assimilation of the realities of capitalism. He then discusses Pascal as the most important "representative" of the bourgeois; on one hand, Pascal accepts a pessimistic Hobbesianism, but on the other he retains his fidelity to Catholicism (that is, Jansenism).

Capitalism, declares Borkenau, "always constitutes a problem for Catholicism."[74] In Pascal, we find a summation of previous bourgeois thought and the inauguration of dialectical thinking. But he strikes a lonely figure compared to other bourgeois thinkers; unlike them, he insisted that bourgeois contradictions were unresolvable and unavoidable. Pascal is a "negative rationalist" who fuses a universal rationalism with a Pyrrhonist pessimism. This pessimism derives from "the basic principles of bourgeois rationalism." He needs these to comprehend social and natural phenomena, although they "are unable to give an account of the bourgeois individual or society as a whole without being contradictory." Consequently, Pascal is "the inventor of negative dialectics," focused on the relation between the whole and the parts. And Borkenau, like Goldmann later, believes Pascal's ahistoricism prevents him from seeing that the world must be changed, not only interpreted.[75]

For Goldmann, dialectical thinking is the hallmark of modernity. The "great sin" it avoids "at all cost" is "taking a unilateral position, *yes* or *no*. . . . The only way to approach human reality . . . is to say *yes and no* and to unite the contrary extremes."[76] Descartes ultimately says yes to the world, believing he can reconcile philosophy and science with faith. For Goldmann, the essential differences between Descartes and Pascal are those between rationalist and dialectical epistemology. Pascal's critique of Descartes demands a new type of knowledge, one in which individual wholes are known dialectically.[77] Again, we find a homology between Goldmann's methodological and political concerns:

> By reducing physics to geometry and bodies to extension, Cartesianism, in the final analysis, divests them of all individual existence; similarly, souls— aside from their union with bodies—can be difficult to differentiate, since in thinking correctly, they must all think the same thing. Finally, there is no specific domain of life which is separated from extension. Thus individuality only has a place within Cartesianism by means of man, by the union of soul and body, and by the passions and errors they engender—by what subsequent rationalists found most difficult to accept in Descartes's work.[78]

In other words, a philosophy that fragments wholes into parts in order to understand them inevitably makes abstractions of those parts, as capitalism abstracts individual human beings. In the end, the starting point is dissolved; the individuals/parts lose concrete existence. In contrast,

> [t]he true recognition of the ontological reality of the individual begins with the philosophers who transcend individualism. Pascal, for whom "the self is hateful," takes the first step towards a theory of knowledge of individual facts, and it is Hegel and Marx, the theoreticians of the absolute spirit and history as expression of collective forces, who elaborate it definitively. They know as well that this mode of knowledge applies primarily not to physics but to biological and above all to human realities.[79]

In other words it is the dialectic of the whole and the parts that allows concrete conception of the "individual," as much in the domain of the human as in that of the natural sciences. Here Goldmann comes close to suggesting a dialectics of nature—although he frequently rejected the concept and, like Lukács, saw its classic statements in Engels's *Dialectic of Nature* and *Anti-Duhring* as mechanistic attempts to understand the physical universe.[80] His real point is this: as Hegel and Marx were distinguished from the Enlightenment and classical political economics by the priority of totality in their thinking, so, too, was Pascal distinguished from Descartes. It was in seeking to go beyond the Cartesian ego that Pascal opened a path to dialectical thinking. Cartesianism induces a mechanistic vision providing understanding of neither whole nor parts.

Thus Pascal says both yes and no to the world, and struggles endlessly between yes and no. He accepts the accomplishments of rationalism and empiricism, but deems them insufficient. Therefore he wagers and strives to supersede them and tragedy, as Kantian man ever unsuccessfully strives beyond *Verstand*, the realm of understanding and scientific knowledge, toward *Vernunft*, the noumenal realm. "Throughout his life," writes Goldmann, "Pascal sought what he, like all Christians, called God; a rationalist would call it truth and glory, and a socialist the ideal community. And they would all be right. . . . I prefer a word which *today* appears more neutral: *totality*."[81]

Goldmann's Pascal first sought "truth" in nature and science, supposing life separable into different hierarchies. Then he turned to the Church, hoping religion might triumph in this world, and thinking he might aid this victory. At the end of his life, Pascal realized that "true greatness" is recognition of human limits and uncertainties, in both the world of nature and that of the Church Militant. Hence the simultaneous necessity for faith and the "rational attitude" of the wager. This takes him beyond Barcos, who embraced faith without reason, and also beyond Augustine, by rediscovering the idea of tragedy; this is the heart of the *Pensées*.[82] Tragedy was necessitated by the very meaning of Pascal's life: his quest for God was the quest for totality. Goldmann, returning to the celebrated "Pensée 353," avows that "no one has better formulated the practical, concrete meaning of [the word totality] than Pascal . . .: 'One does not demonstrate one's greatness by being at one extreme, but by touching both at once, and by filling the space in between.'"[83]

Furthermore, the *Pensées* illustrate a fundamental principle of dialectical aesthetics: there is "a necessary and organic unity between a coherent content and an adequate form."[84] Since Pascal's work assumes a unity of opposites, its style must be fragmentary. Only in fragments can the paradoxes of man—a being in an all-or-nothing quest for absolute values—be validly expressed. But the fragments compose a coherent whole, for they express a worldview. Again, it is solely by a dialectic of whole and parts that Pascal's work is comprehensible. Yet Pascal's thought remains deficient, for it lacks a fundamental of dialectics—the dimension of history. It therefore lacks the dimension of the future. The wager is on an other-worldly totality. Only by historicizing the wager can a fully dialectical position be attained. It is with this in mind—while also mindful of the differences between them—that Goldmann compares Pascal's wager to Kant's practical postulate of God's existence. Both consider God's existence to be a theoretically unprovable assertion although a necessary one "for *non-theoretical reasons*."[85] Goldmann asserts that for Pascal certain, that is, non-paradoxical, proof of God is impossible. He disputes earlier scholarship for contending that since Pascal was a Christian, he was confident of God's existence; such scholarship concluded that the wager was not personal, but intended to persuade freethinkers. The wager fragment is, indeed, part of a dialogue with a nonbeliever, but Goldmann insists that it aims at "Everyman [*tout homme*], Pascal himself included."[86] While for Jansenism, God was a surety and individual salvation a hope, Pascal's wager extends the idea of hope to the very existence of God. Thereby Pascal's thought takes on a character profoundly different from that of Arnauld or Barcos—not because he turns from Jansenism, but because he pushes it to its "final consequences."[87] After Pascal, says Goldmann, such a wager is essential to any philosophy that makes human beings autonomous monads.

Goldmann's wager is essential to the tripartite nature of his work, the three parts composing a totality. For Hegel, philosophy, art, and religion are the three moments of absolute *Geist*, with philosophy as its crown. For Goldmann, philosophy is the conceptual expression of the greatest possible consciousness of historical transindividual subjects; literature or art are their imaginative expressions (Goldmann's second moment). The third moment for Goldmann is a historical wager that brings *Geist* to earth. For Hegel, *Geist* itself binds philosophy, religion, and art in its absolute self; for Goldmann, the bond is considerably less secure for it is a matter of objective possibility. Accordingly, Goldmann's humanism has an existential rather than an essentialist structure. Structuralist Marxists, such as Althusser, accused their humanist counterparts of seeing "the subject of history" in terms of a simplistic expressionist totality. However, Goldmann's subject is not an abstraction called humanity that realizes its inherent self; it is humanity conceived as transindividual subjects objectifying through various forms of creation and the creation of forms.

Goldmann's Racine complements his Pascal: one expresses the tragic vision imaginatively; the other, conceptually. Racine gives us Phèdre dying; Pascal, a concept of death. The sun in *Phèdre* is the hidden God of the *Pensées*. The three elements of the tragic vision are all to be found in Racine—the view of man, the world, and a hidden God. Racine's works are ultimately played out *"in a single instant*: when *man* becomes truly tragic by *the refusal* of the world and life."[88] But not all of Racine's plays are tragedies, according to Goldmann. In those that are, the conflicts are insoluble and linked to fatality and destiny. In those that are not tragedies but "dramas," resolution or irresolution of conflict is fortuitous. *Andromaque*, for example, is a tragic figure by refusing the alternatives before her and choosing death; the play, however, becomes a drama when she decides to marry Pyrrhus and commit suicide, for she thus attempts "to transform her *moral* victory into a *material* victory which will survive her."[89] *Brittanicus* and *Bérénice*, together with *Andromaque*, in Goldmann's interpretation, translate into literature the experience of the pre-1669 Jansenist *solitaires*. *Phèdre*, on the other hand, represents a fundamental change. It expresses the experience of Jansenism between 1669 and 1675, when persecution was revived. As persecution intensified, Racine moved closer to Arnauld and Nicole. But in *Phèdre*, his growing doubts about their compromise come forth—it weighs the scales of their struggle. Goldmann submits that *Phèdre* is "the tragedy of the hope of life in the world without concession, without choice and without compromise, and of the recognition that this hope has a *necessarily* illusory character."[90] *Andromaque* represents Barcos's position; *Iphigénie* represents Arnauld's compromise; and *Phèdre* represents Pascal's simultaneous yes and no.

II

In *The Hidden God*, the tragic vision elaborates the greatest possible consciousness of a social group in crisis at a particular historical juncture, that of absolutism's rise. In his 1964 *For a Sociology of the Novel*, Goldmann's focus and method shifted as a function of the object. The change in the object of inquiry—to the novel from seventeenth-century French classicism—compelled methodological reformulation, a turn from worldviews per se to structural homologies.[91] Concurrently, his politics were reformulated. His study of the history of the novel made problematic his previous insistence that the subject of cultural creation is transindividual. He sought an explanation in the transformative impact of phases of capitalism on the psyche. The novel is "the story of a quest [*recherche*] for authentic values in a degraded mode [*un mode degradé*], in a degraded society, a degradation which, in as much as it concerns the hero, manifests itself primarily by mediation [*la médiatisation*], the reduction of authentic values to the implicit level and their disappearance as manifest realities." It is "the transposition on the literary plane of daily life in individualist society born of production for the market."[92]

What Goldmann means by "degraded" is linked to his use of the notion of reification. As we have seen, Lukács argued that in commodity production for the capitalist market, exchange values increasingly appear as a "second nature," and relations among human beings become mystified, taking on a "phantom objectivity" so that they appear to be relations among things. There is, however, a historical force of resistance—the one commodity that can become self-conscious, the proletariat. Goldmann's discussion of reification, while leaning significantly on Lukács's, moves in important new directions, reaching conclusions further from Lukács than Goldmann would perhaps have liked to admit.

In Goldmann's "La Réification" (1958), his lengthiest treatment of the subject, he defines his object as "the *psychic* and *intellectual* consequences of the existence of production for the market in a purely capitalist society—liberal or monopolist—with little economic intervention by the state." He remarks immediately that this is an abstraction, for no such society ever existed; all capitalisms contain precapitalist survivals, and manifestations of future changes. In other words, Goldmann employs reification and capitalism as ideal-types in order to gauge empirical realities. He notes that, after all, thirty-five years separate his own study from *History and Class Consciousness*, and in that time, "the world has profoundly changed."[93]

Goldmann contends that the theory of reification gives coherence to Marxist texts on the relation between base and superstructure.[94] His dialectical conception of the interaction between consciousness and reality refuses any mechanical conceptualization of cultural, political, and spiritual superstructures as simple reflections of the (economic) base. However, he avows that in capitalism the superstructure does in fact increasingly become such a reflection as reification penetrates all dimensions of life. However, the consequent predominance of the economic and the "quantitative" aspects of life is—as in Arnauld—"a primacy of *fact* and *not right*." It is no law of human nature or thought. It is the product of a specific, historical society:

> In principle, religion, morality, art, literature are neither autonomous realities, independent of social life, nor simple reflexes of it. *In the capitalist world,* however, they tend to become so progressively, and to the extent that their

authenticity is *emptied out from within* thanks to the appearance of an *autonomous* economic whole [*ensemble*] which tends to seize on all manifestations of human life in an exclusive manner.[95]

In precapitalist societies some principle—traditionalist, religious, or rationalistic—governed production and distribution. With the rise of capitalism, exchange relations became dominant and universal, and the production and distribution of commodities became anarchic, regulated solely by the market as an *"external, objective, and blind reality."* Following Marx, Goldmann says that exchange value "transforms the relation between the labor necessary to produce a good and that good itself, into *the objective quality of the object."* The value does not become an actual quality, comparable, say, to color. Instead, a social process occurs "in which value appears *to the consciousness of men* as an objective quality of the commodity."[96] In the precapitalist "natural economy," things were produced for use value. In the market economy, where production is for exchange value, there is no necessary link between production and distribution. Consequently, the qualitative aspects of the objects are rendered implicit, for all commodities become comparable through a quantitative characteristic, exchange value. Use value only reappears when the commodity enters the private sphere of individual usage and leaves the realm of interhuman relations, which itself becomes a domain of the implicit.[97] People become increasingly closed to the qualitative aspects of the natural world, and "social relations among men, and spiritual and psychical realities" are "masked" as capitalism gives them "the appearance of natural attributes of things."[98] The price of a pair of shoes expresses a series of social relations among a cattle breeder, a tanner, the tanner's workers, a shoemaker, a wholesaler, a shoe merchant, and a consumer. But, says Goldmann, these disappear on the market, for one sees solely the price. This is

> the fundamental social phenomena of capitalist society: the transformation of qualitative human relations into *the quantitative attribute of inert things*, socially necessary labor employed to produce certain goods as *value* becomes manifested as *the objective quality of these goods*; reification, which afterwards extends itself progressively to the whole of human psychic life, in which, because of it, the abstract and the quantitative predominate over the concrete and the qualitative.[99]

As a result, people increasingly become passive, faced with a world of things subject to "blind laws," which appear to be independent of their wills, even though they created them. The consequences of reification extend to all realms of life, are multifarious, but are not all negative. Goldmann follows Weber in asserting that once capitalism develops to a certain level of complexity, the modern bureaucratic state, with its rationalized administration and formal procedures of justice, becomes necessary. This institutionalization of reified and abstract laws is a crucial step in eliminating arbitrary political power. Goldmann underlines that with the rise of the market society, the individual and humanism become possible—if only formally—and that this is positive. Echoing Hegel, he distinguishes three "separate and contradictory" sectors of the psychic life of individuals in capitalist society:

1. the private individual in the context of relations with the family and friends;
2. the professional individual engaging in economic activities; and
3. the citizen.

In private life, says Goldmann, reification is least accentuated.[100] In social life, however, economic processes take on "the apparition" of being "an *autonomous power*," and the superstructure appears to express the dominion of the base, not the reverse. While the penetration of reification into all realms of life is a central Goldmannian precept, Goldmann distinguishes two different levels within this process: a level closely linked to the economy (such domains as law and politics) and a level further from it constituting the more "spiritual" realm proper, that is, intellectual, moral, and religious life.[101] Reification, as Goldmann presents it, has as its opposite "authenticity" and the "natural." In "La Réification," Goldmann, with an eye toward cultural questions but with very clear political connotations as well, differentiates "subjective" from "objective" authenticity. Reified capitalism is objectively inauthentic inasmuch as qualitative relations are, by the mediation of exchange value, made implicit and quantified. The individual consciousness is ghettoized and becomes a canton of the private realm, unable to find authentic communal or social expression. One result, says Goldmann with a rare Freudian echo, is that there is an "excess" of "subjective authenticity" expressed in religious, moral, and aesthetic phenomena. This counterpart to objective inauthenticity is the key to the emergence of romanticism, which is based on divorce from the real, inauthentic, objective world.[102]

Reified capitalism was a condition for the development of such positive notions as the individual, liberty, and equality before the law. It also has a corresponding form in the realm of literary creation: the novel. The essence of the novel, says Goldmann, building on Lukács's *Theory of the Novel*, is "the story of a quest, of a hope which *necessarily* fails." It takes, initially, the form of individual biography; to the extent that the failed quest elucidates the milieu of its failure, the novel becomes a social chronicle. What is important, says Goldmann, pointing to Balzac, Mann, and Malraux, among others, is "the problem of human quest in an anti-human world, and describing this world."[103] In other words, what is important is the struggle to be human in a world marked by the opposition of subject and object. In the history of the novel, says Goldmann, this quest is eventually denuded. The abyss between the striving human spirit and the inauthentic social reality it faces appears unbridgeable; the novelist is reduced to simple description of a meaningless, reified world. This was exemplified in the contemporary *nouveau roman*, and especially the work of Alain Robbe-Grillet. In his *Jealousy*, Goldmann avers, *things* alone act.[104]

These perceptions were published five years before *For a Sociology of the Novel*. In "La Réification," he seems to say that in the early novel, the human quest was a protest—explicit or not—against the inauthenticity of the capitalist world. In its later phase, the novel increasingly reflects a reflexive world, as the individual championed by classical bourgeois thought became passive, a cog in the mechanism of developed reified capitalism. Marx and Lukács posited the proletariat as the force that would contest and overthrow capitalism. Goldmann, in "La Réification," embraces this position when he states that capitalist crises and the working class serve as counterweights to reification.[105] However, we can detect also the beginnings of a move beyond the Marxist view of the proletariat, toward the New Left-*autogestionaire* approach of the 1960s. The relation of workers to reification is different from that of all other strata, he writes. The alienated labor and hierarchical relations of the worker with the boss are markedly different from the worker's nonreified relations with coworkers. In capitalism, "more than anyone else, and perhaps alone, the proletariat and the theoreticians who judge the world from its point of view—that is, from the human as opposed to the mechanistic one—are potentially [*virtuellement*]" refusers of reification. They potentially embody a return to the human, "thereby continuing the effort of the great classical thinkers, the spiritual heritage the bourgeoisie let fall from its hands."[106] But Goldmann is quick to underscore that this is a matter of possibility, not necessity. Indeed, while the proletariat, "because of its economic and social situation, is a living protest against the lie and reification of capitalist society, this does not make it less of a constituent element of that society as well."[107]

Whereas Marx described the proletariat as in but not of capitalist society, Goldmann hesitatingly determined that it had, at least to a very significant extent, actually become *of* that society. An array of factors brought traditional Marxist tenets into question. Revolutions in the advanced West had been deflected; they succeeded instead in the Third World, all while the living standards of Western workers rose, thanks both to imperialism and trade union struggles.[108] Furthermore, central planning, be it in the USSR or in modified versions in Western "organized" capitalist economies, had proven to be a threat to the positive achievements of classical capitalism, such as respect for individual liberty and the formal equality of individuals before the law. Planning might weaken reification, but whereas classical socialists believed that "the disappearance of reification brings a return to the concrete, to the meaningful," Goldmann warned of the emergence of societies that would embody the most negative consequences of reification while eliminating its positive dimensions.[109] "The universality of values and, above all, respect for individual liberty, is no more automatically preserved in a socialist society than in a capitalist one," he argued, concluding that the conceptual apparatus of Marxism was no longer adequate to the new situation (although, ironically, he was largely using Marxist concepts in making this argument).[110]

It is a startling conclusion for a student of Lukács, and it indicates quite how far Goldmann had traveled beyond his master. Moreover, as Goldmann turned to the novel and modern literature, he found that his concept of transindividuality had to be recast. Or to be more precise, as his object of study shifted from the tragic world vision of a precapitalist transindividual subject to modern cultural expression in the capitalist world, he found that in the latter, precisely because of reification, the constitutive possibilities of transindividual groups, including the proletariat, were wanting. His study of the novel, and its relation to the phases of capitalism, marks this out.

Goldmann devoted intensive study to Lukács's *Theory of the Novel* and René Girard's *Mensonge romantique et verité romanesque* (1961) in the seminars he conducted in 1961 at the Free University of Brussels. His theoretical introduction to *For a Sociology of the Novel* was the result. In comparing Lukács and Girard, we find Goldmann preoccupied again with the same dynamic he discussed in his "Lukács und Heidegger" appendix to *Kant*. Goldmann contends that Girard's book, which used language that was Heideggerian in origin, constituted a virtual rediscovery of ideas in Lukács book, albeit with modifications.[111]

To see what underlies this claim, and where it leads, we must return to some of the themes of *Theory of the Novel* and follow Goldmann in comparing them to Girard's text. In this book, as we have seen, Lukács historicized the atemporal aesthetic categories of *Soul and Forms*. "The epic and the novel," he wrote, "these two major forms of great epic literature, differ from one another not by their authors' fundamental intentions but by the given historico-philosophical realities with which the authors were confronted."[112] While in *Soul and Forms*, Lukács spoke of "the gods of reality, of history" as "abstinent and rash," in *Theory of the Novel*, he discusses the novel as the epic form of fragmented contemporary society, one in which the individual is "problematic" and "transcendentally homeless." Every art form is defined "by the metaphysical dissonance of life which it accepts and organizes as the basis of a totality complete in itself."[113] The novel stands in the epic of the "integrated civilization" of ancient Greece. In the latter, the "hero" is at home in an "organic—and therefore intrinsically meaningful—concrete totality." It was a rounded, homogenous world, an "extrinsic" totality in which meaning was immanent. The real hero of this epic is actually the community, not the individual.[114] The "secret" of the Greek world, according to Lukács, was "its perfection, which is unthinkable for us." The Greek knew "only answers, but no questions . . . only forms but no chaos."[115] There was no "omnipotence of ethics" in the epic because it came from a world in which individuals were not posited as "autonomous and incomparable."[116] It is our questions, our chaos, our world without extensive totality, that gives us the novel:

> The novel is the epic of a world that has been abandoned by God. The novel hero's psychology is demonic; the objectivity of the novel is the mature man's knowledge that meaning can never quite penetrate reality, but that, without meaning, reality would disintegrate into the nothingness of inessentiality.[117]

Thus if an art form is characterized by the "metaphysical dissonance of life," which it attempts to organize "as the basis of a totality complete in itself," the novel must always seem to be in a process of becoming, rather than being finished.[118] Its "outer form" is biography; its "inner form" is "the process of the problematic individual's journeying towards himself."[119] Irony is its "normative mentality."[120] For irony is an "intuitive double vision," which "can see where God is to be found in a world abandoned by God." It is the "self-surmounting of a subjectivity that has gone as far as it was possible to go"; it is "the highest freedom that can be achieved in a world without God." And in a Godless world, there is an "incommensurability of soul and work, of interiority and adventure" because there is no "transcendental 'place' allotted to human endeavor."[121]

In a Godless world, individuals in quest of totality are ever thrown back upon themselves: "The novel tells of the adventure of interiority; the content of the novel is the story of the soul that goes out to find itself, that seeks adventures in order to be proved and tested by them, and by proving itself, to find its own essence."[122] The problematic indi-

vidual has no recourse but "interiority" because the "is"—the empirical world—is opposed to the "ought"—how it should be. As a result,
Lukács proposed that "whether inner reality is superior to outer reality or vice versa" is "the ethical problem of utopia," that is, whether
"the ability to imagine a better world can be ethically justified and . . .
whether this ability can serve as the starting point for a life that is
rounded in itself." But he insisted on the inadequacy of creating utopia
"by purely artistic means."[123]

Lukács, having once contrasted form and empirical life, next argues
that "the structural categories of the novel constitutively coincide with
the world as it is today."[124] The totalities of ancient Greece and the
Middle Ages are gone, displaced by a world in which "no aims are
directly given." This is the world in which the problematic individual
of the novel strives. It is a world in which human conventions appear
as a "second nature" beyond human beings, and like nature ("first"
nature, that is), these human-made structures appear as senseless necessity: "This second nature is not dumb, sensuous and yet senseless
like the first; it is a complex of senses—meanings—which has become
rigid and strange, and which no longer awakes interiority; it is a char-
nel-house of long-dead interiorities."[125] But—and it is a significant
"but" for Lukács's later development—"[w]hen the structures made
by man for man are really adequate to man, they are his necessary and
native home."[126] Marxism later makes this an historical possibility for
Lukács. The theory of "second nature" becomes that of reification, and
the revolutionary proletariat's historical goal is to create a world in
which structures made by humans are adequate to them; thus would
the tragic vision of *Soul and Forms* be transcended. In *Theory of the
Novel*, Lukács did not yet posit world historical action by the universal class; in its final pages, however, he detected "intimations" of a
"new epoch," expressed abstractly by Tolstoy and portentously by
Dostoyevsky. He asked, Was the latter already the "Homer" or the
harbinger of a new world about to be born?

The place of Dostoyevsky in *Theory of the Novel* must be seen in
terms of two factors: Lukács's typology of the novel and his fascination
with Russia. The typology is based on the "incommensurability" to
reality of the soul of the novel's protagonist, and results in a twofold
division. In the novel of "abstract idealism," the protagonist's vision is
too narrow, and he or she takes his vision for reality; the ought is taken
for the is. *Don Quixote* is its paradigm, and it appears "at the beginning
of the time when the Christian God began to foresake the world." In
Cervantes' novel, we see "the first great battle of interiority against the
prosaic vulgarity of outward life."[127]

The second type of novel is that of "Romantic disillusion." Here, the protagonist's soul is too wide; there is a different kind of incommensurability. He "is no longer significant as the carrier of the transcendent world, as he was in abstract idealism, he now carries his value exclusively within himself."[128] Rather than tilting at windmills, the protagonist withdraws. Examples are Walter Scott's novels and Flaubert's *Sentimental Education*. In Goethe's *Wilhelm Meister*, Lukács saw "an attempted synthesis" that "stands aesthetically and historico-philosophically" between the other two types because its theme "is the reconciliation of the problematic individual, guided by his lived experience of the ideal, with social reality."[129] Goethe's humanist utopianism "steers a middle course between abstract idealism, which concentrates on pure action, and Romanticism, which interiorises action and reduces it to contemplation."[130]

In Dostoyevsky's work, Lukács discerns a movement beyond the novel. If the novel comes of the epoch of absolute sinfulness, "it must remain the dominant form so long as the world is ruled by the same stars."[131] In other words, there was a homology between the novel and its epoch. However, in Tolstoy, Lukács saw "intimations" of a new epoch; in Dostoyevsky, he sees a man of a new age, perhaps its Homer or Dante. Later, after he became a Marxist, Lukács insisted that Dostoyevsky, despite his reactionary politics, stripped "through spontaneous vision, every character, human relationship, and conflict of the reified shell in which they are all presented today and to pare them down, to reduce them, to their purely spiritual core."[132] He projected a utopian vision—and the necessity of revolution despite himself, for "the spontaneous, wild and blind revolt of Dostoyevsky's character's occurs in the name of the golden age."[133]

Girard, writing half a century later, rediscovered Lukács's problematic, according to Goldmann. Girard's book contends that great writers grasp "intuitively and concretely" in their work "the system in which they were first imprisoned together with their contemporaries." Interpretation of literature therefore ought to be systematic; its task is to render explicit what is implicit in the literature itself. Criticism is the "continuation of literature," its aims being to "embrace," to "comprehend," to "articulate" literary "substance." To elaborate, Girard initially turns to Cervantes. Whoever would approximate "perfect chivalry," Don Quixote tells Sancho, ought to imitate "one of the most perfect knight errants," Amadis of Gaul. Amadis, writes Girard, chooses the objects of Quixote's "metaphysical desire." As Quixote's model, Amadis is his "*mediator* of desire" (as Quixote is for Sancho). Since the desire (of Quixote) is defined by an Other (Amadis), there is no simple subject-object relation between desirer and object; rather, mediation creates "triangular desire." Its structure composes a "synthetic metaphor," in which "the mediator is imaginary but not the mediation." He who desires imitates the *desire* of a model, while *believing* he has made a free choice.[134] Girard also sees triangular desire in Flaubert and Stendahl. Emma Bovary's desires are not spontaneous but come of the romantic heroines in the mediocre novels she read as a girl. In *The Red and the Black*, Julian Sorel wants to imitate Napoleon. *The Memoirs of Saint-Helène* are for him what Amadis's chivalry is for Quixote and romances are for Emma Bovary. In Stendhal, the triangle appears as a result of vain individuals (*the vaniteux*). The vain individual is incapable of drawing desires "from his own resources." Thus de Renal, the mayor of Verriéres, negotiates the employ of Julian Sorel to tutor his sons not for the sake of learning but because he fears a wealthy rival, Valenod, may hire him. "The ever-increasing price that the buyer is willing to pay is determined by the imaginary desire which he attributes to his rival." Similarly, Julian will later seek to retrieve Mathilde by pursuing another woman. Girard expresses surprise that "Marxist critics, for whom economic structures provide the archetype of all human relations, have not as yet pointed out the analogy between the crafty bargaining of old Sorel and the amorous maneuvers of his son."[135]

Girard distinguishes "external" from "internal" mediation. The vain individual desires an object because it is desired by another (usually admired) individual. This mediator thereby becomes a rival for the object. In a novel of "external mediation," real rivalry is impossible; Quixote's mediator is (presumably) in heaven. This is not so in "internal mediation"; the mediator of de Renal is Valenod, who is on earth. There is an "enormous spiritual gap" between his vanity and that of Quixote.[136]

A great novelist, for Girard, reveals the mediator, "the imitative nature of desire," which is difficult to perceive because "the most fervent imitation is the most vigorously denied."[137] The imitator revels in the modern illusion of autonomy. For Girard, Proust and Dostoyevsky, like Stendhal, are important novelists of internal mediation. In the "snobbism" of Proust is a caricature of the vanity found in Stendhal. These two writers are novelists of the "bourgeois interregnum," the transition from traditional feudal societies to the most modern ones. They "occupy the upper reaches of internal mediation," while Dostoyevsky, in a Russia that passed from feudal to modern society without an interregnum, "occupies the lowest."[138] The vain person is decidedly modern because "the triumph of vanity coincides with the crumbling of the traditional universe. Men of triangular desire no longer believe but are to get along without transcendency,"[139] For it is Girard's view that "it is in internal mediation that the profoundest meaning of the *modern* is found."[140] Triangular desire has become a "universal structure," which penetrates "the most petty details of daily existence."[141] Stavrogin, in Dostoyevsky's *The Possessed*, is the mediator for the other characters; their ideas come from him, and his image is the anti-Christ. For Dostoyevsky, "[d]enial of God does not eliminate transcendency but diverts it from the *au-delà* to the *en-deçà*." The imitation of Christ becomes the imitation of one's neighbors. Stavrogin's imitators sacrifice all for him in a "deviated transcendency," which caricatures "vertical transcendency," for false prophets proclaim that "in tomorrow's world *men will be gods for each other*" in a paradise which is, in reality, hell.[142]

This is the dilemma of modernity. Stendhal's work seeks to answer one question: "Why are we not happy in the modern world?"[143] The answer: We are *vaniteux*. But great novels conclude with "a *Past Recaptured*," a conversion in which memory ends triangular desire. In *The Red and the Black*, "Julian wins solitude but he triumphs over isolation," and Dostoyevsky's Raskolnikov overcomes his isolation and wins solitude.[144] Goldmann comments:

> Girard implicitly compares his own analysis to Marxism: Marx's *alienation* is analogous to metaphysical desire. But alienation has little correspondence with anything but external mediation and the upper stages of internal mediation. The Marxist analyses of bourgeois society are more penetrating than most but they are vitiated at the outset by yet another illusion. The Marxist thinks he can do away with all alienation by destroying bourgeois society. He makes no allowance for the extreme forms of metaphysical desire, those described by Proust and Dostoyevsky. The Marxist is taken in by the object; his materialism is only a relative progress beyond middle-class idealism.[145]

In comparing Lukács and Girard, Goldmann reinvents his earlier comparison of Lukács and Heidegger in the appendix to *Kant* and anticipates his later, unfinished *Lukács and Heidegger*. *Being and Time* distinguishes the ontological realm, that of being as such and inquiry into it, from the ontic, which is that of beings, of data, of the particular, or inquiry into particular entities. In Girard this becomes the duality of the ontological and the metaphysical. This duality corresponds, says Goldmann, "to the authentic and the inauthentic." For both Lukács and Girard, then, the novel is characterized by a problematic hero's quest for authentic values in a "degraded" world. The degradation is consequent to "a more or less advanced ontological sickness [*un mal ontologique*] . . . to which, within the novel's world [*du monde romanesque*], corresponds an increase of metaphysical desire, that is, degraded desire."[146] Girard discerns the degradation in mediation, while

Lukács finds it in reification ("second nature"). In Girard, argues Goldmann, the degradation of the world of the novel, the progress of ontological sickness, and the growth of metaphysical desire are manifested, to a greater or lesser degree, by a mediation (*une médiatisation*), which progressively increases the distance between metaphysical desire and authentic quest, the quest for "vertical transcendency."[147] Both Lukács and Girard believe that the novelist must supersede the consciousness of the heroes he presents. For Girard, this is accomplished by humor; for Lukács, through irony. Girard believes this supersession is a rediscovery of authenticity in the writing of the novel—it is "vertical transcendence." As Girard puts it, "while remaining the Other, the hero of the novel gradually merges with the novelist in the course of creation" and thus the self and the Other become one.[148] The result is vertical transcendence. For Lukács, in contrast, a literary form expresses an *"essential* content," and consequently Goldmann argues that any transcendence of the novelist must itself be degraded; it must be abstract and not lived concretely.[149] In *Theory of the Novel*, irony is thus an essential means for the novelist, and the irony must be aimed both at the hero and at *the author's own consciousness.* "This is why the story of the degraded quest . . . always remains the sole possibility for expressing essential realities."[150] Ethical and aesthetic problems are linked.

While Lukács and Girard did not write their respective works with specifically sociological aims, Goldmann makes use of them precisely for this purpose. He proposes that the novel is "the transposition on the literary plane of daily life in individualist society born of production for the market." There is "a *rigorous homology* between the literary form of the novel, as defined by Lukács and Girard, and the daily relation of men and goods [*les biens*] in general, and by extension between men and other men, in a society producing for the market."[151] Whereas Racine's tragedies were the literary articulation of the mental structures of the noblesse de robe, Goldmann finds in the novel the transposition of the general categories of a particular society, one dominated by the commodity form, and hence reification.

A homology is a correspondence due to a common source; in it, as Goldmann put it, "one and the same structure . . . manifests itself on two different planes."[152] In biology, the term "homology" refers to structural or functional parallels in different organisms consequent to parallel evolutionary derivation from a common source. To discern a homology, then, the genesis and structure of the commonality must be examined, and this is impossible without seeing the whole. By turning to homologies between socioeconomic and cultural realms within capitalism, Goldmann sought to demonstrate structural correlations, which, because capitalism is a historical phenomenon, must be

grasped both genetically and structurally. It is for this reason that
Goldmann began calling his method genetic structuralism, consciously
in opposition to static models of structuralism, such as those of Lévi-
Strauss, who also made frequent use of the notion of homology.

In *Towards a Sociology of the Novel*, the transindividual consciousnesses of classes or groups are no longer mediators of the socioeconomic and cultural realms; instead, the relation between the two realms
is defined as homologous. Homologies do not, therefore, articulate coherently the consciousness of a social group. Economic life, as Goldmann presents it, is directly transposed into and mediates cultural life,
but not by means of a transindividual subject. In fact, Goldmann now
goes beyond the argument of "La Réification" to assert that the proletariat can no longer be seen as the transindividual basis of cultural con-
testation. Not only was Marxism wrong to believe that the proletariat
would constitute an alternative culture; it was wrong to assume that
reification would destroy culture. Still, in reified society, "collective
consciousness progressively loses all reality and tends to become a
simple reflex of economic life and, ultimately, to disappear."[153] Consciousness becomes increasingly passive. Goldmann initially thought
that while reification "tended to dissolve and integrate into society as
a whole [*la société globale*] different partial groups, thereby removing
their specificity to a certain extent," it was "so contrary to the biological as well as psychological reality of the human individual, that it
would necessarily engender in *all* human individuals . . . reactions of
opposition . . . thus creating a diffuse resistance to the reified world, a
resistance that would constitute a background to novelistic creation [*la
création romanesque*]." However, he now concluded that these claims
were based on "an unexamined *a priori* supposition: that of the existence of a biological nature whose external manifestations could not be
entirely denatured by social reality."[154] Consequently, "authentic" cultural creation and its nature must be grasped otherwise.

Goldmann argues that there is a homology between the liberal capitalist individualism of the nineteenth century and the novel of the
nineteenth century. The novel emphasizes biography and social chronicle; in it a problematic hero strives for authentic values in a degraded
society; it is written by a "problematic individual" who lives in such a
society but is oriented towards authentic values. But while this type of
novel comes of the bourgeois era, it expresses neither the real nor the
possible consciousness of a class. Indeed, Goldmann goes so far as to
say that in Balzac alone is to be found a literary universe structured by
purely individualist values.[155] This is radically contrary to Lukács's
distinction between periods of bourgeois ascension and decline.

Subsequent transformations of the novel lead to a more complex story, homologous to the transformations of the structures of reification. Liberal capitalism—whose internal equilibrium was maintained by the "free" market—was replaced by a capitalism dominated by trusts, finance capital, and monopolies. Concurrently, the notion of the individual modeled on the individual entrepreneur and the novel of the problematic hero dissolve. The individual, like capitalism, enters a period of crisis, whose corresponding literary development is exemplified by Kafka and Joyce. Instead of the problematic hero, we find the "dissolution of the subject" and the emergence of "the nonbiographical character." Liberal capitalism still harbored an ensemble of values that had nontransindividual but nonetheless universal aims—those of liberal individualism. But individualism had been increasingly eliminated "by the transformation of economic life and the replacement of the economy of free competition by an economy of cartels and monopolies."[156] With the post-World War II rise of "organized capitalism" and the consumer society—in which the state and large monopolies regulate the economy and society to avoid crises, especially of overproduction—we find the emergence of the *nouveau roman*. In Alain Robbe-Grillet's fiction, things and objects supersede human beings and their actions. In short, Goldmann presents the story of capitalism as first the triumph of individualism over any notion of the social whole, and then the subversion of individualism, leaving neither collective nor individual actors.

For Goldmann, the novel is an oppositional form of literature. It begins with the problematic hero facing a degraded society. This hero dissolves when capitalism goes into crisis. However, Goldmann devotes most of *Towards a Sociology of the Novel* not to Kafka or Joyce, but to André Malraux, especially his *Man's Fate* (*La Condition humaine*). The reason is easy to discern. This novel about the revolutionary efforts and murderous fate of Chinese Communists during the Shanghai uprising of 1927 embodies Goldmann's dialectic of tragedy and hope. *Man's Fate*, published in 1933, is born, according to Goldmann's scheme, of an age of crisis in values, the era of capitalism in crisis, which, not incidentally, also marked the birth of existentialism, first in the work of the young Lukács, then in Heidegger, and later in the early Sartre. The crisis of individualism brings forth a focus on action and death, both of which are central to Malraux's novel. Goldmann, a Romanian Jew in France writing on Pascal, Racine, and the Jansenist sect and searching for the "authentic human community," saw Marxism not as a dogma modeled on natural science but as a wager on humanity's future; Kyo Gisors, the half-Japanese, half-French leader of a revolutionary community in struggle in China in Malraux's novel, is a man who had been taught by his father that Marxism is a will, not a doctrine. That community composes a problematic *collective* hero in a novel written in an era when, according to Goldmann, the "character" dissolves. Instead of the "I" of the classical novel dissolving, it becomes in Malraux the "We" of revolutionary community—Goldmann's alternative.

Goldmann's deliberation on Malraux—a chapter of more than two hundred pages—is presented as a "preliminary outline of the significative structures *immanent*" in Malraux's work.[157] Goldmann divides Malraux's writings into stages, and says it is the second stage alone that yields novels proper. The products of the first phase—*The Temptation of the West* and *Paper Moons*, for examples—"affirm the death of the Gods and the universal decomposition of values." Their structures are homologous to those of capitalism in crisis. However, in the second stage—that of *The Conquerors*, *The Royal Road*, and *Man's Fate*—Malraux, despite the surrounding crises, creates and believes in "universal and positive" though "*problematic values*."[158] This is transposed into the "problematic heroes" of his novels. The problematic individual does not pose problems, but finds that his "existence and values place insoluble problems before him." He does not, however, grasp them coherently, for if he did, he would be a hero of tragedy, rather than of the novel.[159] Yet he lives his problematic existence authentically. In *The Conquerors*, set during the Hong Kong strike of 1925, Garine's revolutionary role achieves for him a precarious but "authentic sense of his existence." In *Man's Fate*, the hero is collective: the novel's concern is the "problematic community" of Shanghai revolutionaries. Each member, as an individual, finds authenticity the common struggle and, ultimately, in common defeat.[160]

Man's Fate depicts two conflicts—one between the Shanghai revolutionary community and Chiang kai-shek, and one between the Shanghai revolutionary community and the Communist Party leadership in Hankow. It is easy to imagine that Goldmann recalled his own experience in Romania—the attack on him as a Trotskyist—when he underscored the conflicting values incarnated in two different forces and perspectives, "the Trotskyist value of immediate *revolutionary* community and the Stalinist value of discipline."[161] The unproblematic obedience demanded by the Communist Party leadership in Hankow, which leads to the destruction of the Shanghai revolutionaries, is seen by Goldmann as incipient Stalinism. In later novels, however, Malraux, under the impact of Nazism, embraced official Communist Party positions. Consequently, in contrast to *Man's Fate*, he produced works depicting "nonproblematic relations." In *Hope*, his novel about the Spanish Civil War, the subject is "the *non-problematic relation* between the Spanish people and the international proletariat with a Communist

Party that is disciplined and opposed to revolutionary spontaneity."[162] Such spontaneity, in *Man's Fate*, was embodied in the revolutionary community, in opposition to the Hankow Party leaders. Thus the author of *The Conquerors* and *Man's Fate* embraces universal, though problematic, values, while the later Malraux embraces universal, nonproblematic ("transparent"), though menaced, values.[163]

What is crucial in *Man's Fate*, however, is not solely the creation of a collective subject composed of Kyo, May, and Katow, together with the "anonymous militants" on their side. Rather, it is the presentation of the collective hero—the problematic revolutionary community—as the value structuring the novel.[164] In elaborating his argument, Goldmann dwells particularly on love and death in the novel. These forces, which bring people together and end their existence, were important themes in existentialism and, as we have seen, in Goldmann's unpublished "Dialogue dans une Buffet de Gare." There, Goldmann, criticizing Sartre's exposition of love in *Being and Nothingness*, defined eros and the need to act together as fundamental to the human condition. It is in realizing the "We" through action that we approach the "absolute"; "the reality of eros, the community of two [*la communauté à deux*], love," is based on this.[165] In brief, Goldmann fastened the possibility of love between two individuals to the notion of community in general. Love, like art in the "Dialogue," synthesizes sensibility and understanding, and transforms "sexual union into a community of struggle for the ideal," for "the human purpose, the human community in general."[166]

Two decades later, Goldmann argued that in *Man's Fate*, "eroticism is, like the individual, integrated and transcended [*dépassé*] in an authentic and superior community: that of love." That love will become the realization of totality. For Kyo and May it is "organically linked to the revolutionary action of the two partners."[167] They seek a relation with each other based on profound love, equality, and nonpossessiveness. Early in the novel, we learn that May has, on the eve of the insurrection, slept with another revolutionary. She did so out of pity and out of the knowledge that he might well die in the coming upheaval. Yet she sees this act as inconsequential to her relation with Kyo. The sexual act, for her, is not one of emotional surrender. Kyo, on the other hand, feels jealousy. But it is jealousy coupled with a sense of disjuncture, for his politics should preclude such an emotion.

The tension between the two is resolved only when, on the verge of defeat, May accompanies Kyo on his way to the Party headquarters, knowing it likely that he will be seized and executed by the counterrevolution. She is knocked unconscious, and he is captured. After refusing to trade his life for collaboration, Kyo is taken to await execution. But instead of allowing himself to be killed, he acts; he commits suicide. At the hour of death, he feels a great sense of reconciliation, for he is not alone and his death will embody how he lived. He is one with his comrades of revolutionary community, those who will die with him, and those, such as May, who will later carry on and love others. Goldmann calls the relation between Kyo and May a "total union," a *"realized totality,"* for between them it is impossible "to dissociate the private relation from revolutionary activity." Facing his end, Kyo "completely and without reservation retrieves May and his battling comrades at once."[168] In contrast to the relation between Kyo and May is the brutal one between Ferral and Valerie; while Goldmann does not say so, it comes close to embodying Sartre's view of love in *Being and Nothingness.*

Goldmann also finds "realized totality" in the extraordinary death scene, in the same prison, of Katow, the older, experienced, Russian revolutionary. Chiang's henchmen have chosen a particularly gruesome dispatch for the radical leaders—they are incinerated alive in a locomotive engine. Its whistle blows with each burning to remind the other prisoners of their impending lot. Katov, who is wounded, can escape this agony with a cyanide pill. In a final gesture of human solidarity and revolutionary love, he offers it to two terrified younger comrades. As he hands forth the pill, it is dropped. Alas, his sacrifice seems in vain. They scramble to find it, and suddenly, in the dark, for one brief moment, the doomed men discover themselves grasping one anothers's hands. And then the capsule is found. The two young men die, and, soon enough, Katov is silhouetted by the flames, limping to his doom, with all the other prisoners listening as he scrapes along. The whistle calls.

Goldmann finds in these scenes an important contrast to Malraux's earlier works, such as *The Conquerors* and *The Royal Road.* In them, death is the "inevitable reality which rendered all action-bound intramondaine values precarious and provisional, which *retroactively* annihilated them, and reduced [*ramenait*] the hero to the formless, to absolute solitude." However, in *Man's Fate,* death does not break "the links between the individual and the community" but "assures the definitive transcendence of solitude."[169]

For Goldmann, this is also what distinguished *Soul and Forms* from *History and Class Consciousness,* and Heidegger and existentialism from Lukács. Death is not the limit against which the individual is set and the basis for resolute authenticity, but a moment of authentic community, even in defeat. Meaning is found in the "We," not in the "One" or the "One/They" (*Das Man*). While Goldmann does not say so explicitly, the role of time is essential here. The novel's focus is a present moment, but the past and the future are implicit in the present. For though most of the revolutionaries die, the revolution, the future, does not. The author has a totalizing grasp of the revolutionary moment. The hope, the tragedy, the *raison d'étre* of the Shanghai revolutionary community—all these as a whole justify the novel's (French) title: *La Condition humaine*.

III

What was Goldmann's view of modernism, those cultural trends homologous to capitalism in crisis and organized capitalism? The answer is complicated by the extreme schematism of Goldmann's homologies and his argument that in capitalism, especially because of reification, culture and consciousness increasingly become reflexes. His tendency to see the superstructure as a reflection of the base often comes close to the simplistic Marxist paradigms against which he argued. As a consequence he ignores the variety of literary creation in the twentieth-century. However powerful *Man's Fate*, and however forceful Goldmann's reading of it, it is hardly representative of twentieth-century literature. Also, much in British and American literature wouldn't fit Goldmann's categories comfortably. On the other hand, he does provide an array of interesting readings based on his theory. In his studies of Jean Genet, he conceives of modernism—or certain aspects of modernism—as a form of realism. Here (again) he is very much at odds with Lukács's celebrated theories. As Robert Sayre has pointed out, Goldmann's analysis of Genet's play *The Balcony* employs a central Lukácsian concept against itself.[170] Great artistic realism, for Lukács, brings out the historically typical through an individual's experiences. The individual character is not an abstract symbol of historical reality, but is placed within a social and historical totality. Lukács extolled great bourgeois "critical" realists, such as Balzac in the nineteenth century and Mann in the twentieth. Great socialist realism (for example, the works of Gorky) continued and transcended bourgeois realism, thereby becoming the pinnacle of the classical and humanist tradition of the West. Realism reveals what is behind immediate empirical reality.

Lukács's complaint against modernism and its techniques is like his critique, in *History and Class Consciousness*, of bourgeois social science: he thinks they both fetishize surface appearances and do not—indeed, cannot—grasp the whole. This was the source of Lukács's criticism of Brecht's alienation effect. Brecht insisted that as the proletariat had to break with bourgeois civilization, so, too, did art. He chastised

Lukács's notion of realism; it was too restricted. The world of modernism is the world of modern technique, not that of Goethe in Weimar, however great the latter's interest in science. Consequently, Lukács's realism, which insists on presenting to the reader (or audience) a sociohistorical totality that can be opposed to the distortions of the contemporary world produces, in Brecht's view, illusory catharsis. It becomes, ultimately, illusory realism. In contrast, modernist techniques, such as the alienation effect, force an audience to grasp reality actively through disruption.

In *Towards a Sociology of the Novel*, Goldmann defines realism as "the creation of a world whose structure is analogous to the essential structure of the social reality in which the work has been written." The *nouveau roman*, as practiced by Nathalie Sarraute and Alain Robbe-Grillet (as well as the screenplay written by the latter, "Last Year at Marienbad") are examples.[171] Goldmann defends Sarraute and Robbe-Grillet against critics who see their writings as "an ensemble of purely formal experiences and . . . an attempt to evade social reality." In Goldmann's eyes, their work is "born of an effort . . . to grasp [*pour saisir*] the reality of our times in the most essential way."[172]

The *nouveau roman* is homologous to capitalism's development in that there is "more or less [a] radical disappearance of character" and a corresponding reinforcement of "the autonomy of objects."[173] The *nouveau roman* responds to the need for a new novel form consequent to changes in capitalism.[174]

Liberal capitalism extolled the individual; the novel of the problematic hero was its homologue. Capitalism in crisis (the imperialist period) resulted in the repression of the individual, and then organized capitalism yielded a world that appeared to be constituted by objects. In other words, human dimensions become increasingly implicit. Sarraute's work, along with Sartre's *Nausea*, Camus's *The Stranger*, and the work of Joyce, Kafka, and Musil exemplify the second period of capitalism, in which "character" "dissolves." A new period, that of autonomous objects, had been inaugurated, and Robbe-Grillet was its harbinger. Sarraute's focus on psychology and interhuman relations showed that she had not been overwhelmed by reification. However, Robbe-Grillet "focuses on the external manifestations of social life, not recording the essentially psychic and human character of the relations which are at the origins of reification, and the growing autonomy of objects."[175] Individual action has lost all meaning in Robbe-Grillet's novels. In *Le Voyeur*, for example, "the universe is constituted solely by passive *voyeurs* who have neither the intention or the possibility of intervening in social life to transform it qualitatively and render it more human." This, says Goldmann, is realism, for it displays the scope of reification, illustrating the extent to which regulated organized capitalism turns humans into passive voyeurs.

Goldmann's differences with Lukács's theory of realism were captured vividly at the Third International Colloquium on the Sociology of Literature at Royaument in January 1968, when he responded to a paper by Agnès Heller, then Lukács's leading pupil in Budapest. Presenting the ideas of the late Lukács, Heller argued that a valid work [*oeuvre valable*] rests on its coherence "and the fact that it is situated within the meaning of history; works are realist only to the extent that they reflect global historical evolution."[176] While Goldmann acclaimed Lukács's studies of German classicism, he insisted that Lukács's rejection of surrealism, the *nouveau roman*, and Brecht in the name of humanism and realism was radically misconstrued.

Goldmann proceeded with an anecdote that demonstrated that his disagreement with Lukács was deeply rooted and long-standing. He recounted his first meeting with the Hungarian philosopher at the Rencontres Internationales in Geneva after the war. Goldmann approached Lukács after Lukács had lectured on Romain Rolland and Upton Sinclair, and inquired "if he truly believed" that these authors were "among the greatest writers of our time." Lukács responded that they were "as important as Proust or Celine among others. On the other hand, well, no, perhaps not, but valid art is only possible when it is situated in a humanist perspective. While waiting for great writers of this type, one must cite Upton Sinclair and Romain Rolland." Goldmann observed that Lukács's answer was a "response of the nineteenth century."[177]

Moreover, it illustrated why such thinkers as Goldmann wanted to "reclaim" the aesthetics of the Lukács who had written *Soul and Forms* and *Theory of the Novel*. The later Lukács's inability to transcend his "nineteenth-century position" precluded any understanding of modern art, its relation to the historical world, and the role of individuals and social groups in the modern world. Since organized capitalism is a world in which groups lose efficacy, especially as mediators of the socioeconomic and cultural realms, culture divorced from this modern reality is not realist.

Still, in his own analysis of the "realism" of postwar avant-garde theater, Goldmann did not entirely abandon the methodological use of transindividual subjects. Writing shortly after "the historical turning-point" of May–June 1968, Goldmann argued that the "central question" of postwar avant-garde literature was "the nature of the social relations that developed in Western Europe during this period." Thus it was realist "in the best sense of the word."[178] Genet, "the outsider of genius," a nonconformist who had not elaborated an oppositionist ide-

ology, nonetheless expressed "the reality of our times and the problems of today's man better than anyone else."[179]

Goldmann's first extensive discussion of realism, in an essay in *Les
Temps modernes* in 1960 entitled "A Realist Play: Genet's *The Balcony*,"
may have been a product of his correspondence with Lukács concerning *The Hidden God*. Lukács's response to the book was cool, as we
know, because in it Goldmann ignored the former's work after *History
and Class Consciousness*. Much of that work is preoccupied with realism, and Lukács, in the same letter, asked Goldmann to help facilitate
the French translation of one of his books on this subject. Goldmann
did so, securing as translator Maurice de Gandillac, one of France's
preeminent Germanists.[180]

Soon afterward Goldmann began to write on realism instead of
French classicism. His essay on *The Balcony* is, at least implicitly, a
scathing critique of Lukács's antimodernism. Perhaps it was Goldmann's real reply to Lukács's comments on *The Hidden God* as well.
"Today," the essay begins, "the notion of socialist realism has been
severely undermined by the many years during which it meant the
submission of a writer to a given political directive."[181] Since Marxism
saw itself as heir to classical humanism, its greatest literary criticism
focused on classicism and its realism in contrast to romanticism. Realism in this context meant the elucidation of "the essential relationships
that at a particular moment govern both the development of the whole
of social relations and—through the latter—the development of individual destinies and the psychological life of individuals."[182] *The Balcony* did just this. It is a pessimistic play about the transformations
that occurred in the first half of the twentieth century, leading to technocratic, organized capitalist society. The characters of Irma, madame
of the brothel in which the play is set, and the police chief represent,
respectively, two crucial elements of organized capitalism: enterprise
director and state power. In other words, Genet's play is homologous
with the "real" world. Whatever the subjective aims of Genet, whatever his biography, his play coherently elaborates the mental structures homologous to organized capitalism.

Goldmann makes an argument at once similar and different about
the theater of Witold Gombrowicz. His *Ivona, Princess of Burgandia* and
The Marriage were often criticized as incoherent. Goldmann demurs.
The first, he says, is actually a play about the ruling classes of pre–
World War II Europe, and the second is one about the transformation
of Eastern Europe into dictatorships ("People's Democracies"), seen
from a distinct standpoint. "Christian and aristocrat, Gombrowicz . . .
writes from the perspective of a class that is . . . disappearing," but he
nonetheless captures imaginatively what was happening historically.

Goldmann seems to have found a transindividual subject here, though Gombrowicz denied he was an aristocrat and called Goldmann's interpretation "heresy."[183] Writing in 1970, Goldmann claimed that Gombrowicz's 1966 *Operetta* anticipated the May 1968 rebellions; Goldmann claimed to see in it a rejection of the old established order and Stalinism.

More striking, however, was Goldmann's own anticipation of the Events of 1968 in his 1966 study "The Theater of Genet." Here, he offered an appraisal of *The Maids, The Balcony,* and *The Blacks.* He suggested that their basic structure corresponded to "the mental and spiritual structure" of an important segment of the radical Left, the emerging New Left, in France. It is clear that this is the segment with which Goldmann identified, for he was by now a Marxist who no longer believed that the proletariat would play the role ascribed to it by Marxism, yet who still wagered on the development of forces contesting capitalism. The mental and spiritual structures Goldmann discerned in Genet were composed of the following elements: an affirmation of the necessarily antagonistic class nature of Western society; a recognition that the dominant strata of these societies could not be vanquished by violent revolution; a fascination with the political success of "the technocrats of organized capitalism"; and the moral condemnation of this society, combined with the justification of radical struggle against it "in the name of moral, aesthetic, and human values."[184]

This is not only Genet: it is the position of a left-wing intellectual caught between his own analysis of capitalist stability and his quest for "authentic community," in the aftermath of the rise of Gaullism and the impotence of the Left during the Algerian war. Goldmann found Genet's massive play about Algeria, *The Screens,* especially striking. He contended that the rejection by Said, the play's main character, of the three "orders" or realms of the play—the Arab village, the resistance, the kingdom of the dead—corresponds to Genet's rejection of three concepts fundamental to European socialist thought: the oppressive class society, the victorious revolutionary society (which suppresses oppression "but is still founded on constraint") and the vision of a classless, constraintless society of the future. It is through Said/Genet's negative judgment that something positive may emerge. That judgment was expressed in theater just as part of the European Left— that which was to become the New Left—was starting to perceive the inadequacy of the Old Left's revolutionary design. The central problem before the Left was captured in Genet's play. And while Goldmann's homologies here may appear a bit too imaginative, they lead him to close his essay with a startling question: "Is *The Screens* only an isolated, accidental phenomena? Or is it the first swallow which an-

nounces the arrival of Spring,, representing a turning point in the intellectual and social life of today.?"[185]

Spring arrived two years later when students and workers, prominently carrying signs calling for *autogestion* (workers' self-management), brought French society to a halt; in the process, they found
themselves battling the Gaullist government, and also stymied by the
ever-dogmatic French Communist Party. The Events of 1968 disrupted
organized capitalism and the social evolution that had led such Western Marxists as Horkheimer, Adorno, and Marcuse to a pessimism
that Goldmann, publicly and repeatedly, rejected. We will return to
Goldmann's politics in more depth in a future chapter. For the moment, it is important to see that Goldmann, having argued for the realism of the avant-garde in opposition to Lukács, discerned in Genet a
possible consciousness, which was, in its own way, actualized in Paris
in May 1968. Lukács had asked in *Theory of the Novel* if Dostoyevsky
were the Homer of a world to come from Russia shortly before the
Bolshevik revolution; Goldmann similarly saw in Genet the harbinger
of the May Events. While Goldmann's theory of homologies may be
criticized as something of a reversion to economic determinism, at the
end of his analysis of Genet he does something quite different: he discerns "superstructural" intimations of future political developments.

7

Existentialism, Marxism, Structuralism

"In the beginning was the deed." Goldmann often quoted this line from Goethe's *Faust*—Goethe's recasting of the opening of the Gospel of John, traditionally, "In the Beginning was the Word." Action and language symbolize the two cardinal phases of French intellectual debate during Goldmann's lifetime. They were dominated, respectively, by Sartrian existentialism, with its emphasis on man making himself and the world through freely chosen acts, and structuralism, which made language the paradigm for the human sciences. Marxism, however, persistently engaged existentialism and structuralism, sometimes as interrogator, sometimes as antagonist, sometimes as ally, sometimes as alloy.

Postwar France had a powerful Communist Party; Sartre, in the 1950s, embraced the Party, then broke with it, and finally wrote a massive *Critique of Dialectical Reason* with the declared aim of rescuing Marx from it by incorporating existentialism into Marxism. When Sartre's influence waned in the 1960s, displaced by structuralism at center stage of the Latin Quarter, Marxism was still there. Claude Lévi-Strauss, though no Marxist, cited Marx as one of his "mistresses" in developing structuralist anthropology, and the Communist Party philosopher Louis Althusser used structuralist concepts to oppose his own "scientific" Marxism to the humanist variety.

Lucien Goldmann was, in many ways, uniquely situated in these debates, although this was rarely recognized by his peers. He had not come initially from the Gallic intellectual world and had argued in *The Hidden God* for Pascal as representative of a countertradition, which articulated a tragic and incipiently dialectical worldview, to the Cartesian and positivist mainstream in France. Goldmann also closely associated the tragic vision with existentialism and the dialectic, proposing that Lukács's early works were the first texts of modern existentialism, and that they represented a conjuncture between phenomenological structuralism (probably influenced in part by Husserl) and Marxism (which Lukács eventually embraced).[1] *Soul and Forms*, Goldmann contended, envisioned man as a form-creating being who "seeks to give coherent expressions to fundamental attitudes he takes facing life and the universe." Lukács's employment of "form" closely corresponded to the way "structure" was later used. One such form, the tragic vision, corresponded "to the true essence of the human condition and implicitly permits the comprehension of all the others."[2]

French existentialism was deeply indebted to its German predecessors, first and foremost, Heidegger. Goldmann repeatedly characterized the tragic vision with existential language as a necessarily unsuccessful quest for authenticity in an inauthentic world: a demand for absolute values in a relativistic universe, a demand for all or nothing in a world that knows only compromises, and which, because it is not conceived historically is therefore not understood as changeable. The tragic man faces this world in anguish, cognizant of his own limits, the most important being death. The one value accessible to tragic man, says Goldmann, summarizing the young Lukács, is "consciousness of his own limitations and of the non-value of the world, a consciousness which can be translated into action solely as radical refusal of the relativistic world and of life—the tragic attitude."[3] For Goldmann this mode of thinking did not, of course, arise *ex nihilo* in Lukács's mind; its genesis, like that of structuralism decades later, was part of a historical moment.

The impending crisis of capitalism had engendered, on the eve of World War I, a crisis in the idea of the individual, for individualism, in the bourgeois-liberal sense, was being undermined by the growing dominance of large-scale socioeconomic organization. One consequence was philosophy preoccupied with individual limits, angst, and death.[4] The older Lukács, writing after World War II, declared that the "avant-garde of the bourgeois intelligentsia" during this period—who included his younger self—"lived in a sort of permanent carnival of fetishized interiority."[5] Yet in Goldmann's eyes, what was striking about the young Lukács was that despite the calm preceding World War I, Lukács's essay on "The Metaphysics of Tragedy" intimated impending crisis, and thus was its harbinger.[6]

I

In 1909 Lukács wrote an essay on Kierkegaard, which was, like "The Metaphysics of Tragedy," included in *Soul and Forms*. This essay, on the man generally considered the nineteenth-century father of existentialism, was the subject of Goldmann's presentation to *Kierkegaard vivant*, a Paris colloquium organized by UNESCO in April 1964 with the participation of Sartre, Heidegger, Gabriel Marcel, and Karl Jaspers, among others. Goldmann's approach here—as in much of his work—is to construct a dialogue between the thinker at hand, in this case, Kierkegaard, and Lukács. Lukács's superiority is generally proven, but in the process Goldmann customarily reaches his own conclusions, which are not necessarily those of Lukács. This pattern can be seen in all of Goldmann's discussions of existentialism: he counterposed Lukács to Kierkegaard (in 1964), to Heidegger (in 1945 and 1967–1970), and to Sartre (in 1961). We shall consider each of these in turn, following not the chronology of their authorship, but that of existentialist thought.

Kierkegaard's project was famously opposed to Hegel's: when Kierkegaard attacked idealist dialectics for fashioning a rationalist totality, he was criticizing Hegel's system for being a system. For this Danish philosopher, there was only the individual, the ethical self freely making choices. There is no Hegelian *Geist* or rationality structuring the whole, and there can be no ultimate resolution of contradictions. One can choose an "aesthetic," satisfying life; an "ethical" life defined by fidelity to moral law; or a religious life based on an irrational and individual leap of faith in the face of the world's objective uncertainties.

Lukács's essay, "The Foundering of Form against Life: Soren Kierkegaard and Regine Olson," was preoccupied with Kierkegaard's decision to break his engagement with his fiancée, in order to pursue Christianity instead. In Goldmann's commentary, Kierkegaard was presented as "one of Lukács's most important interlocutors," despite Lukács's persistent rejection of Kierkegaard's views. Lukács used Kierkegaard's "act" in order to analyze "the gesture." What is the "life-value" of a gesture, he queried, or rather, "what is the value of form in life, the life-creating, life-enhancing value of form?" Form, he concludes, is the sole means of "expressing the absolute in life" because a gesture is "perfect within itself." What truly distinguishes one life from another is whether it is "absolute or merely relative." The "deep meaning" of Kierkegaard was that he placed "fixed points beneath the incessantly changing nuances of belief." He rejected "middle ways" as well as reconciling "higher unities." Olson could only be "a step on the way that leads to the icy temple of nothing-but-the-love-of-God." Kierkegaard's "heroism" consisted in his desire "to create forms from life," and he walked "to the end of the road he had chosen. His tragedy was that he wanted to live what cannot be lived."[7]

Goldmann contends that, given his tragic worldview, Lukács had to foredoom Kierkegaard's effort to realize a form of the absolute in the relativistic world. It is a gesture—heroic, radical, and authentic, but unfulfillable.[8] In a later work, Goldmann differentiated Lukács from other existentialists on the grounds that in *Soul and Forms*, Lukács displayed little appreciation for Kierkegaardian angst. Yet why Goldmann should see Lukács's exposition as a rejection of Kierkegaard is not very clear, considering Kierkegaard's own rejection of a reconciling dialectic and his insistence on the permanence of contradiction. Kierkegaard is closer to the Lukács of *Soul and Forms* than Goldmann—and possibly Lukács himself—would admit.[9] Perhaps Goldmann saw reconciliation in Kierkegaard's embrace of Christianity.

What is particularly important for Goldmann, however, is to view Lukács's later development in light of the early tragic position. *Theory of the Novel*, Goldmann maintains, represented a fundamental change, for in it Lukács accepted the validity of a life that does not attain absolute values but nonetheless strives for them.[10] However, in *History and Class Consciousness*, a full transformation has taken place. While Lukács still believes that "structuration and the tendency to coherence are the essence of the human condition and cultural creation" (Goldmann's words), he has moved to a historical and dialectical position and can provide answers to the questions he posed in *Soul and Forms*. Having "discovered the fundamental category of the dialectic"—totality—Lukács can affirm "the possibility of authentic life within the framework of historical action" by a collective rather than an individual subject, the proletariat, the universal class whose knowledge of self and knowledge of the whole are one and the same thing.[11] While Goldmann explicitly rejects the apocalypse of *History and Class Consciousness*, he insists that this book provides the answer not only to the problem posed by Kierkegaard and the young Lukács, but to the existentialisms of Heidegger and Sartre. (I use the word "existentialism" broadly here, cognizant of Heidegger's problems with the term.)

Goldmann, by means of Lukács, was an interlocutor of Heidegger from his first book through his last, from the 1944 appendix to *Kant* entitled "Lukács und Heidegger" (hereafter "LH") to his last unfinished work, *Lukács and Heidegger* (hereafter *LH*).[12] In "LH," Goldmann tried to show how parallel sets of questions were posed in the thinking of Lukács and Heidegger, originating in the neo-Kantian milieux of late Wilhelmian Germany (see Chapter 2). At the center of these questions was the problematic relation between a fluctuating world and absolute values. Heidegger's juxtaposition of authentic and inauthentic *Dasein* in *Being and Time* was already present in *Soul and Form*'s distinction between "Life" and relativistic, empirical, daily "life," and *Being and Time* responded to and challenged *History and Class Consciousness*.[13] Heidegger's notion of authentic *Dasein* stands in opposition to Lukács's conceptualization of true consciousness as the creation of subject-object unity and the "We" through class action.

The later Lukács considered Goldmann's argument *"ein Kurio-*

sität."[14] In the 1967 preface to *History and Class Consciousness*, the Hungarian philosopher, while neither embracing nor dismissing Goldmann's claim that Heidegger was responding to him, declared that central preoccupations of his early work, such as "alienation," were "in the air at the time." Lukács declared his lack of interest in "who was first and who influenced whom."[15] Heidegger, speaking to a French disciple, insisted that he knew neither Lukács nor his work before World War II.[16] Whether or not Heidegger knew Lukács, it is difficult to imagine that he was unfamiliar with his work, given their mutual links to Lask and the notoriety of *History and Class Consciousness*. (It is worth noting that Emmanuel Levinas, who studied with Heidegger during the winter term of 1928–1929, made use of the notions of reification and "actual and potential consciousness" in his influential book on Husserl's theory of intuition, published in 1930.)[17] More to the point, is the fact that certain matters were "in the air." For Goldmann, this is not just a question of immediate influences, but, rather, of modes of thinking, the mental structures that came of the crises of European capitalism and life and responses to them. A "new problematic" was "incarnated" first in Lukács's and then in Heidegger's writings, and this can only be discovered through a genetic study of the homologous structure of their work.[18]

Goldmann pursues this by examining the Heidelberg neo-Kantians and the relation between Marxist and "university" philosophy in the early twentieth century. It is within these milieux that the "new problematic" developed, leading on one hand to phenomenology and existentialism, and on the other to Lukácsian dialectical Marxism. While Marxist and university philosophy were "expressions . . . of different sectors of the global society," they were never "radically" separate, and they communicated with each other.[19] Marx and Engels, after all, were educated within the university world of young Hegelianism, and later Marxists were influenced greatly by academic positivism and neo-Kantianism. Marxist and academic philosophies developed homologously, out of the same "global society."

There was, Goldmann argues, a homologous evolution from Marx to Bernstein, Plekhanov, and Kautsky, on one hand, and from Hegel to the neo-Kantians and university positivism on the other. The "new problematic" in Lukács and Heidegger broke from positivism, which had been dominant from the end of the eras of Hegel, Marx, and Kierkegaard until the turn of the twentieth century. *Soul and Forms*, as an existential work, and *History and Class Consciousness*, as a Marxist work, represent "a veritable renaissance."[20] Lukács's turn to Marx occurred only after he had left Heidelberg to join the Hungarian Revolution, and what marked this turn was his insistence on the unity of theory and practice, the identity of subject and object, and the concept of totality. As Goldmann sees it, phenomenology and existentialism also represented a break with traditional bourgeois philosophy, which was based on subject-object dualism, with its accompanying bifurcations of determinism/freedom, power/humanism, knowledge/morality, synchrony/diachrony. Husserl, Heidegger, and Lukács asserted, in Goldmann's words, that

> [m]an is not *opposite* the world which he tries to understand and on which he acts, but *within* this world, of which he is a part; and there is no radical rupture between the meaning that he is trying to find or introduce in the universe, and that which he tries to find or introduce in his own existence. This meaning, common to individual or collective human life . . . is called history.[21]

It is from here that one can delineate the differences among Husserl, Heidegger, and Lukács.

The notion that consciousness must always be *of* something and that the subject exists only in relation to the world, says Goldmann, requires that the idea of a nonempirical transcendental subject that constitutes the world be rejected. The "first fundamental commonality" between Lukács and Heidegger is that they reject the transcendental subject on behalf of a concept (with Hegelian roots) "of man as inseparable from the world of which he is part," and a definition of man's place in the world through historicity.[22] Lukács's theory of history rests on the action of transindividual subjects—specifically, classes—whereas Heidegger's "romantic" view of history does not. But this is just one of the significant differences between them. For Lukács, writes Goldmann, history is made by all human beings and is thus "under a global vector" making progress and reaction meaningful concepts that gauge the growth or diminution of knowledge and freedom. The idea of "progress" is vacuous to Heidegger because authenticity and inauthenticity of the individual are ultimately the only meaningful categories for him.[23] Finally, since Lukács characterizes all human action as historical, there can be no dualism between the human sciences and philosophy, whereas for Heidegger, historical action is the privilege of elite individuals. They alone cannot be addressed by positivist science, for theirs are questions of ontology, of Being writ large, as opposed to the "ontic" world of beings. Heidegger's elites are ever engaged in repetition in their quest for authenticity because they are ever lapsing into inauthenticity. Lukács's history, on the other hand, progresses or regresses.[24]

In brief, Goldmann wants to show that at one and the same moment, there is a "close kinship" (*parenté*) and a "radical difference" between Lukács and Heidegger.[25] He maintains that several terms central to Heidegger's philosophy, notably, "*Sein*" (Being), "*Dasein*" (Being-there), and "*Zuhandenheit*" (readiness-to-hand, more or less translatable as manipulability), are remarkably parallel to the use by Lukács of the terms "totality," "subject" (or "man"), and "praxis." Heidegger's project was a phenomenological inquiry into ontology, that is, into the question of Being. In 1929, shortly after *Being and Time* was published, he defined "the basic question of metaphysics" as "Why are there beings at all, why not rather nothing?"[26] His question concerned the category of categories, as it were, that of "isness," what it means "to be." It thus goes beyond inquiry about various empirical beings, which is the task of science proper, that is, the realm of "ontic" rather than "ontological" inquiry. The former concerns beings (*Seiende*), while the latter concerns Being itself. What Being, he wants to know, makes beings possible; what is the "ground"? In the past, *das Sein* was mistaken for *das Seiende*.

Heidegger maintained that the type of question he asked had been forgotten since the ancient Greeks. It therefore required its own terminology, to be invented by him: humans are the only beings capable of inquiry into their own being and Being in general, so Heidegger classifies human-being as *Dasein* (Being-there). *Dasein*, not as the object of scientific inquiry, not as an entity or thing, but as a Being of meaning, is addressed hermeneutically in *Being and Time* as a first step toward analyzing Being in general.

In analyzing *Dasein*, Heidegger began by rejecting the opposition of subject and object and by insisting on a holistic approach. "Facts" of our existence can only be interpreted within its totality. *Dasein* is not opposite the world, but is always Being-in-the-World, and that world is temporal. We are "thrown" into this world, and our primary involvement with it is not "knowing" it as something opposite to us, but as *Sorge* (care), as engagement with it, for we must make our Being-in-the-World into a project, a future which we actualize. We encounter the world into which we have been thrown either through *Zuhandenheit* (readiness-to-hand), seeing the world as useful, as that which is to be manipulated so that our possibilities are realized, or through *Vorhandenheit* (presence-at-hand), that is, seeing the world as present before us, opposite to us, and there to be known. That which "is" is not atemporal Platonic forms somehow lurking behind appearances, but is rather in our temporal—and thus historical—existence. *Dasein* is activity, not entity. This is why Heidegger insisted that *Dasein*'s "essence" is in *Dasein*'s "existence." When we mistake *Seiende* for *Sein*, we mistake one temporal mode, the present, for the totality, which is trimodal for it contains past and future as well. Understanding the whole of our existence, that is, understanding it within all three temporal modes, necessarily entails grasping our finitude because the future, ultimately, brings death to *Dasein*. Recognizing that we die, that we are each *Sein zum Tode* (Being-towards-Death) is a fundamental criterion of *Eigentlicheit*, authenticity. It compels us to see unceasingly that "possibility" is more crucial than "actuality." Such recognition engenders pursuit of a self-aware, self-determined existence based on one's choices and actions, and taking full responsibility for those choices. Authenticity is fullness of Being of the self-conscious and self-determining "I." But this always requires recognition of death, which I dread; it fills me with "angst." It is an individualizing angst because only I can die *my* death. Authenticity thus demands that I act "resolutely" in full recognition of the fact that I will die; in recognition that *time* is the ontological horizon of my self, and of my being; and that consequently I am free to act in light of this.

Heidegger insists that, thrown into the world, *Dasein* is not isolated but is *Mitsein*, a "being-with" others. "Being-with" implies that we live in an "everydayness" with others, especially at work. However, because we are "being-with" others, we can become not ourselves. We have an inherent tendency to "fall" and become alienated from ourselves as part of "the they"—"*Das Man*." In *Das Man*, the authentic self dissipates. The realm of *Das Man* is that of "chatter," in which there is a losing of self in the "they-self." For Heidegger, "The Self of everyday Dasein is the *they-self*, which we distinguish from the *authentic Self*— that is, from the Self which has been taken hold of in its own way. . . . As they-self, the particular Dasein has been dispersed into the 'they' and must first find itself."[27] Authenticity means being resolute and rejecting *Das Man*; to do so means, one might say, to be conscious of oneself ontologically and not only ontically. This resolution entails "Being-towards-Death," for I die alone not as one with the They. Authenticity requires recognition of death, for that alone gives us our Selves as totalities. Such resolution demands that I act towards the future. I embrace my freedom, I project possibilities; this establishes my *Existenz*, an existential structure corresponding to temporal projection of the future (as opposed to the other two existential structures, "fallenness" in the present, and "facticity" in the past).

This summary presentation of some of *Being and Time*'s complex themes enables us to grasp more clearly Goldmann's presentation of *Sein*, *Dasein*, and *Zuhandenheit* as homologous to Lukács's totality, subject, and praxis. Goldmann argues that both the development of dialectical thought in Hegel and Marx and the philosophical "turn" of the

Heidelberg neo-Kantians were born of the demand to "surmount" the traditional opposition in Western thought of the subject and object of action.[28] He writes:

> The fundamental problematic common to Lukács and Heidegger is that of the inseparability of man from meaning [*du sens*] and the world, that of the identity of subject and object: when man understands the world, he understands the meaning of *Dasein*, the meaning of his Being and, inversely, it is in understanding his own Being that he is able to understand the world. . . . What Heidegger tells us of the category of Being is already there in Lukács in relation to totality. Being is . . . a fundamental reality beginning from which *Dasein* questions. Its character is *temporal, meaningful* [*significant*] and historical.[29]

Sein cannot be separated from, let alone opposed to *Dasein*/the subject (that is, human being). When Heidegger's inauthentic *Dasein* sees the world as *Vorhanden* rather than *Zuhanden*, this parallels Lukács's historical subject's seeing the world as reified rather than as created and creatable through historical praxis.

Heidegger does not name Lukács, but Goldmann contends that his placing of "reification of consciousness" (*Verdinglichung des Bewusstseins*) in quotation marks indicates the context of *Being and Time*, which was published four years after *History and Class Consciousness*, in which "reification of consciousness" is a central theme. This makes manifest "with whom" Heidegger debates and "the place he wants to occupy in relation to him."[30] When, on the last page of *Being and Time*, Heidegger speaks of "reification," he addresses it as a valid and important problem, yet one that has been misplaced on the "ontic" level. Ontological investigation must situate it.[31] Heidegger's problem with Lukács, Goldmann deduces, is that Lukács accords to reification a sociohistorical status lacking ontological foundation. But for Lukács, Goldmann points out, no ontological foundation is possible divorced from social and historical knowledge.[32]

Goldmann also discerns an important parallel between Heidegger's criticism of traditional ontology for opposing subject and object, and Lukács's critique of positivism. Lukács's analysis, however, would have to be situated solely on the ontic level in Heidegger's eyes, and this misses the point of Lukács's denial of the opposition of judgments of fact and judgments of value. On one hand, Lukács and Heidegger agree that

> [t]he world is not . . . given immediately opposite to a knowing consciousness who knows it . . . and who judges it thereafter. Using Piaget's language, the object itself, the formal claim [*la contestation protocolaire*] of positivism—

the presence here of a cigarette lighter—is not a fact, but is already a construction: all thought implies a construction of the subject. There is no given world, the object is constructed, and its inseparability from the subject goes so far as their identity . . . in the social sciences. . . . [O]bjectivity does not exist. There is only and always structuration of the object by the subject.[33]

On the other hand, Heidegger presents his own parallel dualities, those of authentic and inauthentic, ontological, and ontic. He thus separates philosophy from and opposes it to science. When Heidegger tries to transcend traditional ontology and the subject/object dualism, "a two-dimensional spirit" (ontological/ontic) comes to define history. But for Lukács, writes Goldmann, "science and philosophy are inseparable in the understanding and explanation of a single history, which is not immediately given and is 'to be made' in science and praxis."[34] Lukács posits a collective subject of history, whose self-knowledge is knowledge of the whole, making it an identical subject-object. Heidegger's *Dasein* is ultimately singular. Following Marx's "Theses on Feuerbach," which criticized materialists who failed to see that "the object, reality," embodies human activity, Lukács does not counterpose praxis as *Zuhandenheit* to a world that is *Vorhanden*. Seeing the world as *Vorhanden* is a reification, whereas the collective subject recognizes it as human-made. *Zuhandenheit* results when *Dasein* comes across something *Vorhanden* and uses it. The example given in *Being and Time* is of a hammer which is *Zuhanden* when pounding, but is not regarded as the thing "hammer" when it breaks and is just there as pieces. For Lukács, in contrast, *Vorhandenheit* is an essential moment of *Zuhandenheit*.[35] For Heidegger, if the problem of truth is formulated as "adequation of representation of the object," it rests on "the false ontology" of *Vorhandenheit*.[36] Truth has no scientific character. It is part of "the mode" of authenticity as opposed to inauthenticity. For Lukács, the ground of truth is transindividual praxis, which can be scientifically studied. For Lukács, writes Goldmann, "truth is the possibility of orienting oneself in praxis; the scientific conception is derived from the project." Consequently,

> [f]or *Being and Time* history, in as much as it is authentic . . . is the history of individuals who become authentic in isolation and by [making] decisions, before again falling into the inauthentic. History is made [*s'effectue*] each time, beginning from a resolution whose authenticity comes from being-free-towards-death and from the tie this resolute-decision . . . creates between the individual and the community [*Gemeinschaft*] of a people [*Volk*] through the hero from the past whom this individual has chosen, in this decision, to repeat in orienting himself towards the future. Heidegger calls this authentic being-with in the community of a People: *destiny*. It is not a

question of the human community or universal history—which is, according to Heidegger, on the level of chatter—but of the community of a people and of the authentic repetition of earlier heroes. For Lukács in 1923, on the other hand, the subjects of history are groups, collective subjects which are at the same time objects. *Dasein*, this particular form of Being beginning from which action and understanding are possible, is not, according to Lukács, individual, but plural subjects whose possibilities are objective.[37]

Thus while both philosophers speak of meaning revealed in relation to (respectively) *Dasein* or a collective subject, this relation is in one case "determined by the individuality of *Dasein*" and in the other determined by "the collectivity of the subject."

Outside of the brief passage above, Goldmann never develops the comparison between Lukács's collective subject/human community (or universal history) and Heidegger's *Dasein*/ the *Volk* and its destiny. The notion of *Volk* at least raises issues concerning Goldmann's radical contraposition of the transindividual in Lukács and the individual in Heidegger, especially given Heidegger's discussion of *Geschick* (destiny) as *Dasein*-in-community (national community, that is). Goldmann does, however, make a pertinent comparison between the political directions—one might call them homologous directions—taken by the two thinkers in relation to such concepts.

Here, again, Heidegger and Lukács are presented by Goldmann as both similar and opposed. Both rallied to dictators, Heidegger to Hitler and Lukács to Stalin, as a result of what Goldmann calls "their respective global analyses of the meaning of history." In a perverse way, both conceived themselves as akin to Hegel, who, privy to the cunning of reason, perceived Napoleon's world historical role though the emperor himself did not. Each imagined that he, as a philosopher, had grasped reality better than a politician (Hitler or Stalin) did. For example, Heidegger believed that he saw what Hitler, obsessed with anti-Semitism, could not: biological theories of race are situated on the ontic rather than the ontological level. Nonetheless, Hitler was the charismatic, exceptional man who recaptured authenticity in political history, and so Heidegger rallied to him, even though he believed that this Leader, as in every "repetition," would return to the "they," forgetting authenticity and leading ultimately to political catastrophe.[38] For Lukács, Stalin, whatever his personal motivations, represented a transitory Bonapartism necessary to protect the revolution. "Needless to say," remarks Goldmann, "neither Hitler nor Stalin could accept these positions: for the first anti-semitism constituted an essential element of his politics . . .; as for the Stalinists, far from accepting themselves as a transitory phase, they claimed to be realizing socialism in one country and to be constituting a revolutionary force throughout the world."[39] Long after Hitler and Stalin were gone, Heidegger and Lukács still maintained that they, rather than the dictators and their cohorts, had truly understood the historical moment. The proof: Hitler produced catastrophe, and Stalinism helped defeat Hitler. Goldmann doesn't say it, but by such arguments Heidegger and Lukács engaged in remarkable feats of *mauvaise foi*, self-exculpation for their own collaboration with two of history's most repulsive regimes; authenticity is to be found nowhere in their assertions.

What all of this also makes clear is the extent to which Goldmann, in studying Lukács and Heidegger, is in a dialogue with and is criticizing their ideas. *Being and Time*, despite everything (particularly its author), posed important existential questions. And Goldmann—as always—wants to save Lukács from, well, Lukács. This entailed reformulating the subject-object relation in terms of partial identity. But if, as Goldmann maintained, Lukács failed to adequately describe the relation between individual and class consciousness, a *hiatus irrationalis* emerges between the individual and the imputed totality. And this, in turn, poses acutely to Marxism the question of the individual and the specific, which was perhaps the essential concern of existentialism. Goldmann repeatedly warned against a socialism which negated certain fundamental values born of the bourgeois era—the individual, liberty, equality before the law etc. Existentialism, however flawed in Goldmann's mind, insisted on matters he believed urgent. The existentialist who dominated Goldmann's era in France, Sartre, had several bitter exchanges with Lukács. Consequently, Goldmann's essays on Sartre are especially valuable in elucidating Goldmann's own ideas.

II

In 1966 Goldmann hailed Sartre as a "great philosophical thinker" who was "probably the most important French philosopher alive."[40] In an interview conducted jointly for Belgrade Radio-Television and *Praxis*, the dissident Marxist Yugoslavian journal, he declared that existentialism had a positive character and a positive influence on Marxism because it re-posed the question of authenticity and helped Marxism retrieve important elements—humanist ones—of itself.[41] This echoed claims Sartre had made in *Search for a Method*, the long introduction, initiallly published separately, to his *Critique of Dialectical Reason*.

Beginning in the 1940s, Sartre and Lukács were philosophical ships passing each other in a Marxist night, occasionally firing across each other's bows. The first article Goldmann devoted to Lukács after returning to Paris from Switzerland was entitled "Georg Lukács, L'essayiste." It was published in 1950, a time when Sartre's influence was immense. Goldmann's assertion of Lukács's place in the history of existentialism probably took his readers aback. The Lukács known then in Paris was not the Lukács championed by Goldmann. It was a Lukács who had just been deployed by French Stalinists to assault Sartre and existentialism. Sartre replied in kind, yet as one commentator later put it, neither seemed to have read much by the other.[42] Lukács's early works were unavailable in French; the first chapters of *History and Class Consciousness* were translated only in 1957, in the independent Marxist journal *Arguments*, over Lukács's protests,[43] *Souls and-Forms* and *Theory of the Novel* appeared even later.

Moreover, the first work by Lukács to appear in French, one of his worst, could only inspire Sartre's ire. *Existentialisme ou marxisme?* (1949) was not solely philosophical in purpose, for it aimed to assist the French Communist crusade against the "Rassemblement democratique revolutionnaire," a short-lived movement Sartre helped found as a socialist "Third Force," neither Stalinist nor reformist. This was also the context of Lukács's Paris lecture tour in early 1949, which was accompanied by a series of nasty public exchanges with Sartre, particularly by means of interviews of the two philosophers by François Erval in *Combat*. Lukács accused existentialism of being an "indirect apology" for capitalism; Sartre accused Lukács of not being dialectical. Lukács called Sartre a "mediocre academic" who sinned "against intellectual integrity"; Sartre declared that Lukács had thereby defined himself. In his book, Lukács dismissed existentialism as an ideological reflection of "the spiritual and moral chaos of the current bourgeois intelligence," well on its way to nihilism.[44] For Lukács, "two orientations of thought" emerged after the French revolution. One led left to Marx via Hegel. The other turned right, beginning with Schelling and Kierkegaard. Both Marx and Kierkegaard were responses to the collapse of objective Idealism. The former became a dialectical materialist (the only philosophical basis that makes socialism possible, insisted Lukács). The latter immersed himself in a "theological-mystical" worldview.[45] Lukács's ultimate point: there was no "third way" between rationalism (defined here as dialectical materialism) and irrationalism (defined as most other forms of modern thought).

Goldmann had a singular vantage point from which to view the Lukács-Sartre dispute, for unlike the combatants, he had examined the relevant writings of both. Despite his own criticisms of existentialism, Goldmann was undoubtedly unimpressed by Lukács's attacks on Sartre, and his own interest in Sartre grew a decade later with the publication of the latter's *Search for a Method* and *Critique of Dialectical Reason*. Sartre probably encountered the actual text of *History and Class Consciousness* for the first time when it began appearing in translation in *Arguments*. Notably, this was when he was writing the *Critique*. *Search for a Method* focused on central preoccupations of both Lukács and Goldmann, and the latter read it attentively. Sartre's early existential philosophy proclaimed the radical freedom of the individual, who chooses even when claiming not to choose and who is conceived within a Heideggerian and quasi-Hobbesian ahistorical ontology that sees conflict as the essence of interhuman relations. His play *No Exit* had proclaimed that "hell is other people," and in *Being and Nothingness*, Sartre's discussion of *Mitsein* (Being-with others), including the deliberation on love discussed by Goldmann in the "Buffet Dialogue," always presumed conflict to be primary in human relations.

Like Heidegger on reification, so for Sartre it is ontology that provides the foundation for social and historical conflicts. The "we" (the "*nous*") can only take the form of an ensemble of men reduced to an object by the "Look" of a "Third," an Other (for example, a boss and his workers). A plural "subject" exists only through cojoining individual experiences. The "we" can never go beyond the subjectivity of individuals as lone consciousnesses. Thus while Sartre, in 1944, subscribed to the notion of the class struggle, he argued, "When we say a man who's out of work is free, we don't mean that he can do whatever he wants and change himself into a rich and tranquil bourgeois on the spot. *He is free because he can always choose to accept his lot with resignation or to rebel against it*. . . . [H]e is able to choose to struggle—in his own name and in the name of others—against all forms of destitution."[46] Even when addressing the action of groups—here, a class—Sartre always reduces action to individuals and their free choices. He juxtaposed Being-for-Itself, that is, consciousness conceived as a "nothingness" surging out at the world, which it "intends," and Being-in-Itself, that is, opaque, brute matter. The For-Itself becomes translated into the principle of the individual. This ontology posits that there is inevitable conflict between For-Itselves surging forth to make themselves.

When Sartre, in the late 1950s, sought to synthesize existentialism and Marxism, he had to use history as a fundamental category, and this compelled essential transformations in his analyses. Also, the For-Itself/In-Itself division was reinvented as that between praxis and the "practico-inert." The latter is the realm of human products turned against their producers; it is a reified realm. (Notably, Goldmann's essay "La Réification," which dealt extensively with Lukács, appeared in *Les Temps modernes* while Sartre was writing his *Critique*.) Praxis, however, is no longer presented as individuals making choices but as

collectivities of individuals in structured and mediated historical relations. Individuals are no longer simply surging For-Itselves, for Sartre
now tried to describe reciprocal relations. He elaborated on these
themes in the *Critique*, where he distinguished "serial" collectivities (in
which men remain isolated though engaged in the same act, such as
waiting on line for a bus) from authentic, that is, common, group
praxis (such as the storming of the Bastille in 1789).

In *Search for a Method*, Sartre began by asking if it were possible "to
constitute a structural, historical anthropology." Yes, he concluded,
but solely through Marxism, "the only philosophy of our time that we
cannot go beyond." However, the specificity of the individual had
been lost by contemporary Marxists, who deployed Marxism as if it
were an a priori system. The consequence was the dissolution of all
particulars.[47] Marxism became "a pure fixed knowledge," and its practice turned into an "empiricism without principles." Intellectuals serving the Party, habitually, distorted or ignored what was unsuitable,
thereby "violating experience," and "conceptualizing the event *before*
having studied it." Moreover, "Marxism [had] stopped," in part because it had been subordinated to the needs of the Soviet state.[48]

Sartre praised Hegel for not fixating on "frozen paradoxes ultimately referring to an empty subjectivity" and aiming "through his
concepts at the veritable concrete." At the same time, Sartre lauded the
great foe of Hegel's system building, Kierkegaard, for refusing "to
play the role of concept in the Hegelian system," and making progress
"towards freedom" by insisting "on the *primacy* of the specifically real
over thought." Sartre concludes that "Marx rather than Kierkegaard or
Hegel is right since he asserts with Kierkegaard the specificity of
human *existence* and, along with Hegel, takes the concrete man in his
objective reality."[49] For Sartre, a living and heuristic Marxism at once
gives the particular its own meaning and reveals it to be part of a synthetic whole. The problem with contemporary Marxism was that it
"reabsorbed man into the idea," whereas existentialism "seeks him everywhere *where he is*, at work, in his home, in the street." It uses its
concepts as regulative ideas. Consequently Sartre, when speaking of
both sociohistorical realities and method, intentionally refers not to totality or totalities, which indicate fixity, but to "totalizations." Totalization is "never achieved," and "totality exists at best only in the form of
a *detotalized totality*."[50] The problem with contemporary Marxism is
that "the totalizing investigation has given way to a Scholasticism of
the totality."[51] Aided by existentialism, Marxist concepts will become
"keys" and "interpretive schema" instead of "already totalized knowledge." They will thereby be able to reconquer man within Marxism."[52]

Sartre chastised Marxism for becoming a doctrine that "situated" but did not discover. For instance, it tells us that Flaubert's "realism" was tied to the petit bourgeoisie of the Second Empire, but it does not explain why literature was Flaubert's passion or why he wrote what he wrote as opposed to other books. To Lukács's assertion in *Existentialisme ou Marxisme?* that the prewar bourgeois avant-garde indulged in a "carnival of fetishized interiority," Sartre retorts, So what? The practitioners of literary subjectivism proclaimed their intentions openly. Lukács's "lazy Marxism" doesn't study the conduct of particular individuals, but "puts everything into everything," turning "real men into myths" and giving us a "false individuality," which is ultimately "a Hegelian idea . . . which creates for itself its own instruments."[53] This, Sartre suggests, is a species of reductionism:

> Valéry is a petit bourgeois intellectual, no doubt about it. But not every petit bourgeois intellectual is Valéry. The heuristic inadequacy of contemporary Marxism is contained in these sentences. Marxism lacks any hierarchy of mediations which would permit it to grasp the process which produces the person and his product inside a class and within a given society at a given historical moment. Characterizing Valéry as a petit bourgeois and his work as idealist, the Marxist will find in both alike only what he has put there.[54]

To grasp the mediations between the individual and the world, Marxism had need for "auxiliary disciplines" it had traditionally shunned, such as psychoanalysis. A "method which is primarily concerned with establishing the way in which the child lives his family relations inside a given society" is crucial to show the passage "from general and abstract determinations to the particular traits of the single individual."[55] Without incorporating such auxiliaries—including the contributions of positivist sociology, Sartre specifies—Marxism would remain inadequate and partial. An adequately totalizing Marxist method will yield *not* the abstract human being, but, rather, what Sartre classified (in his presentation to the UNESCO symposium on Kierkegaard, and in *The Family Idiot*, his unfinished study of Flaubert, which he called the sequel to *Search for a Method*) as a "universal singular." In Sartre's words, "Summed up and for this reason universalized by his epoch, he in turn resumes it by reproducing himself in it as singularity. Universal by the singular universality of human history, singular by the universalizing singularity of his projects, he requires simultaneous examination from both ends."[56] The method is always a double movement whose epistemology rests on "the truth of metaphysics: the experimenter is a part of the experimental system." One never stands outside the world; the researcher is "outside" of one group that he may study, only to the extent that he is "inside" another.[57] Thus Sartre is contemptuous of positivism in the human sciences, be it a Marxist or a non-Marxist positivism.

Sartre urges against two types of "Idealism": the reduction of the real to the subjective and the denial of subjectivity on behalf of "objectivity." The alternative to these Idealisms is the double movement of the "progressive-regressive method," whose origins he attributes to Henri Lefebvre and whose strength he locates in its dialectical integration of sociology and history.[58] In a sociological study of a rural community, Lefebvre first delineated its "horizontal complexity" by examining the level and techniques of agricultural productivity, and the social structure underlying and being shaped by them. Various aspects of the community were described, ranging from demography and religion to family structure. He then turned to "vertical or historical complexity," that is, how different social formations from different ages coexist within the same community. Vertical complexity complements and acts on the horizontal complexity, all while the horizontal complexity acts on vertical complexity. A picture of this totalization (that is, of the community) is fashioned through three phases: phenomenological description, guided by general theory; an analysis ("analytico-regressive") of reality, including dating it; and a "historico-genetic" effort "to rediscover the present, but elucidated, understood, explained" (Sartre's words, summarizing Lefebvre).[59]

Sartre is seeking, by means of Lefebvre, a method that conceives individuals and their actions at once as singular and as part of the totalization that comprises history. An endless dialectical interplay of different levels of research, corresponding to the different levels of the phenomenon, is required. To "understand" means using both the progressive and regressive movements at once. (In the *Critique* Sartre calls them, using the language of structuralism, diachronic and synchronic). Man is a "signifying being" and it is "the work or the act of the individual which reveals to us the secret of his conditioning." For example, Sartre asks how one comprehends a simple human action, such as that of a friend, with whom I have been sitting, who suddenly goes to open a window because it is too warm. His action is not "inscribed in the temperature." It is "a synthetic conduct which by unifying itself, unifies before my eyes the practical field in which we both are."[60] In the intensity of my discussion with him, I had experienced heat in the room, but only as an "unarmed discomfort," which, along with the intention of his move, is revealed by his act. The progressive moment grasps the "objective result" of his action (which will open the window and allow cool air in). But the moment is inextricably linked to the regressive moment, which reveals the original condition.[61] The progressive movement grasps a synthetic whole of purposeful behavior—a totalization—in a situation whose elements are analyzed in a regressive movement. The latter is external and entails breaking down the object in order to analyze causes; the former is a synthetic movement grasping the whole internal action.

This dual movement synthesizes a Marxist historical approach with an existential psychoanalytical one, asserts Sartre, in opposition to mechanical and schematic Marxisms. When one fails to do this, one reduces Valéry or Flaubert to a petit bourgeois. Or, as Plekhanov did to Napoleon, one turns an individual into nothing more than the role demanded by a historical moment. The real Marx, for Sartre, is Hegel and Kierkegaard at once. To speak of the historical necessities of a moment without simultaneously focusing on individual contingency is, for him, simply uninteresting. To say that a fellow named Bonaparte played the role of dictator, which was required by a military regime to liquidate the revolution, is not just uninteresting; it is obvious. It is like announcing that Valéry was a petit bourgeois. What interests Sartre is

> to show . . . that *this* Napoleon was necessary, that the development of the Revolution forged at once the necessity of the dictatorship and the entire personality of the one who was to administer it, and the historical process provided *General Bonaparte personally* with preliminary powers and with the occasions which allowed him—and him alone—to hasten this liquidation. In short, we are not dealing with an abstract universal, with a situation so poorly defined that several Bonapartes were *possible*, but with a concrete totalization in which *this* real bourgeoisie, made up of real living men, was to liquidate *this* Revolution, in which *this* Revolution created its own liquidator in the person of Bonaparte, in himself and for himself—that is, for those bourgeois and in his eyes.[62]

The scholastic a priorism of contemporary Marxism is not only reductionist in its understanding of individuals (for example, of Flaubert, Valéry, Napoleon), but it also fails to understand collective behavior. (This is a remarkable criticism given that this collective behavior is at the center of Marxist theory. Class, after all, is conceived by it to be the motor of history.)

Stalinized Marxism, Sartre argued, converts the real worker from a real being into a Platonic idea, eternal, universal, true. Just as Plato could approach the Forms only through myths, events became "edifying myths" for Stalinists. Sartre maintains that he wants to look at real human beings acting collectively in history. He wants "to insist on the ambiguity of past facts" and to contend that "the event itself, while a collective apparatus, is more or less marked by individual signs." In Sartre's argument, "the ambiguity of political and social action results

most often from profound contradictions between the needs, the mo-
tives of the act, and, on the other side, the collective apparatus of the
social field—that is, the instruments of praxis."[63] Sartre therefore embraces the proposition that "by becoming conscious of itself the proletariat becomes the subject of History," while simultaneously declaring
that more than one proletariat exists because of the varying developments of different national production groups. His view is "differential"—"not to recognize the solidarity of these proletariats would be as
absurd as to underestimate their *separation*."[64]

But what composes a group? Sartre did not abandon his earlier individualism and has not argued against Stalinist and Marxist a priorism
in order to embrace metaphysical or reified notions of collectivity. Instead, he conceives collectivities as structured and mediated relations
among actual people. This, he insists, is the proper Marxist concept.
"We repeat with Marxism: there are only men and real relations between men." The group is "a multiplicity of relations and of relations
among those relations."[65] In the *Critique* itself, Sartre elaborated his
theory of collectivities and group behavior at length. For our concerns
here, what is essential is his overall purpose when he speaks of the
collective and the individual as real but differentiated and, consequently, in need of a progressive-regressive method to comprehend
them. In *Being and Nothingness*, using Heidegger's *Mitsein*, Sartre
claimed that "Being-for-Others" was an ontologically primary category revealing conflict to be the primary relation among individuals.
The Marxist Sartre, in contrast, posits the possibility of individuals
with others in a historically created action and community. Yet it is
only a possibility, not a necessity, for Sartre also insists on the historical category of contingency. Here, we can again perceive why Sartre
insisted on speaking of totalization and not of totality.

Sartre, one might say, tried to be Hegel and Kierkegaard at once by
being an existential Marx. It was precisely such an ambition that
Lukács denounced without qualification in 1948. For Lukács, dialectical (or Marxist) and existential (including Kierkegaardian) thought
were irreconcilable . (Ironically, this same complaint against Sartre's
Critique was made, from the perspective of the liberal Right, by Raymond Aron: "A descendant of Kierkegaard cannot at the same time be
a descendant of Marx."[66]) Goldmann was no Kierkegaardian, and
while we find him in frequent disagreement with Sartre, there is no
radical rejection of the existentialist philosopher. At the same time,
while Goldmann always placed tragic and existential thought in close
proximity to each other, he distinguished clearly between them, at
least as concerns Sartre's thought. In 1947 Sartre defined "the chief
source of great tragedy" as human freedom. Fate, in ancient tragedies,

"is only the other side of freedom. Passions themselves are freedoms caught in their own trap."[67] Antigone confronts a free choice between family and civic morality. It is "through particular situations that each age grasps the human situation and the enigmas human freedom must confront." Today's problems may not be identical to those of Antigone, but they raise the same questions of choice.[68] For Goldmann, especially in *The Hidden God*, the source of tragedy is not human freedom, but the refusal of the world from within it. Tragic man is not defined by his necessary exercise of choice, but by his quest for a totality, a wholeness, that is unattainable, making the world all and nothing at once. Thus in Racine's *Phèdre*, there is a "solitary dialogue" between Phèdre and the sun, the divinity in all its grandeur, while at the center of Sartre's *The Condemned of Altona*, there is "the same solitary dialogue of the hero with a divinity that has become problematic, the men of the future," who will perhaps be crabs.[69] Finally, in Goldmann's theory it is through transindividual action, or through recognizing its historical possibility, that one moves from the tragic to the dialectical.

Analyzing *Search for a Method* Goldmann, although not accepting Sartre's claim that all of Marxism had stopped (what of his own?), identified with Sartre's critique of mechanistic, positivistic and what Goldmann called "degraded and unilateral" Marxism.[70] Sartre's insistence on the individual and contingency appealed to Goldmann, who had long argued for the importance of individual freedom for socialism and argued that socialism was a wager, not a necessity. Here, we can locate an important link among Kierkegaard, Sartre, and Goldmann, although it is nowhere explicit. Goldmann makes Pascal the father of the dialectic; Pascal has more often been seen as a father of existentialism and Kierkegaard's predecessor. In Kierkegaard's worldview, there is no provable objective truth in Christianity; it requires an existentially based, but ultimately irrational, leap of faith. Goldmann argued that while "reason is an important factor in human life . . . *it is not the whole of man.*" Marxism was a wager in humanity's future comparable to Pascal's: "*Risk, possibility of failure, hope of success* and what is a synthesis of these three in *a faith which is a wager* are the constitutive elements of the human condition."[71]

It is noteworthy that in *History and Class Consciousness*, Lukács responded to the application of the "epithet" "religious" to Marxism by declaring, "What they call faith . . . is nothing more or less than the certainty that capitalism is doomed and that—ultimately—the proletariat will be victorious. There can be no 'material' guarantee of this certitude." But what is Marxist certitude that cannot be guaranteed materially? Perhaps the certitude is more appropriately displaced by a Pascalian wager. Lukács continued: "[T]he so-called religious faith is nothing more than the certitude that regardless of all temporary defeats and setbacks, the historical process will come to fruition *in our deeds and through our deeds.*"[72] But while Lukács is dismissive of "faith," Goldmann embraces it. And so, indeed, did Sartre, in terms almost identical to Goldmann's, accenting humanism, yet also accepting the possibility of failure and the authority of tragedy in ways Lukács, as a Marxist, did not. In a 1975 interview with Sartre in *Le Nouvel Observateur*, the following exchange took place:

> Sartre: Nothing can guarantee success for us, nor can anything rationally convince us that failure is inevitable. But the alternatives really are socialism or barbarism.
>
> Question: *In the end, like Pascal, you are making a wager.*
>
> Sartre: Yes, with the difference that I am wagering on man, not on God. But it is true that either man crumbles . . . or else this revolution succeeds and creates man by bringing about his freedom. Nothing is less sure. In the same way, socialism is not a certainty, it is a value: it is freedom choosing itself as the goal.
>
> Question: *Which therefore presupposes a faith?*
>
> Sartre: Yes, to the extent that it is impossible to find a rational basis for revolutionary optimism, since what *is* is the present reality.

Sartre then adds that it is necessary to pursue radical politics even though success is not guaranteed "and there faith enters in."[73] It is notable that two decades earlier, Sartre had planned to write a play entitled *Le Pari* (The Wager)—in 1955, the year of the publication of Goldmann's *The Hidden God*, although there is no evidence to link the two projects directly.[74]

Of course, the differences between Sartre and Goldmann are as important as any similarities. For Goldmann, the key categories of Sartre's worldview and their literary and philosophical expressions were generated within the context of the "crisis of capitalism." Here, Goldmann becomes curiously contradictory. *Nausea* (1938), he argues, was the first important French novel to present on the literary level an essential "problematic" of the period—the dissolution of the individual (*la disparation du personnage*).[75] *Being and Nothingness* (1943), on the other hand, gives us, by means of its radical Cartesian dualism between For-Itself and In-Itself, the individual opposite the world and society. In any event, Goldmann contends that Sartre's posture is "rigorously amoral" in that the only explicit values he accepts are individual autonomy and free choice. Goldmann cites Sartre's comment in

Being and Nothingness that an ontology cannot formulate an ethics because its concern is not what ought to be but what is.[76] There can be no intersubjective relations among different For-Itselves—not even love, as Goldmann pointed out in the "Buffet Dialogue" of the 1940s when he discussed the concept of love delineated in *Being and Nothingness*. Each lover, through the famous Sartrean "Look," reduces the other to the In-Itself. There is no possibility of a transindividual subject. A new period began, however, with Sartre's 1945 lecture, "Existentialism Is a Humanism." Sartre moved toward a quasi-Kantian position by arguing that individuals, in choosing themselves, must choose humanity writ large. In being responsible for oneself, one must be responsible for all people. The next step, which Sartre would undertake in the 1950s as he moved toward Marxism, was to rework substantially the relation between individuals and collectives.

Sartre, Goldmann notes, began as a prose writer and later became a playwright. This "passage from novel to theater coincides with a transformation of the problematic; that is to say, of the significative structure of writings centered first on purely individual problems [which] afterwards [become] oriented towards the problem of history, oppression and revolution." In other words, it represents the passage from an individual mode, the novel, to a public one, the theater. Notably, while Sartre engages in innovation and modernist prose techniques in *Nausea*, his plays use a very traditional style.[77]

This parallels Sartre's philosophical passage from the individualism of *Being and Nothingness* to the more Kantian "Existentialism Is a Humanism," which endeavors, if unsuccessfully, to go beyond the individual. (Notably, it is the only work Sartre later rejected.) It is obvious to Goldmann that this was a consequence of Sartre's experience of World War II. By the early 1950s, Sartre found himself trying to juggle a (quasi-)Kantian ethic and a disciplined, amoral French Communist Party. Goldmann links Sartre's passage to stylistic "traditionalism" with his movement towards the French Communist Party. For Goldmann, Stalinism was a conservative phenomenon.

From his first theatrical success, *The Flies* (1943), through his last, *The Condemned of Altona* (1959), Sartre's plays are concerned with the relation between individual action (and/or morality) and revolution. But Goldmann contends that Sartre was almost never able to move from the individual to the transindividual. In *The Flies* (1943), there is no collective action against tyranny. There is Orestes, the free individual who takes the burdens of liberty on himself, and kills Aegisthus— alone. When collectivities appear in Sartre's plays, individual characters are never truly integrated into them. Even Hoerderer, the humanist but tough party chief of "Dirty Hands" is at odds with his party. The theme of "Dirty Hands," as well as later plays, such as "The Devil and the Good Lord" and "The Condemned of Altona," is the irreconcilability of morality and efficacy. The one exception, the one Sartrean play in which collective action appears, "The Victors" (*Morts sans sepulchres*) (1946), is judged by Goldmann to be one of Sartre's weakest efforts. In it, imprisoned members of the French Resistance face Nazi torturers in solidarity, but their solidarity is one that also separates them from *the rest* of the Resistance. Consequently, collective action becomes immediate, limited and not generalized.[78]

Sartre's inability to move beyond the individual is also the center of Goldmann's criticisms of *Search for a Method*. These criticisms are, however, tempered by a real appreciation of Sartre's effort. Goldmann is also at pains to demonstrate that Sartre was mistaken in thinking of Lukács solely in terms of *Existentialisme ou Marxisme?*—for *History and Class Consciousness* had laid out the vital issues with which the existential Marxist now wrestled. If, writes Goldmann,

> Marxism became for a period of time . . . an idealist, eclectic or mechanistic positivism, the dialectical positions that Sartre defends based on the concepts of *the project*, of *the primacy of the future*, of *identity* of subject and object [this is Lukács's term; Sartre speaks of identity of the questioner and the questioned] existed already implicitly or explicitly in Marx himself and in an entire sector of post-Marxian Marxist thought, beginning above all with Lukács's work of 1923.[79]

Goldmann might have added that Sartre ignored an entire body of Marxist literature, ranging from the writings of Karl Korsch and the members of the Frankfurt School in Germany to those of the *Arguments* and *Socialsme ou Barbarie* groups in France, and Goldmann's own work as well. Sartre directs his ire principally at French Stalinized Marxism. Undoubtedly, this was partly due to the power of the French Communists and Sartre's complicated relation with them in the 1950s.

Still, Goldmann's point is justified, given Sartre's proclivity to sweeping statements. For one example, Sartre proclaims that "the dialectical knowing of man, according to Hegel and Marx demands a new rationality. Because nobody has been willing to establish this rationality within experience, I state as a fact—absolutely no one, either in the East or in the West, writes or speaks a sentence or a word about us and our contemporaries that is not a gross error."[80] Goldmann rejected both the breadth of such declarations and Sartre's tendency to blame the development of crude Marxist thinking on the historical dilemmas of the USSR. Goldmann thought that these dilemmas were, indeed, important factors, but at the same time he showed impatience with Sartre's position on the Soviets. "It might be interesting," he once commented,

> to undertake a psychological and sociological study of what is at first glance a difficult phenomenon to explain: how a certain number of intellectuals, formed in the critical spirit of Cartesian and liberal academic philosophy, could be so deeply disturbed by the revelation [of Stalin's crimes by Khrushchev] . . . coming from an authority they had trusted—of facts they might easily have known for years by reading available anti-Stalinist texts, leftist or rightist.[81]

Goldmann's criticisms extended to another level. Sartre wanted to fashion a historical and structural anthropology. This was well enough in Goldmann's eyes; however, "the fundamental methodological problem of every human science—above all when situated in a structuralist and historical perspective—resides in the *découpage* of the object of study and particularly the *découpage* of significative structures."[82] To contend, as Sartre did, that auxiliary disciplines, including positivist ones, could be adjoined to and help salvage degraded Marxism was a methodological error. Positivism believes that it reproduces in the human sciences the method of natural science. It separates subject and object and opposes them to each other. Goldmann's methodological writings hold firmly that this is invalid because it forgets that the subject is partially within its object and the object partially within the subject. The *découpage* of positivist method eliminates what Sartre himself called structured relations among individual projects. To salvage bad Marxism through positivism and methodologically erroneous "auxiliary disciplines" was to forget that "[t]he sum of the results of two false methods doesn't constitute a truth."[83] The proper Marxist method for historical and structural anthropology, says Goldmann, has already been defined—as genetic structuralism. (Given Goldmann's own use of Piaget and his classification of Freud as a genetic structuralist, his objection is not really to integrating the work of thinkers who are not Marxist, but to those who do not follow a genetic structuralist and dialectical method, broadly conceived.)

Goldmann questioned Sartre's conception of collective action on the same basis as he criticized Sartre's methodological prescriptions. *"From the concrete point of view of research and explanation of social facts,"* wrote Goldmann, Sartre accorded "a disproportionate measure [*une importance demesurée*] to the mediation constituted by the psychological structure of individuals."[84] Goldmann's point was not to belittle individuality, but to affirm transindividuality: "It goes without saying that *the collective subject* . . . has no autonomous reality outside of organic individuals and individual consciousness."[85] But transindividuality is intrinsic to Marxist method.

Does Sartre fail to conceptualize a truly collective subject because of a recalcitrant methodological individualism? Thomas R. Flynn's excellent study, *Sartre and Marxist Existentialism*, attempts to respond to Goldmann's suggestion that because the idea of the collective subject is intrinsic to Marxism, Sartre, finally, is not a Marxist. In Flynn's reading, Sartre is a "dialectical nominalist," who seeks a methodological and ontological "via media" between holism and individualism. This is why *Search for a Method* and the *Critique* conceive praxis as totalization, "a practical synthesizing activity that transforms a multiplicity of parts into an emerging whole which serves the goal [*sens*, 'direction'] of the ongoing activity." This departs from Sartre's earlier existentialism because it represents the discovery of "mediating factors in experience and in the world that separate and unite individuals." An "epistemology of praxis" now permits Sartre to explain collective action, but, Flynn perceptively notes, Sartre remains unable to reconcile this epistemology with the Cartesian and Husserlian "epistemology of vision" he maintains simultaneously.[86]

Flynn thereby brings into focus why Goldmann maintained that Sartre, ultimately, was an individualist at odds with both genetic structuralism and the notion of the transindividual subject. Sartre's epistemology of vision always individualizes in that it is bound to intentionality of consciousness without a concept of transcendental ego, leading to inevitable conflicts between For-Itselves surging forth. Although Goldmann, no less than Sartre, upholds the view that a group is always composed of individuals, his theory of the subject of history rests on common, that is, transindividual, mental structures. In Goldmann's view, Sartre was never able to transcend Cartesianism, even when his focus shifted from the strictly individual and radical notion of freedom in *Being and Nothingness* to that of collectives and groups in *Method* and the *Critique*. Human liberty, complains Goldmann, is not limited only by external conditions, as Sartre argued. Rather, "men are just as limited by their mental structures which result from those conditions and are to be found in them. However, these conditions and those mental structures don't only place limits on men, they equally create for them a field of possibilities within which they act and modify reality, all while being modified themselves; consequently, they change their field of possibilities."[87]

In a 1966 interview Goldmann took note of a recent declaration by Sartre that he could not conceive anything antecedent of individual consciousness. Here, for Goldmann, was what separated him from Sartre: for Goldmann, it was obvious that before individual consciousness there is history, community, class, and so on, which are dialectically interiorized as individuals act on the world, thereby fashioning transindividual subjects establishing commonalities among individuals. "For Sartre," continued Goldmann, "consciousness is in the final instance an individual phenomena and the collective can only be the result of a sum of mutual contacts among a certain number of individual consciousnesses."[88] As a consequence, when Sartre and Goldmann approach cultural creation as well as history, they begin with different questions. Sartre speaks of the "universal singular" and asks how, at each "conjuncture," one can discover the "indissolubly" linked "singularity of the universal and the universal of the singular."[89] What interests Sartre is not the class background of Flaubert or Valéry, but how, given those backgrounds, they became Flaubert and Valéry. Goldmann wants to elucidate how a social group in a specific era gives rise to mental categories that a writer elaborates in his or her work.[90] Goldmann's *découpage* is not Sartre's. Goldmann did not ask how Pascal, coming from a certain class background, became Pascal, for this would be to pose the question on an individual level. Instead, he asks how transindividual mental structures are formed within a group and how and why they are coherently expressed in the work of the individual Pascal. The *Pensées* are interesting not because an individual named Pascal produced them, but because of their cultural and historical meaning. Similarly, "the problem is not to know what *Madame Bovary* was *for Flaubert*, but what *Madame Bovary* is as an *important cultural work*, that is, [as] a *historical reality* which differentiates it from a thousand other, mediocre writings of the same epoch and the ravings of a lunatic."[91] On the cultural and political-historical planes, a Flaubert or a Napoleon is not "just any individual." Both are privileged individuals "within the ensemble of collective development." Undoubtedly, no serious thinker would claim that *Madame Bovary* or the French Revolution could be studied apart from the individuals known as Flaubert or Napoleon. The issue, in Goldmann's eyes, is that Sartre studies the individual creator by means of psychoanalysis and "the individual lived existence" (*le veçu individuel*) but not as "a *privileged individual* within a process of collective creation." With Sartre's method, Flaubert could be studied just as any other individual.[92] Yet as human facts have both "objective historical meaning" and "objective individual meaning" beyond a creator's conscious intentions, Goldmann proposes that his own transindividual starting point, as opposed to Sartre's individual one, is requisite to anything calling itself a "human science."[93] Sartre fails to provide the basis on which the cultural or historical meaning of Flaubert's texts can be established.

Goldmann never discussed the *Critique* as a whole. To substantiate fully his criticism, he ought to have analyzed Sartre's discussion of collective action in the latter. Furthermore, Goldmann died before the publication of the first volume of *The Family Idiot*. Judging from two essays by Goldmann on Sartre's theater—"Sartre, Genet, Gombrowicz" (1968) and "Problèmes philosophiques et politiques dans le théâtre de Jean-Paul Sartre: L'itineraire d'un penseur" (1970)—he would have maintained his criticisms. But if his criticisms were trenchant in many ways, his conclusions were one-sided. In *The Family Idiot*, Sartre declared that man "is never an individual" but, rather, a "universal singular," and that his subject matter is, "[W]hat at this point in time can we know about a man?"[94] This formulation goes beyond individualism, even if equivocally and without posing Goldmann's trans-individual questions.

Shortly before Goldmann's death, he and Sartre had a short exchange on these matters. Following a brief meeting, Goldmann sent Sartre several of his articles on him. Sartre wrote to Goldmann praising the objectivity of Goldmann's presentation of his ideas as a whole, but denying Goldmann's claim that his work was stymied on the level of individual psychology. This Goldmann would see, Sartre wrote, when *The Family Idiot* was published, for it "has as its proper goal the study of an *oeuvre* by a double procedure: 1. From the man, 2. In itself (that is to say as it appears [to readers through several generations]) and my goal is to show that it can be grasped only through this double study (which reveals also the man himself)."[95]

Within a month of that exchange, Goldmann was dead, and Sartre died a decade later, never having completed his book. It is, consequently, impossible to judge finally whether Sartre would have succeeded in going beyond the individual or if Goldmann was correct in pronouncing him unable to do so. From what we have, it seems to me that Goldmann was vindicated. On the other hand, Goldmann's conclusions, rooted in his methodological antipathy to biography, are extreme. His error is the opposite of Sartre's: Sartre slides too far toward the individual, and Goldmann slides too far away. *Madame Bovary* may be contrasted as an important cultural work to a mediocre one or to the ravings of a lunatic, but does not investigating Flaubert as a "universal singular" help us understand how and why a great cultural work rather than a mediocrity came from his pen? Goldmann thought that Sartre did not ask the essential questions about cultural creation. But why are not Sartre's questions also fundamental, or at least quite interesting? Goldmann relentlessly attacked Marxists who, politically or philosophically, belittled the individual, while arguing against overemphasis on authorial biography in understanding works. These two points are not contradictory, provided that one is not sacrificed on behalf of the other. Sartre's questions, even if they do not elucidate the whole picture, are nonetheless compelling.

In a parallel vein, Sartre's use of "totalizations" is a terminological and conceptual improvement on Lukács's Marxism, for it underscores praxis as dynamic and changing synthesizing processes, whereas "totalities" can appear to be consolidated and reified, like the practico-inert. Goldmann argued, however, that Sartre's opposition of praxis to the practico-inert reproduced the subject-object dichotomy that dialectical thinking seeks to overcome. It paralleled Sartre's earlier Cartesian dichotomy of "For-Itself" and "In-Itself," and thus ignored the partial identity of subject and object. Sartre sees collective action as a sum of individual actions. Since his subject is ultimately individual, the practico-inert is deprived of meaning and confronted by the individual. Conditions, such as the practico-inert, are the consequence of human action and therefore are meaningful as significative structures.[96]

Up to this point, Goldmann's argument seems forceful. However, if one considers the practico-inert as something meaningless to be overcome, a reification, then Sartre's "totalization" takes on a different, valid connotation. Goldmann virtually admitted this at a roundtable discussion at the Kierkegaard conference, where he approvingly cited a criticism of Lukács by Henri Lefebvre. The problem was that Lukács took "totality as a given [*la totalité comme donnée*]." Yet, in history, totality is always in motion:

> We always try, by our behavior and action, to change these totalities, to move forward within the evolution [*le devenir*] of history, to grasp realities as precisely as possible by placing them within broader and broader totalities, but which, of course, we never arrive at objectively. Now if human behavior is always a creation of coherent structures or relative totalities, it is by the very destruction of these totalities that there is history, as all creation of new totalities is destruction [Goldmann intends "destructuration"], transformation of past totalities. Now there is totalization only to the extent that there is detotalization.[97]

Given Goldmann's use of Piaget's notions of structuration and destructuration, to speak of totalization rather than totality makes considerable sense, and Goldmann virtually acknowledged this, although claiming it to be only a terminological concession "to avoid misunderstanding."[98] But it is not simply a terminological matter, particularly since Goldmann himself maintained in the same discussion that "totality" and all other terms in the human sciences are ultimately undefinable because their objects are always in processes of becoming.[99] If so, one should speak of totalization, not totality, for use of the latter term creates a sense of fixity that exists neither in the "whole" of history, nor in transindividual subjects. (In fact, Goldmann increasingly spoke of "relative totalities.") In a perceptive criticism, Jacques Havet responded to Goldmann as follows:

> It seems to me that Mr. Goldmann oscillates between two points of view. On one hand, totality is a given [*donnée*] and on the other, he refers to a double movement of totalization. It seems to me that if totality is undone [*défaite*], if there is an identity of subject and object, and if each movement of the history of totality is called into question, the process of totalization-detotalization is primary and totality cannot be a given, but rather it must be a sort of idea, a regulative idea—rather Kantian terms. But one can then no longer speak of totality except to the extent that totality directs one to an understanding of a totality which is never given as [fully] coherent. Thus consciousness, taking its part in Being, introduces into this totality an element of non-totality.[100]

The "oscillation" Havet discerns is actually the distance Goldmann traveled, both philosophically and politically, from Lukács, although this was at best only partially apparent to Goldmann himself. As Goldmann was wont to point out, an author's intentions and the objective meaning of his work are by no means the same. Lukács's totality was inseparable from subject-object identity. The unity of Being and knowledge was incarnated in the proletariat when the empirical consciousness of proletarians became class consciousness—a unified, coherent total view of the world and self, at once subjective and objective. On the other hand, the theory of the transindividual subject, and Goldmann's insistence that the individual is a member of several transindividual subjects and that identity of subject and object is only partial, assume that the parts are not fully one with the whole. Nontotality is introduced into totality, making totality meaningless unless one speaks instead of totalization and uses totality, as Havet suggests, as a regulative idea. This is what Lukács did not do, and it is what one must do given Goldmann's own theory. After all, Goldmann specifically noted that Lukács had been unable to delineate the structured relations between individual consciousnesses and the consciousness imputed to them.

Consequently, Goldmann's *Lukács and Heidegger* should be seen not only as a dialogue with Lukács, but as an immanent critique of Lukács's thinking, both political and philosophical. For Lukács, argues Goldmann, there is an "inextricable link" between objective possibility and possible consciousness.[101] Yet when *History and Class Consciousness* examined the relations between the bourgeoisie and its possible consciousness on one hand, and the proletariat and its possible consciousness on the other, Lukács was convinced that it was only the proletariat and never the bourgeoisie that could and would finally be truly "globally oriented" (Goldmann's words).[102] The bourgeoisie seeks to make society in its own limited image, believing that with capitalism, history stops, but proletarian class consciousness sees beyond this, for it is the consciousness of the universal class. The proletariat can understand the crises of capitalism, but the bourgeoisie cannot and will be unable to thwart them. Goldmann, however, had concluded that the "organized capitalism" of the post–World War II era, with its regulation of the economy and its consumer culture, had effectively disproved these contentions:

> Lukács asserted that bourgeois consciousness could not understand the crises because such understanding implies the discovery of the transitory and historical character of the capitalist mode of production, and the recognition by the bourgeoisie of its own limits, thereby signifying its own historical condemnation. Now, bourgeois society, far from disappearing as Lukács believed, surmounted the crises and transformed itself into the technocratic society of organized capitalism, which assured a considerable development of the productive forces. This is partly because the theoreticians of the bourgeoisie and its official thinkers integrated, even on the level of economic thought, the whole of the economy.[103]

Consequently, "it is above all the Lukácsian perspective of consciousness that is now the problem."[104] No less problematic is Lukács's concept of totality, for the actual totalizations of the bourgeoisie and the proletariat placed it in question. Ironically, while Goldmann's examination of the encounter between existentialism and Marxism centered on the question of the collective subject, he simultaneously recognized that the Marxist collective subject was not to play its part. That is why tragic thought was so important to Goldmann, and why he and Sartre, whatever their differences on the notion of the transindividual subject, both end up wagering. And it is why Lukács, when writing *History and Class Consciousness* after the Bolshevik revolution, spoke of the "certitude" that the proletariat would incarnate totality, while Goldmann, writing after Hitler and Stalin, wrote of a hidden God.

III

At the UNESCO conference on Kierkegaard, Goldmann noted that a new philosophy, structuralism, was being born. "One day," he commented, "Lévi-Strauss will be more important than Kierkegaard" but "not in himself [*non pas en soi*]." Lévi-Strauss's thinking would be recognized as the intellectual counterpart of technocratic, consumer soci-

ety.[105] If existentialism coherently expressed the traumatized individual of capitalism in crisis, structuralism was a coherent expression of
stabilized "organized capitalism," with its great narcotic—consumerist
culture.

While the word "structure" appears prominently in Goldmann's
work, and while he classified Marxism as a "genetic structuralism," his
use of these words, and his place in the French "structuralist controversy" of the 1960s, is, again, distinct. In the first place, unlike most of
his French contemporaries, his intellectual debts were not to Ferdinand de Saussure's structuralist linguistics, but to Lukács's notion of
form and Piaget's genetic epistemology. Indeed, he was frustrated by
the expropriation of the word "structure" by structuralism. In a 1969
interview, Goldmann simply disclaimed interest in reconciling structuralism with Marxism, insisting that his own use of "structure" long
antedated its current vogue.[106]

Goldmann criticized structuralism as vigorously as he did existentialism, but from the opposite direction. If the problem with Sartre was
his individualism, the problem with structuralism was antihumanism
and ahistoricity. Nonetheless, as Goldmann, though critical of Sartre,
was not entirely at odds with him, so would he criticize structuralism
while upholding the view that the concept of structure was essential to
his own vocabulary. Genetic structuralism provided the alternative to
the flaws of structuralism and existentialism.

Although important structuralists—Althusser and the younger Foucault, for examples—refused the label "structuralist," Goldmann discerned a common problematic in their thinking, and proposed that it
was homologous with "organized capitalism." As J. G. Meriquor appropriately notes, structuralism was more of a style of thought than a
school. Hence it is appropriate to refer to these thinkers as practitioners of it, despite their disclaimers.[107] Briefly examining theoretical antihumanism in the works of Lévi-Strauss, Foucault (in *The Order of
Things*) and Louis Althusser will permit us to situate Goldmann and
genetic structuralism in relation to the trends of structuralism proper.

Public interest in structuralism was, more than anything else, a consequence of the publication in 1955 of Lévi-Strauss's *Tristes tropiques*.
In this remarkable quasi-memoir and in numerous essays and books,
Lévi-Strauss sought to delineate a method inspired, so he declared, by
Marxism, geology, and psychoanalysis. These, his three "mistresses,"
showed that "understanding consists in reducing one type of reality to
another; that the true reality is never the most obvious," but is quite
elusive.[108]

The underlying reality which this anthropologist aimed to uncover
was the unconscious structure of "collective phenomena." He submit-

ted that this structure was universal, to be found in "modern" as well as "savage" man. To discern it, Lévi-Strauss proposed "interpreting society as a whole in terms of a theory of communication."[109] Linguistics, in his view, had made the most progress of all the social sciences. It alone was able "to formulate necessary laws."[110] Language could provide a "logical model" with which to understand "the structure of other forms of communication."[111] In other words, it provided the basis of a generalizable method, like Marx's quest to grasp the inner principles of capitalism, and Freud's fathoming of the structure of the psyche.

Lévi-Strauss, after citing Rousseau's discussion of the state of nature with approval, argued that his own study of

> "savages" permitted the construction of a model of human life which does not correspond to any observable reality, but with the aid of which we may succeed in distinguishing between what is primordial and what is artificial in man's present nature and in obtaining a good knowledge of a state which no longer exists, and which will never exist in the future but of which it is nonetheless essential to have a sound conception of our present state. Solely "at the beginning" does man create something great. Otherwise, and for millennia, he repeats himself."[112]

According to Lévi-Strauss, the rules governing kinship and marriage—rules that "insure the circulation of women among groups"—are homologous to economic rules guaranteeing the circulation of foods and linguistic rules securing "the circulation of messages."[113] The structural linguistics of Ferdinand de Saussure's *Cours de linguistique generale* (published in 1913) provided Lévi-Strauss with his model. Saussure argued that language had to be examined as a meaningful system of signs (*la langue*), rather than in its expressions in acts of speech (*la parole*, the spoken word). *La langue* was a properly social object of linguistics, whereas *la parole* was an ephemeral, even accidental, individualized act, a matter of the person who happens to utter it in a given moment. Consequently, the priority in linguistics had to be synchronic study: language viewed as a structured, systemic whole as opposed to a diachronic, that is, evolutionary or historical, approach.

The synchronic whole is composed of linguistic signs, each of which has two components, the signifier (*signifiant*), which is a signifying form, and the *signified (signifie)*, a concept that is signified. The relation between the two is arbitrary: languages do not name things; for example, there is no natural link between the word "pen" (signifier) and the idea of the instrument with which I write these words. Languages are to be conceived as differential systems within which signs have no positive identities. "Identity is a function of difference within a system."[114] Similarly, if the chessmen are considered part of the system of chess, a single piece can have any shape provided it is distinguished from the others. Identity is conferred by differentiations within the system, not by the actual shape of the king or pawn. Linguistics and chess must, consequently, be approached as holistic enterprises. *La parole* or a pawn is incoherent without the system of differentiations providing its identity, respectively, *la langue* or the rules of chess. Language, then, must address semiotics, the study of systems of signs, not history.[115]

Lévi-Strauss deployed Saussure's linguistic insights in anthropology by presenting cultural phenomena as meaningful systems of signs. Myths were to be studied and compared as languages were by Saussure, that is, on the structural level of codes: matrixes of meanings refer to each other within the system, not to originary meanings. The key is synchrony, not genesis—*la langue*, not *la parole*; the code, not the message. The universal in human nature is to be discovered by synchronic analysis, not through what is immediately manifest at a given moment. History becomes, at best, a discipline complementing Lévi-Strauss's own; it is not to be accorded "a special value." History "unfurls the range of human societies in time," while Lévi-Strauss's task is to do this "in space."[116] The primitive forms of thought Lévi-Strauss studied among inhabitants of South American jungles were conceived by him to be embodiments of structures primordial to all human beings. He was "happy to adopt . . . to a system with no temporal dimension, in order to interpret a different form of civilization."[117] The object of study would be elaborated in terms of its coherent internal structure, exclusive of its genesis or cultural context. As Saussure sought out the abstract model of linguistic structures underlying language, similar to a model in the natural or physical sciences, Lévi-Strauss sought the meaningful system of signs underlying cultural phenomena.

Antihistoricism leads Lévi-Strauss to theoretical antihumanism. The goal of the human sciences is "not to constitute but to dissolve man."[118] He intends this with irony, for his point is not to be inhumane, but to reject "man" as the "subject" of the "human sciences." To those who might object that language, the very structure he uses as a model, was created by men, Lévi-Strauss responds:

> Language, an unreflecting totalization, is human reason which has its reasons and of which man knows nothing. And if it is objected that it is only so for a subject who internalizes it on the basis of linguistic theory, my reply is that this way out must be refused, for this subject is one who *speaks*: for the same light which reveals the nature of language to him also reveals to him

that it was so when he did not know it, for he already made himself understood, and that it will remain so tomorrow without his being aware of it, since his discourse never was and never will be the result of a conscious totalization of linguistic laws.[119]

What Lévi-Strauss opposes is the belief—"humanism"—that the development and unfolding of man's potentialities, accomplishments, and miseries, conceived as the driving force of social life, should be the starting point of analysis. Rather, social life is to be seen as one aspect of the structures of nature in which man, at best, plays certain roles. In his conclusion to *Tristes tropiques*, Lévi-Strauss declares, "The world began without man and will end without him. The institutions, morals, and customs that I shall have spent my life noting down and trying to understand, are the transient efflorescence of a creation in relation to which they have no meaning, except perhaps that of allowing mankind to play its part in creation."[120]

As "humanity" just plays its part in the system, the human sciences (if we can even call them this) cannot be conceived as fundamentally different from natural science. "Man" as subject vanishes from center stage; his self-creation and development through his interaction with nature on the basis of his past history and future hopes become a conceit at worst, a myth at best. In fact, concrete individuals within humanity become myths. In a particularly revealing passage in *Tristes tropiques*, the author recounts his escape from Marseilles at the outbreak of World War II. By chance, he found himself aboard a ship with Victor Serge, whom he perceived as asexual and prim, a "cultural type" as suited to being a monk as to being one of Lenin's comrades. The man was no longer the historically placed individual; for Lévi-Strauss he was no more than an impetus to look beyond what was manifest, beyond the phenomenal Serge, as it were, to the "more subtle correspondences between individuals and *the parts they play*" (emphasis added).[121]

Though Foucault maintained that he had "used none of the methods, concepts, or key terms that characterize structural analysis," his early work, particularly *Les Mots et les choses* (Words and Things, translated as *The Order of Things*) clearly partakes of structuralism's "style of thought." In this book, which defined itself as an archaeological expedition to discover "the epistemological space" in which knowledge is "constituted," the author declares that "God is perhaps not so much a region beyond knowledge as something prior to the sentences we speak."[122] Foucault focused on how the study of language, wealth, and nature in what he called the Classical Age (the seventeenth and eighteenth centuries) was encoded in a "grid" (an "episteme"). As an archaeologist of knowledge, Foucault uncovers and digs into this con-figuration, which, he contended, structured the possibilities of knowl-edge, and which differed from the grids of the Renaissance and mod-ern periods. A culture's basic codes govern "its language, its schemes of perception, its exchanges, its techniques, its values, the hierarchies of its practices" and establish "the empirical orders" with which a man deals and "within which he will be at home."[123] A change in episteme recasts the relation between "words and things."

"Man" as a concept—and thus the entire notion of "human sci-ences"—became possible, according to Foucault, only by modernity's displacement of the Classical episteme. In the Renaissance, the natural world was undifferentiated from man's, and both were believed to be authored by God. Language was interwoven with the world, which partook of its "dissemination of similarities and signatures." It was an age of "interpretation". In contrast, its successor, the Classical Age—the Age of Reason—was one of "analysis." Language was no longer "a thing inscribed in the fabric of the world," but was "dissolved in the functioning of representation; all language had value only as dis-course."[124] Language became transparent. The human and nonhuman realms were separated. Nature was now studied as the naming of the visible, and grammar was studied as verbal order in relation to what it was supposed to represent. Political economy does not yet exist be-cause what was examined was "wealth," not "production." This epi-steme, however, does not provide a grid that isolates or gives a specific domain to "man" as such.[125]

At the center of the Classical episteme was "mathesis," a "universal science of measurement and order." Things were ordered "by means of signs" that constituted "all empirical forms of knowledge as knowl-edge based on identity and difference."[126] Classification, taxonomy, and genetic analysis (the latter revealing the constitution of orders) mark this episteme. It is only with modernity's episteme, beginning roughly in the late eighteenth century, that "man" can be conceived, and the "human sciences" invented. The notion of "man," in Fou-cault's hands, is, in short, a conceit of modernity. In the Classical pe-riod, the person for whom representation exists, is not there: "Before the eighteenth century, *man* did not exist. . . . He is a quite recent crea-ture which the demiurge of knowledge fabricated with its own hands." How was the demiurge so urged? By a rupture with the Clas-sical episteme and the birth of one articulating "a specific domain proper to man." Words no longer represented things.[127] Instead of an episteme that speaks of language as representation, the circulation of wealth and taxonomies, a new episteme is born, whose categories are historical philology, biology, and political economy; in other words, it speaks about speaking, living, and working organisms. It is "man" who speaks, lives, or writes, and he does so in "history" not just in an "order." Thus "man" is "constituted" for the "human sciences," which become sociology, cultural studies, and psychology. All these look beyond what is manifest, searching for abstractions behind the immediately visible. Language is no longer transparent but is an a priori of what can be expressed, even though the speaker is not cognizant of this. Forces "within" man lead to his behavior, but they must be dug out. "The threshold between Classicism and modernity . . . ," wrote Foucault, "had been definitely crossed when words ceased to intersect with representations and provide a spontaneous grid for the knowledge of things."[128]

Here, we can see Foucault's theoretical antihumanism: his "man" is a function of the "episteme," as Lévi-Strauss's "message" is a function of the "code" and Saussure's "*la parole*" is a function of "*la langue*." Since Foucault engages in "archeology," not "history," it is the episteme as a structure, with homologies in different realms, that concerns him, not that which produces ruptures between epistemes. "Man" is "probably no more than a rift in the order of things, or in any case, a configuration whose outlines are determined by the new position he has so recently taken up in the field of knowledge." Foucault finds it "comforting" that "man," this "new wrinkle in our knowledge . . . will disappear again as soon that knowledge has discovered a new form."[129]

This theory of the episteme owes a great deal to Gaston Bachelard's philosophy of science, which stresses the historicity of scientific theory. In the process through which scientific theory is "constructed," he argued, it must overcome "epistemological obstacles," which are often unconscious. These obstacles may be erected by past philosophies of science or metaphysics in general. "Reverie," commonsense thinking, produces "images," while science produces "concepts." Scientific progress depends not on accumulating new "facts" but on "epistemological ruptures" that recast the structure of questions asked and problems posed. The "scientific spirit is essentially a way of rectifying knowledge. . . . [S]itting in judgment, it concerns its historic past. Its structure is its awareness of its historical errors."[130] There is, consequently, an epistemological break between them. There was no "transition" from Aristotelian to Newtonian physics, and then from Newton to Einstein, due to "amassing data, perfecting measurement and making slight adjustments to first principles." A "totally new ingredient" was required; a "transcendental induction" and not an "amplifying induction" inaugurates a new science. Older theories don't "develop" into new ones; the new "*envelop*" the old.[131] It is the community of scientific research—the "scientific city"—that permits the overcoming of reverie in the individual.

Bachelard's "epistemological ruptures" underlie Foucault's theory of the episteme and also the structuralist Marxism of Louis Althusser. The latter had been Bachelard's student at the Ecole Normale Superieur, and Foucault had been Althusser's pupil at the same institution. Althusser's *For Marx* was conceived as an "intervention" against the "dangers" he saw posed to Marxism by "subjectivism" and empiricism, on one hand, and "pre-Marxist"—unscientific, in Althusser's view—notions, such as humanism and Hegelianism, on the other.[132] The seeds of Marxist humanism in France were first planted by the Hegelian revival of the 1930s and 1940s, especially the lectures and writings of Kojève and Hyppolyte. Interest in the young Marx was also fueled in the 1930s by the first French translation, by Henri Lefebvre and Norbert Guterman, of selections of Marx's 1844 manuscripts, with their famous theory of alienation. In the 1950s, arguments for Marxist humanism were put forth by independent theorists, such as Sartre, Lefebvre (who was in the Communist Party until 1957), and Goldmann, as well as Communists like Roger Garaudy.

Marxist humanism gathered particular momentum following Khrushchev's denunciation of Stalinism in 1956, which left French Communists reeling and disoriented. Althusser, an Algerian-born Party member, stated with candor in 1975 that had it not been for Khrushchev's speech "and the consequent liberalization," he would "never have written anything." His "target," was "these humanist ravings, these feeble dissertations on liberty, labor or alienation which were the effects of all this among French Party intellectuals."[133] Humanism, like the images of "reverie" for Bachelard, is an obstacle to science.

To those who saw Marxism as a theory of human liberation, Althusser retorted: "It is impossible to *know* anything about men except on the absolute precondition that the philosophical (theoretical) myth of man is reduced to ashes."[134] Althusser's bonfire aimed to show that all humanism and anthropology were effaced from the works of the "mature" Marx who was a "theoretical anti-humanist." An epistemological break separated the humanist Marx of 1844 from the later "scientific" Marx. While Althusser was compelled repeatedly to redate this rupture, placing it later and later in Marx's career, his point was ultimately that Marx's "problematic" (his framework of concepts and questions) were recast when he became a true Marxist.

Knowledge, according to Althusser, is a form of production. It is a "practice," with the latter term defined as "any process of *transformation* of a determinate raw material into a determinate *product*, a transformation effected by a determinate human labor, using determinate means ('of production')."[135] To recast scientifically the means of production, that is, to recast that which turns the "raw materials" of knowledge (concepts, facts, notions) into a product entails an epistemological rupture between "ideology" and "science." A new problematic is the result. Young Marx, who wrote on alienation, was concerned with fulfilling humanity's essence in the face of the dehumanizing realities of capitalism. This was an ideological approach because "while it really does designate a set of existing relations . . . it does not provide us with means of knowing them."[136] The "scientific" Marx turned from the nebulous notion of "man" and his "essence" to the forces and relations of production. This new system of concepts provided a science of social formations and their history, breaking irrevocably with the reveries of "humanism" and "historicism."

The birth of the new science, historical materialism, "induced" the birth of a new philosophy, dialectical materialism, which was only "implicit" in Marx's writings. Just as Lévi-Strauss and Foucault looked behind what was manifest to, respectively, codes and episteme, Althusser argues that one must read Marx's texts "symptomatically" to discern the problematic structuring his thinking. One can thereby elaborate Marxism's epistemology, which is the basis of its claim to be a science. Althusser saw this as his own task.

Marxism, he argued, conceived the social whole to be composed of four levels of "practice"—economic, political, ideological, and theoretical. The last is the domain of Marx's science. Since material objects are outside our minds, science addresses the "concrete-in-thought" and not the "real concrete." Theoretical practice is therefore apart from the other three practices, and its criterion is not correspondence with the material world per se; a scientist who reconceives an object does not thereby change the object. When Marx's problematic shifted from "man" to "the relations of production," neither "man" nor relations of production changed, just as neither were "in" Marx's mind in the first place—concepts of them were.

The science of society is, consequently, something developed entirely outside daily social practices, presumably by theoretical practitioners, such as Althusser. "No mathematician in the world," he writes, "expects that his theories have to be applied before they are declared verified by the facts. The truth of its theorems is completely furnished by the internal criteria of mathematical practice. We could say the same of all sciences."[137] These assertions lead Althusser to conclude, however, that the criterion of theoretical practice is itself. Why Hobbes, Durkheim, Alfred Rosenberg, or a witch doctor could justifiably not make the same assertion is not explained. On the grounds of Althusser's theory, one could rebuke them no more or less than he. On Bachelard's grounds, one imagines that the "scientific city" plays a mediating role. With Althusser, a Leninist, the location of theoretical practice can only be the Communist Party's intellectuals, the Leninist "Scientific City."

Hegelian and humanist Marxists, according to Althusser, worked with an "unscientific" concept of simple totality, in which everything is "expressive" of, or a moment in, the development of *Geist*. Complexity within this totality is deceptive because a "simple internal principle" is always at work, making everything a manifestation of the unfolding of the subject. The parts "never exist for themselves"; rather, "every concrete difference featured in the Hegelian totality, including the 'spheres' in this totality (civil society, the state, religion, philosophy, etc.), all these differences are negated as soon as they are affirmed: for they are no more than 'movements' of the simple internal principle of totality."[138]

In contrast, the mature Marx conceived a complex totality in which various structures—political, economic, ideological—are relatively autonomous and not ultimately expressive of a simple internal principle. The economy is determinant only "in the last instant," and each structure makes its impact felt on the whole, while simultaneously being affected by it and the other structures. The absence of a simple internal principle means that the parts of the whole are "decentered" and the various levels develop, as structures and in time, relatively autonomously.

A complex notion of "contradiction" is required likewise, and revolution is the result not of a simple crisis but of "overdetermination," "condensation" (or fusion) of contradictions on various levels. History is not the "self-development" of humanity. Rather, men play roles and have various functions in different structures. Synchronic analysis becomes primary. A science of history must concern itself with such structures, for example, the relations of production, and in Althusser's theory these structures parallel Saussure's use of *la langue*, Lévi-Strauss's of codes, and Foucault's of episteme.

Goldmann's theories represented part of the problem structuralism sought to correct. Goldmann insisted on a dialectic between synchronic and diachronic analyses, and on looking at structure and history at once. Whereas for Foucault, "the structure/development opposition" is irrelevant "to the definition of the historical field" and "in all probability, to the definition of a structural method",[139] it is essential for Goldmann. For him every *découpage* had to be inserted in a structurating and destructurating totality (a totalization). Otherwise, method would be imposed on the object rather than being dialectically functional to the object. At the beginning of *The Human Sciences and Philosophy*, Goldmann declared, "Every social fact is a historical fact and vice versa. It follows that history and sociology *study the same phe-*

nomena and that if they both grasp a real aspect of them, the image each gives can only be partial and abstract in so far as it is not completed by the contributions of the other."[140] A complementary analysis of both social structure and historical change is required.

Compare Goldmann's statement to Lévi-Strauss's appreciation of Marx:

> Marx's quality has nothing to do with whether or not he accurately foresaw certain historical developments. Following Rousseau, and in what I consider to be a definitive manner, Marx established that social science is no more founded on the basis of events than is physics founded on sense data: the object is to construct a model and to study its properties and its different reactions in laboratory conditions in order later to apply these observations to the interpretation of empirical happenings, which may be far removed from what had been forecast.[141]

It is evident that both Lévi-Strauss and Goldmann see Marx's chief contribution as lying not in predictions but in method; like Marx, they both insist that it is necessary to look behind what is manifest. Lévi-Strauss views the use of a model as a crucial tool, and Goldmann attaches the same sort of importance to *découpage* or imputation. In other words, both insist that we impose an order on "facts," rather than making a sum of them, in scientific study. But how does Lévi-Strauss imagine that the model of capitalism can be divorced from history and placed in a laboratory? Marx, Goldmann repeated often, delineated a model of the structure of capitalism, but never detached it from history. As he wrote in a letter to Roman Jakobson, Goldmann insisted on "the *temporal* primacy of synchrony" in research, but denied that temporality had a "secondary character."[142] For example, to deploy the notion of possible consciousness is to construct a model of that toward which a transindividual subject's consciousness tends. But this subject is a structure within and through history. To borrow Hegel's phrase, the "naked result" of speaking of structure without genesis "is the corpse of [a] system which has left its guiding tendency behind it."[143] Possible consciousness, like Marx's model of capitalism, must be historically placed; it is a model, but not one standing apart from history. Historical analysis in Marx, contrary to Lévi-Strauss's description, is fundamental, not secondary.

Consider Lévi-Strauss's description of Victor Serge (which Goldmann does not address, but which serves well as an illustration of the problem he perceived in Lévi-Strauss). Lévi-Strauss made Serge a "cultural type" equally suiting an asexual spinster, a Buddhist monk and a comrade of Lenin. Lévi-Strauss looked beyond the "historical event" known as "Victor Serge" to find the "more subtle correspondences" between human beings and "the parts they play." But by setting history aside, Lévi-Strauss became reductionist. His structuralist Serge is what for Sartre was the reductionist Marxist's Paul Valéry. Consider: The historical Serge was a revolutionary and a writer; at different times in his life he embraced anarchism, the Bolshevik revolution, and anti-Stalinist libertarian socialism. He fought on the barricades of Barcelona's syndicalist uprising in 1917, was in besieged Petrograd during the Russian Civil War, was persecuted by Stalin, and had to flee fascism. Was the historical Serge the same "type" as a spinster or a monk? The "event" named Victor Serge whom Lévi-Strauss saw was a man in political defeat, in flight. Failing to place him historically, Lévi-Strauss fashions a caricature. Do we learn anything from Lévi-Strauss's reduction? In contrast, Goldmann would have approached Serge by seeking to understand and explain the coherence of his political and literary activities, and their genesis, within larger structured historical totalities. What distinguished Goldmann from Lévi-Strauss and other structuralists was the question of history, the genesis of structures, and, importantly, their functioning.

Yet it is curious that in distinguishing his own genetic structuralism from nongenetic structuralism, Goldmann misread Saussure as his own ally. The essential link between the subject and structure, Goldmann maintained, was meaning (or "functionality"). This is precisely what the theoretical antihumanism of nongenetic structuralism eliminates. Goldmann proposed that he was "more faithful to Saussure than any linguistic structuralist" because he concurred that linguistic structuralism was valid for "la langue, but invalid for la parole" since "the functionality of language—communication—is universally human whereas the functionality of la parole always refers to a particular subject; it has meaning."[144] This is to assert that la langue is nonmeaningful. Goldmann writes:

> A language can be neither pessimistic nor optimistic because it must equally allow the expression of joy or bad feeling or despair. Inversely, every socialized spoken word [la parole]) is necessarily meaningful within its whole [ensemble]; it says something, although a discourse is a mélange and has several meanings. This is to say that linguistics is the study of systems of means which permit expressions of meanings and not the study of these meanings themselves. No doubt, the latter do not exist without the means to express them, but the choice and the construction of these means in each act of speaking is subordinated to its meaning.[145]

Goldmann partly misinterprets structuralism here, but in so doing he makes a telling point on behalf of his own genetic structuralism. For Saussure, meaning is established through the system of differentiations of signs within *la langue*. This is why the subject, as the positor of meaning, can be "dissolved" by structuralists. Rather than identifying with Saussure, Goldmann should have argued, consistent with his own concept of totality, that it is insufficient to define linguistics as the study of structured means alone. Instead, a dialectical approach would encompass both synchrony and diachrony, with the subject as the link between the two. But in that case, *la langue* cannot be defined as neutral, just as a given set of relations of production cannot be defined as neutral. These sets of means cannot be adequately grasped in and of themselves, for they do not exist in and of themselves. They are historical and change to meet human needs inadequately served by their previous forms. To define a means as neutral is a form of reification because it ignores the extent to which, by their very structure, means impose ways of conceptualizing problems and, in the case of language, consequently help determine how *la parole* is uttered. Otherwise, one must conclude either that languages create and speak themselves or that every time one speaks, one creates a language.

In fact, Saussure did not negate diachronic analysis; like Lévi-Strauss on history, he thought it secondary. Goldmann's contention, however, is that it is insufficient to speak of meaning in terms of language structure alone, although he never addresses directly the extent to which the very structure of language may confer meanings. The salient point for Goldmann is that one must address the one who gives meaning by using the language, in other words, the speaking subject using the language. He writes that "language is bound to every practice [*pratique*] and there is no practice without language; but one must not believe as contemporary structuralists do, that everything is solely language upon language; this is an ideological reduction of praxis, of the fact that everything is action upon action; language presumes theory and language as a moment."[146] Writing to Jakobson, Goldmann summarized his own position in a way consistent with the criticisms we have just made of his comment on Saussure. Goldmann insisted "on the necessity of studying at once and simultaneously meaning and the manner in which it is expressed, the 'what' and the 'how' [*le 'quoi' et le 'comment'*]. But French structuralism is an enterprise of radical elimination of the 'what' and the reduction of the domain of research exclusively to the 'how' which, in my view, cannot be studied in an autonomous way."

He goes on to argue that "the study of meaning demands recourse to what, with extreme irony, our French structuralists call 'the anthropological subject,' which is to say simply that the introduction into research of the men who act, think and speak is for them the supreme crime; the same goes for genetic study, the dimension of development [*du devenir*]."[147] It is for these reasons that Goldmann criticized Lévi-Strauss and especially his appropriation of Marx. In *Structural Anthropology*, Lévi-Strauss embraced a passage in Marx's celebrated preface to *The Critique of Political Economy* to support his own position. Goldmann quotes Lévi-Strauss's comment:

> I do not postulate a sort of preestablished harmony between the diverse levels of structure. They can be, and often are, perfectly contradictory with each other, but the modes of contradiction all belong to the same type [*groupe*]. This is, moreover, what historical materialism teaches when it affirms that it is always possible to proceed [*de passer*] by transformation, from the economic structure or that of social relations to the structure of law, of art, or of religion. But Marx never pretended that these transformations were of a single type, for example that ideology could only reflect social relations as if in a mirror. He thought that these transformations are dialectical, and in certain cases, he went to great pain to recover the indispensable transformation. . . . If we admit, following Marx's line of thought, that infrastructures and superstructures are composed of multiple levels, and that there exist diverse types of transformations.[148]

But Goldmann argues that Marx's text, which maintains that when the relations of production fetter the development of the material forces of production, social conflict and revolution result, makes it quite clear that its author is speaking not of transformation or inversion between infrastructure and superstructure, but of functionality. The relation between the relations of production and the means of production is that of "favoring, of being an element in the development of the behavior of men or, inversely, of being a fetter." It is, in other words, a matter of "functionality," which Goldmann says is a more precise term for what was called "meaning."[149] Functionality, however, brings with it the subject—the transindividual subject in Goldmann's case. Men are not functions of structures, but structures are functional to human needs, all while shaping them and their possibilities. Consequently, they structurate and destructurate as transindividual subjects seek to address new needs.

Goldmann's point is highlighted in a remarkable exchange with Foucault in January 1968, as well as by Goldmann's general critique of Althusser. In a paper on "What Is an Author?" Foucault criticized some of his own formulations in *The Order of Things*. He noted that his "archaeology" of the "discursive layers" in the study of natural history, wealth, and political economy lacked a similar analysis of the relations between an author and his works. This led to ambiguities in his use of the "names" of various authors, since he was preoccupied with finding the rules of the episteme that provided the functional conditions of discourse. As a result he had proceeded not with a social and historical analysis of authors as individuals, but with the relation between an author and the text, focusing on "the author-function."

Goldmann, like Foucault, thought it mistaken to focus on the individual author as subject. But Goldmann's argument was on humanist grounds: his "transindividual subject" articulated that which linked human beings as subjects of knowledge, not that which "dissolved" man. Moreover, for Goldmann, asking, Who speaks? must be complemented by, What does he say?" Nongenetic structuralism, Goldmann complained, rejected the subject on behalf of linguistic, mental, or social structures; men became roles, functions of structures. Genetic structuralism, while rejecting the individual subject, both historically and culturally, did so on behalf of a transindividual one. Structures do not make history, Goldmann insisted; men and women do, although always in signifying and structured ways. Goldmann's riposte to Foucault was to quote a graffito on a Sorbonne wall in 1968: "Structures don't go into the streets." Foucault responded that he did not use the word "structure" and had been trying to define how and in what circumstances the "function" of an author operates, which is not to argue that the "author" is nonexistent. To show how the notion of man emerged for the human sciences is not to say that men had not existed. Goldmann then asked, "A single question: When you admit the existence of man or the subject, do you, or do you not, reduce them to the status of function?" Foucault retorted that he did reduce man to a function, but sought to analyze "the function within which something like an author" could exist. "If I had lectured on the subject, I probably would have analyzed in a similar fashion the subject-function [la fonction-sujet], that is, I would have made an analysis of the conditions in which it is possible for an individual to fill the function of the subject." Jacques Lacan, at this point, sought to rebuff Goldmann by insisting that in May 1968, it was "precisely that structures did take to the streets." The graffito to the opposite effect quoted above only demonstrated that what is often internal "to what may be called an act" is not recognized in itself.[150]

Lacan's assertion throws into focus Goldmann's central objection to structuralism and theoretical antihumanism. Althusser, Goldmann once noted, "asserts the existence of structures within history without relation to human activity."[151] While this encapsulated Goldmann's criticism of the structuralist style of thought in general, it does not mean that he embraced the notion of an individual universal subject of history. He went so far as to assert that making the proletariat such a subject represented a Hegelian residue in Marxism. This obviously included Lukács's vision of the proletariat. At the same time, Goldmann denied that the "Hegel-Lukács" tradition conceived totality as "simple," as Althusser contended. Hegel's totality, he points out, is "given" only at the end.[152] Although he does not do so, Goldmann could have pointed to the beginning of the *Phenomenology of Spirit*, where Hegel distinguishes his notion of the whole from Schelling's. For the latter, the parts were lost in the totality, thereby becoming, in Hegel's famous metaphor, a night in which all cows are black.

We have argued earlier that such a night does appear in Lukács. Indeed, Goldmann's discussion of structuration and destructuration, and his notion of the transindividual subject, imply this. There are subjects in history and culture, and human beings are mere functions of structures or discourses. But when Goldmann speaks of the "subject," he is not substituting "humanity," in a simplistic generic sense for Hegel's *Geist* or Lukács's proletariat. This would entail a teleological view of history as the fulfillment of a human essence postulated at the outset. But Goldmann *wagers* on socialism; his is an existential and not a teleological position. When he speaks of three constituent elements of the human "condition," these are risk, possibility of failure, and hope of success. The "permanence" of the human condition "resides in the potentiality [*la virtualité*] of responding to problems posed by different historical situations by the tendency to elaborate a certain number of fundamental structures which I have called world-views, structures whose number is limited."[153] Hence "man" has no abstract "essence" and is not an essential subject unfolding in history. "Man" as "subject" must be grasped on the basis of various possibilities, which are expressed in the creation of mental structures in the adaptation process and historical action. Man is not "decentered"; he acts on the historical world as it acts on him. Consequently, man is not to be displaced as an object of the human sciences by making him a decentered function of the relations of production. Embracing an unfolding human essence is a type of Idealism, which Goldmann rejected along with making man a decentered function. The latter notion risks turning into mechanical determinism, and this was precisely the danger Goldmann saw in Althusser, despite the latter's criticisms of economic determinism.

A remarkable Marxist paradox emerges: Althusser eliminated the subject of history but still believed that the science of Marxism demonstrated the necessity of proletarian revolution, while Goldmann abandoned belief in the revolutionary role of the proletariat and its status as universal subject, yet refused to yield the concept of man as transindividual subject that acts in history and constitutes the basis for study of social structures and history. Structures, for Goldmann, are composed of men who act, and to conceive of the relations of production,

for example, as anything but structured relations among human beings, is nothing less than a reification. Who creates and sustains these
structures? asks Goldmann. Did they appear *ex nihilo*? Theoretical antihumanism turns structures themselves into reified subjects. But on
the contrary,

> language, structures, relations of production, are not subjects and never pro-
> duce anything. It is men who, engaged in an ensemble of structured rela-
> tions, with a structured consciousness and behavior structured as well, pro-
> duce historical events. It is men who create language within a rigorously
> structured *praxis*, and it is men who, within relations of production having
> a precise significative structure, act, transforming reality and transforming
> the relations of production.[154]

Structure is intrinsic to human relations—but the relations are human,
and structures are made by humans. Thus Goldmann speaks of the
transindividual subject of cultural creation and not an "author-function." Althusser's discussion of "overdetermination" becomes a mode
of reification because it obfuscates who and what provokes social and
political change: not "structures" in abstraction, but, rather, transindividual subjects, collective actors composed of individuals in an ensemble of structured relations at a given historical conjuncture.

Consequently, while Goldmann obviously agreed with Althusser
that theory is not a matter of adding up facts and deriving order from
them, he had little use for Althusser's reading of Marx. He went so far
as to tell one of his classes that "the epistemological break is an
Althusserian joke [*plaisanterie*]."[155] In Goldmann's view, Marx's development from 1844 on represented a process of concretization in which
ideas vague in Marx's youth attained more mature expression. For one
important example, the notion of alienation became the theory of the
fetishism of commodities.[156] Furthermore, since Goldmann insisted on
the methodological dichotomy between human and natural sciences,
he could not accept Althusser's claim that the young Marx was an ideological humanist, while the older Marx was a scientist. Echoing
Hegel's preface to the *Phenomenology*, Goldmann declared, "[Human]
Science will be philosophy, philosophy will be science, or the first will
not be a true science and the second will not be true philosophy."[157] In
the human sciences, knowledge is not "just" science, but consciousness
as well. Thus human science implies taking a position and not pretending otherwise.[158] Lukács's accomplishment, Goldmann once told Althusser in a debate, was his demonstration that "science" in *Capital* had
the same meaning as it had in Hegel: taking a position that at once
demands evaluation *and* authentication.[159]

Goldmann's argument for partial identity inevitably led him to conclude that "theory" cannot be spoken of as an autonomous realm apart from history and transindividual subjects, because the theorist lives within history and transindividual subjects. Althusser's "theoretical practice" becomes, therefore, a species of positivism based on an opposition of subject and object and an inappropriate translation of theories of natural science into the human sciences. For Goldmann, "any pretense [in the human sciences] to a science with definitive and durable non-ideological character is . . . one of the gravest forms of dogmatism, a pretension which is precisely what closes off the possibility of research and the possibility of progress."[160] All forms of nongenetic structuralism, not only Althusser's, were "positivist."

In Paris in the 1960s, nongenetic structuralism, Marxist and non-Marxist, first displaced Sartrean phenomenology and existential Marxism, and then pressed Goldmann's type of independent Marxist humanism to the intellectual sidelines.[161] Goldmann was quite aware of this process. Writing to Jakobson, he was bitter: French structuralism had become "above everything else an ideology and a pressure group on the intellectual and university level" seeking "to eliminate" research on "meaning, the subject of thought, action and language and with them, history."[162] Goldmann sought to explain this sociologically: the popularity of structuralism, which emphasized stasis rather than change, was a product of the stabilization of post–World War II capitalism.

After the war, capitalism became "organized" and increasingly sought to integrate and pacify contesting forces, particularly the proletariat, through rising living standards, guaranteed by state or monopolistic intervention into the economy. Traditional middle classes were being displaced by new, wage-earning "middle strata" composed of the specialists and technicians required by developed industry, technology, and state planning in advanced Western societies. Decision-making was increasingly the prerogative of restricted groups of technocrats in all fields; everyone else was to be satisfied by new and expanding forms of consumption. This, in Goldmann's eyes, resulted in a "contraction" of personality, individualism, and consciousness. The dimension of "the possible" receded from the horizons of men and women. Goldmann not only questioned the traditional Marxist view of the role of the proletariat in such circumstances; he even imagined a general dissolution of the human potential to act collectively, that is, as self-conscious transindividual subjects. The human world would be perceived by men and women as essentially static as they adapted themselves as anonymous individuals seeking to satisfy themselves in a technocratic society.[163] Such a society gives rise to structuralism, in which history, the possible, collective human action are all categories that dissipate, whereas they ought to be central in the human sciences, and consciousness in general. These categories are replaced by synchrony and the vision of man as "decentered."

It was in opposition to structuralism that Goldmann classified his own thought as "generalized genetic structuralism."[164] Just as structuralists came in both Marxist and non-Marxist varieties, so Goldmann declared there to be Marxist as well as non-Marxist genetic structuralism. The most prominent contributors in the latter category were Hegel, Freud, and Piaget. There are, he stipulated, three tenets common to all genetic structuralists:

> 1. They examine human behavior in terms of significative structure;
>
> 2. They seek meaning not in what is immediately manifest, but by integrating an object of study into a "larger relative totality" (for example, a class for Marx, and the unconscious psyche for Freud); and
>
> 3. They maintain that structures are dynamic and not static, and must be analyzed in terms of their genesis.[165]

It may appear surprising that Freud is listed among genetic structuralists considering Goldmann's criticisms of the founder of psychoanalysis. In fact, Goldmann seems to have paid relatively little attention to Freud until the 1960s. In this he was no different from most intellectuals in France, who were generally averse to Freud before Jacques Lacan's Saussure-influenced reading of him. (Lukács was also resolutely hostile to Freud.)

Still, as early as 1957, we find Goldmann praising the richness of Freud's work, while declaring it impossible "to reconcile psychoanalytic explanation of social and cultural facts with their explanation according to historical materialism."[166] Goldmann stressed, as one might expect, the difference between the "subject of libidinal behavior" and the subject of political action and cultural creation. Freud's primary focus was on the individual, Goldmann asserted, and this marked him off from other genetic structuralists. Among other things, such individualism loses sight of the category of "the future." The category of totality is thereby lost. The individual—Goldmann here sounds almost as though he were Lukács appropriating Heidegger on temporality—is limited and sooner or later dies. While Freudianism has "a genetic character," it becomes two-dimensional because its temporal focus is on the present and, especially, the past, but not on the future.[167] Questions of intrasubjectivity and transindividuality are thereby major lacunae in Freud's thought. Still, Freud was a genetic structuralist because of his insistence that apparently insignificant phenomena may be determined to be meaningful if they are inserted in a "global structure" of the individual's consciousness and unconscious, whose genesis is studied from birth.[168]

According to Goldmann, Marxist theory alternated historically between dialectical (that is, genetic structural) and positivist phases. The former was generally characteristic of times of social upheaval, that is, of mass praxis. Goldmann makes a sweeping and highly schematic periodization of Marxist thought in terms of four stages:[169]

1. The dialectical thought of Marx himself was the first stage.

2. The next stage was the "great positivist period" of the late Engels and the Second International. Luxemburg and Trotsky were partial exceptions, while Kautsky and Bernstein, among others, personified it. Among the chief characteristics of positivist Marxism was the insistent separation of facts and values. This expressed the reality of a social democratic movement at a time of relative stability: their socialist "values" seemed far removed from contemporary "facts" and possibilities. Lenin's *Materialism and Empirocriticism*, which Goldmann calls "one of the most mechanical and anti-dialectical works there is" was a product of these tendencies as well.[170]

3. A dialectical revival began near the end of World War I and lasted until the rise of Stalin. This was the era of revolutionary tumult in Russia, Hungary, Germany, and elsewhere. The revival is exemplified by the work of Lukács, Gramsci, Korsch, Luxemburg, and the Lenin of the *Philosophical Notebooks* and *State and Revolution*.

4. In the immediate post–World War II period, there was another revival of dialectical thinking.

Undoubtedly, Goldmann partly had himself in mind in speaking of a post–World War II revival. Yet by the early 1960s, with organized capitalism stabilized and post-Algeria Gaullism consolidated, this revival was challenged by the rise of positivist and nongenetic Marxism, epitomized by Althusser. Goldmann refused to accept this historical stability as permanent, although the picture he drew of organized capitalism placed in question the prospects that contesting transindividual subjects could emerge. Thus, while he was influenced by Marcuse's *One-Dimensional Man*, he criticized its bleakness. Still, the conditions Goldmann identified as giving rise to non-genetic structuralism's negation of the subject left him searching for one. We can see this in his political trajectory.

8

The Hidden Class: Goldmann's Unwritten Politics

GOLDMANN NEVER WROTE a work devoted entirely to politics. This is one reason why he was often viewed solely as a sociologist of culture or, more narrowly, of literature. However, a reconstruction of Goldmann's politics based on both published and unpublished sources demonstrates that this is misleading. In fact, sometime in the 1960s, Goldmann planned a general work entitled *Philosophie et politique*. It seems that all that was written was a three-page outline. Had the book been completed, its preoccupation, it is clear, would have been to delineate the historical relation between theory and politics.

The opening chapter was to mark out "three attitudes" of philosophy toward politics. The first was that of "advice" ("classical philosophy") and the second that of the disinterested observer ("certain currents of contemporary philosophy"). According to the third, "philosophical thought" has "a political effect properly speaking"(*une action politique propre*) adjoined to that of the politician (*du technicien politique*). This perspective may either oppose the intrusion of philosophy into politics or favor it. Goldmann indicates parenthetically that "Hegel and Marxism" fit the latter category.[1] Goldmann's theoretical apparatus, and especially his concept of partial identity, makes it evident that the third attitude is his own. Moreover, one can assemble from his various writings, especially in the 1950s and 1960s, major elements of what would have composed his unwritten *Politics*.

I

It is clear from *Kant* that Goldmann saw his philosophical and cultural work as political; he declared that nothing could of right call itself philosophy, save that whose aim was "the liberation of man and the realization of a true community."[2] Contrary to the neo-Kantian slogan "Back to Kant," the true legacy of the critical philosopher was the attempt to go forward by demanding a new human community, the striving to go beyond the autonomous individual to the ideas of community, universe, and totality. Once again, totality is a matter of method *and* aspiration, for totality is "the most important philosophical category, as much in epistemology as in ethics and aesthetics," and its two principal forms are "the universe and the human community." Goldmann adds that like Lukács, he does not see this totality as preexistent but as a goal to be created by collective human action.

In contrast to philosophers whose premise is the "I," Goldmann proposed "a philosophy of community, of the *we*, which surmounts the oppositions between contemplation and action, the individual and the community."[3] The dialectic between a quest for community and a consciousness of the possibility of tragedy structured Goldmann's politics as all his other works. Consequently. his quest for totality rests on a faith, an aspiration he believes may be discerned in all men and women, reinvented in different times and places in varied garbs. For Pascal, it was a quest for God; for rationalists, it was a quest for truth and glory; for socialists, it is a quest for the ideal community.[4]

Goldmann's concept of socialist community emerged in a highly abstract and vague way in his earliest writings, and often remained so for the next quarter of a century. The community he envisioned is structured homologously to his vision of an adequate comprehension of the relation between a whole and its parts and to his idea of the transindividual subject. It rests on a view of the individual as a "social individual" as defined by Marx in the *Grundrisse*: the being who individuates within, not outside society. Goldmann's quest for community is a quest to transcend—*Aufhebung* in Hegel's sense—the opposition between "individual" and "community" in order to achieve a synthesis of "individual-in-community." In this synthesis, individual liberty and *"la communauté comme le bien suprême"* were inseparable.[5]

In *Kant*, Goldmann distinguished three types of visions of the world (which he also called philosophical systems). The first vision, the atomist/individualist one, has the individual and freedom as its principal ethical referents. Its chief "cosmological" category is the atom or monad, and its primary psychological categories are the image and sensation. Rationalism and empiricism are its chief expressions. In them, the whole can be conceived solely as a composite of independent parts interacting within the framework of a reified universality (*universalitas*). This corresponds to Lask's notion of analytic logic as well as to the model of classical bourgeois society, neither of which can conceive of a whole (or a community) that is not ultimately reducible to individual entities (for example, the individuals acting in their own interests in the model of a liberal market economy). In contrast, the essential categories of the *vision totalitaire* are the whole and the universe. Its basic social referent, says Goldmann, is the collective. "Feeling" (expressed by means of revelation or intuition) is its central ethical term, while its chief "physical category" is the "life principle" (for example, the soul or *élan vital*). In this system, which is more or less the antithesis of the individualist/atomist one, the part or the individual is absorbed entirely and lost in the whole, be the latter defined as God, nation, or class.

The third vision is that of "the Person and the Community," and Goldmann declared it encapsulated in the Kantian formula that the universe and the human community form a whole "in which the very existence of the parts presupposes their union in the whole" while simultaneously, the autonomy of the parts and reality of the whole "constitute reciprocal conditions."[6] Thus "the person *and* the community" provides the "total solution" to the one-sidedness of the other two visions. This dialectical philosophy, Goldmann proposed in the 1940s, was still in its formative period, although crucial steps in its elaboration had been taken by Kant, Hegel, Marx, and Lukács. Its development was, in his eyes, "the principal task of modern thought."[7]

We find in this tripartite scheme the theoretical foundation of Goldmann's politics: the quest for a dialectical transcendence of atomistic individualism (a philosophy that negates community) and collectivism (which negates the individual). The whole, in this vision of socialist community, is not composed of disconnected atoms or egos (in which case it would not really be whole), nor is it to be an undifferentiated totality in which the parts are extinguished. There is a dialectical oscillation between the whole and the parts; human beings individuate themselves within the community. This politics is, however, rooted (again) first and foremost in Goldmann's reading of Kant as a philosopher who believes that man's authentic destiny entails a ceaseless striving for the absolute. As we know, Goldmann identified "the absolute" at various points as totality, noumena, God, and community, but in his analysis, the critical philosophy reached its goal only in the realm of aesthetics, and there only subjectively. Interestingly enough, it is in Kant's aesthetic theory that we find the principle of Goldmann's politics, though he himself does not point to it directly. We already saw the importance of *The Critique of Judgment* for Goldmann's "Dialogue dans une Buffet," written around the time he wrote *Kant*. Likewise, the third *Critique*, which Kant saw as a bridge linking his first two critiques, respectively, on epistemology and moral theory, parallels Goldmann's political vision. Kant sought to demonstrate that there are universally valid intersubjective judgments of taste based on a "harmony" of our faculties of understanding and imagination. Such a judgment is subjective *but* universal in that a given object ought to invoke, but cannot compel, pleasure. It appeals to what is common in all human beings, whatever their individual idiosyncracies. Kant writes:

> The judgment of taste exacts agreements from everyone; and a person who describes something as beautiful insists that everyone *ought* to give the object in question his approval and follow suit in describing it as beautiful. The

ought in aesthetic judgements therefore, despite an accordance with the requisite data for passing judgement, is still only pronounced conditionally. We are suitors for agreement from everyone else, because we are fortified with a ground common to all.[8]

Similarly, Goldmann seeks a socialism that makes the individual part of the whole (the community) on the basis of that which ties the individual as a human being to all other human beings and not because of a compulsion that negates individuality. This will be the socialist kingdom of ends, that is, a socialism of the person and the community.

Where does Lask's emanatist logic, which Goldmann sometimes calls a view of history, fit into the threefold division of philosophical systems? In *The Human Sciences and Philosophy*, Goldmann stipulated two key components of emanatism. The first is the idea that all human realities must be understood as emanating from or expressive of something more profound, usually "supraindividual," for example, a *Volksgeist* or Objective Spirit. This would seem to place emanatism within the *vision totalitaire*. Goldmann tells us that it is precisely its emphasis on the whole that gives the emanatist perspective its value. Simultaneously, however, he asserts the validity of the analytic critique of this position. More often than not, the supraindividual entities postulated by emanatism are speculative and metaphysical in nature.[9] The second key emanatist idea is, according to Goldmann, accepted by Marxism. This is the notion that "the totality [*l'ensemble*] of individual consciousnesses" is not to be regarded as an "arithmetical sum" of autonomous entities. Rather, each consciousness must be grasped in terms of its relation with the whole and the other individual parts.[10]

In *The Human Sciences and Philosophy*, Goldmann is not clear how the first concept of emanatism (which subsumes the part under the whole) and the second (which apparently does not) are to be reconciled. In any event, the latter leads us to Goldmann's claim that both analytic and emanatist conceptions are inadequate and need to be synthesized on a higher level.[11] How? By the very principles of what he later called transindividuality:

> For dialectical materialism, there is no supra-individual consciousness. Collective consciousness, the consciousness of a class, for example is only the ensemble of individual consciousnesses and their tendencies resulting from the mutual influence of men on one another and on nature.[12]

Discussing *Kant*, we saw that for Goldmann, communication implies that individuals must transform what is immediately given to them in experience in such a way that their comprehension allows similar apprehension by other persons. This was a question of the forms of experience and communication, or, in the language of genetic structuralism, of mental structures. There is, Goldmann suggests, a minimum of form necessary to render understanding possible between human beings.

There would also be a maximum that would correspond to "an ideal community."[13] Goldmann implies that as ideal communication is structured, so, too, is the ideal community. (He thus anticipates some themes later developed by Jürgen Habermas.) Again, Goldmann's notions of totality, community, and the transindividual subject have the same structure, which is that of his concept of the relation between the whole and the parts. Underlying it is a quest for a whole man, one not beset by the dualisms that reified capitalist society generates by *its* very structure: dualities of form and content, fact and value, subject and object, community and individual, whole and parts. In a reified world, man as subject increasingly perceives himself as an object among others; he lives in a universe of objects which appear external to him, although he created them. "Form," that which orders experience and enables communication with others, is confronted by the "content" of social relations—atomistic, egoistic individuals selfishly pursuing their own goals. Common ends in a cooperatively organized society would, in contrast, unite form and content by uniting man's essential sociability with cooperative communal relations. Form and content would be common to the lives of all as part of an apparently fully, or almost fully, self-conscious transindividual subject. This, then, would be an "authentic" human community.

What precisely Goldmann meant by "authentic" can be discerned by placing this word in two contexts: the theory of reification and the conclusions Goldmann drew from his study of the relation between the thought of Lukács and that of Heidegger. In one discussion of reification Goldmann wrote, following Marx and Lukács, that "the natural, healthy relation among men and goods is in effect that of production consciously regulated for future consumption, by the concrete qualities of objects, by their *use value*."[14] In production for the market, exchange value mediates all social relations, rendering use value secondary and "implicit" in consciousness. For example, when I purchase clothes on the market, their manufacturer is indifferent to their actual use. For the manufacturer, the clothes are solely a means to ensure more exchange values:

> In economic life, which is the most important part of modern social life, all authentic relations with the qualitative aspect of objects and human beings [*des objets et des êtres*] tend to disappear—in relations between men and things as well as in inter-human relations—in order to be replaced by a me-

diated and degraded relation of purely quantitative exchange values. Naturally, use values continue to exist and even govern, in the last instance, the whole of economic life; but their impact [*leur action*] takes on an *implicit* character, exactly like that of *authentic values in the novel's world*.[15]

In the novel, Goldmann found a "degraded" quest by a "problematic individual" in search of "authentic values" in a world where all manifest values—all transindividual relations—appear to be absent. The rise of capitalism and the primacy of the category of exchange value in all aspects of life begot the first system in which economics per se dominates every mode of existence. This leads Goldmann to distinguish between "subjective" and "objective" authenticity: "To the extent that the influence of the economy on other domains of life grows progressively, while inversely, the influence of these domains on economic life tends to disappear, the result is a paradoxical situation in which *in the best of cases* spiritual life attains a subjective authenticity which is the counterpart of its objective inauthenticity."[16]

Goldmann contended that reification presses individual consciousness into its own canton, as it were. Thus there can be an excess of subjective authenticity in moral, religious, and aesthetic phenomena, as a counterpart to the encompassing objective inauthenticity of socioeconomic life. Among other things, it is this, in Goldmann's view, which explains romanticism, which was engendered by a divorce from reality.[17] On the other hand, the dominant tendency under capitalism is for religion, art, and morality to lose their autonomy and become, increasingly, reflexes of economic life. While in principle these domains are neither autonomous nor simple reflexes of economics, their "authenticity" is emptied out as they become more and more enmeshed in market relations, and the "apparition" of an autonomous economic whole penetrates all human manifestations and remakes them in its own image.[18]

In these passages, "authenticity" clearly denotes something based on qualitative human needs, that is, needs not derived from or dependent on quantitative factors. "Authenticity" rests on the distinction between use and exchange value, with the former viewed as "natural" and "healthy," qualitative and immediate. The latter is reifying, quantitative, mediated, and "unhealthy." Classical Marxism, Goldmann tells us, saw in the disappearance of reification—that is, in the supersession of capitalism and the market—a return to "the human" and "the meaningful."[19] This does not, however, represent a nostalgic effort to recreate the medieval world. When Goldmann, in contrasting a "natural economy" to a market one, defines "natural" to mean "all the forms of economic organization implying a body [*une organisme*] of planning production and consumption," he is quick to add that its modern form is quite different from the organization of production and consumption" by a peasant family.[20] Goldmann, like Marx, saw important positive features in the development of capitalism, but Goldmann, unlike Marx, emphasized the ideas of individual liberty, tolerance, equality before the law. These resulted from the collapse of the old medieval "totality." He is looking, we repeat, for "*Aufhebung*" of totalizing community, which negates the individual, and of egoistic individualism, which negates community. However, the Marxist return to "the human," as Goldmann presents it, would seem to carry this implication: since in capitalism relations among individuals and their objectifications appear as relations among things, authentic relations must in some way eliminate the mediation of the market in human interaction. Thereby, man would recognize his own powers at play and recognize himself in the world of objects he creates, rather than perceiving that world and other human beings as things external to and beyond him. The *endziel* would seem to be an identity of subjective and objective authenticity, in other words, the dialectical attainment of a historically created human totality that banishes inauthenticity.

Abolished, too, would be the conditions that engendered the tragic vision, the rupture that so obsessed young Lukács between the (authentic) Life of absolute values and the (inauthentic) life of quotidian empirical existence. Goldmann, we know, compared Lukács's distinction between Life and life in *Soul and Forms* and between empirical and imputed class consciousness in *History and Class Consciousness* to Heidegger's distinctions between the ontological and the ontic (in the appendix to *Kant*, Goldmann attributed Heidegger's distinction to Lask) and authenticity and inauthenticity.

If for Goldmann, Being and totality function similarly in the respective philosophies of *Being and Time* and *History and Class Consciousness*, and if authentic/inauthentic *Dasein* in Heidegger parallels not only Life/life in Lukács's *Soul and Forms* but true and false consciousness in *History and Class Consciousness*, then authenticity in the (Lukács-inspired) Goldmannian sense must mean the self-conscious self-determination of the "We," and the latter must be understood ultimately as a self-conscious transindividual subject, a fully realized human community unmediated by the mechanisms of capitalism, which engender reification. Inasmuch as *Being and Time* is a response to *History and Class Consciousness*, "from the community of the 'We,' only the 'They' [*l'on*] remains" in Heidegger.[21] However, ontology demonstrates to Heidegger that *Dasein* must "fall" repeatedly into inauthenticity, whereas for Goldmann, totality as the authentic human community is conceived as a goal to be historically established by collective human action. Indeed, the "We" is constituted in this action.

But how shall this "We" make its appearance? And what form shall it take? Lukács's answer to both questions was consistent: the revolutionary proletariat. It is an irony of Goldmann's intellectual journey that when he began to specify his own answers to these questions in the late 1950s and in the 1960s, he was compelled to reject this key element in Lukács's system on the basis of his own understanding of the development of capitalism. As his philosophical analyses diverged from Lukács's in essential ways, so too would his politics. Having insisted that philosophy stands within and not outside the world, and having contended that subject-object identity can only be partial, Goldmann could not escape important ramifications concerning the "totality" he had proposed to create. There was a *hiatus irrationalis* between his *endziel*, his concept, and political possibility. Consequently, he began to seek another possibility: "revolutionary reform" and the elaboration of the authentic community as *autogestion*, workers' self-management.

II

Goldmann's typology of the development of capitalism was highly colored by the "New Working Class" school of theorists in France, especially former French Communist Party member Serge Mallet and André Gorz, the political editor of *Les Temps modernes*. In addition, Herbert Marcuse's *One-Dimensional Man* influenced Goldmann significantly, although he had serious reservations about its conclusions. While Goldmann was close friends with both Marcuse and Mallet— the latter referred to himself as a "genetic structuralist"—Goldmann had no personal relation with Gorz.[22] Importantly, Goldmann's typology and the evolution of his political concepts were tightly linked to the political upheavals of the late 1950s. In June 1959, Goldmann declared that the events of the previous three years—Khrushchev's denunciation of Stalin, the invasion of Hungary, the war in Algeria— compelled many socialist intellectuals, obviously including himself, to rethink their positions, and, as we have seen, he wrote to Lukács expressing concern that intellectuals of the Left were going to throw out the Marxist baby with the Stalinist bathwater. The consolidation of Gaullism filled Goldmann with dread, and it was an article by Mallet analyzing the birth of the Fifth Republic that led Goldmann to seek him out.[23]

The politics espoused by Goldmann, Mallet, and Gorz in the 1960s were radically at odds with both the Communists and the Socialists (the SFIO), as they imagined *autogestion* to be the embodiment of socialist community. In this, Goldmann, Gorz, and Mallet anticipated the slogans of May 1968. Although Goldmann never actually joined it, he was close to the most important political party identified with the French New Left, the Parti Socialiste Unifie (PSU), founded in 1960 as a breakaway from the mainstream socialists. Mallet served in the PSU political bureau (Gorz influenced it but did not enroll, being, in his word, "allergic" to joining parties).[24]

Goldmann's advocacy of *autogestion* rested on his concept of community and on his understanding of the development of capitalism, an understanding that led him to conclude that history had disproved the classical Marxist paradigm. It will be useful to recapitulate and flush out Goldmann's analysis at this point. Liberal capitalism, we recall, lasted roughly until the eve of World War I. In it, the market reigned, the "abstract individual" was the key reference point, and the process of reification, a necessary result of production for the market, caused the disappearance "of any community dimension from the consciousness of individuals."[25] Instead of the community, we have the deification of the egoistic competitor, who is viewed as the embodiment of human nature rather than as a product of history. Individualist philosophies (rationalism, empiricism) predominate, and the notion of totality beyond the atomized ego recedes from consciousness: "transindividual values" (which Goldmann saw exemplified in the ideas of morality, faith, aesthetics, and charity) are subsumed under exchange values. Reification rules. Since the commodity form is this society's ultimate frame of reference, homo economicus, a being who understands and acts in the world primarily through the medium of exchange values, reigns as well. Economics comes to dominate all aspects of life; human consciousness, which "in *its own right* [*en droit*]" is not "a passive reflex of social life," tends to become one "to the extent that the development of an *autonomous economy* empties it of all efficacy."[26] The reified society and the mental structures generated within it preclude certain types of cultural creation and encourage others. The bourgeois world, contended Goldmann, could not produce cathedrals and epics, for these require the structuring of consciousness by the transindividual, by the collective, not by the reified world of liberal individualism, whose "classic epoch" is the nineteenth century.[27] Characteristic of the culture of this period is the "novel of the problematic hero" in which the individual is extolled but unable to attain self-realization in a society supposedly dedicated to that self-realization.

In this world, regulated theoretically by the liberal market, there was an additional contradiction of particular importance: its structure was composed of two opposed sectors, one strongly hierarchical and one democratic. The hierarchical structure was to be found in the workplace, in schooling, and in offices and government and was modeled on the family, in which the father was the chief. It was, as such, a "quasi-monarchical" sector. Alongside it was a "democratic" sector of "free enterprise," a realm of economic competition, individual decisionmaking, and responsibility, which also had social and political parallels. This democratic sector was restricted, however, for it was the domain of the *notables* (the traditional middle classes), who were autonomous, their authority resting on individually or family-owned enterprises. The reproduction of the generalized system of social hierarchy, Goldmann argued, was facilitated especially by educational institutions, particularly the universities and the upper levels of the lycées (high schools) which were largely the private preserve of the children of the notables. Here the obedient child who was disciplined by the quasi-monarchical (and patriarchal) family, was transformed into an autonomous individual—a future quasi-monarch over his own family and factory, capable of decisionmaking and authoritative roles.[28]

The ensuing transitional period of "capitalism in crisis" lasted approximately until the close of World War II. The crisis was due to the disruption of the political, social, and economic equilibrium of the earlier phase as trusts and monopolies displaced individually and family-owned enterprises. Western capitalism underwent severe structural traumas as the regulation of the economy through free market competition was undermined. Concurrently, and importantly, markets abroad for capital were sought. But the markets available for the penetration of capital were shrinking precisely when they were increasingly required for imperialism.[29] The cumulative effect of these developments was continued crises in the form of wars, revolutions, and depressions. Capitalism, unsuccessfully, sought to stabilize itself. At the same time, the socialist movements proved unsuccessful, although the severity of these crises led many Marxists to believe erroneously that the downfall of capitalism was on the morrow.

This period engendered a crisis in the idea of the individual, whose economic importance seemed to dissipate with the ascendance of trusts, monopolies, and finance capital. What emerges now are philosophies stressing the limits of the individual, angst, and death. In the—rather schematic—picture Goldmann gives, first liberal capitalism suppresses precapitalist transindividual values in the name of the individual, and next the individual is jeopardized by capitalism's ensuing evolution:

> If the behavior of the individual can no longer be based, in effect, on transindividual values (since individualism suppressed them) or on the undeniable value of the individual (now put in question), thought had to necessarily focus itself [se centrer] on the difficulties of this foundation, on the limits of the human being as an individual and the most important of these limits, death.[30]

This is, of course, the context of the birth of existentialism, Lukács's essay on tragedy, Heidegger's philosophy, and various forms of twentieth-century irrationalism. Finally, the "novel of the nonbiographical character" replaces that of the "problematic hero," and the Western value crisis is expressed with particular acuteness in Malraux's novels.

It required "organized capitalism" (organization carried out by the state and monopolies) to restabilize the advanced societies of the West in the post–World War II period. Not only is capitalism now "organized"; it fashions and is fashioned by a "technocratic" and "consumer" society. An "internal transformation of the relation between the middle classes and the ruling group" has taken place. A "generalized system [une generalisation] with an authoritarian and hierarchical character replaces the synthesis of an authoritarian and hierarchical sector with a liberal and democratic one which characterized the period of 1848–1912."[31] The development of monopolies, trusts and finally state regulation undermined the notables on one hand, and on the other, required the development of new strata of salaried specialists, or "technicians," to carry out the plans of society's new organizers, the "technocrats."

The consequence of this for Marxist theory is momentous. It was Goldmann's claim that organized capitalism had been successful in its goals of regulation and stabilization. He never explicates the relation between the "technocrats" and the "bourgeoisie" under advanced capitalism, but argues that society is increasingly organized and thoroughly administered from top down, with crucial decisions being made by a decreasing number of technocrats in various realms—production, culture, education, and so on—and carried out by technicians. These technocrats aim at the organization of society, or at least the economy, as a whole. The Marxist/Lukácsian claim that the ruling

class/strata could never master crises because they cannot attain a totalizing perspective appears to have been invalidated. Goldmann
writes:

> [B]ourgeois society, far from disappearing as Lukács believed, surmounted
> the crises and transformed itself into a technocratic society of organized
> capitalism which has assured a considerable development of productive
> forces. This is, in part, due to the integration . . . of the whole of the economy
> [into the thought of] the theoreticians of the bourgeoisie and their official
> thinkers.[32]

Goldmann goes further in his departure from traditional Marxism and
Lukácsianism. He argues that instead of the middle strata of society
becoming proletarianized as class structure simplified and polarized
(between the proletariat and the bourgeoisie, as Marx projected), there
was now a technocracy of the state, monopolies, and trusts, which
was making decisions for the society as a whole, and dependent
"wage-earning middle strata" of technicians and specialists, who
were displacing the traditional middle classes. "For the independent
artisan and entrepreneur," he writes, "has been substituted the highly
remunerated 'technician,' the specialist, *le pompiste*, the branch man-
ager of an apparently autonomous store which is in reality greatly dependent on corporations [*des trusts producteurs*]."[33] Members of the
new middle strata have a decent enough income and a professional
culture, but unlike the notables, they are dependent and do not com-
pete economically. They carry out instructions, rather than making autonomous decisions. With the disappearance of the independent notables, the liberal and democratic ideologies linked to them are also
threatened.[34]

So, too, the structures of dominance in the family and education are
transformed, and here the contradictions of organized capitalism are
to be discerned. In the nineteenth century the fathers of notable families were quasi-monarchs in the enterprise and the home, but now they
were "*executants*" in the workplace, and this leads to a loosening of
hierarchical structures in the family. The educational institutions of society now have a new role as well. Whereas they once took the child
who was obedient to a quasi-monarchical father and turned him into
an autonomous, decisionmaking being able also to be a quasi-monarch, organized capitalism requires disciplined and limited specialists
instructed in the technical information required to make a hierarchical,
regulated society function smoothly. Coming from a more liberalized
family structure, the youth of the new middle strata confront more and
more "magisterial and authoritative" teachers—even though the com-

plexity of technical and scientific knowledge progress, Goldmann says, actually demands collaborative efforts and open discussion. The educational environment produces profound tensions, and this will be a conceptual point in Goldmann's understanding of why May 1968 happened.[35]

As late as his essay on reification, Goldmann, though already pointing to the effects of the transition to organized capitalism, still argued that the proletariat was in but not of reified society and that it was the counteragent to reification. A decade later, however, he had concluded:

> There has never been a proletarian revolution and no part of the proletariat has ever oriented itself towards conflict with all the other social groups it should have wanted to eliminate in order to create a classless society in which it would itself disappear: no part of the proletariat's evolution has been spontaneously revolutionary.[36]

And the proletariat was not going to become the identical subject-object of history, for it had become increasingly integrated into Western consumer society. Thanks to the success of the technocrats, rising standards of living were provided for workers. The entire society and the workers in it were becoming increasingly integrated, and oppositional forces were becoming less and less potent. The Marxist schema had to be revised, if not entirely rejected, and more important, the proletariat could no longer be spoken of as the universal class. The concept of the revolutionary proletariat, Goldmann bluntly declares, was perhaps the weakest link in Lukács's theory; it was "possible" that "the proletariat [was] not an exception to the law which says that each group seeks its own survival and dominance," not only on the level of real consciousness, but on that of objective possibility.[37] "Objective possibility," Goldmann wrote, "requires the coincidence of a group's external situation and adequate mental structures."[38] With a rising standard of living and the permeation of all aspects of life by reified thinking—the creation of what Marcuse called "One-Dimensional Man"—in short, with the success of organized capitalism's integration of contesting forces, authentic socialist community might well be beyond the possible consciousness of the proletariat. Proletarian revolution could no longer be considered part of the proletariat's class consciousness. The unhappy outcome of the Soviet experience, for Goldmann, was one additional important factor leading to this.[39]

In liberal capitalism, the perspective of totality was lost because of the deification of the atomized, egoistic individual. Hope for retrieval—or rather, reinvention—of totality had been placed in the proletariat. But in organized capitalism, if the perspective of totality was to be found anywhere, it was in the technocracy. Thesis had become antithesis; those who, according to Lukács, ought to grasp totality do not, while those who theoretically should be unable to do so do grasp it.[40] The consequences, in Goldmann's view, are potentially devastating to humanist hopes. The perspective of totality on the part of the technocrats and its effects—the continued rationalization of society and its administration together with technological advance, linked to the values of rampant consumerism—threatened to produce a "Golem with the face of an angel," a being unable to think of "the possible" since he is satisfied and numbed by the latest commodities and diligently performs his tasks in order to obtain more commodities and relax in a "*Club Mediterranée* of the mind."[41]

Though the theory of the revolutionary proletariat might be unsound, Goldmann still insisted that he was a Marxist, arguing that the theory of reification was the cornerstone of all valid Marxist analysis. The theory of reification provided the key to understanding both contemporary society and, indeed, Marx's work itself: "[O]nly the theory of reification permits understanding the coherence of all the Marxist texts concerning the relations between 'infrastructure' and 'superstructure.'"[42] In "La Réification," he at once adhered to a more traditional Marxist view of the working class and began making observations that point to coming changes. He presents the following four points.

1. Reification is a psychological and intellectual result "of the existence of production for the market in a pure capitalist society—liberal or monopolist—with little economic intervention by the state." It is "an *inevitable* consequence of the market economy" (emphasis added).[43] Because of reification in liberal capitalism, relations among human beings, their labor, and its products appear as relations among things beyond those who create them. Exchange value and quantitative categories take precedence over use value and qualitative categories, as the economy dominates all aspects of life. The fetishized commodity becomes the central category of social life and consciousness. The implication is clearly that reducing the impact of the market will reduce reification.[44]

2. On the other hand, Goldmann emphasized that it was the market economy that had led initially to the emergence of the values of the individual, liberty, and equality before the law. He complained that under capitalism, these values are merely formal; however, this was not to deride the values, as was the case with numerous other Marxists, but instead to demand that their formality be transcended and fully expressed in a socialist society. A socialist society, Goldmann reiterated tirelessly, could not do without them.

3. The proletariat had nothing to gain from capitalism's continuation and, despite reification, found in itself a form of human solidarity that portended possible alternatives to class society in the future. The workers are, he tells us, "potentially [*virtuellement*] a living protest" against reification and capitalism.[45] While maintaining this claim, Goldmann explicitly recognized the influence of rising living standards, the general impact of state intervention in the economy, and the deleterious effects of Stalinism on socialist hopes.

4. There were, Goldmann noted, significant gaps in the Marx/Lukács analysis of reification. Since this phenomenon is so "tightly linked" to production for the market and the absence of economic planning in classical liberal capitalism, planning ought, in principle, to weaken reification. This, Goldmann insisted, was partly the case in the USSR, but it was accompanied by an undermining of liberty and the formal equality of individuals, a possibility classical Marxism failed to envision.[46]

These points have important ramifications for organized capitalism as well, for they will help lead Goldmann to the conclusion that nationalization of the means of production and suppression of reification in and of themselves are insufficient for the creation of a humane socialist society. In fact, "universal values and respect for individual liberty" would be guaranteed no more than under capitalism.[47] New dangers were to be discerned both in communist command economies and in the planning and administration of organized capitalism. Like organized capitalism, the centralized economy of the USSR made necessary a hierarchical society composed of a small group of active rulers and a large, passive population.[48]

Where this analysis eventually led Goldmann can be seen in a preface he wrote in 1969 for an Italian translation of "La Réification." Looking back, he chastised himself for failing to account sufficiently for the evolution of capitalism after Marx and Lukács. Echoing *One-Dimensional Man*, Goldmann wrote:

> [N]either Marx, Lukács, nor later myself (and this is most unpardonable for me as I was writing in 1959 [*sic*]) thought that reification would extend itself much further [*beaucoup plus loin*] and suppress even the functions, importance, and the existence of the individual in the consciousness of men. Now this is in reality what was produced, at least tendentially. [It] was the natural consequence of the disappearance of the individual in the economy, and his replacement by transindividual organisms, i.e., monopolies and trusts.[49]

With no individual or apparent transindividual subject at hand—although with increasingly powerful transindividual organisms dominating society—the question of collective action for change became vital. Looking at the question from the perspective of cultural creation in *Towards a Sociology of the Novel*, Goldmann wrote:

> The old Marxist thesis which saw in the proletariat the only social group capable of constituting the foundation of a new culture due to the fact that it wasn't integrated into reified society, began from the traditional sociological model [*representation*] which supposed that all important and authentic cultural creation can be born only from a fundamental accord between the mental structure of the creator and that of a partial group, one that is relatively large but with universal aims. In reality, the Marxist analysis has demonstrated itself to be insufficient, at least for Western society. Far from remaining foreign to reified society and opposing it as a revolutionary force, the Western proletariat has largely integrated itself, and its political and trade union activities—far from overthrowing this society and replacing it by a socialist world—have permitted it to assure itself a relatively better off place than had been foreseen by Marx's analyses.
>
> And nonetheless, cultural creation has not ceased, although it is more and more menaced by reified society.[50]

Goldmann seems to argue in several places that oppositional and critical thought was being reduced to a few rebellious writers, such as Genet. He turned to the works of Mallet and Gorz for an alternative to the dismal implications of his analyses.

Goldmann's discussion of the "new middle strata" was his contribution to the broader debate within the French Left as to whether these trained strata would be political assets to the Left or to the Right. In separate endeavors, both Mallet and Gorz concluded that the emergence of such sectors composed what might be a new political avant-garde.[51] Mallet wrote of the creation by advanced capitalism of a "new working class," constituted of the new wage-earning strata of which Goldmann spoke, and the traditional (blue-collar) proletariat. This new working class was conceived as a "collective worker"; as a result of the evolution of technocratic society and advances in technology, earlier distinctions between productive and nonproductive labor were becoming decreasingly important. Nonetheless, the members of the middle strata, highly educated as they are, would, Mallet proposed, take greater and greater interest in the workplace and become increasingly restless in their role as executors of decisions made by others. Both Mallet and Gorz envisioned a syndicalist struggle toward *autogestion* led by these advanced sectors, for whom impoverishment was not a relevant issue. "Hunger calls for food to eat," wrote Gorz. "But what does emptiness, boredom, dissatisfaction with life and the world call for? There is no predetermined answer to this question; we have reached a stage where needs could be no longer those of the 'human animal' but those—potentially creative—of the 'human man.' "[52]

Qualitative demands, not only quantitative ones for higher living standards, would be raised by the new middle strata. And qualitative demands composed the heart of the political strategy advocated by Gorz, Mallet, and Goldmann—a strategy of "revolutionary reformism." Structural reforms would be sought in the workplace, but the purpose of such reforms would not be amelioration of capitalism's ills and consequent enhancement of the integrative capacities of an apparently ever-expanding system. Instead, qualitative demands would undo the system, for human needs, not the logic of the system, would be the focus of reform. In particular, reform would aim at continued democratization of the labor process and increased autonomy within and eventual control over the workplace by the workers.

Among the goals of revolutionary reformism were socialization of investment; the subordination of production to the needs of the workers in the plants; and ever-increasing responsibility for the unions at the expense of management at all levels of enterprises, including union control of personnel decisions, organization of work, the division of labor, and training schools and programs. Obviously union democracy was a premise of this entire endeavor. Step by step, the capitalist structure of factories would be compromised as the workers themselves, through their unions, extended control over all aspects of the labor process. The specialists produced by "neocapitalism" (Gorz's term) for its own needs would take the lead in this transformation because their own educations would lead them to raise qualitative questions about daily work and life rather than solely quantitative issues of financial recompense. Following a protracted struggle, a direct clash with the ruling class and its power was likely. The society envisioned by the victory of revolutionary-reformist forces would be a decentralized one, based on workers's self-management, as opposed to a centrally planned economy with power concentrated in state hands. For Gorz, Mallet, and Goldmann, socialism meant increasing the self-determination of the worker in the workplace and in daily life: when they spoke of workers' power, they meant just that.

Goldmann argued that whereas Marcuse's *One-Dimensional Man* viewed the evolution of the West as a "sort of catastrophe without end," a new agent of possible socialist transformation was to be found in the new working class.[53] Similarly, the "end of ideology" proclaimed by sociologists such as Daniel Bell represented the triumph of technocratic ideology—which would have to be undone for revolutionary reformism to succeed. The struggle between capitalism and socialism thus became a struggle for the consciousness of the new working class. Goldmann, like Gorz, believed the members of the new middle strata, on account of their education, job security and income, would slowly begin to revolt against their work situation. Their meaningless roles as well-remunerated executants would propel them to press for structural reforms, with the goal of taking on more meaningful responsibilities and leading the way in the direction of self-management. This theory was based on a law of diminishing quantitative returns: the higher the standard of living of the technicians, the less value they would find in struggling only to increase it.[54] Theirs was an *"intégration contestatrice"* with a *"pensée contestatrice,"* challenging hierarchy and bureaucracy.[55] They would consequently be the cutting edge of a struggle toward *autogestion* and would bring the traditional proletariat with them.

A fundamental Marxist dictum was reversed (again) by Goldmann: it was not those with nothing but their chains to lose who would lead the way to socialism, but an avant-garde composed of secure and well-paid but qualitatively dissatisfied wage earners. In addition, Goldmann turned on its head the thesis that a proletarian *political* revolution had to precede socialist economic transformation. He suggested instead a process of change,

> which bears a considerable resemblance to the development of the bourgeoisie inside feudal society; in this latter case the seizure of economic power and a great increase in the social importance of the rising class *preceded* the seizure of political power which was, moreover, depending on the country involved, at first revolutionary in nature (England, France), but also, subsequently, evolutionary and reformist (Germany, Italy).[56]

Revolutionary structural reforms would, as such, subvert capitalism from within, lead toward self-management, and finally, at the end or far along the path of social change, lead to political revolution, possibly peacefully, possibly violently.

Goldmann knew well that he would be accused of "revisionism" by "orthodox" Marxists. The final chapter of *Philosophie et politique* would have confronted this by analyzing three issues: (1) "[t]he [d]angers of a reformist evolution without qualitative transformation"; (2) "[t]he [p]ossibility and hope of a reformist evolution resulting in a qualitative transformation and a cultural renaissance"; and (3) "[t]he problem of workers' control [*la gestion ouvrière*]." These three points, each of which is discussed by Goldmann in various published writings, link his politics into a whole.

Goldmann remained radically opposed to traditional social democratic reformism on philosophical and political grounds. Bernstein's classical formula that the movement was all and the end nothing was irreconcilable with a dialectical understanding of the relation between means and ends. To lose this dialectic was to lose sight of the very quest for individual-in-community, for a civilization qualitatively different from previous societies. Along with Gorz, Goldmann insisted that he was advocating not just reforms but revolutionary reforms that would engender qualitative transformation and would in themselves embody the means-ends dialectic. (One may perhaps discern here a long-term Austro-Marxist influence on Goldmann, for Otto Bauer and his colleagues spoke of a revolutionary reformism, though not in precisely the same sense. Gorz was of Austrian origin and was certainly familiar with the ideas of the Austro-Marxists). Explicating Lukács's critique of Bernstein, Goldmann asserted that the author of *History and Class Consciousness* recognized what the German revisionist did not: that "the end penetrates each given element at each given moment. The end is not separated from the means which it structures, while it is, for its part, structured by them constantly."[57]

There was an issue on which Goldmann—and Lenin—partially concurred with Bernstein: the revolutionary potential of the traditional working class. Goldmann, as we have seen, frequently constructed an unorthodox analytic division of socialist history. Instead of the traditional partition of radical Left, orthodox center, and revisionist Right, Goldmann proposed a twofold distinction based on attitudes toward the proletariat. On one hand were those who saw the proletariat as a revolutionary class, entirely unintegrated into capitalist society and radically opposed to all other classes; on the other hand were those who believed that the proletariat had been at least partially integrated into capitalism and unable to bring about socialism on its own.[58] Rosa Luxemburg is an obvious example of the first category; Goldmann, Lenin, and Bernstein all fit into the second, although they had dissimilar political programs. In Chapter 5 of Goldmann's *Philosophie et politique*, on "Socialist Thought in the Western Capitalist World," social democracy and Stalinism were to be studied as "two forms of ideology, apparently oppositional, in reality integrated into existing social structures." Actually, Goldmann's classificatory schemes—one based on a division of attitudes toward the proletariat and one providing a unity of opposites (social democracy and Stalinism)—represent the application by Goldmann of different criteria of *découpage* of his object. In each case he brings out a political contrast that highlights his own *autogestionaire* vision of politics.

III

Goldmann never wrote a detailed program for a *société autogestionaire*, although "the problem of workers' control" was to culminate the concerns of the last chapter of *Philosophie et politique*, just before its conclusion. He did, however, delineate its broad principles on several occasions, both in public discussions and in essays, most importantly in a July 1968 "Débat sur l'autogestion," which also included Mallet, among others, under the auspices of *Le Nouvel Observateur*. Then, and often before, he maintained that economically and politically *autogestion* meant self-determination of the daily lives of men and women, but that it also embodied the hope that a "whole man" might be created, one who was not fragmented by capitalism. That Goldmann was alert to the difficulties inherent in his aspirations was clear in the outline for a film script he composed in 1964. This was for a documentary (never realized) about Yugoslav experiments in workers' self-management. In preparation, Goldmann traveled to Yugoslavia, where he visited various factories and participated in the Pula Film Festival. He envisioned a film closely examining the problems of self-management, aimed at a Western audience. The goal was

> to show *autogestion* as a revolutionary attempt to resolve human problems, and notably those of the relation between the individual and the community, an attempt which confronts many difficulties, due partly to the insufficient maturity and inadequately adapted psychology of the workers who take part in it; an attempt which, however, has among other things, by its simple existence, an educative function and which must result not only in a modernization of the productive forces of the country, but also in the realization of a new psychology, the creation of a new man capable of dominating these modern productive forces in a human society, [an attempt] which could indicate the way to the solution of a certain number of fundamental human problems that are hard to solve in other social and economic [forms].[59]

Goldmann recognized that there were vast differences between the underdeveloped Yugoslav economic base and advanced Western European capitalism. And he knew that the Yugoslav experiment, a product of Tito's struggle with Stalin, emerged in a land where political power had been seized by the Communist Party in advance of any socioeconomic structural (revolutionary) reforms. The Yugoslav leader, before breaking with the Kremlin, had been more Stalinist than Stalin himself. Yugoslav *autogestion* hardly came of a scenario of revolutionary reformism. Goldmann hoped that the Yugoslav experiment would eventually construct the basis for a "synthesis . . . of the socialist historical consciousness and . . . individual liberty and tolerance" by demonstrating that *"the suppression of private property in the means of production is not incompatible with the market."*[60]

Though indebted to what he saw in Yugoslavia, Goldmann admitted that the real ancestors of his own notion of *autogestion* were Proudhon and Spanish anarchism. The ideas of Proudhon and Spanish anarchism, it should be pointed out, are significantly akin to the anarchosocialist romanticism (of such figures as Gustav Landauer) that did so much to shape the vision of community Goldmann embraced as a youth in Ha-Shomer ha-Tsair. Ultimately, Goldmann's *autogestion* did represent a form of anarchism, for in his view "radical *autogestion* is synonymous with the suppression of the state."[61]

This was, Goldmann recognized, a distant prospect, and perhaps a utopian aspiration. In the meantime, he argued that the immediate goal of revolutionary-reformist politics in the West ought to be an increasingly self-managed society. In that society, there would be a balance between decentralization and "democratic planning," which aimed to guarantee socialization of investment and to secure consideration of long-term socioeconomic needs of the society as a whole. Traditional Marxism envisioned socialism as the suppression of the market, socialization of the means of production, and the establishment of an overall system of economic planning. The aim, wrote Goldmann, should be a system that would synthesize

1. the rationally organized production of goods;
2. the substantive realization of the values of individual liberty, equality, and community;
3. "the qualitative aspects of psychic life and inter-human relations which characterize precapitalist societies"; and
4. the elimination of exploitation and class divisions, which had been characteristic of primitive communism.[62]

The experience of the previous century, Goldmann contended, showed this formulation to be unsustainable. Furthermore, the evils of Stalinism, while undoubtedly the product of particular historical circumstances, were integrally linked to the abolition of the market and its replacement by an economy controlled entirely by a central authority.[63] The alternative was democratic, self-managed market socialism that abolished the formality but substantively incarnated the values of liberty, equality, and tolerance, without which "socialist man," as Goldmann conceived him, could not be created.

In the organization of a democratic and socialist society, Goldmann distinguished between *autogestion* per se and direct democracy. The latter was chiefly a form of state structure, whereas the former's primary concern was "social relations in the domain of work, it being understood that an important transformation [in this domain] must also have considerable influence on the state and political life since the economic, the social and the political intersect."[64] He did not assume that self-managed socialism would entail a complete elimination of the division of labor because special competencies would inevitably be required in industries and therefore specialized technical and educational levels would be needed in certain tasks. Particularly in large factories, *autogestion* would entail elected representative committees of workers, who would vote regularly on all questions:

> *Autogestion* does not mean . . . making all decisions at the base. It implies, first of all—and this is essential—respect for competencies. It is obvious, especially, given the complexity of management of modern enterprises, that the latter can only be entrusted to a group of technicians, extremely competent specialists, on the level of primary decisions for all small and medium sized problems of everyday management as well as for major choices.[65]

The important task, however, was to prevent this from becoming the basis of privilege and hierarchy. The essence of *autogestion* lay in placing "l'instance suprême de decision" in the hands of the personnel themselves (or their representatives) in matters of serious consequence. This would generally be a right of control "*post-gestion*," an approbation or disapproval that occurs after the technicians formulate a given policy. Some decisions are beyond the capacities of many workers.[66] Goldmann envisioned a *comité de directeurs*, which would be held accountable to a *conseil de gestion* representing the workers as a whole.

The workers in a self-managed enterprise would hold rights similar to those of shareholders (*les actionaires*) in liberal capitalism, with the important difference that they would participate in the day-to-day production process. Daily decisions on their part would primarily concern their own workshops—which would be generally within their competence—and not the factory as a whole. However, control of the enterprise would ultimately be in their hands because they would elect the *conseil de gestion*.[67] The very existence of the latter would ultimately render trade unions, as they exist under capitalism, functionless. Within a system of self-management and "democratic planning," unions would therefore have a pedagogical role as promoters and defenders "of the general interests of the working class."[68]

This role was important because, in Goldmann's view, *autogestion* faced an intrinsic danger of replacing "individual egoism" by the "local collective of egoism" of an enterprise. Such egoism potentially gives rise to frictions among neighboring enterprises or industries. One task of the unions is education to mitigate against such eventualities. For *autogestion* to succeed, it is imperative "to create an atmosphere, a collective consciousness, a psychological state" of workers so that they recognize long-term and not just short-range interests of both their enterprises and society as a whole. In the final analysis, "one of the fundamental aspects of *autogestion* must be precisely its transformative effect on men."[69]

Goldmann's film was to explore the Yugoslavian case but also raise broader questions concerning *autogestion*. The first part was to combine various images with a text to provide viewers with the following background information. Yugoslavia was an agrarian country in which agricultural laborers comprised the majority of the population, industry was largely artisanal and not yet highly developed, and the average income was $175 per annum. After the country was liberated from the Germans, a Soviet-style planned economy was initiated, but with increasing bureaucratization and Tito's rupture with the USSR, an attempt was made to create "an original democratic and antibureaucratic socialism" by means of *autogestion*. In the first stage, workers' councils and management committees elected by the factory employees were established to make decisions on crucial questions. The program subsequently was broadened to encompass a variety of economic sectors, and later the powers of the councils were expanded to additional important domains, including investment and work security. *Autogestion* was later extended into noneconomic realms, such as municipal management and public administration, hospitals, theaters, and schools.

As Goldmann presented it, in the Yugoslavian context, *autogestion* had at least three crucial tasks: (1) to promote industrialization of the country without the great hardships and disparities of wealth that had accompanied Western European industrialization; (2) to "create . . . democratic counterpoints to the inevitable development of strata of technicians, administrators and politicians situated at the nerve centers of economic, administrative, juridical and political power"; (3) to assure a high enough level of culture for the population and to "create the conditions for a true fusion between public and social life, work and what the Yugoslavs call life outside work, and which we call private life."[70]

The next part of the film was to examine the quotidian workings of *autogestion*, again emphasizing its differences from Western capitalism and bringing out inherent difficulties. Scenes were to show the election of a workers' council, and then the council debating how to divide revenues among the economic needs of the enterprise, the collective needs of the workers (for example, establishing a library or other public institution), and salaries. Goldmann wanted to film controversies between technicians and workers and among the workers themselves about such issues as how funds ought to be deployed. The *comité de gestion* would be shown debating investment priorities for the upcoming year and the problems of coordinating the needs of its enterprise with those of other factories pursuing their own interests. Viewers would also observe a meeting of the workers' council in which a dispute about priorities occurred between the council members and the elected director of the enterprise, who would then be shown being ousted. From the more general management level, the documentary would turn to a directly managed workshop. Here a discussion would be occurring about productivity and the hiring and firing of workers.

At this point, Goldmann planned segments presenting self-management beyond the workplace: the administrative council of a school (composed of representatives of teachers, parents, and students), a chamber of a municipal council discussing the establishment of a school, a meeting of a housing committee in a neighborhood. A scene in the Federal Parliament—the summit of "the pyramid of *autogestion*"—would show the adoption of "a general economic plan which constitutes the framework within which the autonomy of the economic units is situated." Next shown would be a class at the Workers's University of Zagreb (a course teaching subjects and skills needed by workers for *autogestion*, such as preparation of an annual account for an industrial enterprise) and a meeting of a union organization. In the third part of the film, two daily lives were to be explored: that of a member of the *comité de gestion* who had not yet obtained good housing and that of a technician who was a member of a municipal council and lived quite comfortably. The two men were to be examined carrying out their responsibilities and interacting both with their coworkers, who had given them their respective mandates, and with their families. The film was to close with three discussants considering the importance and difficulties of the experiment in *autogestion*.

The scenario makes clear that Goldmann, however utopian some of his assertions about the establishment of authentic community, had a sense of the problems, both large and small, of *autogestion*, particularly in Yugoslavia. Of course he could not foresee the complete collapse of not only *autogestion* but the entire Yugoslav state and society within two and a half decades. It is striking that there is no discussion at all of the role of the Communist Party in his discussions of Yugoslavia. This would have been understandable in discussing his hopes for establishing *autogestion* in the West through a syndicalist struggle of revolutionary reformism, but not when he was outlining a film concerned with self-management in an existing one-party state.

Be that as it may, considerable realism can be discerned as well in Goldmann's approach to student radicalism and the events of May 1968, in which *autogestion* was a prominent slogan. The upheaval was greeted by Goldmann with enthusiasm—especially the demands for *autogestion* made by students and then by workers. He felt that the emergence of the Prague Spring was a reason for great optimism, too. It seemed—at last—that in both East and West, one-dimensional societies were being unhinged. What could be more of a protest against technocracy than some ten million French students and workers disrupting an ossified and authoritarian university system, closing down factories in a general strike (in which a prominent role was played by the new middle strata), and battling the police and the regime, all when there was no immediate economic crisis? Qualitative demands by students and workers for control over their lives were the order of the day, and Goldmann felt that his refusal of Marcuse's earlier pessimism had been justified.

While Goldmann drew parallels between the events in France and Czechoslovakia—both were revolts against hierarchy—he wrote little of substance about the Prague Spring. At the time of the Soviet invasion of Czechoslovakia, Goldmann was in Korčula, Yugoslavia, at one of the regular meetings of Western Marxist intellectuals there (the "summer school" organized by the Yugoslav Marxist humanist journal *Praxis*, on whose editorial advisory board Goldmann served). He joined his colleagues in a unanimous denunciation of Moscow's actions. Early in 1969, Goldmann participated in the Stockholm Conference sponsored by the Bertrand Russell Foundation to protest the Soviet aggression. He had previously joined Western leftists in censuring repression in Communist countries. In late 1968, for example, at the initiative of *Praxis*'s Gajo Petrović and Rudi Supek, Goldmann joined André Gorz, Erich Fromm, Jürgen Habermas, and others castigating the dismissal of six professors, including Leszek Kolakowski, from Warsaw University. The statement denied that the victimized academics were "revisionists" and declared that limitations on philosophical and sociological thought were injurious to the socialist idea: "[The] editorial committee of *Praxis* regards humanistic democratic socialism as the unique progressive perspective for contemporary humanity [and believes that it] cannot be successfully developed without . . . exchanges of thought freely conducted and on an equal footing."[71] (*Praxis* itself was later suppressed by Belgrade).

Goldmann composed several essays on the French student movement (not all were published), publicly supported the student/worker rebellion, and signed petitions calling for the "democratic transformation of the French university."[72] While his writings on the student revolt were nuanced differently at different moments, he saw in it "the first manifestation of a historical turning point," in which the key demand was to transform current social relations in the direction of *autogestion*.[73] Goldmann had already suggested that there were parallel contradictions in the working world and in that of the students. In the first case, he hoped, the technicians would lead the way to qualitative demands for transformation because of the contradiction between their cultural and educational levels and the tasks they were supposed to do. In the rapidly expanding educational world of organized capitalism, the university, which formerly turned the obedient children of notables into autonomous beings, now had to take children of more liberal technicians and by means of a hierarchical teacher-student relation turn them into obedient dischargers of the future.

In "Étudiants et société," an unpublished article written evidently in early spring of 1968 (and to which a note was appended indicating that events had surpassed it), Goldmann doubted if the students would ultimately find ways to link their demands to a broader movement. Since the students were not engaged directly in—and universities were relatively marginal to—the basic productive processes, it was obvious to him that the students by themselves could not overturn society. The disjuncture between university and production was one reason why students who wanted to transform society as a whole issued (Marcuse-like) utopian demands. For Goldmann, the real question was how to formulate student demands on a basis that would promote broad-based transformation, rather than enunciating a "simple radical negation" that might become a "utopian abstraction without practical outlet." Lacking such a strategy, the student rebellion might degenerate into a type of Ludditism, becoming "an anarchic and transitory phenomenon, an episode or a precursor, depending on the later evolution of Western capitalism."[74] The crucial step had to be a linkage of the students to the workers through a common call for *autogestion*.

When Goldmann saw something like this happening in May 1968, he revised his position and became enthusiastic. Now he would proclaim, in another unpublished essay written in mid-June 1968, "With the May Days in France, it is a new world, a new historical epoch which knocks on the doors of History. For future historians, these days will mark the first external manifestation of an historical turning point like the French revolution, like the workers' demonstrations of June '48."[75] Marcuse's pessimism and the proclamations of the end of ideology were proven wrong; the "equilibrium" of the previous years had been shattered. Might a new transindividual subject be emerging?

If so, Goldmann was discerning by late July a hiatus between its actions and its consciousness. In a letter (to Frank Benseler, Lukács's German publisher), he wrote that the character of the movement was "extremely complex" and required "careful sociological analysis." Goldmann noted that much had been said about the "considerable gap" between "the real behavior of the students and workers and the conceptualization on the level of consciousness." Whereas in 1789 or 1917, extensive theoretical analyses had been elaborated by earlier thinkers, in 1968 the movement, by and large, elaborated as it went along. While the movement focused on how to adjust and humanize the workplace through such ideas as *autogestion*, it tended to neglect "everything concerning the state in the strict sense of the word." For instance, Goldmann noted that during the large demonstration of May 7, 1968, student marchers did not pause in front of parliamentary buildings. Those buildings seemed irrelevant to them. When de Gaulle turned the political situation into an electoral issue, "a movement which had 9–10 million participants and which had profoundly shaken French society was entirely unrepresented by any of the formations soliciting the votes of citizens" (except for the PSU, which made some effort, but with little success). Similarly, the major parties, from the Communists to the Right, were uncomprehending of the Events. Still, Goldmann emphasized that a series of basic concepts had "penetrated the collective consciousness in the course of events, notably *autogestion*, radical democracy" and especially an insistence on delimiting competencies and privileges attributed to individuals. Even if functional differentiations were necessary in a modern economy, hierarchical relations, the movement believed, could be replaced by those of camaraderie and cooperation.[76]

But the movement was not victorious. This led Goldmann to a process of reevaluation, which was cut short by his death in October 1970. He was clearly torn—again—between dialectical hope and a fear that his wager might have been lost. While his public optimism generally remained firm, this was not always the case in private. In 1969 he began questioning the basic terms of Marxist discourse and even wondered aloud if the very term "socialism" had lost its operative value.[77] At the same time, despite the restabilization of France and the reinstitution of Stalinism in Czechoslovakia, Goldmann spoke of 1968 as a year in which one had witnessed, if only for a brief moment, revolutionary transindividual actions of momentous proportions. Hegel, he remarked, watched Napoleon's army march into Jena and declared to a friend that he had seen the spirit of world history riding through town on horseback. Although Napoleon was finally defeated, and Restoration followed, half a century later it became clear that Hegel had indeed been right. Something new had been born and the ancien régime, though perhaps not fully vanquished, had suffered a mortal blow. Sounding rather like the Lukács of 1923, Goldmann declared that in 1968 "we have seen the spirit of the world in the streets of European cities."[78]

Between 1968 and 1970, Goldmann became increasingly reflective and concluded that while his pre-1968 socioeconomic and political analyses were sound, they were also too unilateral. For one thing, though the proletariat had not fit Marx's description of it, May 1968 demonstrated that it still had a powerful role to play.[79] It remained a critical factor intervening in and promoting social change, even if not as a "universalizing" historical agent. Thus Goldmann still projected a "contesting" role for the new working class.[80] At the time of his death, he still wagered that technocracy would be challenged by a counter-politics and a counterculture—a challenge resting on combining the forces of the new working class, disenchanted intellectuals, and the "disinherited" (for examples, immigrants, American blacks).

IV

Goldmann protested that his was a worldview of dialectical hope, that it was as a dialectician that he analyzed tragedy. Yet by comparing his own wager to Pascal's and by accepting the possibility of failure, Goldmann acknowledged that, potentially, he was a tragic dialectician. Pascal the tragedian opened a path to the dialectic and therefore hope, according to Goldmann's theory; Goldmann the dialectician, by accepting the possibility of a historical dialectic unfulfilled, opened the possibility of a tragic Marxism. This brings him in fact to an existential dialectic, that is, to one that never attains ultimate synthesis. Here, we can see how the homology between Goldmann's method and politics was structured by his departures from Lukács—especially from the young Lukács, whom he described in 1968 as guilty of "leftist revolutionary illusions, the belief that the ideal world was for tomorrow."[81]

In the end, Goldmann not only rejected Lukács's theory of the revolutionary proletariat, but also his formulations of totality, subject-object identity, and the relation between empirical and possible consciousness. Goldmann's thought, like Lukács's, remains a whole. While it does not attain Lukács's heights in *History and Class Consciousness*, it saves Lukács from Lukács, but only by revealing the problems of Lukács's work—and, one might say, by making Lukács something other than Lukács.

Totality, for Goldmann, meant the use of significative structure in method and the aspiration to authentic community in politics. Lukács spoke of totality as the all-pervasiveness of the whole over the parts, while Goldmann spoke instead of an oscillation between the whole and the parts. Lukács spoke of the ideological and the economic "merging" and of the "subordination" of the parts to the whole, while Goldmann defined science as "precisely the effort to distinguish and not to confuse the parts and the whole."[82] The difference between the two positions has crucial political consequences, for one is all-embracing, easily engendering a radically centralist politics, while the other does the opposite. In 1957 Goldmann and Maximilien Rubel disputed the interpretation of Marx in the pages of *Les Temps modernes*. Rubel scornfully pointed to those passages of *History and Class Consciousness* in which party discipline is described as complete subordination of the individual's personality and declared, *"Voilà:* here is the famous dynamic totality."[83] While Rubel was arguing against a defense of Lukács by Goldmann, his criticisms of "Lukács and his Party of the Totality" are implicit in Goldmann's own attenuations—transformations—of Lukács. These culminated in Goldmann's championing not of Leninism, much less Stalinism, but of the decentralized vision of *autogestion*.

Goldmann contended that the more *autogestion* developed, and the wider it spread, the more decentralized and self-determining a society would be, and the more socialist and free it would become. However, "the more *autogestion* is extended, the more it constitutes in certain respects—although possessing a socialist character—a return to a liberal economy."[84] Yet it was precisely the classical liberal (bourgeois) economic order that shattered all possibility of totality and "transindividual values." We thus arrive at another Goldmannian paradox. As a Lukácsian, he insisted that the consequences of the liberal market economy—reification, abstract individualism, disappearance of the "We," and notions of totality/community—were the greatest of evils, incarnations of dehumanization. But as a Goldmannian, he perceived that some form of liberal economy was required to guarantee the socialist community he espoused—a socialism that did not negate the positive features engendered by the rise of market economies. Indeed, in "La Réification," Goldmann went so far as to suggest that the erosion of reification brought dangerous ramifications.[85] It was a matter of no and yes: The market creates reification and a vision of the world radically at odds with the idea of authentic community, but it is at the same time a prerequisite of a truly free community, and not only because capitalism creates technological, economic, and industrial development as Marx argued. The essential question became

> to what extent the suppression of private property in the means of production, tied to far-reaching decentralization, to a forceful reduction (but not suppression) of central planning, and finally to the maintenance of the market and consequently of an economic sector of social life, can permit the creation of a socialist society which will suppress the negative elements of reification and extreme quantification, while simultaneously safeguarding and reinforcing traditional values linked to the market, notably individual liberty, equality and tolerance?[86]

In the final analysis, is not Goldmann's advocacy of market socialism the recognition that socialist community, conceived as *autogestion*, is something less than "totality"? that subjective and objective authenticity, like subject and object, cannot be one and the same? If reification is a necessary result of a market economy, if central planning threatens the humanist values born of the market, and if *autogestion* implies a return to some of the characteristics of the liberal phase of capitalism, then some form of reification must survive in Goldmann's socialist community. It would be "inauthentic" in some regard, for the quantitative would still intrude—perhaps in new, different, and more limited ways—on the qualitative. If we accept Goldmann's claim that the disappearance of the market has dire consequences for human freedom, but that such freedom is merely formal without the context of socialist community, then just as Pascal insisted on standing not in the middle, but at both extremes at once, so Goldmann was saying yes and no at the same time. Here, as in the relation between subject and object, partiality, not totality, has become reality. But it was the inability to grasp totality, or the aspiration to an unattainable totality, that Goldmann himself defined as characteristic of tragedy. He, despite himself, stood at this threshold.

Totality, for Lukács, was predicated on total subject-object identity; for Goldmann, only partial identity is attainable. Yet what sense can we make of what is now the necessary consequence of Goldmann's position—partial totality? It can make methodological sense inasmuch as totality becomes solely a heuristic and regulative concept and knowledge is conceived, as Goldmann indeed conceived it, as a dialectic between the whole and the parts, assuming that a definitive conclusion or picture is never formed. Again, it would seem that in this case, Sartre's term, "totalization," is preferable, particularly since partial identity in its political application suggests that neither the proletariat nor anyone else can attain complete self-knowledge or knowledge of historical, socioeconomic totality. Modification of political goals is inescapable. Totality—as opposed to actual totalizations—becomes a political ideal and will not be actualized by the victory of socialism as Goldmann conceived it. Lukács's totalizing and indeed apocalyptic conception—the union of knowledge and reality in the proletariat and the transcendence of all oppositions in life—must therefore be abandoned. Goldmann did so.

Goldmann's shift from Lukács might be summarized as follows. A form of *hiatus irrationalis* between concept and reality was unavoidable. Once it is granted that empirical consciousness will not merge totally with the ideal-type of imputed consciousness, once it is recognized that real consciousness results from the obstacles empirical life places before "possible consciousness" and that the result is transindividual mental structures that are structurating and destructurating in various ways and to various degrees, then one must recognize that the tendency toward an imputed consciousness by the transindividual structures of a class or group (the proletariat, for example) may be vitiated or precluded by the empirical individuals in the class or group.

Does totality become a hidden God? Goldmann, we know, embraces the notion, rejected with chagrin by most Marxists, that Marxism did, indeed, resemble a religion. Echoing Feuerbach, he presented Marxism as a godless religion of man. A messianism with a transcendent supernatural being as its focus, he once commented, is more primitive than a messianism without it, just as magic preceded theism, which in turn preceded atheism.[87] It was Christian culture and its concept of transcendence, he argued elsewhere, that provided the intellectual universe permitting the creation of socialist thought.[88] In *The Hidden God* he goes very far in comparing his own faith to Augustinianism. This was almost natural considering the Augustinianism of Pascal and the Jansenists and Goldmann's claim that Pascal was the first dialectician. But this is misconceived, and the misconception illuminates the problem of totality in Goldmann's thought in a striking way. Goldmann's argument rested on viewing the roles of God and history as correlates, respectively, in Augustinianism and Marxism.[89] The Augustinian view of the world—and Pascal's—is based on the doctrine of original sin and the belief that grace is the unmerited gift of God. There is nothing an individual, let alone a group of individuals, can do to expiate guilt and attain salvation, for no act has efficacy in attaining grace. Humanity is damned; no one knows in this life if he or she is redeemed and admitted to the City of God, which is never of this world. In Goldmann's Marxism, humanity is saved by collective action in history; in Augustinianism, we stand condemned, with no remedy possible by our own hand, and hope is a function of something entirely beyond humanity. A wager based on Augustinianism must be rigorously antihumanist, and beyond historical action. It has no guarantee, just as Goldmann's has none, but Goldmann's is based on historical possibilities created by those living in history of bringing the City of God to earth.

"In the beginning was the deed," said Goethe's Faust. For Goldmann, Pascal's tragedy lies ultimately in an ahistorical vision, while the Marxist humanist wager is historical, dialectical, and immanent. Yet it is not only a matter of historical action: to transcend tragedy, Pascal would have had to become Hegel, who, despite his protestations that he was an orthodox Lutheran, was no Augustinian. An argument for the secular religiosity of Marxism would have been better served had Goldmann compared it with those Jewish and Christian millenarian traditions that rested not only on faith but also on belief in a messianic future hurried directly by human action. One can find perhaps the best modern example of this in an anti-Christian argument made by Marx's contemporary, Moses Hess. The young Hess, as a "Spinozist," rejected the Christian dualism between the City of God and City of Man in order to argue that the messianic impulse entailed human action to make *this* world holy, as opposed to seeking a salvation not of this world. "In the beginning was the deed": similarly, Goldmann wagered that human actions would realize human words in a human totality; in this consisted the radicality of the human rupture with Augustinian Christianity. But "totality," Goldmann told us, is undefinable; any human science is based ultimately on concepts undefinable in a definitive way because they are always in genesis. His totality thus seems at once to be like Hegel's *Geist* and like the God of the Jews, whose positive features they were neither able nor permitted to describe.

Yet it is Kant's God—so different from Hegel's—that is crucial in comparison, and this brings us back to Havet's criticism of Goldmann at the Kierkegaard symposium. Having remarked that Goldmann wavered between speaking of totality as a given reality and, because of the processes of structuration and destructuration, speaking of it as a double movement of totalization and detotalization, Havet asserted that totality thereby became not given, but a regulative idea—"a rather Kantian term." However, "totality" could therefore only direct understanding and never be coherently present; there must be "an element of non-totality" introduced into totality.[90] This, in brief, encapsulates the problems of Goldmann's politics and method—his aspiration to totality.

As Kant asserted that God's existence, though unprovable, was a necessary practical postulate and regulative idea of reason, and as Pascal wagered on his hidden God, Goldmann wagers on totality. But totality, it seems, was more than he had counted on. He finds in the end—though he never openly admits—that it is unattainable. He seems to have reinvented, also without admitting it, the *hiatus irrationalis*. In this sense, the objective meaning of Goldmann's oeuvre and intellectual journey transcended his various presentations of his own ideas. There are hints that he knew this. The second chapter of *Philosophie et politique* was to be on the "relations and more precisely the inevitable conflicts between the philosopher and the politician." He had pointed to such inevitable conflict decades earlier in the letter to Duclos that we mentioned in chapter 2. He wrote to her that philosophy "knows man as such," whereas "party politics must resolve the tasks of the day." Philosophy's concern was the future, but party activities—politics—centers on the present. "Can we make a *philosophy* of the present," he asked, "and would it be Marxist?" He could provide no definitive answer when he posed this question at the end of World War II, and he still could not by the time of his death, after the hidden God had become the hidden Class.[91]

9

Between Yes and No

GOLDMANN PROPOSED in 1957 that meaningful Marxist theoretical work had been accomplished in recent decades solely by *franc-tireurs* (partisans, snipers), who were inevitably branded heretics.[1] Clearly, the remark was self-referential: Goldmann was a Marxist heretic who insisted on his faith while discarding belief in one of its central tenets, the world historical role of the proletariat. In the early 1960s, notably at a colloquium on "Heresy and Society in Pre-Industrial Europe," Goldmann, seconding another scholar's comment, pointed to two characteristic features of heresy: "choosing [to] distance [oneself] from the religious community and the fact of belonging to it."[2] He immediately added that heresy is usually a reaction to the development of new social and economic—he should have added political—circumstances.

There is perhaps another, secularized way of making this last point: method and theory must be functional to their objects, not vice versa. In a sense, Goldmann was more of a dialectician than the author of *History and Class Consciousness*. If method, as Goldmann contended, is "not an end in itself" and if making method autonomous is "positivism in the worst sense," then Lukács's definition of orthodox Marxism as exclusively (*ausschliesslich*) a matter of method is itself a species of positivism, even though his intent was to counter dogmatic forms of Marxism.[3] It is noteworthy that in his later literary studies, after he had publicly renounced *History and Class Consciousness*, Lukács's methods and aesthetic criteria did not fundamentally alter according to his object of study, whether it was German classicism or literary modernism. This is perhaps one reason why he could not appreciate modernism— why the older Lukács would, for instance, write compellingly on Goethe and obtusely on Kafka.

Goldmann made method a function of his object, emphasizing worldviews when investigating seventeenth-century French classicism and homologies when exploring twentieth-century literature. Importantly, Goldmann's politics, in contrast to Lukács's, were a function of what he perceived to be the changing nature of capitalism. When reality proved that the proletariat was not to be the identical subject-object of history, Lukács did not distance himself from his "religious community." Instead, he insisted all the more fiercely on his membership in it, renouncing his own "heresies." Fidelity to the "means"—the party—

was paramount. But Goldmann, the faithful heretic, insisted on the possibilities of an egalitarian humanism and identified himself as belonging to "Marxism," all while distancing himself from its fundamentalist variants and embracing a non-Leninist, decentralized notion of market socialism.

Goldmann may be situated between the antitheses of Lukács and Adorno. If for Lukács, in 1923, the perspective, indeed, the reality, of totality was to be attained by history's identical subject-object, thereby making Hegel's "whole" and "true" one, Adorno, echoing Lask and the neo-Kantians, argued for "non-identity thinking." His "negative dialectics" rested not on the proletariat but on a critique of the "despotic" deployment of concepts as tools of knowledge. If one assumes identity of thought and reality, then concepts, as generalizations, erase the specificity of what we try to know.[4] While philosophy cannot avoid operating with concepts, he cautioned against turning this "into the virtue of their priority." Instead, he sought a philosophy "that extinguishes the autarky of the concept" and recognizes that it is "entwined with a non-conceptual whole."[5]

The thesis of nonidentity warns against a conceptual whole; this is what prompted him to claim that "the whole is the false."[6] For Adorno, as for Lukács and Goldmann, totality was a question of both method and aspiration, and consequently, if there is a *hiatus irrationalis* (Adorno does not use the term) between concept and reality, if theory and praxis had not become one, that is why theory—philosophy— lived on: "the attempt to change the world misfired."[7]

Since the revolution had imploded, Adorno sought incarnation of philosophical truth in art. *Wahrheitsgehalt* (truth content) was the Other of—and presented an alternative to—the reified existing social reality. It is, in this sense, utopian and redemptive, for it is not a means to something else. "Whereas in the real world all particulars are fungible," he wrote in his unfinished, posthumously published *Aesthetic Theory* (1969), "art protests against fungibility by holding up images of what reality itself might be like, if it were emancipated from the patterns of identification imposed on it."[8] However, as Richard Wolin notes, since Adorno, first and foremost, conceived art works as "vehicles of philosophical truth, in his approach the entire pragmatic side of works of art—their role in shaping, informing, and transforming the lives of historically existing individuals—falls by the wayside."[9] Indeed, by the end of his career, he had little to say about political possibilities available to such existing individuals, and, in contrast to Goldmann's embrace (albeit critical) of the student Left in France, Adorno found himself angrily at odds with its German counterparts.

Lukács, already in 1962, had targeted the political implications of

Adorno's position. Adorno had taken up "residence in the 'Grand Hotel Abyss,'" which was "equipped with every comfort" but sat "on the edge of an abyss, of nothingness, of absurdity. And the daily contemplation of the abyss, between excellent meals or artistic entertainments, can only heighten the enjoyment of the subtle comforts offered."[10] The question Lukács dared not pose was, Were the only options the Grand Hotel Abyss and the abysmal Leninist lodgings in which he had ensconced himself? Or, to put it another way, were the only options acceptance of a *hiatus irrationalis* between concept and reality and seeking to fill it with the party?

Goldmann's answer, for all his admiration of both Adorno and Lukács, was no, as can be seen in his exchange with Adorno at the Third International Colloquium on the Sociology of Literature at Royaument in January 1968. The two began in agreement that dialectical method cannot be separated from its object. "Description" and "understanding" (*Verstehen*) of a literary object, Adorno argued, could not be separated either, for to describe adequately this object, one must understand it. In his draft introduction to *Aesthetic Theory*, Adorno (in a section that partly reproduced his discussion with Goldmann), defined *Verstehen* as

> the ability to become aware of the spiritual content of the work by experiencing its many sides. This refers to the work's subject matter, appearance and intention as much as to its truth or falsehood. . . . Works of art are not properly understood until aesthetic experience confronts the alternatives between true and false. . . . Comprehending a work of art as a complex of truth entails recognition that it is also untrue: no art work escapes complicity with untruth, the untruth of the world outside.

It is because truth "is an essential quality of works of art" that they are capable of aesthetic cognition, something quite different from scientific cognition of natural objects. The artwork, Adorno says, "is always simultaneously itself and something other than itself"; thus "aesthetic truth-content" is "the transcendent dimension of illusion in which illusion transcends itself."[11]

Understanding, Adorno maintained at Royaument, must entail "the moment of critique." Using Ibsen's play *The Wild Duck* as an example, he submitted that there are several levels of understanding. One level is factual (grasping what happens in the play), and another apprehends what is "signified," that is, why the author has characters say or do something. Finally, there is the level of "the idea" of the play—in the case of *The Wild Duck*, "the idea of culpability as a product of subjective rectitude."[12] Together, these levels ought to reveal not merely the author's subjective purposes, but the truth content of the work, and it is this that "decides" its "aesthetic quality." Through "the intermediary of truth-content," philosophy and art "converge"; it is the work's truth content that "communicates" with philosophy without becoming an abstraction "beyond" the artwork. Still, by "its participation in truth-content," art becomes "more than it is" and knowledge of art makes explicit what has "crystallized" in the work.[13]

One does not—cannot—approach the artwork as if one were a tabula rasa, "forgetting everything" like a fool. Rather one must "mobilize whatever transcending knowledge" one possesses and "make it disappear into the experience of the very thing during immanent analysis." Paradoxically, "to understand something purely in itself, in an immanent manner" one must always know something in advance, one must know "more than what comes of the thing itself." For example, one deploys such categories as "myth" or "exchange society" in analyzing a play even though these do not appear "in categorial form" in the work itself. (Adorno insists that truth content arises "through the structure of the art-work and not conceptually." How this bears on the use of categorial forms is unclear, at least to me.)[14] Truth content is always "that which transcends the work." To grasp truth content one must, therefore, always "transgress" the work's pure immanence, just as knowledge that is "pre-immanent" is brought to the immanent work "in order to master it." Consequently, Adorno insists on the dual character of the artwork—it is at once something social and something autonomous and opposed to social reality. This implies that aesthetic criteria alone cannot enable one to judge the work's quality. Truth content establishes the moment in which "art in its truth is more than art," and a method of literary criticism "worthy of man" would render "this dialectic visible, concretizing it in particular aesthetic experience."[15]

One can readily see that Adorno's theory is radically at odds with the realist, systematic aesthetics of the later Lukács. In response, Goldmann, who the day before had defended Adorno in debate with Lukács's student Agnès Heller, now emphasized his own debt to the early Lukács against Adorno. What differentiated his approach from Adorno's, he proposed, was first of all his notion of "transcendence" of a text, and second, whether systematizing is required for philosophical understanding. For Adorno, transcendence means deploying something nonaesthetic, which is "situated on the general level of critique," to evaluate art—that is, truth content, which is dependent on "philosophical culture and critical knowledge." But Goldmann insisted that while art and philosophy are closely linked, there is a vital difference between them. A work of art "is not philosophical. The work of art is a universe of colors, sound, words, concrete characters. There is no death; there is Phèdre dying; there is color on the canvas." When critics address the work, they use concepts, but these translate something nonphilosophical—something that composes "a total universe"—into a philosophical system. The latter does not "transcend" the artwork, but is its systematic "corollary." But Adorno, on behalf of nonidentity thinking, resists systems.

Without fully articulating it, Goldmann apparently teased out a contradiction within Adorno's argument. He implies that contrary to the nonidentity thinking he espoused, Adorno reduces—or comes close to reducing—artistic judgement to something other than itself, imposing philosophical culture on the nonconceptual (the "total universe" of the artwork). Philosophical culture, the author of *Aesthetic Theory* admitted, requires concepts and thus systematizing. Adorno, Goldmann seems to be saying, wants to have his artistic cake nonconceptually, but eat it philosophically if the judgment of aesthetic taste depends on philosophical critique. Echoing Piaget's distinction between accommodation and assimilation in the adaptive process, and using a somewhat strained formulation (using ill-conceived terminology in my view), Goldmann declares this to be a question of the relation between "criticism" and "dogmatism" in approaching culture. Adorno's focus is exclusively on the moment of "criticism", whereas the older Lukács is trapped in dogma, seeking to systematize at all costs however much reality contradicts his system. Nonetheless, Goldmann abjures criticism, which "eliminates the system," for without systematizing, without systematic projection of totalities—here, Goldmann strikes a Kantian motif—the mind would be unable to orient itself in the world. Dogmatism is an "affirmation within each work . . . of a human ideal—not only the *no* but also the *yes*—of the potentials of unity in human life."[16] The task is to avoid reductionist systematizing, which "simplifies and eliminates antagonism," as well as Adorno's "excess of critical spirit." Thus Goldmann remains ever the dialectician, conceiving dogma and criticism to be at once parallel and necessary to each other. Goldmann, proponent of the thesis of partial identity in contradistinction to Adorno's nonidentity theory, therefore affirms that to which Adorno is averse, a principle of "global understanding." Adorno's demarcation of different levels of understanding is valuable, he agrees, but only so long as it is recognized that each level is partial and that it is only the work's meaning as a whole that allows integrating these levels. This, however, means that the work cannot be judged solely by truth content: Adorno is guilty of "intellectualism." Philosophy and art may express the same worldviews, but one does so on a conceptual level, and the other on a nondiscursive level. "Art is art," Goldmann maintained; "literature is literature and no more than that. It only corresponds to philosophy on the level of world-view."[17] One must always ask, "[T]ruth content in relation to what?" To determine the truth content of a work, "I know of no criterion other than taking the text and discovering a structure, a model" in it that allows elucidation of its internal coherence. However, understanding and explanation must be linked, and explanation, in Goldmann's sense, is not a matter of philosophical transcendence. Rather, it is transcendence of the work on the level of structure, particularly social structure. "Explanation establishes a very precise type of relation, one of understanding, that is functional [*L'explication, c'est une mise en relation d'un type trés précis, compréhensif c'est-à-dire fonctionnel*]." That is why Goldmann explained Racine by Jansenism, while understanding Jansenism as a structure. One studies an artwork as a totality "equivalent to and situated on the same level as a philosophical work" by establishing it as "a function of human aspirations within a given global structure."[18] In the abstract, Goldmann admits, one might, having obtained a certain level of philosophical culture, grasp 90 percent of a text "immanently," as Adorno would like. However, in practice, this is virtually impossible. "I am not a positivist," Goldmann averred, "but I am very positive: the thesis I want to establish is that in research to obtain understanding on a positive level of 90% of the text, there must be control step by step." Again, he stresses that understanding and explanation must be dialectically entwined.[19] Adorno's philosophical translations of artworks are remarkable, said Goldmann, but he inevitably situates the work in relation to his own philosophy and a contemporary critical perspective, not in relation to the dogmatic—systematic—confirmation by and embodiment in the work of the spirit of its own times. This subordinates art to "truth," and makes a work's value dependent finally "on its critical function, its *Wahrheitsgehalt*." Goldmann, however, upheld a Kantian definition of validity, "historicized by Lukács in the Hegelian and Marxist sense." The criterion of a "valid" artwork was nonconceptual surmounting of the "tension between an extreme richness and an extreme unity, a very rich universe and a rigorous structuration."[20] "Transcendence" is not solely a matter of critique; it takes form in a worldview embodying a coherent projection of socially and historically placed human possibilities, expressed conceptually in philosophy and nonconceptually in art and literature. The tragic worldview of the noblesse de robe, via Jansenism, took philosophical form in Pascal's *Pensées* and artistic form in Racine's theater. The former gives us the concept of death; the latter, Phèdre dying.

In his distinction between criticism and dogmatism, Goldmann had also reinvented the dialectic of yes and no that he had explicated in his analyses of Arnauld, Barcos, and Pascal. "Pensée 353," we know, had particular power for him as a refusal of middle grounds and extremes at the same time: "One does not show one's greatness by being at one extreme, but by touching them both at the same time and filling up all the space in between."[21] If one takes Lukács and Adorno as the extremes, Goldmann sought to do just this. Half a year before his debate with Adorno, Goldmann formulated his opposition between dogmatism and criticism, and then situated himself as follows: "The dialectical spirit is above all the attempt to maintain the two opposed extremities of the chain while remaining always on guard against the deformations which can go either in one direction [un sens] or the other."[22]

Is it possible to maintain the two extremities, to touch them both at once, indeed, to full the space between them? To synthesize Life and life, as young Lukács would have had it? Or is this an ambition for the identity of the City of God and the City of Man (to use an Augustinian formulation for a possibility Augustine would have denied)? Goldmann's own claim of partial identity, taken to its logical conclusion argues against this prospect. The necessary corollary, moreover, is acceptance, at least partially, of the profane—an acceptance that demands secular thinking and acceptance of the tragic possibility along with any insistence on dialectical hope. As in the case of Kant's urge toward an unattainable totality, Goldmann was impelled to surpass partial identity, while finally recognizing (though sometimes only implicitly) that it was not possible.

Yet if Goldmann had been led, by genetic epistemology and the theory that the bases of knowledge, mental structures, were structurating and destructurating totalities, to reject Lukács's notion of the identical subject-object of history, Piaget's concepts also precluded a principle of nonidentity. Goldmann would have likewise rejected what has become known as postmodernism as one-sided, on the grounds that this style of thought dissolves any notion of totality; and postmodernists would have to reject Goldmann's dialectical demand for both a critical posture and global understanding.

If Goldmann conceived the rise of structuralism, with its emphasis on static categories, to be partly a function of the consolidation of organized capitalism and, more specifically, the stabilization of French society under the Fifth Republic, he would, in all probability, have perceived the rise of postmodernism among left-wing (and formerly left-wing) intellectuals in the 1970s as a function of the failure of May 1968's emancipatory and global, if rarely coherent, aspirations.

Perhaps Foucault's trajectory, his politics, and his appeal best symbolize this transition. Save for a short period in the Communist Party in his early years, Foucault only became engaged directly in radical politics after 1968. In the mid-1960s, when he was writing *The Order of Things*, which had a stronger structuralist motif than any of his other works and was initially perceived as right-wing by many critics, he apparently had no misgivings about energetically participating on a government commission under the auspices of a Gaullist minister of education.[23] In the 1970s, he became the champion of radical micropolitics, lashing out at power, which he perceived to be enmeshed everywhere, yet not globally structured in society. Postmodernism, one could say, is enmeshed in fragmentation, and Goldmann, as he sought to show in analyzing the fragments of Pascal's *Pensées*, perceived fragmentation itself as a way—a human way—of orienting oneself in the world; fragmentation was itself a structure that is incomprehensible without reflective systematizing and the effort to elucidate both critical and dogmatic dimensions.

Goldmann's insistent humanism would have placed him no less at odds with the theoretical antihumanism that, pursuant to structuralism, pervaded postmodernism. Theoretical antihumanism was, more often than not, entwined with a contempt for liberal values, and Goldmann, though not a liberal, always upheld the importance of liberal principles for radical values. When left-wing (or formerly left-wing) antihumanists negated liberalism, it was to break with it and to place themselves in opposition to it. The contrast between Goldmann and Foucault could not be sharper in this regard. The problem with French education, Foucault complained, while serving on the Gaullist education commission, was that "the most insipid psychology, the most antiquated humanism" reigned in the existing system—the same "humanism" that was his enemy as a radical activist and theorist in the 1970s.[24] When the humanist Goldmann "transcended" liberalism, he did so in the specifically Hegelian sense of negating and preserving at once, absorbing what was vital in it into socialism, while annulling its abstractions.

After all, he conceived socialist humanism as the culmination and not the annulment of Western culture, though, for him, the specter of tragedy haunted Marxist hopes. Where postmodernists say no and scorn dialectical thinking as a humanist throwback, Lucien Goldmann insisted on yes and no. A wager of transcendence, the authority of tragedy, his work was animated by dialectical movement:

> I am like a train
> rushing for many years now
> between the city of Yes
> and the city of No.
> My nerves are strained
> between the city of No
> and the city of Yes . . .
>
> (*Yevgeny Yevtushenko*)[25]

Abbreviations Used in the Notes _____

THE FOLLOWING abbreviations are used in the notes. Full bibliograpical information is to be found in the Select Bibliography following the notes.

Works by Lucien Goldmann

Cc   *La Création culturelle dans la société moderne*
Dc   *Le Dieu caché*
Epp   *Epistémologie et philosophie politique*
HG   *The Hidden God* (English translation of *Le Dieu caché*)
Ipk   *Introduction à la philosophie de Kant*
Kant   English tanslation of *Ipk*
"LH"   "Lukács et Heidegger" (the appendix, subsequently dropped, to the 1945 edition of *Ipk*)
LH   *Lukács et Heidegger* (the unfinished book Goldmann was writing when he died in 1970)
Mensch   *Mensch, Gemeinschaft und Welt in der Philosophie Immanuel Kants* (original German edition of *Ipk*)
Msh   *Marxisme et sciences humaines*
Rd   *Recherches dialectiques*
Shp   *Sciences humaines et philosophie*
Sm   *Structures mentales et création culturelle*
Sr   *Pour une sociologie du roman*

Works by Georg Lukács

GK   *Geschichte und Klassenbewusstsein* (original German version of *History and Class Consciousness*)
HCC   *History and Class Consciousness*
SF   *Soul and Forms*
TN   *Theory of the Novel*

Other Publications

Kv   *Kierkegaard vivant* (proceedings of UNESCO symposium)
Sg   *Le Structuralisme génétique* (edited by Annie Goldmann, Sami Naïr, and Michel Löwy)

Archives

EHESS   École des Hautes Études en Sciences Sociales, Goldmann's papers in the Sociology of Literature section
AGA   Annie Goldmann Archives (private collection)

Notes

Introduction

1. Lucien Goldmann, "Eppur si muove," in *Power and Humanism* (Nottingham: Spokesman Books, 1974), p. 40.

2. Herbert Marcuse, "Some General Comments on Lucien Goldmann," in *Lucien Goldmann et la sociologie de la littérature: Hommage à Lucien Goldmann* (Brussels: Editions de l'Université de Bruxelles, 1974), pp. 51–52.

3. Alasdair MacIntyre, "Pascal and Marx: On Lucien Goldmann's Hidden God," in *Against the Self-Images of the Age* (New York: Schocken Books, 1971), p. 79; Jean Piaget, "Bref Témoignage," in *Lucien Goldmann et la sociologie de la littérature*, pp. 53–54.

4. Lucien Goldmann, *Dc*, p. 337.

5. I would note as well that despite his interdiction, he made considerable use of the lives of Pascal and Racine.

6. Allen Bloom, *The Closing of the American Mind* (New York: Simon and Schuster, 1987), p. 352.

7. Irving Howe, *Politics and the Novel* (New York: Columbia University Press, 1992), p. 212.

8. Marcuse, "Some General Comments," p. 52.

9. Edward Said, "Travelling Theory," in *The World, the Text, and the Critic* (Cambridge, Mass.: Harvard University Press, 1983), pp. 234–35.

10. *SF*, p. 153.

11. Interview with Annie Goldmann, Paris, June 25, 1980.

12. J. Piatier, "Thèses en Sorbonne: Pascal, Racine et le Dieu caché de l'univers tragique," *Le Monde*, February 22, 1956; id., "De Saint Augustin à Karl Marx," *L'Express*, February 21, 1956.

13. See André Blanchet, "Pascal est-il le precurseur de Karl Marx?" *Études*, March 1, 1957; Samï Nair and Michel Löwy, *Lucien Goldmann ou la dialectique de la totalité* (Paris: Editions Seghers, 1973), p. 14.

14. Leszek Kolakowski, *Main Currents of Marxism*, Vol. 3 (Oxford and New York: Oxford University Press, 1978), p. 325; Julia Kristeva, *The Samurai* (New York: Columbia University Press, 1992), p. 10.

15. Witold Gombrowicz, *Diary*, Vol. 3 (Evanston, Ill.: Northwestern University Press, 1993), p. 153.

16. Interview with Henri Lefebvre, Paris, June 19, 1980.

Chapter 1

1. Lucien Goldmann, "Sur la peinture de Chagall," in *Sm*, pp. 418–19.

2. Lucien Goldmann, Discussion following his presentation of "Sur la peinture de Chagall," in Maurice de Gandillac, Lucien Goldmann, and Jean Piaget, eds., *Entretiens sur les notions de génése et de structure* (Paris and the Hague:

Mouton and Co., 1965), pp. 169–70. It should be noted, however, that if relatively few Jews became artists, among those who did were many leading figures in modern art.

3. Isaac Deutscher, "The Non-Jewish Jew," in id., *The Non-Jewish Jew and other Essays* (London: Oxford University Press, 1968), p. 27.

4. Quoted in Robert R. King, *History of the Romanian Communist Party* (Stanford: Hoover Institution Press, 1980), pp. 23–24.

5. Michael Shafir, "'Romania's Marx' and the National Question: Constantin Dobrogeanu-Gherea," *History of Political Thought*, Summer 1984, pp. 303–4.

6. Leon Trotsky, "Amid Difficulties," originally in *Kievskaya Mysl*, no. 218, August 9, 1913, trans. in id., *The Balkan Wars: Wartime Correspondence, 1912–13* (New York: Monad Press, 1980), p. 376.

7. Hugh Seton-Watson, *Eastern Europe between the Wars, 1918–1945* (New York: Harper Torchbooks, 1967), p. 75; King, pp. 10–11, 20.

8. Nicholas M. Nagy-Talvera, *The Green Shirts and the Others* (Stanford: Hoover Institution Press, 1970), p. 47.

9. Irina Livezeanu, "Fascists and Conservatives in Romania: Two Generations of Nationalists," in Martin Blinkhorn, ed., *Fascists and Conservatives: The Radical Right and the Establishment in Twentieth-Century Europe* (London: Unwin Hyman, 1990), p. 220.

10. Leon Trotsky, "Dobrogeanu-Gherea," *Kievskaya Mysl*, nos. 236, 238, August 27, August 29, 1913, trans. in id., *The Balkan Wars*, p. 408.

11. For examples of Rakovsky's denunciation of government anti-Semitism, see the passages quoted in S. Bernstein, *Les Persécutions des Juifs en Roumanie* (Copenhagen: Edition du Bureau de l'Organisation Sioniste à Copenhague, 1918), pp. 63–65.

12. See Michael Kitch, "Constantin Dobrogeanu-Gherea and Rumanian Marxism," *Slavonic and East European Review*, January 1977, pp. 74, 86.

13. Ghita Ionescu, *Communism in Rumania* (London: Oxford University Press, 1964), pp. 7, 12–13, 21.

14. King, pp. 18–20.

15. Ibid., pp. 33–35; Ionescu, p. 18.

16. Lucien Goldmann, unpublished, untitled autobiographical fragment, in AGA. Goldmann wrote the fragment in Tunis shortly before his marriage there to his second wife, Annie, a Tunisian Jew.

17. Eliyahu Feldman, "Botoşani," *Encyclopedia Judaica*, Vol. 4 (Jerusalem: Keter Publishing Ltd., 1971), p. 1271; Salo Baron, *The Jews of Rumania: Report to the American Jewish Congress* (New York: American Jewish Congress, 1930), p. 6.

18. Christian Rakovsky, "An Autobiography," in id., *Selected Writings on Opposition in the USSR, 1923–30* (London and New York: Allison and Busby, 1980), p. 71.

19. Philip Gabriel Eidelberg, *The Great Rumanian Peasant Revolt of 1907: Origins of a Modern Jacquerie* (Leiden: E. J. Brill, 1974), pp. 1, 207–8.

20. See Leon Trotsky, "The Jewish Question," *Kievskaya Mysl*, nos. 226, 229, 230, August 17, 20, 21, 1913, trans. in id., *The Balkan Wars*, pp. 413–14.

21. Eidelberg, pp. 37, 202. My discussion of the arendaşi, the specifics of 1907, and its background are culled largely from Eidelberg's study.

22. Ibid., pp. 23, 201.

23. Ibid., pp. 155, 189, 202.

24. Quoted ibid., p. 224.

25. Ibid., p. 233; Seton-Watson, p. 77.

26. Bernstein, *Les Persécutions*, pp. 14, 19–20.

27. Goldmann told this to his first wife, Jeannine Quillet. Letter to the author from Quillet, February 24, 1988. Goldmann was married to Quillet in Paris in 1948, and they divorced in 1955. Details also provided in an interview with Mrs. H. Tismaneanu, Philadelphia, November 23, 1988.

28. Dosarul (File) No. 499 *bis*, Studentului Goldman T. Lucian, Archives of the Law Faculty of the University of Bucharest.

29. Interview with Mihail Leonescu, Bucharest, July 5, 1990.

30. Interview with Romanian sources who wish anonymity; Interview with Annie Goldmann, Paris, June 3, 1980. The circumstances of his father's death were related to me by a Romanian who requested confidentiality, but was in a position to know the details.

31. Goldmann's Liceu certificate in Dosarul (File) 499 *bis*, Studentului Goldman T. Lucian, Archives of the Law Faculty of the University of Bucharest; Statistics on the Laurian in *Al 69 Lea An 'Liceul Laurian' Din Botoşani, 1927–28* (Botoşani: Tipografia B. Saidman, 1928), p. 79, on file at the Liceul Laurian, Botoşani; Letter to the author from Simon Katz, Bucharest, undated (written in 1981); Interview with Mihail Leonescu, Bucharest, July 5, 1990.

32. Letter to the author from David Zoller, April 18, 1981. My portrait of Goldmann's period in Ha-shomer ha-Tsair is based primarily on correspondence and an interview with Zoller, in Rehovot, Israel, July 10, 1980, and an interview with Prof. S. Z. Feller of the Hebrew University Law School, a schoolmate of Goldmann's in Botoşani, June 22, 1990, in Jerusalem.

33. Elkana Margalit, "Social and Intellectual Origins of the Hashomer Hatzair Youth Movement, 1913–1920," *Journal of Contemporary History* 4 (April 1969), p. 34.

34. Ibid., pp. 36–37.

35. Ibid., pp. 44–45.

36. Elkana Margalit, *Ha-Shomer ha-Tsair—Me-adat Nearim le Marxism mahpkhani (1913–1926)* (Ha-Shomer ha-Tsair: From Youth Community to Revolutionary Marxism, 1913–1926)(Tel Aviv: Tel Aviv University and Ha-Kibbutz ha-Meuhad, 1971), pp. 149–54 and 292–96.

37. Interview with Joseph Gabel, Paris, June 25, 1980.

38. Zoller's word was *emunah*, the traditional Hebrew for "faith" or "belief."

39. I wish to thank Ionel Bejenaru, a local historian in Botoşani, for providing me with details of the Circle when I visited Botoşani in July 1990.

40. Goldmann, "Autobiographical Fragment," AGA.

41. Lucien Goldmann, *Curriculum Vitae*, p. 1, in AGA. This curriculum vitae, prepared by Goldmann himself in the late 1950s, contradicts the dating of his stay in Vienna in several brief biographical accounts of him; cf. S. Naïr and M. Löwy, *Goldmann* (Paris: Editions Seghers, 1973), p. 11; Mary Evans, *Lucien*

Goldmann: An Introduction (Sussex: Harvester Press, 1981), p. 1; and Annie Goldmann, "L'Auteur," in Lucien Goldmann, *Situation de la critique racinienne*. These place him in Vienna during the school year of 1933–1934. It is possible that Goldmann returned for a visit to the Austrian capital that year, the year in which the Left was defeated there, but his studies in Vienna were in 1930–1931, according to his own account and that of an acquaintance who knew him there but prefers to remain anonymous.

Several Austrian socialists, including Adler and Julius Braunthal had ties to and expressed sympathetic interest in the Zionist Left. In 1931 Adler wrote a foreword for a Ha-Shomer ha-Tsair publication and two years later addressed an anniversary celebration in Vienna for another left-wing Zionist group, the Poale Zion. See J. Jacobs, "Austrian Social Democracy and the Jewish Question in the First Republic," in Anson Rabinbach, ed., *The Austrian Socialist Experiment: Social Democracy and Austro-Marxism, 1918–1934* (Boulder and London: Westview Press, 1985) pp. 161–62.

42. Goldmann's file at the University of Bucharest indicates that he first matriculated in the academic year 1931–1932. He apparently remained in Vienna until the fall of 1931. A certificate signed by the Romanian consul-general in Vienna dated November 16, 1931, declares: "The Royal Legation of Romania in Vienna certifies that Mr. Lucian Goldmann born 20 June 1913, possessor of national passport number 853289 issued by the police station of Botoşani on 13 October 1930 following information received by the Population Bureau in that locality, is registered at this bureau beginning Oct. 10 of this year and lives until today at Vienna Porzellangasse 25. This certificate was issued at the request of the above named to assist him in inscribing at the law faculty in Bucharest." Dosarul (File) 499 *bis*, Studentului Goldman T. Lucian, Archives of the Law Faculty of the University of Bucharest.

43. Lucien Goldmann, *Introduction à la Philosophie de Kant* (Paris: Gallimard, 1967), pp. 65–66.

44. The *Rechtsphilosophie* and *Fichtes Idealismus und die Geschichte* are in Vol. 1 of E. Lask, *Gesammelte Schriften* (Tübingen: J.C.B. Mohr, 1923). The *Rechtsphilosophie* is translated as "Legal Philosophy" in *The Legal Philosophies of Lask, Radbruch, and Dabin*, with introduction by E. Patterson (Cambridge, Mass.: Harvard University Press, 1950).

45. Among them were Léon Duguit, a positivist in orientation; François Gény, who contended that "objective reason" demonstrated what is "objectively just"; Rudolf von Jhering, who elaborated a sociology of law; and Hans Kelsen, the neo-Kantian legal positivist. For short surveys of these thinkers see Arnold Brecht, *Political Theory* (Princeton: Princeton University Press, 1959).

46. "Vorwort" to Lucien Goldmann, *Mensch, Gemeinschaft und Welt in der Philosophie Immanuel Kants* (Zurich and New York: Europea Verlag, 1945), n.p. My description of the University of Bucharest is based in part on telephone interviews with Charles Gruber (Paris, June 18, 1987) and Liviu Floda (New York, March 11, 1988), both of whom were students in the law faculty shortly before or at the same time as Goldmann, as well as an interview with Ion Filatti, G. Tasca's grandson (June 18, 1987).

47. Baron, p. 9.

48. Interview with Leonte Răutu, Bucharest, July 7, 1990; Interview with Mihail Dragomirescu, Bucharest, July 5, 1990.

49. Lucien Goldmann, *Sociologia Literaturii*, with preface by Miron Constantinescu and introduction by Ion Pascadi (Bucharest: Editura Politică, 1972). On Constantinescu, see Vladimir Tismaneanu, "Miron Constantinescu or the Impossible Heresy," *Survey* 28: (Winter 1984), p. 123.

50. Notably, none of Goldmann's Romanian acquaintances with whom I spoke remembered him speaking of Lukács at this time.

51. My depiction of life in the Schuller is primarily based on interviews, conducted in Paris, Philadelphia, and Bucharest between 1987 and 1990, with Leonte Răutu, Cristina Boica, Hermina Tismaneanu, Mihail Florescu, and Mihail Alexandru, who all frequented the dormitory in the early 1930s. The quote is by Alexandru.

52. Accounts conflict. His membership in the UCY was confirmed to me initially in correspondence with Răutu and Florescu. Anna Toma, in a phone conversation (in Bucharest on July 12, 1990), concurred. Mircea Bălănescu, a friend in both Botoşani and Bucharest, denied that Goldmann was in either the UCY or the RCP.

53. King, pp. 22–23.

54. This article was described to me by a source who wishes to remain unnamed. I was unable to find it either in the library of the Romanian National Academy or in the West. It should be noted that the theme of "the other side of the Grant Bridge" reappeared in Goldmann's article on the novels of N. D. Cocea, discussed below.

55. Interview with Ernst Erdöes, Zurich, August 2, 1987. Pătrăşcanu served as the Romanian justice minister for the RCP in 1944; he was purged in 1948 and shot six years later.

56. King, p. 27.

57. Interview with Mircea Bălănescu, Bucharest, July 2, 1990. Bălănescu was then Eugene Bendl.

58. See Scarlat Callimachi and S. Cris-Cristian, *Călători şi scriitori străini despre Evreii din Principatele Româneşti* (Jassy: Institutul de Arte Grafice 'Brawo,' 1935).

59. See Eugene Simion, "Préface: Tableau d'une Époque," in Eugene Ionesco, *Non* (Paris: Gallimard, 1986), for a brief survey, from which I draw, of Romanian intellectual life from the end of World War I through 1934.

60. Eugène Ionesco, *Non* (Paris: Gallimard, 1986), pp. 71–72.

61. Interview with Cristina Boica, Paris, December 23, 1987.

62. I summarize from Michael Shafir, "Sociology of Knowledge in the Middle of Nowhere: Constantin Dobrogeanu-Gherea," *East European Quarterly*, September 1985, pp. 327–29. Gherea's inversion of Marxist causality and its inconsistency with Plekhanov is pointed out by Kitch, pp. 76–77.

63. In the following, I paraphrase and quote from C. Al (Lucien Goldmann), "Romanele Lui N. D. Cocea," *Clopotul*, no. 30, April 13, 1934, p. 2.

64. Lucien Goldmann, "Un Grand Polémiste: Karl Kraus," originally in *Lettres* 4 (Geneva: 3e année, 1945), reprinted in *R*, p. 231.

65. Or to another planet. Kraus's preface to *The Last Days of Mankind* begins: "The performance of this drama, whose scope of time by earthly measure would comprise about ten evenings, is intended for a theater on Mars." Karl Kraus, *The Last Days of Mankind* (New York: Frederick Unger, 1974), p. 3.

66. Goldmann, "Un Grand Polémiste," p. 232.

67. Ibid., p. 232.

68. Ibid., p. 234.

69. It should be noted, however, that Lukács himself praised Anatole France—indeed, in the same breath as Thomas Mann—as a major realist in his 1938 essay on "Marx and the Problem of Ideological Decay" in his *Essays on Realism* (Cambridge, Mass.: MIT Press, 1981), p. 149. Also see his praise of Anatole France in his 1955 *The Historical Novel* (Harmondsworth: Penguin Books, 1981), pp. 248–49, 308–9.

70. Goldmann, "Un Grand Polémiste," p. 234.

71. Lucien Goldmann, "La Réification," in *Rd*, n. 2, pp. 97–98.

72. Interview with Leonte Răutu, Bucharest, July 7, 1990; Interview with Mihail Dragomirescu, Bucharest, July 5, 1990.

73. Interview with Răutu.

74. Telephone interview with Joseph Bujes, Los Angeles, May 20, 1990.

75. Interview with Bălănescu, Bucharest, July 2, 1990.

76. Leszek Kolakowski, in a letter to the author (May 8, 1981), states that Goldmann told him that he had been in a Trotskyist group for a period. At least two other Romanian sources, who wish to remain anonymous, assert that Goldmann was accused of Trotskyism. One told me in 1980 that his father, an RCP official, mentioned to him often that " 'Gică' Goldmann the Trotskyist was thrown out of the party." Goldmann told a friend in Geneva that he had become a Trotskyist in Romania. Interview with Pierre Engel, Geneva, June 23, 1989.

77. According to Helena Solomon, with whom Goldmann regularly discussed politics in these years. Interview, Tel Aviv, March 12, 1989.

78. This notion of "community" undoubtedly came from Ha-Shomer ha-Tsair and not Trotsky, who elaborated no such concept.

79. Letter from Răutu, 2 January 1988; Letter from a source who wishes to remain unnamed.

80. Interview with Carol Neuman, Paoli, Pennsylvania, June 6, 1990; Telephone interview with Joseph Bujes, Los Angeles, May 20, 1990; Interview with an anonymous source.

81. Interview with Bălănascu.

82. Interviews with Bălănescu, Florescu, and Boica.

83. Her husband served as *chef de bureau* of the Communist Ministry of Health after the war.

84. Lucien Goldmann, Letter to Madeleine Duclos, 1945. Courtesy Madeleine Duclos Garepuy. The letter is not dated by Goldmann, but Duclos noted the year after receiving it.

85. See Mic, *Dictionar Enciclopedic* (Bucharest: Editura Stiintifica si Enciclopedica, 1978), p. 1316; C. I. Gulian, *Marxism și Structuralism* (Bucharest: Editura Politică, 1976), pp. 173–87.

Chapter 2

1. Victor Eftimiu, "Parisul ăi Studenţimea" (Paris and Students), *Viaţa Studenţească*, December 15, 1934, p. 2. Copy in the library of the Romanian Academy, Bucharest.

2. Lucien Goldmann, untitled poem, AGA.

3. Interview with Joseph Gabel, Paris, June 25, 1980; Telephone interview with Joseph Bujes, Los Angeles, May 20, 1990. See also the short description of Goldmann in Helène Elek, *La Mémoire d'Helène* (Paris: Maspero, 1977) p. 166.

4. Vincent Descombes, *Modern French Philosophy* (Cambridge: Cambridge University Press, 1980), pp. 8–9.

5. *Ipk*, p. 308. Lukács had not been entirely silent, although his work after *History and Class Consciousness* was inaccessible to Goldmann in the 1940s (Lukács was in Moscow). In any event, Lukács renounced precisely those early works to which Goldmann was attracted.

6. See Mounier's late summary of his ideas (he died in 1950) entitled *Personalism* (Notre Dame and London: University of Notre Dame Press, 1952), pp. xxiv, 2, 70.

7. Mounier, pp. 12–13. See also ibid., pp. 16, 30, 105.

8. Dorothy Margaret Eastwood, *The Revival of Pascal: A Study of His Relation to Modern Thought* (Oxford: Clarendon Press, 1936), pp. 13–16.

9. André Suarès, *Puissances de Pascal* (Paris: Emil Paul, 1923), quoted in Eastwood, p. 196.

10. Pierre Engel, "Quelques souvenirs sur Lucien Goldmann," a private correspondence with the author; see also Goldmann's *curriculum vitae* from the 1950s in AGA.

11. Interview with Gabel, 1980; Interview with Annie Goldmann, June 3, 1980; Letter from Goldmann to Duclos, 1945.

12. Interview with Madeleine (Duclos) Garepuy, Toulouse, June 19, 1987.

13. This was a story that Duclos heard but which I could not confirm. However, there exists a photo of Goldmann with a group of children, apparently in Switzerland.

14. Manès Sperber, *Ces temps-là: Au delà de l'oubli* (Paris: Calmann-Lévy, 1979), pp. 218–19.

15. The description of Gierenbad is based on the testimony of two refugees who were interned with Goldmann, Joseph Spielmann, currently of Strasboug (telephone interview, July 5, 1992, and memo to the author, September 30, 1992), and Menahem Wieviorka (interview, Paris, July 5, 1992).

16. All the poems are in AGA. Some may be translations of the work of others, although I was unable to identify any as such, save for the Brecht song mentioned below.

17. Préface à la première édition, *Ipk*, p. 18.

18. See Ferdinand Tönnies, *Community and Society* (New York: Harper Torchbooks, 1963); and Michael Löwy, *Georg Lukács: From Romanticism to Bolshevism* (London: New Left Books, 1979). Löwy's valuable book has especially informed my understanding of romantic anticapitalism and its impact on the intelligentsia in Hungary and Germany.

19. Georg Lukács, Preface to *TN*, p. 19.

20. *TN*, p. 63.

21. Interview with Yvonne Moser, Zurich, August 2, 1987. Spoerri maintained a warm relationship with Goldmann through the 1960s, and it seems Goldmann had as much of an impact on him as he had on Goldmann. After a visit to Goldmann in Paris in 1966, Spoerri wrote to him: "I've learned a lot and I've begun to understand that I am much closer to you and your ideas than I had previously thought." Th. Spoerri to Goldmann, September 9, 1966, AGA.

22. Interview with Moser; Interview with Irene Petit, Paris, June 22, 1987.

23. Interview with Henri Gouhier, Paris, July 22, 1980. Gouhier, to whom *The Hidden God* is dedicated, was Goldmann's adviser for it as his *doctorat d'état*.

24. Lucien Goldmann, "Les Conditions sociales et la vision tragique du monde," in *Échanges sociologiques: Cercle Universitaire de la Sorbonne* (Paris: Centre du Documentation Universitaire, 1948), p. 91.

25. *Ipk*, p. 16.

26. Lucien Goldmann, "Lukács et Heidegger," in *La Structuralisme génétique*, p. 211. This was the first appearance in French of the essay, which did not appear in any of the French editions of Goldmann's study of Kant. A translation from the German into English appears in *The Philosophical Forum* 23, nos. 1–2, Fall–Winter 1991–1992, a special issue dedicated to Goldmann. I have translated from the French, though making modifications based on the original German and the English translation cited above.

27. Ibid., pp. 214–15.

28. Ibid., p. 215.

29. Ibid.

30. Ibid., p. 217.

31. Ibid., pp. 216–17.

32. Ibid., p. 218.

33. Ibid., pp. 217–18.

34. Ibid., p. 217 n. 1. Goldmann does not treat Heidegger's discussion of nation and fate at all, despite their importance in *Being and Time*. A Swiss friend recalls Goldmann, during World War II, making vituperative comments about Heidegger's collaboration with the Nazis. Pierre Engel, "Quelques souvenirs. . . ."

35. All quotes from this "Dialogue" are from the typescript in AGA. A precise dating of the piece is impossible. Its tone and preoccupations indicate that it was probably written during Goldmann's Zurich period or shortly thereafter. Also, it refers to *Being and Nothingness*, which appeared in 1943, while Goldmann was in Zurich, as Sartre's most recent work.

36. See Immanuel Kant, *The Critique of Judgement*, J. C. Meredith, trans.(Oxford: Oxford University Press, 1978), pp. 14–18.

37. "Dialogue," p. 1.

38. Ibid.

39. Kant, *Judgment*, p. 62.

40. Ibid., pp. 62–63.

41. "Dialogue," p. 1.

42. Ibid., p. 2.

43. Ibid.

44. Ibid.

45. Ibid.

46. Ibid.

47. Goldmann retained a consistent, critical, but also sympathetic interest in Sartre throughout his career. While in Switzerland he saw a production of Sartre's play *Les Mouches*. Spoerri wrote an essay on it, and *Kant* mentions Sartre several times, usually coupled with Heidegger. See, for example, pp. 14 and 25 in *Mensch, Gemeinschaft und Welt in der Philosophie Immanuel Kants*. In the 1960s Goldmann wrote essays on Sartre's *Question de méthode* and on his theater.

48. G.W.F. Hegel, *Phenomenology of Spirit* (reprint, Oxford: Oxford University Press, 1977), p. 114 (par. 187).

49. Jean-Paul Sartre, *Being and Nothingness* (New York: Washington Square Press, 1966), p. 477.

50. Ibid., pp. 480, 482.

51. Ibid., p. 475.

52. "Dialogue," p. 5.

53. Ibid., p. 6.

54. Ibid., p. 3.

55. Ibid., p. 4.

56. Howard E. Gruber and J. Jacques Vonèche, Summary of Piaget's *Recherche*, in *The Essential Piaget* (New York: Basic Books, 1977), p. 43.

57. Jean Piaget, "Bref témoignange," in *Lucien Goldmann et la sociologie de la littérature: Hommage à Lucien Goldmann* (Brussels: Editions de l'Université de Bruxelles, 1974), p. 54.

58. See Piaget's comments on Marx and Lukács, and in praise of Goldmann, in his *Introduction à l'épistémologie génétique*, Vol. 3, *La Pensée biologique, la pensée psychologique et la pensée sociologique* (Paris: PUF, 1950), pp. 198–202, 249, 250–51.

59. Jean Piaget to Fred Pollack, September 22, 1945, AGA.

60. Lucien Goldmann to Georg Lukács, May 29, 1963, Lukács Archives, Budapest.

61. Theodor Adorno to Lucien Goldmann, October 15, 1963, AGA.

62. See "Préface à la première édition," *Ipk*, p. 18.

63. Interviews with Annie Goldmann, Paris, June 3, 1980, and July 8, 1987; Interview with Yvonne Moser, Zurich, August 1, 1987. Goldmann told his wife of a "disastrous" dinner in Paris at which Lukács, Sartre, and Goldmann were present. Almost certainly this would have been in early 1949 when Lukács, during a visit to Paris, engaged in a slugfest with Sartre through the press, and published his *Existentialisme ou marxisme*, one of his worst books. I was unable to find anyone else who knew of or attended this dinner.

64. Author's conversation with Ferenc Fehér and Agnès Heller, May 12, 1987; see also Ferenc Fehér, "Lucien Goldmann, the 'Mere Recipient' of Georg Lukács," *Philosophy and Social Criticism* 1: pp. 23–24. Unless Lukács's memory

was imprecise, his dating of this story indicates that Goldmann's plan to write on Pascal and Racine dated to at least the mid-1940s.

65. Copy at the Lukács Archives, Budapest.

66. Georg Lukács to Lucien Goldmann, October 1, 1959, AGA.

67. Ibid.

68. Lucien Goldmann to Georg Lukács, October 14, 1959, Lukács Archives, Budapest.

69. Ibid.

70. Lucien Goldmann to Georg Lukács, November 14, 1962, and Georg Lukács to Lucien Goldmann, December 1, 1962, Lukács Archives, Budapest.

Chapter 3

1. August Comte, *Cours de philosophie positive*, Vol. 1 (Paris: Bachelier, 1839), p. viii, quoted in Gertrude Lenzer, Introduction to *August Comte and Positivism: The Essential Writings* (New York: Harper Torchbooks, 1975), p. xlviii.

2. Emile Durkheim, *Socialism* (reprint, New York: Collier Books, 1962), pp. 141–42.

3. "The Assayer," in *The Discoveries and Opinions of Galileo* (New York: Doubleday and Co., 1957), p. 238.

4. R. Harré, *The Philosophies of Science* (Oxford: Oxford University Press, 1972), pp. 128–30. I have made considerable use of this judicious account in the following pages, together with the invaluable survey by John Lossee, *A Historical Introduction to the Philosophy of Science* (Oxford: Oxford University Press, 1980).

5. John Lossee, *A Historical Introduction to the Philosophy of Science* (Oxford: Oxford University Press, 1980), p. 54.

6. Ibid., p. 81.

7. Comte, *Cours de philosophie positive*, quoted in Lenzer, *Auguste Comte and Positivism*, p. 182.

8. Rene Descartes, *Discourse on Method* (reprint, Indianapolis: Library of Liberal Arts, 1960), p. 15.

9. Comte, quoted in Russell Keat and John Urry, *Social Theory as Science* (London: Routledge and Kegan Paul, 1975), p. 73.

10. Comte, *Cours de philosophie positive*, in *Auguste Comte and Positivism*, pp. 219–20.

11. Comte, "Plan of the Scientific Operations Necessary for reorganizing Society," in *Auguste Comte and Positivism*, p. 54.

12. J. S. Mill, *A System of Logic*, reprinted in *Philosophy of Scientific Method* (New York: Hafner Press, 1974), p. 356.

13. Ibid., p. 332.

14. Ibid., p. 307.

15. Emile Durkheim, *The Rules of Sociological Method* (reprint, New York: Free Press, 1966), p. 14.

16. Heinrich Rickert, *The Limits of Concept Formation in Natural Science: A Logical Introduction to the Historical Sciences* (Cambridge and New York: Cambridge University Press, 1986), pp. 13, 17.

17. Richard E. Palmer, *Hermeneutics* (Evanston, Ill.: Northwestern University Press, 1969), pp. 13, 86.

18. Ibid., p. 87.

19. Quoted in Rudolf A. Makkreel, *Dilthey: Philosopher of the Human Studies* (Princeton: Princeton University Press, 1975), p. 223.

20. Wilhelm Dilthey, "The Construction of the Historical World in the Human Studies," in *Selected Writings* (Cambridge: Cambridge University Press, 1979), p. 175.

21. David Frisby, Introduction to Theodor Adorno et al., *The Positivist Dispute in German Sociology* (London: Heinemann, 1976), p. xxi n. 35.

22. Wilhelm Dilthey, *Pattern and Meaning in History* (New York: Harper and Row, 1962), p. 123.

23. Dilthey, "Construction," p. 194.

24. Ibid., p. 93.

25. Wilhelm Dilthey, "Ideas about a Descriptive and Analytical Psychology," in *Selected Writings*, p. 90.

26. Dilthey, "Ibid.," p. 89.

27. Dilthey, "Drafts for a Critique of Historical Reason," in *Selected Writings*, p. 208.

28. Dilthey, "Construction," p. 195.

29. Ibid., p. 177.

30. Dilthey, "Fragments of a Poetics," in id., *Poetry and Experience: Selected Writings*, Vol. 5 (Princeton: Princeton University Press, 1985), p. 223.

31. Dilthey, "The Development of Hermeneutics," in id., *Selected Writings*, p. 262.

32. Dilthey, "Construction," p. 203.

33. Dilthey, "Ideas," pp. 93, 94; "Construction," p. 244.

34. Dilthey, "Construction," pp. 178, 180.

35. Dilthey, "The Types of World-View and Their Development in the Metaphysical Systems," *Selected Writings*, p. 146.

36. Ibid., p. 139.

37. Ibid.

38. Ibid., pp. 147–48.

39. Ibid., p. 149.

40. Ibid., pp. 149–51.

41. Ibid., pp. 151–52; Makkreel, pp. 346–47.

42. Dilthey, quoted in Makkreel, p. 348.

43. Rüdiger Bubner, *Modern German Philosophy* (Cambridge: Cambridge University Press, 1981) p. 121.

44. Wilhelm Windelband, *A History of Philosophy* (New York: Macmillan and Co., 1893), p. 9.

45. Ibid., p. 680.

46. Wilhelm Windelband, *An Introduction to Philosophy* (New York: Henry Holt and Co., 1921), p. 31.

47. Wilhelm Windelband, "History and Natural Science," *History and Theory* 19, no. 2 (1980): p. 175.

48. Ibid., p. 174.

49. Ibid., p. 178.

50. Ibid., p. 185.

51. Ibid., pp. 181–82.

52. This point is stressed by Guy Oakes's introduction to Wilhelm Windelband, "History and Natural Science," p. 168.

53. My discussion of Lask is greatly indebted to Oakes's excellent discussion entitled "Rickert's Theory of Historical Knowledge," his introduction to Rickert, *Limits*.

54. Emil Lask, "Legal Philosophy," reprinted in *The Legal Philosophies of Lask, Radbruch and Dabin*, trans. K. Wilk (Cambridge, Mass.: Harvard University Press, 1950) p. 4.

55. Ibid., pp. 4–5.

56. Ibid., pp. 5–6.

57. Ibid., pp. 16–17.

58. Ibid., p. 29.

59. Ibid., p. 10.

60. Ibid., p. 11.

61. Emil Lask, *Fichtes Idealismus und die Geschichte, Gesammelte Schriften*, Vol. 1 (Tübingen: Verlag von J.C.B. Mohr, 1923), pp. 29–30.

62. Ibid., pp. 172–73.

63. Ibid., p. 174.

64. See Guy Oakes, "Rickert's Theory of Historical Knowledge," Introduction to Rickert, *Limits*, pp. xiv-xv.

65. Ibid., p. xv; id., *Weber and Rickert: Concept Formation in the Cultural Sciences* (Cambridge, Mass.: MIT Press, 1988), p. 50; Goldmann, *Kant*, pp. 65–66.

66. Oakes, "Rickert's Theory," p. xv.

67. Max Weber, "Roscher's 'Historical Method,'" in id., *Roscher and Knies: The Logical Problems of Historical Economics*, trans. with introduction by Guy Oakes (New York: Free Press, 1975), pp. 66–67.

68. Lask, *Fichtes Idealismus*, p. 30.

69. Ibid., p. 66.

70. Ibid., p. 72.

71. Lask, "Legal Philosophy," pp. 6–7.

72. Ibid., p. 12. Translation slightly amended.

73. Ibid., pp. 13–14.

74. Ibid., p. 21.

75. See Oakes, "Rickert's Theory," p. xii.

76. Rickert, *Limits*, p. 43.

77. Ibid., p. 27.

78. Ibid., pp. 39–40.

79. Ibid., p. 37.

80. Ibid., p. 52. Rickert acknowledges a debt to Georg Simmel in this formulation.

81. Heinrich Rickert, *Science and History: A Critique of Positivist Epistemology* (Princeton: D. Van Nostrand Co., Inc., 1962), p. 71.

82. Rickert, *Science and History*, p. 19.

83. Ibid., pp. 28–29.

84. Rickert, *Limits*, p. 141.

85. Ibid., p. 150.

86. Ibid., p. 151.

87. Ibid., p. 146.

88. Ibid., pp. 64–65.

89. Ibid., p. 121.

90. Rickert, *Science and History*, p. 27.

91. Ibid., p. 88.

92. Ibid., p. 140.

93. Ibid., pp. 95–96.

94. Weber, "Roscher's 'Historical Method,'" pp. 216–17 n. 22.

95. Ibid., pp. 217–18.

96. Max Weber, "'Objectivity' in Social Science and Social Policy," in id., *The Methodology of the Social Sciences* (New York: Free Press, 1949) p. 90.

97. Max Weber, "The Meaning of 'Ethical Neutrality' in Sociology and Economics," in id., *Methodology*, p. 42.

98. Max Weber, "Knies and the Problem of Irrationality," in id., *Roscher and Knies*, pp. 166, 176.

99. Max Weber, *Economy and Society* (Berkeley: University of California Press, 1978), p. 5.

100. Ibid., p. 8.

101. Ibid., pp. 8–10.

102. Weber, "Knies," p. 125.

103. Weber, *Economy and Society*, p. 12.

104. Weber, "Knies," pp. 184–86.

105. Weber, "'Objectivity,'" p. 72.

106. Max Weber, "Critical Studies in the Logic of the Cultural Sciences: A Critique of Eduard Meyer's Methodological Views," in id., *Methodology*, p. 180. Meyer's discussion of Marathon appeared in *On the Theory and Method of History* (1900).

107. Weber, "Critical Studies," p. 175.

108. Weber, "The Meaning of 'Ethical Neutrality,'" p. 1.

109. Weber, "'Objectivity,'" p. 53.

Chapter 4

1. *HCC*, p. 27. Emphasis omitted.

2. Ibid., p. 1.

3. Ibid., p. 198.

4. Ibid., p. xxiii.

5. Heinrich Rickert, *Wilhelm Windelband* (Tübingen: J.C.B. Mohr, 1915), p. 19, quoted in Jeffry T. Bergner, *The Origins of Formalism in Social Science* (Chicago and London: University of Chicago Press, 1981), p. 149 n. 38.

6. In the following discussion I draw on my own discussion in "Portrait of the Young Lukács," *Dissent*, Summer 1987.

7. Lukács's letter to Leo Popper, October 26, 1909, in *Selected Correspondence, 1902–1920* (New York: Columbia University Press, 1986), p. 100.

8. George Simmel, "How Is History Possible?" in D. Levine, ed., *On Individuality and Social Forms* (Chicago and London: University of Chicago Press, 1971), p. 3.

9. Georg Simmel, *The Philosophy of Money* (Boston and London: Routledge and Kegan Paul, 1987), pp. 78–79.

10. Ibid., p. 128.

11. Ibid., pp. 210–11.

12. Simmel, *Philosophy of Money*, pp. 232–34. In making the Greeks his point of comparison, Simmel was within the traditions of both romanticism and classical German philosophy and literature as well. This was a favored motif of Hegel and Goethe, and it reappears prominently in Lukács's pre-Marxist works, such as *The Development of Modern Drama* and *Theory of the Novel*.

13. Simmel, *Philosophy of Money*, p. 280.

14. Ibid., p. 454.

15. Ibid., p. 56.

16. *TN*, p. 20.

17. J. M. Bernstein, *The Philosophy of the Novel: Lukács, Marxism and the Dialectics of Form* (Minneapolis: University of Minnesota Press, 1984), p. 87.

18. G.W.F. Hegel, *Philosophy of Right* (reprint, London and New York: Oxford University Press, 1967), p. 106, par. 147.

19. Ibid., p. 92, par. 138.

20. *TN*, p. 66.

21. Ibid., pp. 31, 67.

22. Ibid., pp. 62, 71.

23. Ibid., p. 34.

24. Ibid., pp. 56, 34.

25. Ibid., pp. 33, 37.

26. Ibid., pp. 66, 80, 88–89.

27. Ibid., p. 93.

28. Ibid., pp. 63–64.

29. *HCC*, pp. 2–3.

30. See Louis Althusser, *For Marx* (Harmondsworth: Penguin Books, 1969), p. 77.

31. See John Cottingham, *The Rationalists* (Oxford and New York: Oxford University Press, 1988), p. 42.

32. G.W.F. Hegel, *Phenomenology of Spirit* (Oxford: Oxford University Press, 1981), p. 3, par. 5.

33. *Hegel's Logic: Being Part One of the Encyclopedia of the Philosophical Sciences)* (Oxford: Oxford University Press, 1975), p. 3, par. 1; Hegel, *Phenomenology*, p. 11, par. 2.

34. Hegel, *Phenomenology*, pp. 178–79, par. 295.

35. Friedrich Engels, *Anti-Dühring* (Moscow: Progress Publishers, 1969), p. 16.

36. Friedrich Engels, *Dialectics of Nature* (New York: International Publishers, 1979), p. 26.

37. Windelband, *History of Philosophy*, p. 655; Rickert, *Science and History*, p. 153 n. 3.

38. Karl Marx, *Capital*, Vol. 1 (Moscow: Progress Publishers, 1965), p. 372 n. 3.

39. Ibid., pp. 19–20.

40. G.W.F. Hegel, *The Philosophy of History* (New York: Dover Books, 1956), p. 25.

41. *Hegel's Logic*, p. 187.

42. Karl Marx, *Grundrisse* (Middlesex: Penguin Books, 1973), pp. 99–100.

43. Ibid., p. 84.

44. Ibid.

45. *Conversations with Lukács* (London: Merlin Press, 1974), p. 100.

46. *HCC*, p. 7.

47. Ibid., p. 34.

48. Ibid., pp. 8–10.

49. Ibid., p. 8.

50. Ibid., p. 27.

51. Ibid., pp. 17, 34.

52. Ibid., pp. 27–28.

53. Ibid., p. 13.

54. In English: *HCC*, p. 27. In the original German: Georg Lukács, *Geschichte und Klassenbewusstsein* (hereafter *GK*) (Darmstadt and Neuwied: Luchterhand Verlag, 1968), p. 94.

55. *HCC*, p. 34; *GK*, p. 105. "Darum verlieren für sie 'ideologische' und 'ökonomische' Probleme ihre gegenseitige starre Fremdheit und fliessen ineinander über."

56. Hegel, *Phenomenology*, p. 9, par. 16.

57. *HCC*, p. 320; *GK*, p. 486.

58. *HCC*, p. 21.

59. Karl Marx and Friedrich Engels, *The Holy Family*, Vol. 4 of *Collected Works* (reprint, New York: International Publishers, 1975) p. 37; *HCC*, p. 46; *GK*, p. 119.

60. *HCC*, p. 51.

61. Ibid.

62. Ibid., p. 70.

63. Ibid., p. 80.

64. Ibid., pp. 40–43.

65. Lucien Goldmann, "Reflections on *History and Class Consciousness*," in István Mészáros, ed., *Aspects of History and Class Consciousness* (London: Routledge and Kegan Paul, 1971), p. 71.

66. The following discussion of the origins of Lukács's theory is particularly indebted to and draws from the excellent presentation in Andrew Feenberg, *Lukács, Marx and the Sources of Critical Theory* (Totowa, N.J.: Rowan and Littlefield, 1981) esp. pp. 59–70.

67. Marx, *Capital*, Vol. 1, p. 72.

68. *HCC*, p. 89.

69. Ibid., p. 90.

70. Ibid., p. 184.

71. Ibid., pp. 111–12.

72. Ibid., p. 121.

73. *Hegel's Logic* (Encyclopaedia), p. 14, par. 10.

74. Immanuel Kant, *Critique of Pure Reason*, Norman Kemp Smith trans. (reprint, New York: St. Martin's Press, 1965), p. 306.

75. Herbert Marcuse, *Reason and Revolution* (Boston: Beacon Press, 1960), p. 121.

76. György Markus, "Ideology and its Ideologies: Lukács and Goldmann on Kant" (paper presented at the conference "Dialectique et sciences humaines: Lukács-Goldmann," Cerisy-la-Salle, August 1979), p. 17. I am grateful to Dr. Markus for providing me with a copy of his original lecture. See also *HCC*, p. 134.

77. *HCC*, p. 124.

78. Ibid., p. 120.

79. Ibid., p. 123.

80. Ibid., p. 142.

81. Ibid., pp. 145–46.

82. Ibid., p. 147.

83. Ibid., p. 168.

84. Ibid., p. 178.

85. Ibid., p. 186.

86. Ibid., p. 23.

87. Ibid., p. 43.

88. This question is raised by T. B. Bottomore in "Class Structure and Social Consciousness," in I. Mészáros, ed., *Aspects of History and Class Consciousness*, p. 55.

Chapter 5

1. Lucien Goldmann, "La Réification," in *Rd*, pp. 64–65.

2. Lucien Goldmann, "Vorwort," in *Mensch*, p. 6. I will refer to the German edition of this book only when it differs with or contains materials absent from the French versions.

3. Lucien Goldmann, *Ipk*, p. 18.

4. "Préface à la présente édition," *Ipk*, p. 11.

5. Henri de Man, "Gutachten über Lucien Goldmann: *Mensch, Gemeinschaft und Welt in der Philosophie Immanuel Kants*," (unpublished typescript dated November 25, 1944, AGA), p. 1.

6. *Mensch*, p. 16. This comment seems to have been dropped from later editions.

7. *Ipk*, p. 22.

8. Ibid., p. 199.

9. See the prefaces to the first French edition and the 1967 French edition in *Ipk*, p. 18 and pp. 12–13, respectively.

10. Ibid., p. 132.

11. Ibid., p. 135.

12. Ibid., pp. 253–58.

13. Ibid., p. 65.

14. Ibid., p. 35 n. 1.

15. Ibid., pp. 36–37.

16. Ibid., p. 40.

17. Ibid.

18. Ibid., pp. 145, 151

19. Ibid., p. 409.

20. *Kant* (English trans.), p. 145.

21. *Ipk*, p. 150.

22. See "Idea for a Universal History with a Cosmopolitan Purpose," in Hans Reiss, ed., *Kant's Political Writings* (Cambridge: Cambridge University Press, 1971), p. 41.

23. *Ipk*, p. 127.

24. Ibid., p. 167.

25. Ibid., p. 164.

26. Markus, p. 18.

27. Lukács: *HCC*, p. 124; Goldmann: *Ipk*, p. 133.

28. *Ipk*, p. 235.

29. Ibid., p. 236.

30. Lucien Goldmann, "Propos dialectiques: Y a-t-il une sociologie marxiste?," in *Rd*, pp. 287–88.

31. Ibid., p. 281.

32. Ibid., p. 286.

33. Ibid., p. 288.

34. Ibid., p. 289.

35. Max Adler, "Kant und der Marxismus," in T. B. Bottomore and P. Goode, eds., *Austro-Marxism* (Oxford: Oxford University Press, 1978), p. 61; T. B. Bottomore, Introduction to *Austro-Marxism*, p. 20; Leszek Kolakowski, *Main Currents of Marxism* Vol. 2, (Oxford: Clarendon Press, 1978), p. 261.

36. Max Adler, "Kausalität und Teleologie," in *Kant-Studien*, Vol. 1 (Vienna, 1904), p. 380, quoted in Kolakowski, *Main Currents*, Vol. 2, p. 264.

37. *Ipk*, p. 159. One can see here another link between Goldmann and Mounier, who also argued that communication is the fundamental human attribute. See Emmanual Mounier, *Personalism* (Notre Dame and London: University of Notre Dame Press, 1952), ch. 2.

38. *Ipk*, pp. 160–61.

39. Ibid., p. 161.

40. Goldmann, "La Psychologie de Jean Piaget," in *Rd*; *Ipk*, p. 13.

41. *Dc*, pp. 13–14.

42. Hegel, *Phenomenology*, p. 23, par. 40.

43. *Dc*, p. 16.

44. Thomas Hobbes, "De Cive," in id., *Man and Citizen* (Garden City, N.Y.: Anchor Books, 1972), p. 92.

45. Hegel, *Phenomenology*, p. 13, par. 24.

46. *Hegel's Logic*, p. 20, par. 15.

47. *Dc*, pp. 14–15. Goldmann seems to downplay, if not ignore, Hume's skepticism.

48. Pensée 72, in the Brunschvicg edition, as translated by Philip Thody in *HG*, pp. 6–7.

49. Goldmann was concurring with a comment by Theodor Adorno during their exchange at a congress on the sociology of literature. See "Décrire, comprendre et expliquer" (unpublished proceedings of the IIIe Colloque International de Sociologie de la Littérature, Royaument, January 1968, EHESS), p. 297–99.

50. *Dc*, p. 7.

51. Marx W. Wartofsky, "From Genetic Epistemology to Historical Epistemology: Kant, Marx and Piaget," in L. S. Lieben, ed., *Piaget and the Foundations of Knowledge* (Hillsdale, N.J.: Erlbaum, 1983), p. 1.

52. Jean Piaget (London and Henley: Routledge and Kegan Paul, 1977), p. 28.

53. Ibid., p. 47.

54. Howard E. Gruber and J. Jacques Vonèche, Introduction to *The Essential Piaget* (New York: Basic Books, 1977), pp. xxx–xxxii.

55. Ibid.

56. Jean Piaget, *Psychology and Epistemology* (Middlesex and New York: Penguin Books, 1977), p. 11.

57. Jean Piaget, *Genetic Epistemology* (New York: W. W. Norton and Co., 1971), p. 2.

58. Jean Piaget, *The Psychology of Intelligence* (Totowa, N.J.: Littlefield, Adams and Co., 1976), p. 8.

59. Jean Piaget, *Structuralism* (New York: Harper Colophon Books, 1970), pp. 6–7.

60. Piaget, *Genetic Epistemology*, p. 13.

61. Lucien Goldmann, "L'Épistémologie de Jean Piaget," in *Rd*, p. 130.

62. Piaget, *Structuralism*, p. 120.

63. Goldmann, "La Psychologie de Jean Piaget," 126; on Piaget's notion of circularity, in *Rd*, see ibid., p. 131.

64. See Piaget's comments in *Introduction à l'épistémologie génétique*, Vol. 3 (Paris: Presses Universitaires de France, 1950), p. 202. Piaget specifically cites Goldmann's article on him on this point.

65. Karl Marx, *Capital*, Vol. 1 (reprint, Moscow: Progress Publishers, 1965), p. 177.

66. Goldmann, "La Psychologie de Jean Piaget," in *Rd*, p. 123.

67. Piaget, *Introduction à la épistémolgie génétique*, Vol. 3, p. 249.

68. Ibid., p. 249.

69. Lucien Goldmann, "La Dialectique aujourd'hui," in *Cc*, p. 162.

70. Goldmann, "La Réification," in *Rd*, p. 64 n. 1.

71. Lucien Goldmann, "Pensée dialectique et sujet transindividual," in *Cc*, p. 131.

72. Lucien Goldmann, "Genèse et structure," in *Msh*, p. 18.

73. See, for example, Goldmann's negative comments on Dilthey in *Shp*, p. 138 n. 1, and in "L'Apport de la pensée marxiste à la critique littérature," *Arguments*, January–March 1959, p. 45.

74. Goldmann, "Genèse et structure," in *Msh*, pp. 20–21.

75. *Shp*, p. 28.

76. Ibid., p. 29.

77. Goldmann, "Épistémologie de la sociologie," in *Epp*, p. 27.

78. Lucien Goldmann, "Sujet et objet en sciences humaines," *Raison présente*, January–March 1971, p. 101.

79. Lucien Goldmann, "Liberté et valeur," in *Atti del XII Congresso Internazionale de Filosofia*, Vol. 3 (Florence: Editore Sansoni, 1958), p. 185.

80. *Shp*, p. 34.

81. Goldmann, *LH*, pp. 148–49.

82. *Shp*, p. 40.

83. Ibid., p. 48.

84. Ibid., p. 44.

85. Lucien Goldmann, "Remarques sur la théorie de la connaissance," in *Épistémologie/Epistemology: Actes du XIe Congrès Internationale de philosophie* (Amsterdam: North Holland Publishing Co.; Louvain: E. Nauwelaerts, 1953), pp. 91–94.

86. *Shp*, p. 44.

87. Lucien Goldmann, "Les sciences humaines doivent-elles intégrer la philosophie?" in *Epp*, p. 171.

88. *Shp*, p. 54.

89. *Dc*, p. 25.

90. Lucien Goldmann, "Reflections on *History and Class Consciousness*," in *Epp*, p. 72.

91. "Dialogue," p. 4.

92. "The person," Mounier argued in a late work, "could . . . be defined as a movement towards a transpersonal condition which reveals itself in the experiences of community and of the attainment of values at the same time." *Personalism*, p. xxiv.

93. Goldmann, "Épistémologie de sociologie," p. 25.

94. Goldmann, "Reflections on *History and Class Consciousness*," p. 72.

95. Goldmann, "Sujet et objet en sciences humaines," p. 93.

96. Lucien Goldmann, "Structure: Human Reality and Methodological Concept," in R. Macksey and E. Donato, eds., *The Structuralist Controversy* (Baltimore and London: Johns Hopkins University Press, 1972), p. 101.

97. Lucien Goldmann, "La Structuralisme génétique et analyse stylistique," in *Linguaggi nella società nella technica* (Milan: Edizioni di Communita, 1970), p. 159.

98. Lucien Goldmann, "Ideology and Writing," *Times Literary Supplement*, September 28, 1967, p. 903.

99. Lucien Goldmann, "Pouvoir et humanisme," in *Msh*, p. 327.

100. *Shp*, p. 124.

101. Ibid., pp. 124–25.

102. Goldmann, "La Réification," in *Rd*, pp. 100–101.

103. Goldmann, "L'Épistémologie de Jean Piaget," p. 134.

104. Max Weber, " 'Objectivity' in Social Science," in *The Methodology of the Social Sciences* (New York: Free Press, 1949), p. 103.

105. *Shp*, p. 92.

106. Ibid., p. 109.

107. *Dc*, p. 26.

108. Goldmann, "Épistémologie de sociologie," p. 29.

109. *Dc*, p. 26.

110. *Shp*, pp. 109–10.

111. See the different presentations in the first two parts of *Dc*; in Lucien Goldmann, "Thèses sur l'emploi du concept de vision du monde en histoire de la philosophie," in *L'Homme et l'histoire: Actes du Vie Congrès de philosophie de langue française* (Paris: Presses Universitaires de France, 1952); and in id., "La Philosophie des lumières" and "Valăry et la dialectique: A propos de *Mon Faust*," both in *Sm*.

112. Goldmann, "Thèses sur l'emploi," p. 400.

113. *Shp*, p. 125.

Chapter 6

1. *Dc*, p. 13.

2. Ibid., p. 27.

3. Lucien Goldmann, "Thèses sur l'emploi du concept de vision du monde en histoire de la philosophie," in *L'homme et l'histoire: Actes du Vie Congrès des Sociétés de philosophie de langue française* (Paris: PUF, 1952), p. 399.

4. *Dc*, p. 26–27.

5. Ibid., p. 30.

6. Ibid., p. 33.

7. Perry Anderson, *Lineages of the Absolutist State* (London: Verso, 1979), p. 86; Franklin L. Ford, *Robe and Sword* (Cambridge, Mass.: Harvard University Press, 1962), p. 35.

8. See Ford, *Robe and Sword*, pp. 20–21; and A. Lloyd Moote, *Louis XIII, The Just* (Berkeley: University of California Press, 1991), pp. 62–64.

9. Moote, *Louis XIII*, p. 296.

10. Gerald R. Cragg, *The Church and the Age of Reason 1648–1789* (Harmondsworth: Penguin Books, 1970), p. 29.

11. *Dc*, p. 54. Goldmann rarely discussed classical theories of tragedy, and he admitted, with candor, his own ignorance of Shakespeare. See *Dc*, pp. 56–57 n. 2.

12. Georg Lukács, *SF*, p. 154.

13. Ibid., p. 153.

14. Ibid., pp. 152–53.

15. Ibid., p. 156–57.

16. Ibid., p. 162.

17. Ibid., p. 160.

18. Lucien Goldmann, Presentation on Kierkegaard and Lukács in *Kierkegaard vivant* (Paris: Gallimard, 1966), p. 127.

19. *SF*, p. 173.

20. Ibid., p. 153.

21. *Dc*, p. 51.

22. Martin Jay makes a similar point in his chapter on Goldmann in *Marxism*

and Totality (Berkeley and Los Angeles: University of California Press, 1984), p. 316.

23. *Ipk*, p. 61.

24. See *Ipk*, p. 37.

25. Lucien Goldmann, "Pascal et la pensée dialectique," *Empédocle: Revue littéraire mensuelle* 7 (January 1950): pp. 50–51.

26. This transcendence must be conceived in the purest Hegelian sense of negation *and* conservation. Goldmann wants to affirm the ideas of the individual, of liberty, and of equality before the law, but not in their bourgeois form. See Goldmann's "Lumières et dialectique," in *Epp*, pp. 73–74. One must note that Goldmann's view of the medieval world is either an overstatement or an ideal-type. It is historically tenuous to assume it approximated the all-encompassing condition of which he speaks.

27. *Dc*, p. 38.

28. G.W.F. Hegel, *Phenomenology of Spirit*, A. V. Miller trans. (Oxford and New York: Oxford University Press, 1977), par. 347.

29. Ibid., par. 377.

30. Ibid., pars. 379–80.

31. Ibid., par. 386.

32. Ibid., pars. 386, 389.

33. Ibid., par. 206.

34. Ibid., p. 207.

35. Ibid., par. 391.

36. *Dc*, p. 54.

37. Hegel, *Phenomenology*, par. 441.

38. Ibid., par. 451.

39. See the discussion in Charles Taylor, *Hegel* (Cambridge and New York: Cambridge University Press, 1975) ch. 6.

40. Hegel, *Phenomenology*, pars. 449–450.

41. Ibid., par. 466.

42. Ibid., par. 452.

43. *Dc*, p. 45.

44. Ibid.

45. Ibid., p. 64.

46. "On ne montre pas sa grandeur pour être à une extremité, mais bien touchant les deux à la fois et remplissant tout l'entre-deux." Pensée 353, quoted in *Dc*, p. 206.

47. *Dc*, p. 66

48. *Dc*, p. 75–76.

49. *Dc*, pp. 120–23.

50. While focusing on Marx and Engels and making no reference to Goldmann, Perry Anderson has advanced a contrary Marxist analysis, which rejects the notion of a balance of class forces. Absolutism, he argues, was consequent to the economic crises of the fourteenth and fifteenth centuries. The end of serfdom should not be conflated with that of feudalism, because even after serfdom was abolished, the social conditions of production remained essentially intact, with cash rent paid to lords as a replacement of the previous ex-

traction of labor or produce from the serfs. Consequently, the aristocracy retained both political and economic power under absolutism; while the form of exploitation had changed, it was still a feudal system, and absolutism was a *"redeployed and recharged apparatus"* for aristocratic domination. Its goal was to secure the nobility and repress popular uprisings, not to mediate between clashing classes. For whatever tensions may have manifested themselves between the nobility and the new state apparatus, that apparatus in fact sustained the class power of the nobility after a change in the structure of feudal property had occurred. Perry Anderson, *Lineages of the Absolutist State* (London: Verso Books, 1979), pp. 17–24; on France especially, see ibid., pp. 85–108. Anderson makes no reference to the accounts in Goldmann's book or to those of Henri Lefebvre's in his studies of Pascal.

51. *Dc*, p. 130.

52. Ibid., p. 129.

53. Ibid., p. 133.

54. Ibid.

55. Ibid.

56. Ibid., pp. 140–41.

57. See Lucien Goldmann, Introduction to *Correspondence de Martin de Barcos, Abbé de Saint-Cyran, editée et presenté par Lucien Goldmann* (Paris: Presses Universitaires de France, 1956), p. 1.

58. Alasdaire MacIntyre, "Pascal and Marx: On Lucien Goldmann's *Hidden God*," in *Against the Self-Images of the Age* (New York: Schocken Books, 1971), p. 77. For Goldmann's differing classifications, see *Dc*, pp. 55 n. 1, 158, 164.

59. *Dc*, p. 164.

60. Ibid., p. 17–178.

61. Ibid., pp. 165, 169–70.

62. Ibid., p. 65 n. 1.

63. Goldmann, Introduction to *Correspondence de Martin de Barcos*, pp. 10–11.

64. MacIntyre, p. 78.

65. *Dc*, p. 179.

66. Ibid., pp. 179–80.

67. Jean Mesnard, *Pascal, His Life and Works* (London: Harvill Press, 1952), pp. 67–69; Georg Lukács, *The Destruction of Reason* (London: Merlin Press, 1980), pp. 114–16.

68. See Henri Lefebvre, *Descartes* (Paris: Editions Sociales, 1947); id., *Pascal* (Paris: Les Editions Nagel, 1949, 1954), esp., Vol. 2, p. 240. Also see Michel Löwy's discussion in "Goldmann et Lukács: la vision de monde tragique," in A. Goldmann, M. Löwy, and S. Nair, eds., *Le Structuralisme génétique: l'oeuvre et l'influence de Lucien Goldmann* (Paris: Denoël/Gonthier, 1977), p. 114.

69. My description of the personal relation between the two men is based on my interview with Lefebvre, June 19, 1980. Lefebvre gives his own overview of the clashes in *La Somme et la reste*, Vol. 2 (Paris: La Nef de Paris, 1959), esp. p. 567. Some of the exchanges, along with contributions by Spoerri and Henri Gouhier—Goldmann's adviser for *The Hidden God*—are in *Blaise Pascal: L'Homme et l'oeuvre* (Paris: Les Editions de Minuit, 1956).

70. Lefebvre, *La Somme et la reste*, Vol. 2, p. 570.

71. Ibid., p. 571; Interview with Lefebvre, June 19, 1980.

72. Lefebvre, *La Somme et la reste*, Vol. 2, pp. 571–72.

73. Franz Borkenau, *Der Übergang von feudalen zum bürgerlichen Weltbild* (Paris, 1934), p. 13. Goldmann denied having read Borkenau. See Martin Jay, *Marxism and Totality* (Berkeley and Los Angeles: University of California Press, 1984), p. 315.

74. Ibid., pp. 484, 489.

75. Ibid., pp. 491, 545, 541, 559.

76. *Dc*, p. 187.

77. Ibid., p. 268.

78. Ibid., p. 270.

79. Ibid.

80. Ibid., p. 274 n. 1.

81. Ibid., p. 202.

82. Ibid., pp. 204–5.

83. Ibid., p. 206.

84. Ibid., p. 218.

85. Ibid., p. 331.

86. Ibid., p. 326.

87. Ibid., p. 330.

88. Ibid., p. 351.

89. Ibid., p. 358.

90. Ibid., p. 421.

91. Jacques Leenhardt argues that Goldmann has, in fact, two different theories, one of worldviews and one of homologies. It seems to me, however, that Goldmann is being a faithful dialectician by reformulating method according to the object. For Leenhardt's argument, see Eva Corredor, "Interview with Jacques Leenhardt," *Diacritics*, Fall 1977.

92. Lucien Goldmann, *Pour une sociologie du roman* (Paris: Gallimard, 1964), pp. 35–36. While I have quoted the original text, which reads, "un mode dégradé," this is very possibly a typographical error for *un monde dégradé*, a degraded world.

93. *Rd*, pp. 64–65.

94. Ibid., p. 66.

95. Ibid., pp. 67–68.

96. Ibid., pp. 69–71.

97. Ibid., pp. 76–77.

98. Ibid., pp. 77–78.

99. Ibid., p. 78.

100. Ibid., p. 84 n. 1.

101. Ibid., p. 86.

102. Ibid., p. 89.

103. Ibid., p. 91.

104. Ibid., p. 92.

105. Ibid., p. 93.

106. Ibid., pp. 95, 98.

107. Ibid., p. 99.

108. Ibid., p. 95, 99.

109. Ibid., pp. 102–3.

110. Ibid., pp. 104–5.

111. *Sr*, p. 22.

112. *TN*, p. 50.

113. Ibid., p. 71.

114. Ibid., pp. 66–67.

115. Ibid., pp. 30–31.

116. Ibid., p. 66.

117. Ibid., p. 88.

118. Ibid., pp. 72–73.

119. Ibid., p. 80.

120. Ibid., p. 84.

121. Ibid., pp. 92–93, 97.

122. Ibid., p. 89.

123. Ibid., p. 115.

124. Ibid., p. 93.

125. Ibid., pp. 63–64.

126. Ibid., p. 63.

127. Ibid., pp. 103–4.

128. Ibid., p. 117.

129. Ibid., p. 132.

130. Ibid., p. 135.

131. Ibid., p. 152.

132. Georg Lukács, "Stavrogin's Confession," in *Reviews and Articles* (London: Merlin Press, 1983), p. 45.

133. Georg Lukács, "Dostoyevsky," in *Marxism and Human Liberation* (New York: Dell Books, 1973), p. 197.

134. René Girard, *Desire, Deceit and the Novel* (Baltimore and London: Johns Hopkins University Press, 1965), pp. 1–5.

135. Ibid., pp. 6–7.

136. Ibid., pp. 8–9.

137. Ibid., pp. 14–15.

138. Ibid., p. 44.

139. Ibid., p. 66.

140. Ibid., p. 92.

141. Ibid., pp. 95, 104.

142. Ibid., pp. 59–61.

143. Ibid., p. 115.

144. Ibid., pp. 294, 295, 297.

145. *Sr*, p. 26.

146. Ibid., pp. 26–28.

147. Ibid., p. 28.

148. Girard, *Desire*, p. 300.

149. *Sr*, p. 33.

150. Ibid., pp. 31–32.

151. Ibid., p. 36.

152. Ibid., p. 40.

153. Ibid., p. 45.

154. Ibid., p. 48 n. 1.

155. Ibid., p. 54.

156. Ibid., pp. 49–50.

157. Ibid., pp. 61–62.

158. Ibid., pp. 62–63, 84.

159. Ibid., p. 195, n. 1.

160. Ibid., pp. 195–96.

161. Ibid., p. 157 n. 1 and accompanying text.

162. Ibid., p. 96.

163. Ibid., p. 84.

164. Ibid., pp. 157–60.

165. "Dialogue," p. 3.

166. Ibid.

167. *Sr*, pp. 176, 178.

168. Ibid., pp. 185–86.

169. Ibid., p. 187.

170. See Robert Sayre, "Goldmann and Modern Realism: Introduction to *The Balcony* Article," *Praxis* 2, no. 4 (1978): p. 117.

171. *Sr*, p. 324.

172. Ibid., p. 283.

173. Ibid., pp. 287–88.

174. Ibid., p. 287.

175. Ibid., p. 301.

176. In "Décrire, comprendre et expliquer," p. 66. Heller's comments were made in German and translated by Goldmann into the French that appears on the typescript.

177. Lucien Goldmann, Comments on Agnès Heller's "Sur l'aesthetique de Georg Lukács," in "Décrire, comprendre et expliquer," pp. 32–33.

178. Lucien Goldmann, "Genet, Sartre, Gombrowicz" (unpublished typescript, signed July 1968, EHESS), pp. 1, 44.

179. Ibid., p. 27.

180. Lukács to Goldmann, October 1, 1959, Lukács Archives; Goldmann to Lukács, October 14, 1959, Lukács Archives.

181. Lucien Goldmann, "Genet's *The Balcony*: A Realist Play," *Praxis* 2, no. 4 (1978): p. 123.

182. Goldmann, "Genet's *The Balcony*," p. 123.

183. Goldmann, "Sartre, Genet, Gombrowicz," p. 36. See also Goldmann's "Le Théâtre de Gombrowicz" and "A propos d'Operette de Gombrowicz," both in *Sm*. Gombrowicz's comment is in a letter he sent to Goldmann, December 17, 1966, AGA.

184. Lucien Goldmann, "Le Théâtre de Genet," in *Sociologie de la littérature. Rechereches récentes et discussions*, 2d ed. (Brussels: Editions de l'Université de

Bruxelles, 1973), pp. 27–28. This was originally a paper presented at a conference in Cologne in 1966 and published in *Les Cahiers de la Compagnie Madelene Renaud—Jean-Louis Barrault* 57, November 1966.

185. Goldmann, "Le Théâtre de Genet," p. 34.

Chapter 7

1. Lucien Goldmann, "L'esthétique de jeune Lukács," in *Msh*, p. 228. Goldmann writes that *Soul and Forms* was "the true foundation of the modern philosophy of existence." See "LH,"p. 215.

2. Lucien Goldmann, "Présentation," in *Kv*, p. 127.

3. Ibid., pp. 130–31.

4. Ibid., pp. 128–29.

5. Georg Lukács, *Existentialisme ou marxisme?* (Paris: Editions Nagel, [1948] 1961), p. 84.

6. Goldmann's former student, Michel Löwy, has argued, persuasively in my view, that this claim is misplaced. Rather than intimating the crisis, Lukács's agony was rooted in his hatred of the stability, however illusory, of the immediate prewar period. His aesthetic-philosophical idealism—and absolutism—was therefore rooted first and foremost in his unrealizable romantic anticapitalism, as opposed to anticipation of crisis and war. See Michel Löwy, "Goldmann et Lukács: La Vision du monde tragique," in *Sg*.

7. Georg Lukács, *SF*, pp. 28, 31, 36, 40. I have used the standard English translation rather than translating into English Goldmann's translation of German into French in his "Présentation."

8. Goldmann, "Présentation," pp. 131–32.

9. *LH*, p. 114.

10. Goldmann, "Présentation," p. 147.

11. Ibid., pp. 148–49.

12. *LH* was edited and published posthumously in 1973 by Youssef Ishaghpour. Consequently, it is an unfinished and fragmentary, if intriguing, work. It includes an introductory essay that Goldmann wrote the summer before his death and transcripts of his seminars at the École Pratique des Hautes Études during 1967 and 1968. For a valuable discussion of Goldmann on Lukács and Heidegger, see Ishaghpour, "Avant-propos," in *LH*. Unfortunately, this essay was eliminated from the English translation.

13. "LH," p. 217 esp. n. 1.

14. Lukács to Benseler, June 3, 1962, Lukács Archives.

15. Georg Lukács, "Preface to the New Edition (1967)," in *HCC*, p. xxii.

16. Jean-Michel Palmier, "Tragique et finitude chez Lukács et Heidegger: Quelques remarques sur l'interprétation de Lucien Goldmann," in *Sg*, p. 247 n. 2.

17. See Emmanuel Levinas, *The Theory of Intuition in Husserl's Phenomenology* (Evanston, Ill.: Northwestern University Press, 1973), pp. xxxv, 12, 20.

18. *LH*, p. 60.

19. Ibid., pp. 60–61.

20. Ibid., p. 63.

21. Ibid., pp. 65–66.

22. Ibid., p. 67.

23. Ibid.

24. Since my concern is Goldmann's interpretation of Heidegger rather than Heidegger himself, I have generally avoided disputes about interpreting Heidegger. One exception is necessary, however. Ernest Joos, in *Lukács's Last Auto-critique: The Ontology* (Atlantic Highlands, N.J.: Humanities Press, 1983), declares that "as a teacher" he "cannot decline . . . the obligation to oversee Goldmann's teaching with regard to Lukács and his relation to Heidegger" (p. 79). Taking many of Goldmann's statements out of context and ignoring the unfinished nature of *LH*, Joos insists that Goldmann saw only similarities between Lukács and Heidegger. This allows him to state that the differences between them are "irreconcilable" (p. 91), cannot be viewed under a common rubric, and are therefore fruitlessly compared. Goldmann's real purpose must have been "to embellish Lukács's role in the shaping of Western intellectual history" (pp. 96–97). Joos misconceives entirely Goldmann's method and purposes. In the first place, Goldmann is quite clear: the thought of Lukács and Heidegger is "homologous and related, with fundamental differences of orientation which return on the level of every problem. Their perspectives are different and must not, in any case, be confused"(*LH*, p. 120). Goldmann aims not to identify Lukács and Heidegger, but to fashion a structural homology between their systems of thought and to trace it genetically. Moreover, Joos's accusation of "embellishment" ignores Goldmann's initial presentation of these ideas in the "LH" of 1944, when neither Lukács or Heidegger was in the intellectual headlines. Indeed, given Heidegger's behavior during World War II, his name could hardly have embellished anyone at the time. As Joos cites the original French edition of *LH*, and since the opening sentence of Ishaghpour's "Avant-propos" to it points to the 1944 essay, Joos cannot feign ignorance of the earlier text. Goldmann's purpose was not to "reconcile" Lukács and Heidegger. As Ishaghpour notes, it was to engage in a dialogue, primarily with Lukács, whose concepts are significantly modified by Goldmann or, on the political level, rejected outright. To rebut Goldmann's "embellishment" of Lukács, Joos argues that "the apolitical nature of Heidegger's philosophy makes for a kind of universality in its application that Lukács's politically oriented writings lack from the very beginning." Considering the importance of Lukács's pre-Marxist writings for Goldmann's argument, such as the decidedly apolitical *Soul and the Forms*, together with Goldmann's substantial criticisms of the politics of *History and Class Consciousness*, and considering the ample debates since the 1940s over the relation between Heidegger's philosophy and his Nazi affiliation, Joos's characterization of Heidegger is at least open to debate.

25. *LH*, p. 75.

26. Martin Heidegger, "What Is Metaphysics?" in *Basic Writings* (New York: Harper and Row, 1977), p. 112.

27. Martin Heidegger, *Being and Time* (New York and Evanston, Ill.: Harper and Row, 1962), p. 167.

28. *LH*, p. 71.

29. Ibid., pp. 106–7.

30. Ibid., p. 73.

31. The two passages to which Goldmann points in *Being and Time* read as follows:

"One of the first tasks will be to show that to begin research by starting from the immediately given Me and the subject, is to miss the phenomenal aspect of *Dasein*. Any idea of the subject, if it is not based upon a fundamental ontology, falls into this ontological error of the subject, no matter what the effort is to defend it on the ontic level against the 'substance of the soul' and the 'reification of consciousness.' First, reification must be ontologically justified for one to be able to speculate about what one positively comprehends when a non-reified being of the subject, the soul, the consciousness, the person, etc." (*Being and Time*, p. 72).

"That past ontology worked with the concept of things and that the danger of the reification of consciousness exists has been known for a long time. But what does reification mean? What is its origin? Why is being understood, above all, by starting from what is there [*Vorhanden*], what is given, and not from instrumentality (*Zuhanden*), which is nevertheless nearer? Why does this reification continuously predominate? What is the positive structure of consciousness which sees to it that reification is not adequate for it? Does the distinction between consciousness and thing suffice to pose the ontological problematic? Are the answers to these questions forthcoming? Can one even seek an answer as long as the question about the meaning of Being is not posed or clarified?" (*Being and Time*, p. 487).

32. *LH*, p. 73.

33. Ibid., p. 95.

34. Ibid., pp. 96–98.

35. Ibid., p. 103.

36. Ibid., p. 104.

37. Ibid., p. 118. Goldmann uses *être-pour-la-mort* for Heidegger's *Sein zum Tode* and *être-avec* for *Mitsein*.

38. Ibid., pp. 77–78. I paraphrase Goldmann's presentation.

39. Ibid., p. 78. Heidegger would not have accepted Goldmann's claim either. During a seminar in which both were participants, Goldmann took Heidegger to task "violently" for the latter's embrace of Nazism. According to one observer, "Heidegger responded serenely and very precisely that his work had nothing in common with national socialism. Many of us dreaded that the session would turn prickly, but this was not the case because even Goldmann, who openly presented himself as Heidegger's detractor, was impressed by the art of his interpreter. . . . " Walter Biemel, "Le Professeur, le penseur, l'ami," in *Martin Heidegger* (Paris: Les Cahiers de l'heure, 1983), p. 135.

40. Lucien Goldmann, "En Cours d'élimination," a contribution to a symposium on "L'Existentialisme vingt ans après," in *Arts*, March 23–29, 1966, p. 10.

41. "Structuralisme, marxisme, existentialisme: Un Entretien avec Lucien Goldmann," by Iliga Bojovic, *L'Homme et la société* 2 (October–December 1966): pp. 117–18.

42. Pierre Furter, "La Pensée de Georges Lukács en France," *Revue de théolo-*

gie et de Philosophie, 1961, no. 4, p. 353. Goldmann's article, "Georg Lukács, L'essayiste," is reprinted in *Rd,* having originally appeared in *Revue d'esthétique,* 1950, no. 1.

43. See in particular "Une Protestation de G. Lukács," *Arguments* 1, no. 3 (April–May 1957), and "Une Déclaration de G. Lukács concernant l'Édition Française d'*Histoire et conscience de classe, Arguments,* no. 20, 4e trimestre 1960.

44. See *Combat,* January 13, 20, February 3, 1949; and Georg Lukács, *Existentialisme ou marxisme?* (Paris: Editions Nagel, [1949] 1961), p. 19.

45. Lukács, *Existentialisme ou marxisme?* pp. 13–15, 17.

46. Jean-Paul Sartre, "A More Precise Characterization of Existentialism," in *Selected Prose Writings of Jean-Paul Sartre,* Vol. 2 (Evanston, Ill.: Northwestern University Press, 1974), p. 159, translation of "A Propos de l'existentialisme: Mise au point," *Action,* December 29, 1944, p. 11. This was a response to Communist attacks on Sartre shortly after World War II.

47. Jean-Paul Sartre, *Search for a Method* (New York: Vintage Books, 1963), pp. xxxiv, 8, 21–22.

48. Ibid., pp. 21–23.

49. Ibid., pp. 12, 16, 14.

50. Ibid., p. 79.

51. Ibid., p. 28.

52. Ibid., pp. 27, 83.

53. Ibid., pp. 57, 53.

54. Ibid., p. 56.

55. Ibid., p. 61.

56. Jean-Paul Sartre, *The Family Idiot,* Vol. 1. (Chicago and London: University of Chicago Press, 1971), p. ix. See also *id.,* "L'Universal singulier," in *Kv.*

57. Ibid., pp. 32, 76.

58. Ibid., p. 51 n. 8. Lefebvre himself expressed astonishment that this method was attributed to him, claiming that it was simply Marx's method. See Remi Hess, *Henri Lefebvre et l'aventure du siècle* (Paris: Éditions A. M. Metailie, 1988), p. 192.

59. Hess, *Henri Lefebvre,* pp. 51–52 n. 8.

60. Ibid., p. 153.

61. Ibid., p. 154.

62. Ibid., p. 83.

63. Ibid., pp. 125, 124, 130, 115.

64. Ibid., p. 89.

65. Ibid., p. 76.

66. Raymond Aron, *Marxismes imaginaires: D'un sainte famille à l'autre* (Paris: Gallimard, 1970), p. 45. Lukács's argument is on page 7 of *Existentialisme ou marxisme.* In the republication of this book in 1961, Lukács declared that he had not changed his view of existentialism, although he noted that Sartre had done so by turning to Marxism.

67. Jean-Paul Sartre, "For a Theatre of Situations," in *Sartre on Theater* (New York: Pantheon Books, 1976), p. 3.

68. Ibid., p. 5.

69. Goldmann, "Sartre, Genet, Gombrowicz," p. 25 n. 2.

70. Lucien Goldmann, "Jean-Paul Sartre, *Question de méthode*," in *Msh*, p. 243.

71. *Dc*, pp. 43, 337.

72. *HCC*, p. 43.

73. "Self-Portrait at Seventy," interview with Jean-Paul Sartre by Michel Contat, in *Life/Situations* (New York: Pantheon Books, 1977), pp. 84–85. Originally in *Le Nouvel Observateur*, June 23, 30, July 7, 1975.

74. In an article entitled "Connaissance de Sartre," Collette Audry says that Sartre described the play he was planning to write as being about a destitute refugee couple debating whether the wife should have an abortion. The husband advocates the abortion on the grounds that the child will live a poverty-stricken life, but the wife demurs. A supernatural character lets them see the child's future, which is, indeed, miserable. Nonetheless, the wife prevails, wagering, "He'll pull through alright and that he'll transform his life, however wretched it is." In the second act, the child is grown; he lives and dies in affliction, but by his own "contribution"—his choices and free acts—he makes his woeful life "sublime." See *The Writings of Jean-Paul Sartre*, Vol. 1, *A Biographical Life*, compiled by Michel Contat and Michel Rybalka (Evanston, Ill.: Northwestern University Press, 1974), pp. 319–21.

75. Goldmann, "Genet, Sartre, Gombrowicz," p. 12.

76. Lucien Goldmann, "The Theater of Sartre," *Drama Review* 15 (Fall 1970): p. 104. In French, see, "Problèmes philosophiques et politiques dans le théâtre de Jean-Paul Sartre. L'itineraire d'un penseur," in *Sm*.

77. Goldmann, "Sartre, Genet, Gombrowicz," pp. 11–12.

78. Ibid., pp. 15–17, 21.

79. Goldmann, "Jean-Paul Sartre, *Question de méthode*," p. 246.

80. Sartre, *Search for a Method*, p. 111.

81. Lucien Goldmann, "Sartre's Theater," p. 116.

82. Goldmann, "Jean-Paul Sartre, *Question de méthode*," p. 251.

83. Ibid., p. 253.

84. Ibid., p. 255.

85. Ibid., p. 249 n. 1.

86. Thomas R. Flynn, *Sartre and Marxist Existentialism* (Chicago and London: University of Chicago Press, 1984), pp. 86, 90.

87. *LH*, p. 123.

88. "Structuralisme, marxisme, existentialisme," p. 117.

89. Sartre, "L'Universal singulier," p. 63.

90. Goldmann, "Jean-Paul Sartre, *Question de méthode*," p. 250.

91. Ibid., p. 257.

92. Ibid., pp. 255–56.

93. Ibid., p. 256 n. 1.

94. Sartre, *Family Idiot*, Vol. 1, p. ix.

95. Jean-Paul Sartre to Lucien Goldmann, September 5, 1970. Goldmann sent the articles, which included both the study of *Question de méthode* and the essay on Sartre's theater, with a brief cover letter dated September 2, 1970. Both letters in AGA.

96. *LH*, p. 122.

97. Lucien Goldmann, Comments at Deuxième séance de table ronde, in *Kv*, pp. 267–68.

98. Ibid., p. 272.

99. Ibid., pp. 274–75.

100. J. Havet, Comments at Deuxième séance de table ronde," in *Kv*, pp. 269–70.

101. *LH*, p. 125.

102. Ibid., p. 129.

103. Ibid.

104. Ibid., p. 130.

105. Goldmann, Comments at Deuxième Séance, p. 294.

106. Lucien Goldmann interviewed by Jasmina Alic, "Filosofski Angazman i Angazovanje Filozofa" (The Commitment of Philosophers and Committed Philosophy), *Lica* (Sarajeva, July–September 1969). I have used the typescript of the French version at EHESS, p. 4.

107. J. G. Meriquor, *From Prague to Paris: A Critique of Structuralist and Post-Structuralist Thought* (London: Verso, 1986), p. 2.

108. Claude Lévi-Strauss, *Tristes tropiques* (New York: Pocket Books, 1977), p. 50.

109. Claude Lévi-Strauss, *Structural Anthropology* (New York: Basic Books, 1962), p. 83.

110. Ibid., p. 33.

111. Ibid., p. 83.

112. Lévi-Strauss, *Tristes tropiques*, pp. 446–47, and p. 466. This is a highly selective use of Rousseau, who, in an important footnote to the *Discourse on the Origins of Inequality*, explicitly stated that humans could not return to life in the woods "with the bears" because the processes of civilization had thoroughly destroyed their "original simplicity." Rousseau's portrait of human development is anything but a story of repetition, and he insists on how different the people of his age are from "savages." Lévi-Strauss's parallel is tenuous at best. See Jean-Jacques Rousseau, *The Social Contract and the Discourse on the Origin of Inequality* (reprint, New York: Washington Square Press, 1973), p. 253.

113. Lévi-Strauss, *Structural Anthropology*, p. 83.

114. Saussure, quoted in Jonathan Culler, *Ferdinand de Saussure* (Ithaca, N.Y.: Cornell University Press, 1986), p. 38. In this summary, I have relied significantly on, and occasionally paraphrase, Culler's lucid account.

115. See Culler, pp. 104–7.

116. Claude Lévi-Strauss, *The Savage Mind* (Chicago: University of Chicago Press, 1966), p. 256.

117. Lévi-Strauss, *Tristes tropiques*, p. 93.

118. Lévi-Strauss, *Savage Mind*, p. 247.

119. Ibid., p. 252.

120. Lévi-Strauss, *Tristes tropiques*, p. 472.

121. Ibid., pp. 12–13.

122. Michel Foucault, *The Order of Things* (New York: Vintage Books, 1973), pp. xiv, xi–xii, 298.

123. Ibid., p. xx.

124. Ibid., pp. 35, 43.

125. Ibid., p. 318.

126. Ibid., pp. 56–57.

127. Ibid., pp. 308–9.

128. Ibid., p. 304.

129. Ibid., p. xiii.

130. Gaston Bachelard, *The New Scientific Spirit* (Boston: Beacon Press, 1984), p. 172.

131. Ibid., p. 60.

132. Louis Althusser, *For Marx* (Middlesex: Penguin Books, 1969), pp. 12–13.

133. Quoted in Arthur Hirsch, *The French New Left: An Intellectual History from Sartre to Gorz* (Boston: South End Press, 1981), p. 171.

134. Althusser, *For Marx*, p. 229.

135. Ibid., p. 166.

136. Ibid., p. 223.

137. Louis Althusser, in Louis Althusser and Etienne Balibar, *Reading Capital* (London: New Left Books, 1977), p. 75.

138. Althusser, *For Marx*, pp. 203–4.

139. Michel Foucault, *The Archaeology of Knowledge* (New York: Pantheon Books, 1972), p. 11

140. *Shp*, p. 19.

141. Lévi-Strauss, *Tristes tropiques*, p. 50.

142. Lucien Goldmann to Roman Jakobson, June 4, 1969, AGA.

143. Hegel, *Phenomenology*, p. 69.

144. Lucien Goldmann, "Pensée dialectique et sujet transindividuel," in *Cc*, pp. 141–42.

145. Lucien Goldmann, Preface to *Sm*, p. xv.

146. *LH*, p. 103.

147. Lucien Goldmann to Roman Jakobson, June 4, 1969. Jakobson's letter to Goldmann is dated May 28, 1969. Both in AGA. Goldmann sent an analysis of Baudelaire's "Les Chats" to Jakobson, whose own discussion of it is a classic of structuralist analysis in literature. In his reply, Jakobson wrote that he saw his own perspective as complementary and not necessarily hostile to Goldmann's.

148. Lévi-Strauss, quoted in Goldmann, "Pensée dialectique," pp. 129–130.

149. Ibid., pp. 130–131.

150. See Discussion of Michel Foucault, "Qu'est ce qu'un auteur?" in *Bulletin de la société française de philosophie*, (July–September 1969), pp. 96–103.

151. *LH*, p. 166.

152. Goldmann, Comments at Deuxième séance," p. 275.

153. Lucien Goldmann, "Reponse à Elsberg et Jones," *Sociologie de la littérature: Recherches récentes et discussions*, 2d ed. (Bruxelles: Editions de l'Université de Bruxelles, 1973), p. 216.

154. Lucien Goldmann, "Ideologie et marxisme," *Epp*, pp. 150–51.

155. At the École Pratique des Hautes Études, recorded by Michel Löwy. See "A Propos de *Grundrisse*," in Sami Naïr and Michel Löwy, *Lucien Goldmann ou la dialectique de la totalité* (Paris: Éditions Seghers, 1973), p. 157.

156. Goldmann avoided using the word "alienation" and preferred to follow Lukács in speaking of "reification." He explained that "alienation" seemed to him a "very vague [term] and . . . everyone designates something different [by it]—usually something I don't like." Still, "this said, I believe we speak of alienation every time that in a given society, in given social conditions, there is a fundamental rupture between the needs of man . . . for clear consciousness, for a comprehension of happiness, for authentic community with other men, and concrete conditions in which he lives." "Structuralisme, marxisme, existentialisme," *L'Homme et la société*, October–December 1966, p. 111.

157. Ibid.

158. Lucien Goldmann, Discussion following his presentation of "Philosophie et scientisme," in *Chacun peut-il philosophe?* 9e Conference-débat de Cercle Ouvert (Paris: La Nef, 1957), p. 57.

159. Ibid., p. 17.

160. Goldmann, "Structuralisme, marxisme, existentialisme," p. 110.

161. Goldmann, like Sartre, did have an important influence on the early work of one Marxist who was to become a central figure in structuralist Marxism, Nicos Poulantzas. See Poulantzas's use of the concept of worldview in *Nature des choses et droit: Essai sur la dialectique du fait et de la valeur* (Paris: Bibliothéque de Philosophie du Droit, 1965), esp. pp. 172–85, 212–15, 296–97.

162. Goldmann to Jakobson, June 4, 1969, AGA.

163. Lucien Goldmann, "La Révolte des lettres et des arts dans les civilisations avanceés," in *Cc*, p. 60.

164. Lucien Goldmann, "L'Epistémologie de la sociologie," in *Epp*, p. 46.

165. Lucien Goldmann, "Le Sujet de la création culturelle," in *Msh*, pp. 95–97.

166. Lucien Goldmann, "Propos dialectiques," in *Rd*, p. 268.

167. Goldmann, "Le Sujet de création culturelle," p. 101.

168. Lucien Goldmann, "Génése et structure," in *Msh*, p. 24.

169. They are elaborated most extensively in "Ideologie et marxisme," in *Msh*, and in "Reflections on *History and Class Consciousness*," in I. Mészáros, ed., *Aspects of History and Class Consciousness*.

170. Goldmann, "Reflections on *History and Class Consciousness*," p. 66.

Chapter 8

1. Lucien Goldmann, "Projet pour un ouvrage intitule *Philosophie et politique*" (Unpublished typescript, AGA), p. 1.

2. *Ipk*, p. 309.

3. Ibid., pp. 60–61.

4. *Dc*, p. 202.

5. Lucien Goldmann, "Le matérialisme dialectique est-il une philosophie?" in *Rd*, p. 18.

6. *Ipk*, p. 64.

7. Ibid., p. 64.

8. Immanuel Kant, *The Critique of Judgement*, J. W. Meredith, trans. (Oxford: Oxford University Press, 1980), p. 82. See also ibid., pp. 53–60.

9. *Shp*, p. 133.

10. Ibid.

11. Goldmann is inconsistent in placing Hegel within these categories. In *The Human Sciences and Philosophy* he identified Hegel's Objective Spirit as an example of the first idea of emanatism, a position that brings him close to Althusser's later argument on expressive totality. In *Kant*, however, Goldmann generally places Hegel with the representatives of the vision of "the person *and* the community." The latter is consistent with his objections to Althusser's views on Hegel and Marx. See *Shp*, pp. 132–33; and *Ipk*, p. 133.

12. *Shp*, p. 133.

13. *Ipk*, p. 160.

14. *Sr*, p. 37.

15. Ibid., p. 38.

16. Lucien Goldmann, "Civilisation et economie," in *L'histoire et ses interprétations*, p. 83.

17. Goldmann, "La Réification," in *Rd*, p. 89.

18. Ibid., p. 68.

19. Ibid., p. 102.

20. Ibid., p. 73.

21. "LH," pp. 217–18.

22. Gorz and Goldmann only met twice, and while the latter cited the former frequently, Gorz never read Goldmann's work. Interview with André Gorz, Paris, June 18, 1980.

23. Lucien Goldmann, "Lumières et dialectique," in *Epp*, p. 74; Interview with Annie Goldmann, Paris, June 25, 1980.

24. Interview with André Gorz, Paris, June 18, 1980.

25. *LH*, p. 164.

26. Lucien Goldmann, "La Démocratie économique et la création culturelle," in *Epp*, p. 218.

27. Lucien Goldmann, "Réification et créativité—planification et liberté" (unpublished lecture given at Korçula, Yugoslavia, 1967, EHESS), pp. 8–9.

28. Lucien Goldmann, Untitled paper prepared for Conference à la Societé Française de Sociologie, March 23, 1969, EHESS, pp. 5–6.

29. Goldmann's views on imperialism are especially indebted to Fritz Sternberg. See Goldmann's "Un Bilan desabusé. A propos de Fritz Sternberg: *Kapitalismus und Sozialismus vor dem Weltgericht: Marx und die Gegenwart*," *Arguments* 1 (February–March 1957); and his "Problèmes de théorie critique de l'économie," in *Rd*.

30. *Sr*, pp. 90–91.

31. Lucien Goldmann, "Naissance d'un monde" (unpublished typescript, June 15, 1968, EHESS), p. 14.

32. *LH*, p. 129.

33. Lucien Goldmann, "De la rigueur et de l'imagination dans la pensée socialiste," in *Msh*, p. 318.

34. Goldmann, "Naissance d'un monde," pp. 14–15.

35. Lucien Goldmann, Untitled paper prepared for Conference à la Societé Française de Sociologie, March 23, 1969, EHESS, pp. 6–7.

36. *LH*, p. 136.

37. Ibid., p. 133.

38. Ibid., p. 124,

39. See Goldman "De la rigueur," pp. 323–24.

40. Lucien Goldmann "La Révolte des lettres et des arts dans les civilisations," in *Cc*, p. 54.

41. Lucien Goldmann interviewed by Lorenzo Batallon, "El Gran Problema de la Sociedad Contemporanea Es el Humanismo Amenazado por la Technocracia?" *El Nacional* (Caracas), November 1, 1964; and "Pouvoir et humanisme," in *Msh*, p. 349.

42. *Rd*, p. 66.

43. Ibid., p. 64 n. 1 and p. 68.

44. See *Rd*, p. 70 n. 1.

45. Ibid., p. 99.

46. Ibid., pp. 101, 103.

47. Ibid., p. 104.

48. "De la rigueur," *Msh*, p. 325.

49. Lucien Goldmann, "Premessa a 'La reificazione,'" *Ideologie* 8 (1969). I quote from the unpublished French typescript version at EHESS, p. 3.

50. *Sr*, pp. 33–44. What he refers to as the "traditional sociological model" appears to be his own theory.

51. For overviews of the debate, see George Ross, "Marxism and the New Middle Classes: French Critiques," *Theory and Society* 5 (March 1978), and Mark Poster, *Existential Marxism in Postwar France* (Princeton: Princeton University Press, 1975), pp. 362–70.

52. André Gorz, *Strategy for Labor* (Boston: Beacon Press, 1967), p. x.

53. Goldmann, in Lucien Goldmann, Serge Mallet, et al., "Débat sur l'autogestion," in *Autogestion: Études débats, documents*, Cahier 7 (December 1968), p. 60.

54. Goldmann, "Reflections on *History and Class Consciousness*," p. 81.

55. Lucien Goldmann, "Pourquoi les étudiants?" in *L'Homme et la société* 8 (1968): p. 8.

56. Goldmann, "Reflections on *History and Class Consciousness*," p. 81.

57. *LH*, p. 111.

58. See Goldmann's "Pour une approche Marxiste des études sur le Marxisme," in *Msh*, pp. 224–25.

59. Lucien Goldmann, "Annexe au Protocole: Projet de Film sur l'Autogestion" (Typescript, EHESS), pp. 1–2.

60. Lucien Goldmann, "La Philosophie des lumières," in *Sm*, p. 218; id., "Économie et sociologie: À propos du Traité d'Économie politique d'Oscar Lange," in *Msh*, p. 218.

61. Goldmann, "Débat sur l'Autogestion," p. 90.

62. Goldmann, "Economie et sociologie," pp. 213–16.

63. Goldmann, "La Philosophie des lumières," p. 124.

64. Goldmann, "Débat sur l'autogestion," p. 59.

65. Ibid., p. 67.

66. Ibid., pp. 67–68.

67. Ibid., pp. 68–69.

68. Ibid., p. 69.

69. Ibid., pp. 70, 67.

70. Lucien Goldmann, "Projet d'un film," pp. 1–3. In the text, in addition to quoting directly, I paraphrase and summarize Goldmann's presentation.

71. Goldmann's unpublished notes, "Korçula 1968" (typescript, EHESS), p. 5; and "Declaration of the Editorial Committee of the Review *Praxis*," *Praxis*, no. 2, (1968): pp. 465–67.

72. See Alain Schnapp and Pierre Vidal-Naquet, eds., *The French Student Uprising: November 1967—June 1968* (Boston: Beacon Press, 1971), pp. 495–96.

73. Goldmann, Unpublished notes, "Korçula, 1968," p. 4.

74. Lucien Goldmann, "Étudiants et société," (typescript, EHESS), pp. 8–12.

75. Goldmann, "Naissance d'un monde," p. 1.

76. Lucien Goldmann to Frank Benseler, July 24, 1968, AGA.

77. Lucien Goldmann, "Révolution et bureaucratie," *L'Homme et la société* 21 (July–September 1969): p. 79.

78. Lucien Goldmann, "Eppur si muove," in *Power and Humanism* (Nottingham: Bertrand Russell Peace Foundation, 1970), pp. 50–51.

79. Lucien Goldmann, Préface to *Msh*, pp. 50–51.

80. See ibid., p. 10; and Sami Naïr's reporting of statements by Goldmann to his students in Naïr's "Goldmann's Legacy," *Telos* 48 (Summer 1981): p. 147.

81. Lucien Goldmann, Comments on Agnès Heller's "Sur L'aesthetique de Georges Lukács," in "Décrire, comprendre, et expliquer" (unpublished proceedings of the *IIIe Colloque Internationale de Sociologie de la Littérature, Royaument, January 1968, EHESS), pp. 33–34*.

82. Lucien Goldmann, "Ideologie et marxisme," in *Epp*, p. 135.

83. Maximilien Rubel, "Mise au point non dialectique," *Les Temps modernes* 142 (December 1957): p. 1140. Rubel was responding to Goldmann's criticisms of his recent book, *Karl Marx*, in *Les Temps modernes* two months earlier. Goldmann's essay, "Y a-t-il une sociologie marxiste," is reprinted in *Rd*.

84. Goldmann, "Débat sur l'autogestion," p. 66.

85. Goldmann, "La Réification," p. 104.

86. Goldmann, "Économie et sociologie, p. 218.

87. Lucien Goldmann, Discussion in *L'Histoire et ses interprétations: Entretiens autour de Arnold Toynbee sous la direction de Raymond Aron* (Paris and the Hague: Mouton and Co., 1961), p. 139.

88. Goldmann, "La Réification," p. 91 n 1.

89. See *Dc*, pp. 99, 193 n. 1, 295, 244–45.

90. Havet, Comments at Deuxième séance, pp. 269–70.

91. Goldmann, "Projet pour une ouvrage," p. 1; Goldmann to Madeleine Duclos, 1945, personal archive of Madeleine Duclos-Garepuy.

Chapter 9

1. "Propos dialectiques," in *Rd*, p. 261. The "partisan" metaphor was originated by Lukács.

2. Discussion in *Hérésies et sociétés dans l'Europe préindustrielle XIe–XVIIe siècles*. Proceedings of colloquium at Royaument edited by Jacques le Goff (Paris and the Hague: Mouton and Co., 1968), p. 15.

3. Goldmann was concurring with Theodor Adorno's statement that when one overvalued method and failed to make it functional to the object, one succumbed to the "general tendency" of our times "to substitute means for ends." "Décrire, comprendre et expliquer," pp. 297/9 (Goldmann) and 297/1 (Adorno). For a partial translation into English of the exchange between Goldmann and Adorno, see appendix 3 to Lucien Goldmann, *Cultural Creation in Modern Society* (St. Louis: Telos Press, 1977), pp. 131–47. Lukács's statement is in *GK*, p. 59.

4. He writes: "In truth, all concepts, even philosophical ones, refer to nonconceptualities, because concepts on their part are moments of the reality that requires their formation, primarily for control of nature. What conceptualization appears to be from within, to one engaged in it—the predominance of its sphere without which nothing is known—must not be mistaken for what it is in itself." Theodor Adorno, *Negative Dialectics* (New York: Seabury Press, 1977), p. 11.

5. Ibid., pp. 11–12.

6. Theodor Adorno, *Minima Moralia* (London: New Left Books, 1974), p. 50.

7. Adorno, *Negative Dialectics*, p. 2.

8. Theodor Adorno, *Aesthetic Theory* (London and New York: Routledge and Kegan Paul, 1984), pp. 122–23.

9. Richard Wolin, "Mimesis, Utopia and Reconciliation: A Redemptive Critique of Adorno's *Aesthetic Theory*," in Wolin, *The Terms of Cultural Criticism* (New York: Columbia University Press, 1992), p. 75.

10. *TN*, p. 22. The statement is in the new preface for the book's republication, but Lukács cites his own earlier use of the metaphor of the "Hotel Abyss" in his discussion of Schopenhauer in *The Destruction of Reason* (London: Merlin Press, 1980), p. 243.

11. Adorno, *Aesthetic Theory*, pp. 475–76, 396, 398.

12. "Décrire, comprendre et expliquer," pp. 297/2–4; *Aesthetic Theory*, p. 475.

13. Ibid., pp. 297/30, 5, 31.

14. Ibid., p. 297/35.

15. Ibid., p. 297/9.

16. Ibid., pp. 297/10–11, 23, 12–13.

17. Ibid., p. 297/14.

18. Ibid., pp. 15–16.

19. Ibid., p. 297/17.

20. Ibid., p. 297/19.

21. Thody's translation in *HG*, p. 184.

22. Lucien Goldmann, "Critique et dogmatisme dans la création littéraire," in *Msh*, p. 46. The lecture was at a conference in London on "The Dialectics of Liberation."

23. Didier Eribon, *Michel Foucault* (Cambridge, Mass.: Harvard University Press, 1991), pp. 136, 164.

24. For the Foucault quote, see James Miller, *The Passion of Michel Foucault* (New York: Simon and Schuster, 1993), p. 172.

25. "The City of Yes and the City of No" (1964), in *Yevtushenko: The Collected Poems, 1952–1990* (New York: Henry Holt and Co., 1991), pp. 154–55.

Select Bibliography _____

THIS BIBLIOGRAPHY IS DIVIDED into two parts. The first covers primary materials and is subdivided into books and articles by Goldmann or edited by him, collections published under Goldmann's direction and interviews with Goldmann and discussions and symposia in which he participated. The second part of the bibliography covers secondary materials. Goldmann's writings are listed in their French versions (in which most of them were originally written and published). In a few cases, works by Goldmann appeared solely in languages other than French and are listed in the original published version. An asterisk indicates that the work was published in a language other than French but I used the unpublished French version on file in the Sociology of Literature section of the Ecole des Hautes Etudes en Sciences Sociales in Paris (EHESS). This is a Select Bibliography, and in constructing it I have made use of three other bibliographies of Goldmann's work: that of Brigitte Navelet and Eduard Tell in *Hommage à Lucien Goldmann. Lucien Goldmann et la sociologie de la littérature* (see below under Secondary Sources); that of Ileana Rodriguez and Marc Zimmerman in the English translation of *La Création culturelle dans la société moderne* (see below under Primary Sources, Books and Articles); and Marc Zimmerman's "Bibliography of Lucien Goldmann," in *A Critical Bibliography of French Literature*, Vol. VI, part 3, edited by Douglas W. Alden and Richard A. Brooks (Syracuse, N.Y.: Syracuse University Press, 1980). For a listing of the English translations of Goldmann's articles, these should be consulted. English translations are listed below only for Goldmann's books.

Primary Sources: The Works of Lucien Goldmann

Books and Articles

"Actualité de la pensée de Karl Marx." *L'Homme et la société*, April, May, June 1967.
"L'Apport de la pensée marxiste à la critique littéraire." *Arguments*, January–March 1959.
"Au sujet du 'plan' des Pensées de Pascal." *Bulletin de la Société d'Étude du XVIIe siècle* 23 (1954).
"Un Bilan désabusé: A propos de Fritz Sternberg: *Kapitalismus und Sozialismus vor dem Weltgericht: Marx und die Gegenwart*." *Arguments*, February–March 1957.
"Civilisation et économie." In *L'Histoire et ses interprétations: Entretiens autour*

de Arnold Toynbee sous la direction de Raymond Aron. Paris and the Hague: Mouton and Co., 1961.

"Conditions de l'interprétation dialectique." In *L'Ambivalance dans la culture Arabe*. Paris: Anthropos, 1967.

"Les conditions sociales et la vision tragique du monde." In *Echanges sociologiques: Cercle de sociologie de la Sorbonne*. Paris: Centre de Documentation Universitaire, 1948.

Correspondance de Martin de Barcos, Abbé de Saint-Cyran editée et presenté par Lucien Goldmann. Paris: Presses Universitaires de France, 1956.

"En Cours d'élimination." *Arts*, March 23–29, 1966.

La Création culturelle dans la société moderne. Paris: Denoël/Gonthier, 1971. Translated into English as *Cultural Creation in Modern Society*. Introduction by William Mayrl. Trans. by B. Grahl. St. Louis: Telos Press, 1976.

"La Critique n'a rien compris." *France-Observateur*, February 6, 1964.

"Débat sur l'autogestion" (with Serge Mallet). *Autogestion*, December 1968.

"La Denuncia sociologica e culturale." In *Participazione, denuncia, escorcismo nel teatro*. Venice: La Biennale di Venezia, l968.*

"Diderot, la pensée des lumières et la dialectique." *Médecine de France* 136 (1962).

Le Dieu caché: Étude sur la vision tragique dans les Pensées de Pascal et dans le théâtre de Racine. Paris: Gallimard, 1959. Translated into English as *The Hidden God: A Study of Tragic Vision in the Pensées of Pascal and the Tragedies of Racine*. Trans. by P. Thody. London and Henley: Routledge and Kegan Paul, 1964.

Epistémologie et philosophie politique: Pour une théorie de la liberté. Paris: Denoël/Gonthier, 1978.

Essays on Method in the Sociology of Literature. Edited and trans. with an introduction by William Q. Boelhower. St. Louis: Telos Press, 1980.

"Être et dialectique." *Les études philosophiques*, April–June 1960.

"Faust de. . . ." *Théâtre populaire* 32 (1958).

The Hidden God. See *Le Dieu caché*.

"L'Hotel du libre-échange de Georges Feydeau et Maurice Desvallières." *Théâtre populaire* 22 (1957).

"Ideology and Writing." *Times Literary Supplement*, September 28, 1967.

"Ces intellectuels sans attache." *Le Nouvel Observateur*, March 11, 1965.

Introduction à la philosophie de Kant. Paris: Gallimard, 1967. This is a new edition, with a new preface, of *La communauté humaine et l'univers chez Kant. Études sur la pensée dialectique et son histoire* (Paris: Presses Universitaires de France, 1948). The latter is a slightly modified translation, with a new preface, of Goldmann's thesis for the University of Zurich, originally published as *Mensch, Gemeinschaft und Welt in der Philosophie Immanuel Kants. Studien zur Geschichte der Dialektik* (Zurich and New York: Europea Verlag, 1945). The 1967 edition in French serves as the basis of the English translation, *Immanuel Kant*, trans. by R. Black (London: New Left Books, 1971).

"Introduction aux premiers écrits de Georg Lukács." *Les Temps modernes*, August 1962.

"Liberté et valeur." In *Atti del XII Congresso Internazional de Filosofia*. Vol. 3, *Liberta e valore?* Florence: Editore Sansoni, 1958.

"Littérature (Sociologie de la)." In *Encyclopaedia Universalis*, Vol. 10. 1971.

"Le Livre et la lecture dans les sociétés industrielles modernes." *Le Drapeau*, October 1965.

"Lukács (György)." In *Encyclopaedia Universalis*, Vol. 10. 1971.

"Lukács et Heidegger." In A. Goldmann, S. Naïr, M. Löwy, et al., *Le Structuralisme génétique*. Paris: Denoël/Gonthier, 1977. This is the French translation of the original appendix to the Swiss (German-language) edition of Goldmann's book on Kant, subsequently dropped from the French and English editions. For an English translation, see "Lukács and Heidegger," *Philosophical Forum*, Fall–Winter 1991–1992.

Lukács et Heidegger. Fragments posthumes établis et présentés par Youssef Ishaghpour. Paris: Denoël/Gonthier, 1973. Translated into English as *Lukács and Heidegger*. Trans. by William Q. Boelhower. London: Henley; Boston: Routledge and Kegan Paul, 1977.

"Lukács et Kierkegaard." In *Kierkegaard vivant*. Paris: Gallimard, 1966. Presentation to UNESCO symposium.

"Marilyn, ce négatif de notre époque." *France-Observateur*, September 6, 1962.

"Marx, Lukács, Girard et la sociologie du roman." *Médiations* 2 (1961).

Marxisme et sciences humaines. Paris: Gallimard, 1976.

Mensch, Gemeinschaft und Welt in der Philosophie Immanuel Kants. See *Introduction à la Philosophie de Kant*.

"La mort d'Adorno." *La Quinzaine littéraire*, September 1–15, 1961.

"Note sur le problème de l'objectivité en sciences sociales." In *Psychologie et épistémologie génétique: Thèmes Piagétiens. Hommage à Jean Piaget avec une bibliographie complète de ses oeuvres*. Paris: Dunod, 1966.

"Pascal et la pensée dialectique." *Empédocle*, January 1950.

"Phèdre . . . et Nathan le Sage." *Théâtre populaire* 38 (1960).

"Philosophie et scientisme," in *Chacun peut-il philosophe?* Proceedings of the Ninth Meeting of the Cercle Ouvert. Paris: La Nef, 1957.

"Une pièce réaliste: *Le Balcon* de Genet." *Les Temps modernes*, June 1960.

"La Place d'Andromaque dans l'oeuvre de Racine." *Cahiers de la Compagnie Madeleine Renaud-Jean Louis Barrault*, November 1962.

"Port Royal d'Henri de Montherlant." *Théâtre populaire*, January–February 1955.

Pour une sociologie du roman. Paris: Gallimard, 1965. Translated into English as *Towards a Sociology of the Novel*. Trans. by A. Sheridan. London: Tavistock Publications Ltd., 1975.

"Pourquoi les étudiants?" *L'Homme et la société*, April, May, June 1968. Roundtable discussion, including Goldmann.

Power and Humanism. Nottingham: Spokesman Books, 1974. A translation of the title essay, originally in Goldmann's *Marxisme et sciences humaines*, with Goldmann's "Eppur si muove," a paper he presented to the Bertrand Russell Peace Foundation Stockholm Conference on Czechoslovakia, February 1969.

Préface to F. Dumont, *La Dialectique de l'objet économique*. Paris: Editions Anthropos, 1970.

Préface to G. Namer, *L'Abbé, Le Roy, et ses amis. Essai sur le Jansénisme extrémiste extra-mondaine*. Paris: SEVPEN, 1964.

"Premessa a 'La reificazione.'" *Ideologie* 8 (1969).*

"Présentation de l'exposition 'Antonio Bueno e Silvio Loffredo alla Galleria G.3O di Parigi." *Eco d'arte*, June 1969.

"Problèmes d'une sociologie du roman." *Cahiers internationaux de sociologie*, January–June 1962.

"Quelques remarques sur la philosophie de Th. W. Adorno." *Allemagne d'aujourd'hui*, November–December 1957.

"La Question religieuse et le socialisme." *Bulletin de la société d'études Jaurèsiennes*, June 1960.

Racine. Paris: L'Arche, 1970. A reprint, with minor deletions, of *Jean Racine, dramaturge* (Paris: L'Arche, 1956). Translated into English as *Racine*. Trans. by A. Hamilton. Introduction by Raymond Williams. Cambridge: Rivers Press Ltd., 1969.

Recherches dialectiques. Paris: Gallimard, 1959.

"Reflections on History and Class Consciousness." In I. Mészáros, ed., *Aspects of History and Class Consciousness*. London: Routledge and Kegan Paul, 1971.

"Remarques sur la théorie de la connaissance." In *Epistémologie/Epistemology: Actes du XIe Congrès International de Philosophie*. Amsterdam: North Holland Publishing Co.; Louvain: E. Nauwelaerts, 1953.

"Romanele Lui N. D. Cocea." *Clopotul*, no. 30, April 13, 1934.

Sciences humaines et philosophie. Paris: Editions Gonthier, 1966. Originally published in 1952 by Presses Universitaires de France. Translated into English as *The Human Sciences and Philosophy*. Trans. by Hayden V. White and Robert Anchor. London: Jonathan Cape, 1969.

Situation de la critique racinienne. Paris: L'Arche, 1971. "Sociologia de la literatura" (with Jacques Leenhardt). *Diario*, May 8, 1968.*

Sociologia Literaturii. Preface by Miron Contantinescu. Introduction by Ion Pascadi. Bucharest: Editura Politică, 1972. Romanian translations of various literary essays.

"Structuralisme génétique et analyse stylistique." In *Linguaggi nella societal nella tecnica*. Milan: Edizioni di communita, 1970.

"Structure: Human Reality and Methodological Concept." In Richard Macksey and Eugenio Donato, eds., *The Structuralist Controversy*. Baltimore: Johns Hopkins Press, 1972.

"Structure de la tragedie racinienne." In Jean Jacquot, ed., *Le Théâtre tragique*. Paris: Éditions du centre nationale de la recherche scientifique, 1962.

Structures mentales et création culturelle. Paris: Éditions Anthropos, 1970. The lengthy opening essay of this collection has been translated as *The Philosophy of the Enlightenment: The Christian Burgess and the Enlightenment*. Cambridge, Mass.: MIT Press, 1973.

"Sujet et objet en sciences humaines." *Raison présente*, January–March 1971.

"Thèses sur l'emploi du concept de vision du monde en histoire de la philosophie." In *L'Homme et l'histoire: Actes du VIe Congrès des sociétés de philosophie de langue française*. Paris: Presses Universitaire de France, 1952.

Weltflucht und Politik: Dialektische Studien zu Pascal und Racine. Neuwied am Rheim and Berlin: Hermann Luchterhand Verlag, 1967. This contains a new article, "Pascal und Port Royal," and translations from *Recherches dialectiques*.

Collections Published under Goldmann's Direction

Critique sociologique et critique psychoanalytique. Brussels: Éditions de l'Université de Bruxelles, 1970.

Littérature et société. Problèmes de methodologie en sociologie de la littérature. Brussels: Éditions de l'Université de Bruxelles, 1967.

Problèmes d'une sociologie du roman. Special issue of *Revue de l'Université Libre de Bruxelles* 2 (1963).

Sociologie de la littérature. Recherches récentes et discussions. 2d ed. Brussels: Editions de l'Université de Bruxelles, 1973.

Interviews and Symposia in Which Goldmann Participated

"Arta si discipline umane." *Romania Literaria*, June 18, 1970. Discussion in *Atti del XII Congresso Internazional de Filosofia*. Vol. 2, *L'uomo e la natura*. Florence: Editore Sansoni, 1960.

Discussion of A. J. Ayer, "La mémoire." *Bulletin de la société française de philosophie*, October–December 1956.

Discussion of Jacques Derrida, "La Différence." *Bulletin de la société française de philosophie*, July–September 1968.

Discussion in colloquium on Descartes. In *Cahiers de Royaument, Philosophie II*. Paris: Les Éditions de Minuit, n.d.

"El grand probleme de la sociedad contemporanea es el humanismo amenazado por la tecnocracia?" *El Nacional*, November 1, 1964.

"Entrevista con Lucien Goldmann." *Zona Franca*, November 1964.

"Filozofski Angazman i Angazovanje Filozofa" (The Commitment of Philosophers and Committed Philosophy). *Lica*, July–September 1969.

Discussion of Michel Foucault, "Qu'est-ce qu'un auteur?" *Bulletin de la société française de philosophie*, July–September 1969.

Discussion of Georges Gursdorf, "Les Sciences humaines et la philosophie." *Bulletin de la société française de philosophie*, July–September 1963.

Discussion of Georges Gurvitch, "Structures sociales et multiplicité des temps." *Bulletin de la société française de philosophie*, July–December 1958.

Discussion in *Hérésies et société dans l'Europe préindustrielle XIe–XVIIe siècles*. Edited by J. Le Goff. Paris and The Hague: Mouton and Co., 1968.

Interview on the Middle East, "Israel-Palestine." April 1970.

Interview, "Revista de la Universidad de Mexico." April 1964.

Discussion in *Littérature et stylistique—Les visages de la critique depuis 1920—Molière, Cahiers de l'Association Internationale des Études Françaises*, March 1964.

Discussion of Gabriel Marcel, "L'Être devant la pensée interrogative." *Bulletin de la société française de philosophie*, January–March 1958.

Discussion in colloquium, *La Philosophie analytique. Cahiers de Royaument, Philosophie IV*. Paris: Editions de Minuit, 1962.

Discussion in *Quel avenir attend l'homme?* Paris: Presses Universitaires de France, 1961.

"Recontre/Lucien Goldmann. Un precurseur de la 'pluridisciplinarité.'" *Le Devoir*, October 4, 1969. An interview/article by Pierre Tadros.

Discussion in "Sociologie de la 'construction nationale' dans les nouveaux états." *Revue de L'institut de sociologie de l'Université Libre de Bruxelles*, nos. 2–3 (1967).

Discussion in *Structuralisme et marxisme*. Introduction by V. Leduc. Paris: Union General d'Editions, 1970. Originally a symposium in February 1968, this includes a lengthy presentation by Goldmann.

"Structuralisme, marxisme, existentialisme: Un Entretien avec Lucien Goldmann." *L'Homme et la société*, October–December, 1966. This is the transcript of an interview with Goldmann for Belgrade Radio-Television. The published French version is incomplete. The full interview, in French, is on file at the EHESS.

Discussion in "Sur les rapports entre la mythologie et le rituel." *Bulletin de la société française de philosophie*, July–September 1956.

Secondary Sources

Adorno, Theodor. *Aesthetic Theory*. London and New York: Routledge and Kegan Paul, 1984.

———. *Negative Dialectics*. New York: Seabury Press, 1973.

———. *Minima Moralia*. London: New Left Books, 1974.

Althusser, Louis. *Essays in Self-Criticism*. London: New Left Books, 1976.

———. *For Marx*. Middlesex: Penguin Books, 1969.

———. *Lenin and Philosophy*. New York and London: Monthly Review Press, 1971.

———, and Etienne Balibar. *Reading Capital*. London: New Left Books, 1977.

Anderson, Perry. *Considerations on Western Marxism*. London: New Left Books, 1976.

———. *Lineages of the Absolutist State*. London: Verso, 1979.

Arato, Andrew, and Paul Breines. *The Young Lukács and the Origins of Western Marxism*. New York: Seabury Press, 1979.

Aron, Raymond. *German Sociology*. Glencoe, Ill.: Free Press, 1957.

———. *Marxismes imaginaires*. Paris: Gallimard, 1970.

Bader, Wolfgang. *Grundprobleme der literaturtheorie Lucien Goldmanns*. Frankfurt am Main: Peter Lang, 1979.

Barthes, Roland. *On Racine*. New York: Hill and Wang, 1964.

Baum, Hermann. *Lucien Goldmann. Marxismus contra Vision Tragique*. Stuttgart: F. Fromann Verlag, 1974.

Belleville, Pierre. *Une Nouvelle Classe Ouvrière*. Paris: R. Julliard, 1963.

Bénichou, Paul. *Les Morales du grand siècle*. Paris: Gallimard, 1948.

Bergner, Jeffrey T. *The Origins of Formalism in Social Science*. Chicago and London: University of Chicago Press, 1981.

Blanchet, André. "Pascal est-il le précurseur de Karl Marx?" *Études*, March 1, 1957.

Borkenau, Franz. *Der Übergang vom Feudalen zum Bürgerlichen Weltbild: Studien zur Geschichte der Philosopie der Manufakturperiode*. Paris: F. Alcan, 1934.

Bottomore, Tom, and Patrick Goode, eds. *Austro-Marxism*. Oxford: Clarendon Press, 1978.

Brady, Patrick. "Socio-criticism as Genetic Structuralism: Value and Limitations of the Goldmann Method." *L'Esprit Créateur*, Fall 1974.

Caute, David. "After Lukács: The Literary Criticism of Lucien Goldmann." *Times Literary Supplement*, July 14, 1966.

———. "A Portrait of the Artist as a Midwife: Lucien Goldmann and the Transindividual Subject." *Times Literary Supplement*, November 26, 1971.

Clark, Terry Nichols. *Prophets and Patrons: The French University and the Emergence of the Social Sciences*. Cambridge, Mass.: Harvard University Press, 1973.

Cohen, Mitchell, "The Concept of Community in the Thought of Lucien Goldmann." *Praxis International*, Summer 1986.

———, ed. *Lucien Goldmann: Tragedy and Dialectics*. Special issue of *The Philosophical Forum* 23, nos. 1–2 (fall–winter 1991–1992).

Comte, Auguste. *Auguste Comte and Positivism: The Essential Writings*. Edited by G. Lenzer. New York: Harper Torchbooks, 1975.

Crispini, Franco. *Lo Structuralismo dialettico di Lucien Goldmann*. Naples: Libreria Scientifica, 1970.

Crouzet, Michel. "Racine et le marxisme en histoire litteraire." *La Nouvelle Critique* 79 (November 1956).

Daix, Pierre. *Nouvelle Critique et art moderne*. Paris: Le Seuil, 1968.

de Boisdeffre, Pierre. "Le Destin de Jean Racine." *Combat*, March 26, 1956.

Demetz, Peter. "Wandlüngen der Marxistischen Literaturkritik: Hans Mayer, Ernst Fischer, Lucien Goldmann." In W. Paulsen, ed., *Der Dichter und seine Zeit: Politik im Spiegel der Literatur*. Heidelberg: Lothar Stiehm Verlag, 1970.

"De Saint Augustin à Karl Marx." *L'Express*, February 21, 1956.

Descombes, Vincent. *Modern French Philosophy*. Cambridge: Cambridge University Press, 1980.

Dilthey, Wilhelm. *Selected Writings*. Edited by H. P. Rickman. Cambridge and New York: Cambridge University Press, 1979.

Doubrovsky, Serge. *The New Criticism in France*. Chicago and London: University of Chicago Press, 1973.

Duvignaud, Jean. "Le Marxisme est-il arreté?" *Les Lettres Nouvelles*, May 1956.

Eastwood, Dorothy Margaret. *The Revival of Pascal: A Study of His Relations to Modern French Thought*. Oxford: Clarendon Press, 1936.

Foa, Vittorio. "Les luttes ouvrières dans le développement capitaliste." *Les Temps modernes*, September–October 1962.

Foucault, Michel. *The Order of Things: An Archaeology of the Human Sciences*. New York: Vintage Books, 1973.

Fromm, Erich, ed. *Socialist Humanism*. Garden City, N.Y.: Doubleday, 1966.

Gandillac, M., L. Goldmann, J. Piaget, et al. *Entretiens sur les notions de genèse et de structure*. Paris and The Hague: Mouton and Co., 1965.

Gardner, Howard. *The Quest for Mind: Piaget, Lévi-Strauss and the Structuralist Movement*. New York: Alfred A. Knopf, 1973.

Geras, Norman. "Althusser's Marxism: An Assessment." In *Western Marxism: A Critical Reader*. London: New Left Books, 1977.

Ginsburg, Herbert, and Sylvia Opper. *Piaget's Theory of Intellectual Development*. Englewood Cliffs, N.J.: Prentice Hall, 1979.

Girard, René. *Desire, Deceit, and the Novel*. Baltimore and London: Johns Hopkins University Press, 1965.

———. "Racine poète de la gloire." *Critique*, June 1964.

Glucksmann, Miriam. "Lucien Goldmann: Humanist or Marxist?" *New Left Review* 56 (July–August 1969).

Goldmann, Annie, Sami Naïr, Michael Löwy, et al. *Le Structuralisme génétique: L'Oeuvre et l'influence de Lucien Goldmann*. Paris: Denoël/Gonthier, 1977.

Gorz, André. *Strategy for Labor*. Boston: Beacon Press, 1967.

Groethuysen, Bernard. *The Bourgeois: Catholicism vs. Capitalism in Eighteenth Century France*. New York: Holt, Rinehart, and Winston, 1968.

Hawthorn, Jeremy. *Identity and Relationship*. London: Lawrence Wishart, 1973.

Hegel, G.W.F. *Hegel's Logic: Being Part One of the Encyclopedia of the Philosophical Sciences*. Oxford: Clarendon Press, 1975.

———. *The Phenomenology of Mind*. Trans. by A. V. Miller. Oxford and New York: Oxford University Press, 1981.

Heidegger, Martin. *Being and Time*. New York and Evanston, Ill.: Harper and Row, 1962.

Heller, Agnès, and Ferenc Fehér. *The Grandeur and Twilight of Radical Universalism*. New Brunswick, N.J.: Transaction, 1991.

Heller, Agnès, ed., *Lukács Revalued*. Oxford: Blackwell, 1983.

Heyndels, Roudolphe. "Vision du monde et réification: Reflexion sur la sociologie de la littérature de Lucien Goldmann." *Revue de l'institut de sociologie de l'université libre de Bruxelles*, no. 1 (1974).

Hirsch, Albert. *The French New Left: An Intellectual History from Sartre to Gorz*. Boston: South End Press, 1981.

Hommage à Lucien Goldmann. Lucien Goldmann et la sociologie de la littérature. Brussels: Editions de l'Université de Bruxelles, 1975.

Horkheimer, Max. *Critical Theory*. New York: Seabury Press, 1972.

Horkheimer, Max, and Theodor Adorno. *Dialectic of Enlightenment*. New York: Seabury Press, 1972.

Howard, Dick, and Karl E. Klare. *The Unknown Dimension: European Marxism since Lenin*. New York and London: Basic Books, 1972.

Huaco, George. "Ideology and Literature." *New Literary History*, Spring 1973.

Jay, Martin. *Marxism and Totality*. Berkeley and Los Angeles: University of California Press, 1984.

Kant, Immanuel. *Critique of Judgement*. Trans. by J. C. Meredith. Oxford: Clarendon Press, 1978.

———. *Critique of Practical Reason*. Trans. by L. W. Beck. Indianapolis: Bobbs-Merrill Co., 1956.

————. *Critique of Pure Reason*. Trans. by N. H. Smith. New York: St. Martin's Press, 1965.

Kolakowski, Leszek. *Main Currents of Marxism*. 3 vols. Oxford: Clarendon Press, 1978.

————. *Positivist Philosophy*. Middlesex: Penguin Books, 1972.

————. *Towards a Marxist Humanism*. New York: Grove Press, 1969.

Lask, Emil. *Fichtes Idealismus und die Geschichte*. Vol. 1 of *Gesammelte Schriften*. Tübingen: J.C.B. Möhr, 1923.

————. "Legal Philosophy." In E. Lask, G. Radruch, and J. Dabin, *The Legal Philosophies of Lask, Radbruch and Dabin*. Cambridge, Mass.: Harvard University Press, 1950.

Laurenson, Diana, and Alan Swingewood. *The Sociology of Literature*. London: Paladin, 1972.

Leach, Edmund. *Claude Lévi-Strauss*. Middlesex: Penguin Books, 1976.

Leduc, Victor, ed. *Structuralisme et marxisme*. Paris: Union Generale d'Éditions, 1970.

Leenhardt, Jacques. "Lecture critique de la théorie goldmanniene du roman." In C. Duchet, ed., *Sociocritique*. Paris: Nathan Université Information, 1979.

————. "Towards a Sociological Aesthetic: An Attempt at Constructing the Aesthetic of Lucien Goldmann." *Sub-Stance* 15 (1976).

Lefebvre, Henri. *Au-delà du structuralisme*. Paris: Anthropos, 1971.

————. *L'Idéologie structuraliste*. Paris: Anthropos, 1971.

————. *Pascal*. 2 vols. Paris: Éditions Nagel, 1949, 1954.

————. *La somme et la reste*. 2 vols. Paris: La Nef, 1959.

Lévi-Strauss, Claude. *The Savage Mind*. Chicago: University of Chicago Press, 1966.

————. *Structural Anthropology*. New York: Basic Books, 1967.

————. *Tristes Tropiques*. New York: Pocket Books, 1977.

Löwy, Michael. *Georg Lukács—From Romanticism to Bolshevism*. London: New Left Books, 1979.

Lukács, Georg. *Goethe and his Age*. London: Merlin Press, 1968.

————. *History and Class Consciousness*. Cambridge, Mass.: MIT Press, 1971.

————. *Lenin*. Cambridge, Mass.: MIT Press, 1971.

————. *Political Writings 1919–1929*. London: New Left Books, 1972.

————. *Realism in Our Time*. New York: Harper Torchbooks, 1971.

————. *Soul and Form*. London: Merlin Press, 1974.

————. *Theory of the Novel*. Cambridge, Mass.: MIT Press, 1971.

————. *The Young Hegel*. London: Merlin Press, 1975.

MacIntyre, Alasdair. *Against the Self-Image of the Age*. New York: Schocken Books, 1971.

Macksey, Richard, and Eugenio Donato. *The Structuralist Controversy*. Baltimore: Johns Hopkins Press, 1972.

Mallet, Serge. "Après le referendum: Perspective nouvelles." *Les Temps modernes*, November–December 1958.

————. *Essays on the New Working Class*. St. Louis: Telos Press, 1975.

————. *The New Working Class*. Nottingham: Spokesman Books, 1975.

Mandrow, Robert. "Tragiques XVIIe siècle: A propos de travaux récents." *Annales*, no. 2, (1957).

Marcuse, Herbert. "A Reply to Lucien Goldmann." *Partisan Review*, Winter 1971–1972.

————. *One-Dimensional Man*. Boston: Beacon Press, 1969.

Margalit, Elkana. *Ha-Shomer ha-tsair—Me-adat Nearim le Marxism Mahpkhani 1913–1936*. (Ha-Shomer ha-tsair—From Youth Community to Revolutionary Marxism). Tel Aviv: Tel Aviv University and Ha-Kibbutz ha-meuhad, 1971.

————. "Social and Intellectual Origins of the Hashomer Hatzair Youth Movement 1913–1920." *Journal of Contemporary History*, April 1969.

Mayrl, William W. "Genetic Structuralism and the Analysis of Social Consciousness." *Theory and Society*, January 1978.

Mellor, Adrian. "The Hidden Method: Lucien Goldmann and the Sociology of Literature." *Working Papers in Cultural Studies*, Spring 1973.

Mesnard, Jean. *Pascal, His Life and Works*. London: Harvill Press, 1952.

Mészáros, István, ed. *Aspects of History and Class Consciousness*. London: Routledge and Kegan Paul, 1971.

————. *Lukács's Concept of Dialectic*. London: Merlin Press, 1972.

Mounier, Emmanuel. *Personalism*. Notre Dame and London: University of Notre Dame Press, 1952.

Naïr, Sami. "Goldmann's Legacy." *Telos*, Summer 1981.

Naïr, Sami, and Michel Löwy. *Lucien Goldmann ou la dialectique de la totalité*. Paris: Éditions Seghers, 1973.

Oakes, Guy. *Weber and Rickert: Concept Formation in the Cultural Sciences*. Cambridge, Mass.: MIT Press, 1988.

Palmier, Jean-Michel. "Goldmann Vivant." *Praxis* 3/4 (1971).

Pascal, Blaise. *Pensées*. New York: E. P. Dutton and Co., 1958.

Patri, Aime. "Une interprétation pascalienne du Marxisme." *Preuve*, May 1956.

Piaget, Jean. *The Essential Piaget*. Edited by Howard E. Gruber and J. Jacques Vonèche. New York: Basic Books, 1977.

————. *Genetic Epistemology*. New York: W. W. Norton and Co., 1971.

————. *Insights and Illusions of Philosophy*. New York: New American Library, 1971.

————. *Introduction à l'épistémologie génétique*. 3 vols. Paris: Presses Universitaires de France, 1950.

————. *The Place of the Sciences of Man in the System of the Sciences*. New York: Harper Torchbooks, 1970.

————. *The Psychology of Intelligence*. Totowa, N.J.: Littlefield, Adams and Co., 1976.

————. *Structuralism*. New York: Harper Colophon Books, 1970.

Piatier, J. "Thèses en Sorbonne: Pascal, Racine, et le Dieu caché de l'univers tragique." *Le Monde*, February 22, 1956.

Picard, Raymond. *New Criticism or New Fraud?* Washington State University Press, 1969.

Poster, Mark. *Existential Marxism in Postwar France*. Princeton: Princeton University Press, 1975.

Pouillon, Jean. "Le Dieu caché ou l'histoire visible." *Les Temps modernes*, November 1957.

Rickert, Heinrich. *The Limits of Concept Formation in Natural Science: A Logical Introduction to the Historical Sciences*. Cambridge and New York: Cambridge University Press, 1986.

————. *Science and History: A Critique of Positivist Epistemology*. Princeton: D. Van Nostrand Co., 1962.

Roelens, Rudolphe. "Les Avatars de la Médiation dans la sociologie de Lucien Goldmann." *L'Homme et la société*, January, February, March 1970.

Ross, George. "Marxism and the New Middle Classes: French Critiques." *Theory and Society*, March 1978.

Rudich, Norman. "The Marxism of Lucien Goldmann in The Philosophy of the Enlightenment." *Praxis* (Berkeley) 3 (1976).

Said, Edward. *The World, the Text, and the Critic*. Cambridge: Cambridge University Press, 1983.

Sanders, Scott. "Towards a Social Theory of Literature." *Telos*, Winter 1973–1974.

Sayre, Robert. "Goldmann and Modern Realism: Introduction to the *Balcony* Article." *Praxis* (Berkeley) 4 (1978).

————. "Lowenthal, Goldmann, and the Sociology of Literature." *Telos*, Fall 1980.

————. "Lucien Goldmann and the Sociology of Culture." *Praxis* (Berkeley), Winter 1976.

Schnapp, Alain, and Pierre Vidal-Naquet. *The French Student Uprising: November 1967–June 1968*. Boston: Beacon Press, 1971.

Sebag, Lucien. *Marxisme et structuralisme*. Paris: Payot, 1964.

Sturrock, John, *Structuralism and Since*. Oxford and New York: Oxford University Press, 1981.

Swingewood, Alan. *The Novel and Revolution*. London and Basingstoke: Macmillan, 1975.

Tretin, Bruno. "Les doctrines néocapitalistes et l'idéologie des forces dominantes." *Les Temps modernes*, September–October 1962.

Weber, Max. *The Methodology of the Social Sciences*. New York: Free Press, 1949.

Weiman, Robert. "French Structuralism and Literary History: Some Critiques and Reconsiderations." *New Literary History*, Spring 1973.

Willey, Thomas E. *Back to Kant: The Revival of Kantianism in German Social and Historical Thought 1860–1914*. Detroit: Wayne State University Press, 1978.

Williams, Raymond. "Literature and Sociology: In Memory of Lucien Goldmann." *New Left Review* 67 (May–June 1971).

————. *Marxism and Literature*. Oxford: Oxford University Press, 1977.

Windelband, Wilhelm. *A History of Philosophy*. New York: Macmillan, 1893.

————. "History and Natural Science." *History and Theory* 19, no. 2 (1980).

————. *An Introduction to Philosophy*. New York: Henry Holt and Co., 1921.

Wolin, Richard. *The Terms of Cultural Criticism*. New York: Columbia University Press, 1992.

Zima, Pierra. *Goldmann, dialectique de l'immanence*. Paris: Editions Universitaires, 1973.

Zimmerman, Marc J., "Genetic Structuralism: Lucien Goldmann's Answer to the Advent of Structuralism." Ph.D. diss., University of California at San Diego, 1975.

———. "Lucien Goldmann: From Dialectical Theory to Genetic Structuralism." *Berkeley Journal of Sociology* 28 (1978–1979).

———. "Polarities and Contradictions: Theoretical Bases of the Marxist-Structuralist Encounter." *New German Critique*, Winter 1976.

Index